Lecture Notes in Computer Science 15468

Founding Editors

Gerhard Goos
Juris Hartmanis

AF173232

The series Lecture Notes in Computer Science (LNCS), including its subseries Lecture Notes in Artificial Intelligence (LNAI) and Lecture Notes in Bioinformatics (LNBI), has established itself as a medium for the publication of new developments in computer science and information technology research, teaching, and education.

LNCS enjoys close cooperation with the computer science R & D community, the series counts many renowned academics among its volume editors and paper authors, and collaborates with prestigious societies. Its mission is to serve this international community by providing an invaluable service, mainly focused on the publication of conference and workshop proceedings and postproceedings. LNCS commenced publication in 1973.

John T. Murray · María Cecilia Reyes
Editors

Interactive Storytelling

17th International Conference
on Interactive Digital Storytelling, ICIDS 2024
Barranquilla, Colombia, December 2–6, 2024
Proceedings, Part II

Editors
John T. Murray 🆔
University of Central Florida
Orlando, FL, USA

María Cecilia Reyes 🆔
Universidad del Norte
Atlántico, Colombia

ISSN 0302-9743   ISSN 1611-3349 (electronic)
Lecture Notes in Computer Science
ISBN 978-3-031-78449-1   ISBN 978-3-031-78450-7 (eBook)
https://doi.org/10.1007/978-3-031-78450-7

This Springer imprint is published by the registered company Springer Nature Switzerland AG
The registered company address is: Gewerbestrasse 11, 6330 Cham, Switzerland

If disposing of this product, please recycle the paper.

Preface

These two volumes constitute the proceedings of the 17th International Conference on Interactive Digital Storytelling (ICIDS 2024). ICIDS is the premier conference for researchers and practitioners concerned with studying digital interactive narrative forms from various perspectives, including theoretical, technological, socially aware, and applied design lenses. Organized by ARDIN (Association for Research in Digital Interactive Narratives), the annual conference is an interdisciplinary gathering that combines theoretical inquiry, empirical research, and artistic expression. The conference featured an academic session presenting the papers published in these volumes, workshops, a doctoral consortium, and a parallel art exhibition. The papers presented in these two volumes are organized under the following topical sections:-

Part I: Theory, History, and Foundations; Social and Cultural Contexts; Interactive Narrative Design; Applications and Case Studies.
Part II: Virtual Worlds, Performance, Games, and Play; Tools and Systems; Late-Breaking Works.

In 2024, ICIDS' host country was Colombia, marking the first time a traditionally Global-North conference was held in Latin America. For this reason, efforts were made to invite organizers, authors, and attendees to position in this territory and to acknowledge the continents' research and accomplishments in interactive digital storytelling. This resulted in a larger inclusion of organization and program area chairs as well as program committee members from Latin America.

The host city was Barranquilla, a city surrounded by different kinds of water bodies: the Caribbean Sea, the Magdalena River, and the Mallorquín Swamp, an ecosystem where migratory species from both hemispheres mingle. Barranquilla was also the city that received most migrants coming to Colombia from Europe and the Middle East during the 19th and 20th centuries. The natural and human forces that led to the formation of the city's landscape inspired the main theme of the conference: "STREAMS" or "CORRIENTES" in Spanish. With this topic we drew attention to flow and movement, exchange, convergences, and divergences within the various ecosystems and belief systems that we inhabit and are part of. In this sense, we invited the interactive narrative global community to think about our field within posthumanist, multispecies, and pluriversal contexts.

STREAMS ~ CORRIENTES looked into the collisions of different streams of thought that converge into and extend the Interactive Digital Narratives field, following the question: What epistemologies are shaping the IDN landscape and enriching our understanding of interconnectedness among humans, but also with other species and machines? This topic also invited us to revisit the current streams that push us forward in IDN research and practice. How will IDN as a field respond to rapidly changing socio-political movements, especially concerning issues of identity, representation, and social justice? How do IDNs understand, operationalize, and be critical of emerging technological currents such as generative AI?

As it is vital for the IDN community to give space to historically marginalized epistemologies, we invited authors from the "Global Souths" (in plural), to reflect on how alternative views and applications from our territories deepen our understanding of interactive digital narratives, narrative structures, themes, audiences, and applications. Although we encouraged authors to consider possible connections to this theme, there was no requirement that papers or workshops reflect the theme as it was meant only as inspiration.

ICIDS 2024 received 75 submissions. 7 papers were desk rejected, leaving 68 papers that were peer reviewed: 34 full papers, 22 short papers and 12 Late-Breaking Works papers. Following the review process, the Program Committee accepted 21 full papers, 9 short papers, and 11 Late-Breaking Works, for a total of 41 papers. The acceptance rate of the conference was 60%. As in previous ICIDS, the program was divided into six main areas: Applications and Case Studies; Interactive Narrative Design; Social and Cultural Contexts; Theory, History, and Foundations; Tools and Systems; and Virtual Worlds, Performance, Games, and Play. The Late-Breaking Works track introduced in 2023 continued this year and was presented at the conference as posters.

All papers were subjected to a rigorous double-blind review procedure, utilizing an organized and comprehensive review process, much like in previous years. A minimum of three reviews per paper were completed before the decision, with additional reviews solicited on the recommendations of reviewers. In addition, we included a rebuttal phase, and final decisions were made at virtual program chairs' meetings. However, we still welcome feedback from both authors and reviewers to help us continue to refine and strengthen the way that we run the conference.

ICIDS also accepted 14 thesis proposals, whose authors received feedback and mentoring at the Doctoral Consortium, 4 workshops, and 20 artworks to be showcased at the Art Exhibition. As has become the rule for ICIDS, this conference was fully hybrid for the paper sessions, workshops, doctoral consortium, posters, and art exhibition. We want to express our deep gratitude to the program committee members who provided high-quality reviews, critical analysis, and insightful discussions to authors and the community. We also want to extend our appreciation to the program area chairs: Ágnes Bakk, Jonathan Barbara, Dan Cox, Emily Johnson, Chloe Anne Milligan, Alex Mitchell, Frank Nack, Augusto Salazar Silva, Anastasia Salter, Cláudia Silva, and Ulrike Spierling. We also thank our keynote speakers: Irene Lema (Colombia), Mirjam Palosaari-Eladhari (Sweden), Vincent Morisset and Caroline Robert (Canada), and Elder Tobar Panchoaga (Colombia) for enriching our field and conference with their presentations about decolonial thinking, hyperlocal IDN production, GenerativeAI and IDN, and artist's authoring process merging narrative and interactivity.

Finally, we thank the sponsors who made ICIDS 2024 possible: Springer Nature, Universidad del Norte, the Archeological Museum of the Karib People *MAPUKA* for hosting the Art Exhibition, and the Transmedia Laboratory Álvaro Cepeda Samudio *LACS* for providing the streaming of the conference.

December 2024

John T. Murray
María Cecilia Reyes

ARDIN, Association for Research in Digital Interactive Narratives

ARDIN's purpose is to support research in Interactive Digital Narratives (IDN) in a wide range of forms, be that video and computer games, interactive documentaries and fiction, journalistic interactives, art projects, educational titles, transmedia, virtual reality and augmented reality titles, or any emerging novel forms of IDN.

ARDIN provides a home for an interdisciplinary community and for various activities that connect, support, grow, and validate said community. The long-term vision for the suite of activities hosted by ARDIN includes membership services, such as a community platform, job postings, and support for local gatherings, but also conferences, publication opportunities, research fellowships, and academic/professional awards. ARDIN publishes a monthly newsletter and holds a monthly online social, where both established researchers and graduate students share their ongoing work in an informal setting. In 2024 we launched the Journal of Interactive Narrative, published in collaboration with ETC press (https://journal.ardin.online/). There are also several committees and task forces, listed below.

ICIDS is the main academic conference of ARDIN. Additional international and local conferences are welcome to join the organization. The Zip-Scene conference, focused on eastern Europe, is the first associated conference. Diversity is important to ARDIN. The organization strives towards gender balance and the representation of different people from different origins. Diversity also means to represent scholars at different levels of their careers. No ARDIN member shall discriminate against any other ARDIN member or others outside of the organization in any way, including but not limited to gender, nationality, race, religion, sexuality, or ability. Discrimination against these principles will not be tolerated and membership in ARDIN can be withdrawn based on evidence of such behavior.

The association is incorporated as a legal entity in Amsterdam, the Netherlands. First proposed during the ICIDS 2017 conference in Madeira, Portugal, the association was officially announced at ICIDS 2018 in Dublin, Ireland. During its foundational year, members of the former ICIDS Steering Committee continued to serve as the ARDIN board as approved by the first general assembly at ICIDS 2018. The current board structure and membership were approved at the second general assembly at ICIDS 2019 in Utah, and, as of November 2024, ARDIN has more than 400 members.

More information about ARDIN can be found at https://ardin.online/.

Committees

The Promotion and Advancement committee is led by Hartmut Koenitz and Josh Fisher with the help of Luis Bruni and Colette Daiute. The aim of this committee is to create a tenure equivalency document and recruit a team of expert reviewers for tenure and examination. Those interested should reach out to Hartmut Koenitz (hkoenitz at gmail.com).

The IDN in Education committee is led by Jonathan Barbara. This committee will be looking into how IDN can become a part of school (K-12) curricula and will be producing a white paper with recommendations. Students are also welcome to join as task force members. Those interested should reach out to Jonathan Barbara (barbaraj at tcd.ie). The Graduate Student Committee, led by Anca Serbanescu, provides a space for students to meet, discuss, and develop initiatives for emerging scholars within ARDIN. The goal of the ARDIN Graduate Student Committee is to foster a collaborative and nurturing environment that supports PhDs and early career researchers. Contact Anca Serbanescu (ankaserbanescu at gmail.com) for information on activities and how to get involved.

Task Forces

The Task Force on Inclusive Pricing Structure is led by Agnes Bakk. This task force has been looking into how to adjust registration for membership and conference registration according to GDP, and results have been a major input for this year's multi-tiered registration system.

The Task Force on ARDIN Outreach is led by María Cecilia Reyes. Aims of this task force are to create awareness about IDN and around ARDIN, and to build partnerships with industry, art, and education institutions, among other key stakeholders. Contact María Cecilia Reyes (mcreyes at uninorte.edu.co) for more information or to get involved.

Organization

General Chair

María Cecilia Reyes   Universidad del Norte, Colombia

Program Committee Chairs

John T. Murray   University of Central Florida, USA
María Cecilia Reyes   Universidad del Norte, Colombia

Art Exhibition Chairs

Gabriela Muñoz-Barrios   Universidad del Norte, Colombia
Mark C. Marino   McMaster University, Canada

Workshop Chairs

Christian Roth   HKU University of the Arts, The Netherlands
Paola Harris-Bonet   Universidad del Norte, Colombia

Doctoral Consortium Chairs

Hartmut Koenitz   Södertörn University, Sweden
Clàudia Silva   ITI-LARSyS—IST, University of Lisbon, Portugal

Virtual Chairs

Andrea Cancino-Borbón   Universidad del Norte, Colombia
Jonathan Barbara   Saint Martin's Institute of Higher Education, Malta

Financial Management Chairs

Frank Nack   University of Amsterdam, The Netherlands
María Angélica Díaz Granados   Universidad del Norte, Colombia

Local Chair

Juan Pablo Osman   Universidad del Norte, Colombia

Local Organizers

Vanessa García Bermejo   Universidad del Norte, Colombia
Alfredo Sabbagh   Universidad del Norte, Colombia
Daniela Pabón   Arqueológico de los Pueblos Karib, MAPUKA,
                                    Colombia
Sebastián Florez   Universidad del Norte, Colombia

ARDIN Officers and Board

Executive Board

Hartmut Koenitz   Södertörn University, Sweden
Frank Nack   University of Amsterdam, The Netherlands
Lissa Holloway-Attaway   University of Skövde, Sweden
Alex Mitchell   National University of Singapore, Singapore
Ágnes Bakk   Moholy-Nagy University of Art and Design,
                                    Hungary

General Board

Luis Emilio Bruni   Aalborg University, Denmark
Clara Fernandez-Vara   NYU, USA
Joshua A. Fisher   Ball State University, USA
Andrew Gordon   University of Southern California, USA
Mads Haahr   Trinity College Dublin, Ireland
Michael Mateas   UC Santa Cruz, USA
Valentina Nisi   University of Madeira, Portugal/Carnegie Mellon
                                    University, USA

Mirjam Palosaari Eladhari	Södertörn University, Sweden
Tess Tanenbaum	UC Irvine, USA
David Thue	Carleton University, Canada/Reykjavik University, Iceland

ICIDS Program Committee Area Chairs

Theory, History, and Foundations

Frank Nack	University of Amsterdam, The Netherlands
Dan Cox	University of Central Florida, USA

Social and Cultural Contexts

Cláudia Silva	ITI-LARSyS—IST, University of Lisbon, Portugal

Tools and Systems

Ulrike Spierling	Hochschule RheinMain, Germany
Augusto Salazar Silva	Universidad del Norte, Colombia

Interactive Narrative Design

Alex Mitchell	National University of Singapore, Singapore
Ágnes Bakk	Moholy-Nagy University of Art and Design, Hungary

Virtual Worlds, Performance, Games, and Play

Jonathan Barbara	Saint Martin's Institute of Higher Education, Malta
Emily Johnson	University of Central Florida, USA

Applications and Case Studies

Anastasia Salter	University of Central Florida, USA
Chloe Anne Milligan	Pennsylvania State University

Late-Breaking Works

John T. Murray	University of Central Florida, USA
María Cecilia Reyes	Universidad del Norte, Colombia

Art Exhibition Jury

Itoro Bassey	BBC, Nigeria
Toni Celia	Dirección Arte y Cultura, Universidad del Norte, Colombia
Astrid Ensslin	University of Regensburg, Germany
Erika Fulop	University of Toulouse, France
Anna Nacher	Jagiellonian University, Poland
Vinicius Pereira	Universidade Federal de Mato Grosso, Brazil
Edgar Plata	Universidad del Norte, Colombia
Mike Russo	Interactive Fiction Author, USA

Program Committee

Amnah Ahmad	Google Deepmind, USA
David Antognoli	Columbia College Chicago, USA
Pratama Atmaja	University of Pembangunan Nasional "Veteran" Jawa Timur, Indonesia
Ágnes Karolina Bakk	Moholy-Nagy University of Art and Design, Hungary
Paulo Bala	ITI-LARSyS, Portugal
Jonathan Barbara	Saint Martin's Institute of Higher Education, Malta
Mattia Bellini	University of Tartu, Estonia
Jessica L. Bitter	Hochschule RheinMain, Germany
Erika Blanco	Universidad del Norte, Colombia
Justin Bortnick	University of Pittsburgh, USA
Jason Boyd	Toronto Metropolitan University, Canada
Sarah Brown	University of Florida, USA
Alex Calderwood	Montana State University, USA
Andrea Cancino-Borbon	Universidad del Norte, Colombia
Sherol Chen	Passion Talks, USA
Angeliki Chrysanthi	University of the Aegean, Greece
Jordan Clapper	Washington State University, USA
Dan Cox	University of Central Florida, USA

Joseph Livingston Crawford-Visbal   Pontificia Universidad Católica del Perú, Peru
Colette Daiute   City University of New York, USA
Giuliana Dettori   CNR-ITD, Italy
Kath Dooley   University of South Australia, Australia
Sabrina Durling-Jones   RISEBA University, Latvia
Daniel Echeverri   Masaryk University, Czechia
Mirjam Eladhari   Stockholm University, Sweden
Carl Erez   University of California, Santa Cruz, USA
Jamie Fawcus   Skövde University, Sweden
Iliana Ferrer   Autonomous University of Barcelona, Spain
Caitlin Foley   UMass Lowell, USA
Arnau Gifreu-Castells   University of Girona, Spain
Kyle Gonzalez   University of California, Santa Cruz, USA
Andrew Gordon   University of Southern California, USA
Mads Haahr   Trinity College Dublin, Ireland
Paola Harris   Universidad del Norte, Colombia
Wolfgang Heiden   Bonn-Rhein-Sieg University of Applied Sciences, Germany
Lissa Holloway-Attaway   University of Skövde, Sweden
Jussi Holopainen   City University of Hong Kong, China
Taylor Howard   University of Central Florida, USA
Andrés Isaza-Giraldo   Universidade de Lisboa, Portugal
Shi Johnson-Bey   University of California, Santa Cruz, USA
Akrivi Katifori   University of Athens, Greece
Jack Kelly   University of California, Santa Cruz, USA
Hartmut Koenitz   Södertörn University, Sweden
Victoria Lagrange   Kennesaw State University, USA
David Lamas   Tallinn University, Estonia
Vincenzo Lombardo   Università degli Studi di Torino, Italy
Anahí Lovato   Universidad Nacional de Rosario, Argentina
Kirk Lundblade   University of Central Florida, USA
Abhilash M   University of Amsterdam, The Netherlands
Péter Kristóf Makai   Kazimierz Wielki University, Poland
Derek Manns   University of Central Florida, USA
Mark Marino   University of Southern California, USA
Terhi Marttila   ITI/LARSyS, Portugal
Michael Merriam   University of Central Florida, USA
Chloe Milligan   Pennsylvania State University, Berks, USA
Snežana Milosavljević Milić   University of Niš, Serbia
Alex Mitchell   National University of Singapore, Singapore
Gabriela Muñoz   Universidad del Norte, Colombia

Frank Nack	University of Amsterdam, The Netherlands
Thomas Neteler	H-BRS University of Applied Sciences, Germany
Jorge Palinhos	CEAA-ESAP; ESACT-IPB; ESTC-IPL, Portugal
Dave Pape	University at Buffalo, USA
Lucas Pereira	Instituto Superior Técnico, Portugal
Dimitra Petousi	Athena Research & Innovation Center, Greece
Andrew Phelps	American University, USA
Derek Reilly	Dalhousie University, Canada
Juan-David Rodas	Universidad de Antioquia, Colombia
Rebecca Rouse	University of Skövde, Sweden
Svetlana Rudenko	Haunted Planet Studios, Ireland
Morgan Sammut	Lambda Literary, USA
Ben Samuel	University of New Orleans, USA
Anca Serbanescu	Politecnico di Milano, Italy
Yotam Shibolet	Utrecht University, The Netherlands
Samuel Shields	University of California, Santa Cruz, USA
Cláudia Silva	IST, University of Lisbon, Portugal
Lyle Skains	Bournemouth University, UK
Caighlan Smith	Memorial University of Newfoundland, Canada
Mel Stanfill	University of Central Florida, USA
Yuqian Sun	Royal College of Art, UK
Michel Andrés Toledo	Universidad Viña del Mar, Chile
Mauricio Vásquez	EAFIT, Colombia
Jorge Vázquez-Herrero	Universidad de Santiago de Compostela, Spain
Diego Zavala	Tecnológico de Monterrey, Mexico
Hongwei Zhou	University of California, Santa Cruz, USA
Alejandro Ángel Torres	Universidad Jorge Tadeo Lozano, Colombia

Keynotes

Interactivity as a Starting Point

Vincent Morisset and Caroline Robert

AATOAA, Montréal, Canada

Abstract. For two decades, Caroline and Vincent have combined crafts-manship and technology in their projects. The experiences, where visitors are invited to become participants, put into perspective our relationship with others and the way we look at the world around us. In this presentation, Caroline and Vincent present a vast array of projects they've developed in the past years (interactive videos, installations in public spaces, XR, mobile project, net art).

Bio: *Vincent Morisset and Caroline Robert* of Montreal-based studio AATOAA (aat oaa.com) are known for their long collaboration with Arcade Fire. They have won numerous awards, including an Emmy, a Grammy, a Golden Pencil, many Webbies, and the Art Directors Club Tomorrow Award. Their work has been presented at many museums and festivals around the world, including Sundance, the Venice Biennale, SXSW, SIGGRAPH, Sonar+D, TIFF, the Japan Media Arts Festival, and the Cooper Hewitt.

From Dystopia to Indigenous Futurism: Codex of the Future, in Search of Alternative Futures

Elder Manuel Tobar Panchoaga

Specialist in Digital Humanities, Indigenous Futurism,
and Immersive Storytelling

Abstract. *Codex of the Future* aims to propose new ways of envisioning possible futures, taking Indigenous Futurism—or ancestral futurism—as its starting point. In this talk, Elder Manuel Tobar Panchoaga will explore the methodological and conceptual approach of his work with Indigenous communities in Colombia, as well as the development of a spiritual universe that integrates immersive technologies, paper engineering, oracles, and spirals of time.

Bio: *Elder Manuel Tobar Panchoaga* is a Social Communicator with a Master's Degree in Digital Humanities; he has specialized in the creation, design, and production of multiplatform digital narrative projects. He has experience as a producer and director of web comics, animated shorts, interactive exhibitions, and immersive experiences in Virtual Reality and Augmented Reality.

He works at the intersection between art, technology, and narrative from where he has designed projects that portray the armed conflict in Colombia and historical memory as well as advising and directing work teams for entities such as the National Library of Colombia or the Gold Museum Network of the Bank of the Republic.

His latest project focuses on ancestral futurism where he explores his indigenous roots, rituality, and spirituality and weaves a bridge with his work in the world of technology, science fiction, and narrative.

Dust to Pointclouds: From Hyperlocal Narratives into Worldbuilding

Irene Lema

New Media Director/Communications Strategist

Abstract. How is narrative -and form- transformed by interactions with technology, production challenges, and the voices and minds of the rightful owners of the story? How does it also change the end-user experience? What questions arise about inclusive design and creation involving technology?

Born in the town of Palenque, just a couple of hours from Barranquilla, *El Beat* is a story about music, rebellion, and resistance. Shaped by the voices of the palenquero people, it has evolved into a cross-platform project that stages the story of the African Diaspora in Latin America. Several years later, this living project continues to transform in diverse venues around the world, from Cartagena to Seoul.

Bio: *Irene Lema* is a pioneer in cross-platform and expanded reality (XR) in Latin America. Her expertise includes digital and new media. Her work has been show-cased at prestigious international festivals, including SXSW in Austin, RedSea in Saudi Arabia, and FICCI in Latin America. She has been a fellow at the Sundance Institute Interdisciplinary Program and has received several awards, such as the Transmedia (2019) and the Documentary Creation Award (2010) from the Colombi-an Film Development Fund, as well as the New Media Fund from Proimagenes-Canada Media Fund (2017). She has been speaker at multiple spaces, like the MIT doc lab – worlding initiative.

She has a background in filmmaking and animation, with diverse experience writing, directing and producing for film, tv, and major media. Irene is particularly interested in the intersection of narrative, technology, and global changes.

Co-creative Interactive Narratives in the Age of GenAI

Mirjam Palosaari-Eladhari

Stockholm University, Sweden

Abstract. In this keynote, we explore the evolving landscape of interactive digital narratives (IDNs) by examining the emerging possibilities of co-creating with AI. I will start by considering the rich history of creatively using systems and machines for storytelling – such as tarot, I-Ching, RPGs, MUDs and others which blend generative aspects and audience participation.

In the present day, machine-learning approaches such as small and large language models (SLMs and LLMs) have further transformed the landscape of IDNs. These tools grant access to vast reservoirs of knowledge, allowing creators to experiment with storytelling structures from cultures beyond their own. This keynote will examine critical questions: How valuable are machines in crafting IDNs compared to narratives drawn from human creativity and lived experience? What does it mean for construction of stories when audiences are increasingly able to infuse their personal stories—known as "bleed"—into the narrative? How can we creatively and ethically use Generative AI and co-create fitting representations of the human condition for the twenty-first century?

Bio: Mirjam Palosaari Eladhari is an Associate Professor at the Department of Computer and System Sciences at Stockholm University and a resident scholar at the University of Arts, Crafts and Design in Stockholm (Konstfack). Her research centers on AI-based game design and interactive narratives, with a primary focus on co-creation. She explores how interactors can contribute to games and narratives to reflect on their own existence and discover new perspectives. Her work spans various application areas, including tabletop story-making games and games for mental health. She has worked on interactive experiences since the late 1990s (initially as a game programmer), did her PhD on agents and narratives in virtual worlds, and was instrumental in a team of scholars which coined the expression "AI-based game design" in 2011.

Contents – Part II

Tools and Systems

Late Breaking Works

Contents – Part I

Applications and Case Studies

Virtual Worlds, Performance, Games and Play

WILDWOOD: Southside Chicago Worldbuilding Through Interactive Digital Narrative

E. M. Alexander(✉)

University of Maryland College Park, College Park, MD 20742, USA
emaphd6@gmail.com

Abstract. From the archive to the screen, Black digital humanists regularly engage interactive digital media as a tool of social justice-based creative place-making. In this short paper, Alexander examines interactive digital narrative as a radical worldbuilding platform, particularly for marginalized communities, and outlines a theoretical framework for Black futurist worldbuilding. This framework culminates in *WILDWOOD*, an afro-solarpunk interactive digital narrative that visions a rewilded future for one Southside Chicago neighborhood. *WILDWOOD* incorporates elements of tabletop roleplay game storytelling and interactive digital narrative methods, using hypertext fiction and chance as digital worldbuilding tools. The game explores community histories and futures through Black speculative placemaking, offering tools to imagine new visions of Black worlds and space to enact through immersive digital narrative play.

Keywords: Afro-solarpunk · Black digital humanities · Black speculative · Chicago · Creative placemaking · Digital media · Greater Englewood · Hypertext fiction · Interactive narrative · Narrative change · Social justice · Southside Chicago · Tabletop role play gaming · Twine · Twine writing · Worldbuilding

1 :: *Wild Seeds*

When it comes to worldbuilding, power is play, just as play is power. In "The Political Power of Play," Adeline Koh writes that "to reimagine the world is to create the potential to change it. Play is, in brief, serious business. To play is to imagine; to imagine is political because it allows us to envision a different order, a different system, a different way to separate economic resources and power" [1]. Playing through worldbuilding translates dreams about what society could be into temporary virtual realities, asking participants to imagine how they might reach that world and how they would live once they got there.

As a worldbuilding tool, interactive digital narrative crafts a space for a player/reader to "shape the narrative," their movement through a given world, "through their choices, actions, and interactions" [2]. This offers a uniquely engaging reading practice on the digital page, but also offers a way for unfamiliar users to play through a "counternarrative…by presenting a different perspective on socially relevant topics…these features empower interactive digital narratives as a means for sharing perspectives and experiences, enabling self-expression for all the different actors involved," engaging the

J. T. Murray and M. C. Reyes (Eds.): ICIDS 2024, LNCS 15468, pp. 3–14, 2025.
https://doi.org/10.1007/978-3-031-78450-7_1

player/reader in the process of imagining and constructing a new world alongside the author [2]. In this way, interactive digital narrative is not simply a neat multimedia presentation format, but a key tool for narrative change through immersive play.

For those of us at the sociopolitical margins, this play is a critical practice. If you've encountered my work before, you likely saw or heard a mention of Greater Englewood [3], the Southside Chicago neighborhood where I am originally from and where much of my immediate family still lives. I find Greater Englewood fascinating as a distant resident and interdisciplinary researcher. The neighborhood's dominant sociocultural narrative, its world origin myth, is one of violence, trauma, and destitution, like neighborhoods on the South and West sides of the city, and myriad working-class Black and Brown neighborhoods in many other urban cities. The brightest escape, never to return, and everyone else is left to rot. This is a narrative believed by many outsiders, encountering Greater Englewood through sensational news stories amplified by tyrannical politicians as justification for totalitarian policing. The story is also believed by many insiders, who have a nuanced lived experience as actual residents but learn the same story of ruin from the media reinforced by their experiences of real structural inequality, shaped by years of neglect and disinvestment.

To be clear, the desolation of structural disinvestment is a very real force in the community, but so is the power of care and the possibility of joy, exhibited in the multimodal activism platforms of social justice organizations working in the community. I am incredibly curious about this little neighborhood thriving at the nexus of Black power and anti-Black oppression. How could a space so neglected simultaneously be so beautiful, full of spirit? *WILDWOOD* first seeded itself in my mind as a project seeking to make sense of that dichotomy.

In the following short paper I discuss *WILDWOOD*, an experiment in Black futurist worldbuilding through interactive digital narrative design. Though I discuss *WILD-WOOD*'s game mechanics and technical elements, the paper privileges an exploration of the cultural, theoretical, and aesthetic basis for this piece, taking up the conversation in progress within interactive digital narrative considering narrative change as a form of social justice. This illuminates the possibilities of digital narrative worldbuilding for inner-city neighborhoods like Greater Englewood. Not simply a fun space of escape, worldbuilding through interactive digital narrative is an effective strategy for collectively envisioning and growing new futures through play.

2   :: *Wild Buds*

WILDWOOD's seeds began to root and sprout in the dirt of Black digital and experimental methods (popularly known as Black digital humanities, or BlackDH). According to Kimberly Bain, BlackDH is the intertwining of methodology and theory in service of "interrogating and mapping" and refashioning the complicated relationship between technology and the African diaspora; it is a "call to study how we read, how we think, and how we become invested" [4] in anti-Black systems of thinking, knowing, and producing. This practice involves using and understanding technology in relation to and in service of Black self-narrative, Black community (re)creation, and Black world making, often through collective effort. For example, the above analysis comes from an article co-written with a dear friend; as is a common theme in my BlackDH community, that article began as a way for us to collaboratively analyze and theorize our own relationship to and personal histories of the technologies we interact and produce with.

Interrogating and refashioning how we think and produce Black and digital together is not simply breaking apart what already exists, not simply turning away from, but the genesis of something altogether different, seeding and flowing Black technocultures in new directions. Fundamentally, BlackDH demands that we create with an eye toward the affordances of digital technologies and the lessons of cultural knowledge. As Marisa Parham explains, our field compass is set to navigate "what digital affordances could bring to Black diasporic texts…[n]to because the texts were necessarily resistant or because we were unsure, but because we wanted so desperately to have critical forms that could sometimes show and not tell, forms that could express relationality differently, that could foreground media materiality, and because we…come from traditions wherein direct telling and explication are less valued than other modes of knowledge transfer" [5].

When I think about cultural theories of Black expressive traditions, and how to name Blackness in digital production, my mind goes to Barbara Christian's claim that we are a race for theory, "but in forms quite different from the Western form of abstract logic…our theorizing (and I intentionally use the verb rather than the noun) is often in narrative forms, in the stories we create, in riddles and proverbs, in the play with language, since dynamic rather than fixed ideas seem more to our liking. How else have we managed to survive with such spiritedness…women, at least the women I grew up around, continually speculated about the nature of life through pithy language that unmasked the power relations of the world. It is this language, and the grace and pleasure with which they played with it, that I find celebrated, refined, critiqued in the work…a written figure which is both sensual and abstract, both beautiful and communicative" [6]. I'm interested in the capacity of interactive and immersive narrative methods (digital or otherwise) to create dynamic texts both sensual and abstract, beautiful and communicative, in response to the power relations of the world, with spirit, grace, and pleasure; in other words, to world build.

As adrienne maree brown writes in *Emergent Strategies: Shaping Change, Changing Worlds*, "we must imagine new worlds that transition ideologies and norms, so that no one sees Black people as murderers, or Brown people as terrorists and aliens, but all of us as potential cultural and economic innovators […]. This is collaborative ideation— what are the ideas that will liberate all of us? The more people that collaborate on that ideation, the more that people will be served by the resulting world(s). Science fiction is simply a way to practice the future together…emergent strategies are ways for humans to practice complexity and grow the future through relatively simple interactions" [7]. As an element of narrative change through interactive design, worldbuilding shifts from a leisurely escape into a strategy for evaluating radical ideas and playing through essential skill sets in service of liberation.

For example, Grow Greater Englewood [8], a Southside Chicago-based land and food justice collective, grounds its community agricultural work in historical recovery through storytelling; a form of narrative worldbuilding grounded in real-world action. Their belief is that in addition to land ownership and foodway sovereignty, we community residents must be rooted in our full, radical, sustainable history to bloom new futures.

The organization works to build a new world through on-the-ground activism (including literally feeding neighborhood residents and teaching them how to grow food in their own backyards), but also by collecting and interactively sharing community narratives. In addition to hosting community storytelling sessions, they have plans to create a virtual reality experience showcasing the Englewood Village Farms network and community narratives relating to land, food, family, future, and justice. No matter what the core issue is, much of the Southside Chicago activism I encounter involves a storytelling component. If the only histories residents ever learn about themselves are negative, how can the community imagine a positive future for itself? If the community cannot imagine a positive future, how can we count on anything to improve? Social justice means growing and sustaining new cultural forms as much as it means ending structural oppression; giving the people their bread, and their roses too.

Interactive digital narrative offers a unique space to explore and play through this radical science fiction practice. As outlined in the INDCOR workgroup whitepaper "Addressing Societal Issues in Interactive Digital Narratives," this creative method "combines systemic representation and self-guided exploration…provid[ing] ways to represent complex issues and enable understanding through participatory engagement, since audiences can explore them as interactors, making their own choices, picking perspectives, and using the opportunity for replay to revisit earlier decisions and encounter different perspectives" [9]. Player/readers are not simply passive audience members, but become part of the narrative world through choice, and observers of the worldbuilding process through reaction.

The last item in the INDCOR outline is particularly pertinent to a call for narrative change, in that a desire for success and mastery over an interactive narrative (a desire for some version of winning, even in a narrative game that eschews such hierarchies) may lead player/readers to return to the beginning of the narrative and play/read again, with any shifted responses leading to a completely different experience of the world. In many ways, interactive digital narratives allow for a kind of imaginative flexibility that an on-the-ground justice organization may not have the capacity for. Ultimately, even the most radical justice organizations must exist within the boundaries of our shared material reality, addressing the immediate needs of the populations they serve, needs often so urgent and critical that there is no opportunity to go back to the beginning and start over again. Interactive narratives are "helpful in the understanding of the causes and consequences of decisions and choices that impact societal contexts…sustain[ing] different perspectives, sensibilities, and/or emotional experiences concurrently," [9] presenting these perspectives in a way that maximizes their potential for exploration and learning without direct impact on the social context itself. In simpler terms, a player/reader can make a single error or come to understand the error of their ways over time and are still afforded the opportunity to try again (and again, and again, ad infinitum). In this sense, the dynamism of an interactive digital narrative is rooted not only in the affordances of player/reader choice, but in the generative possibilities of playtesting the consequences of our actions. Digitally, a player/reader can refine their choices before enacting them in the real world.

Inspired by Christian's call to create dynamic texts with spirit, grace, and pleasure, *WILDWOOD* builds a digital narrative world that shifts in response to the player/reader's choices and chances. Writing this work of interactive fiction is a way for me to collaboratively world build with myself, moving between the roles of author, player/reader, and researcher as I iteratively build a world, create conflict, envision responses, parse the results, and create new conflicts to give the world its substance. The project is also an invitation to other player/readers to engage with me in the practice of envisioning and enacting new stories about Greater Englewood. Specifically, afro-solarpunk stories.

Why ground my methodology in this genre? Solarpunk culture envisions a radically sustainable world where humanity and technology work in concert with the environment instead of against it, demanding the disavowal of un- and anti-sustainable capitalist structures. This can take many shapes and function at many scales, from fully off the grid eco-village living to neighborhood composting services, but is always grounded in grassroots collective organizing; sustainability for the people, by the people. Solarpunk aesthetics are almost completely overgrown with wild flora and fauna, but not entirely; a visualization of balance between the built and natural environments. Afro-solarpunk places Black life at the center of this cultural data visualization.

Worldbuilding in this way is the work of intersectional environmentalism, defined by Leah Thomas as "environmentalism that advocates for the protection of both people and the planet...[it] also aims to create space for a more complete and inclusive retelling of environmental or natural history, one that embraces all cultural contributors to sustainability and environmentalism" [10]. Environmental justice requires not only new actions and new structures, but new stories about how they intertwine to fashion our surroundings, rooted in lessons of history.

Upon first encountering the term solarpunk, I immediately began imagining what a solarpunk Greater Englewood would look like. What if every vacant lot was a forage garden and every abandoned building a solar-powered greenhouse? How would the community be different, and how would it stay the same? Initially an aesthetic thought experiment, I began to spend afternoons convened with Greater Englewood activists and evenings visioning Black speculative futures. I visited the Englewood Nature Trail [11], a stretch of formerly abandoned freight train tracks anchored by the Grow Greater Englewood farmland purposefully allowed to grow over and re-wild into an elevated nature preserve. This helped me realize that folks were already experimenting with strategies to enact the afro-solarpunk future I envisioned. Over time my research questions shifted: how might I imagine and write a world where Greater Englewood has solved some of the world's greatest environmental challenges? How can I help to flesh the skeletal world these community leaders have already begun to sketch? How might I construct a future narrative for a neighborhood that is very invested in and actively works toward social and environmental futurity but is rarely spoken of as such?

WILDWOOD takes the player on a journey through a socially and technologically radical version of Greater Englewood, combining interactive digital narrative with the randomness and luck of a role-playing game to explore playing through one narrative of radical Black futurity. As a theoretical and aesthetic practice, interactive digital storytelling grounded in BlackDH is an ideal method to experiment with afro-solarpunk worldbuilding. In response to the power relations of the world, in response to the impulse to enhance and transform the networks that link us, *WILDWOOD* uses digital storytelling as a tool of justice with digital methods of interactivity and choice to craft a dynamic text full of spirit, playtesting strategies for the future.

3 :: *Wild Woods*

Building *WILDWOOD* has been a journey through technoculture, blending experiments in interactive cultural storytelling with lessons in new media methods. The project uses digital hypertext fiction to platform a narrative of Black futurity laced with role-playing game mechanics. In so doing, these methods offer a capacious framework for speculative Black worldbuilding.

Though not a role-playing game by strict definition, *WILDWOOD* is heavily influenced by role-playing games as an interactive narrative theory and structure. For context, role-playing games facilitate a group of players taking on a character role and playing through a story sketched out by a game master (GM), collaboratively advancing the narration through player choices and dice rolls. Role-playing games come in many forms, including in person and online; tabletop role-playing games take place around a table and as such are heavily narrative, as opposed to advancing the story through movement as in live action role-playing (LARP-ing). Across media, role-playing games facilitate a journey through a world, a journey involving collaboration (between the players and the GM), accountability (in that players are responsible for the consequences of their actions), and luck; a framework for playtesting life. 2024 is the fiftieth anniversary of the release of *Dungeons & Dragons* [12], perhaps the most famous tabletop role-playing game in existence, and there have been numerous articles profiling different groups, from autistic children [13] to connection-starved adults during the pandemic [14], to former athletes [14], to Texas death row inmates [15], using the game as a tool of real-world healing, connection, and presence through storytelling and problem solving, despite being set in a fictional world.

Role-playing games offer a critical interactive narrative framework. It's less about being able to act out a story as an elven warrior princess guarding a medieval tower dungeon, though we Black queer elven warrior princesses are certainly part of the un-televised revolution. Rather, it's about the possibilities of real-life collective world-building. Outlined by Karen Schrier, Evan Torner, and Jessica Hammer in their article "Worldbuilding in Role-Playing Games," worldbuilding combines the "act of designing and constructing believable fictional universes" with the "process of…link[ing] together individual stories scattered across multiple media" [16]. Worldbuilding offers fictional universe rules within which characters can sketch their own stories, collaboratively building a new universe as individual stories branch and intersect. Players are dropped into a skeletal world outlined by the GM, and the world is fleshed through actions and reactions, much like reality. And yet, though players meet as characters in a fictional world, this engagement serves to re-imagine if not "re-enchant" [16] the real world; as the authors posit, "most fictional worlds present us with lenses with which to view familiar aspects of our own that have been accentuated, transformed, and lain bare" [16]. Even as we create fictional worlds, those worlds are still constructed in relation to the world we occupy, calling into question elements of our own reality by playing through a narrative of their escape. As an interactive digital narrative framework, role-playing games can spark as many inquiries about the real world as there are pathways and modes of engagement with the fictional digital world.

Tabletop role-playing games are exciting to consider for their imaginative possibilities but playing them is a different story. A true tabletop role-playing game allows for endless choices because the GM and players shape the narrative together in real time, meaning that multiple people need to be present in the same place at the same time for an ideal tabletop experience. This is where text-based gamebooks come into action. Gamebooks (such as the popular *Give Yourself Goosebumps* [17] series, a choose-your-own-adventure spin-off of the *Goosebumps* children's horror story series) are like tabletop role-playing games in that they ask a player/reader to inhabit a specific character and build a narrative shaped by individual choice and interventions of luck, but a player/reader's choices are bounded by what is written in the text. The world of the text may not be endlessly open, but nevertheless the narrative pathways through that world are many, and so too are the exploratory possibilities for the player/reader.

Exploring narrative pathways necessitates an interface platform that can dynamically yet seamlessly move a player/reader through those pathways, and can allow for an infinite combination of possible pathways to unfold during creation and gameplay. *WILDWOOD* is built with Twine [18], a platform for writing hyperlinked texts that often take the form of interactive narratives. A unique writing and content management system, Twine is a powerful platform that can be impactful at any development scale and ability level. I've played some complex Twine stories that combine narrative and media into a rich multimodal landscape. I have also played Twine stories comprised solely of words, such as Anna Anthropy's *Queers In Love At The End of The World* [19], that hit me harder in ten seconds than some novels do in 400 pages. Interactive fiction urgently pulls the reader into the world of the game, and the Twine platform streamlines this process.

At its root level, Twine works by allowing the author to hyperlink ideas, thoughts, concepts, frames, and other media elements into an author-designed narrative network. SugarCube v2 [20], the Twine story format behind *WILDWOOD*, allows for a greater level of customization and interactivity by allowing authors to edit and script the interface code. Hyperlinking within the flow of writing was very simple, meaning that narrative creation was inherently imbued with interactivity from my first moments of writing (as opposed to writing a non-interactive narrative and trying to fit gameplay within the reader's role). Twine helped to productively shape my writing practice in this way; once I was in the mindset and the keystroke pattern of setting up challenges, creating possible solutions to choose from, and determining the effects of those choices on the main character, it became much easier to write a continuous interactive narrative. Not unlike living life, we can theorize and plan endlessly but eventually we must act and react. Writing interactive fiction, let alone playing/reading it, has been no different.

With SugarCube Twine, I was also able to build complex game and interface mechanics such as dice rolls and saved character statistics into the narrative, allowing for the main character's ability composition to continually update as the story progresses and the character's world grows. Rolls and character stats add an element of chance to the game, which helps keep the narrative unpredictable. Moreover, such mechanics allow the game to shift and modulate according to how effectively (relative to their individual mental, physical, and emotional wellness) a player/reader travels their journey. Really, health points and ability modifiers are no different from gaining and learning from lived experience in the real world, further expanding the potential of interactive digital narrative to affect meaningful material change.

WILDWOOD is a story permanently in progress, mirroring the real world as a story permanently in progress. Each chapter stands alone as its own narrative unit, exploring themes and elements of the real world, infinitely linking together to build and broaden the world of the narrative. The player/reader inhabits the world as the nameless main character, allowed to fully immerse into the narrative as themselves, a reality augmented by ability modifiers, health points, and checks on both throughout the game. *WILDWOOD* begins slowly, to allow the player/reader to acclimate to and learn the world, but rapidly picks up steam as choices are made that shape how the main character's journey unfolds.

The player/reader is first introduced to the world of *WILDWOOD* through the following introductory text [21]:

> *You find yourself in Wildwood, in the year 2099.*
>
> *This region was once known as Greater Englewood, a section of the traditional homeland of the Three Fires Confederacy between the indigenous Potawatomi, Odawa, and Ojibwe nations.*
>
> *After the land was stolen and sold to Paul Cornell, cousin of Cornell University founder Ezra Cornell, it was incorporated as the south side of Chicago.*
>
> *The land passed many decades as a white middle- and working-class residential area, until the arrival of Black southern families led many white residents to flee.*
>
> *As Black families made the neighborhood their home, they faced increasing inaction and a lack of sustainable investment from the city government. The trees they couldn't get the city to trim grew large; the potholes they couldn't get the city to fill grew larger. The people exhausted every avenue of civic engagement, straying at times into civil disobedience, but were met at every turn by thoughts and prayers.*
>
> *Brought on by years of neglect (written as thoughts and prayers) by city, state, and national government, coupled with fear and disgust from other citizens, the community began to rewild. As the Rewilding took place, those outside the community assumed that those inside would kill each other off as resources diminished; a problem finding its solution. So, the outsiders offered their thoughts and prayers and never entered.*
>
> *But the people didn't kill each other off. They formed a self-sustaining community around the Rewilding, flowing with the massive environmental changes this brought on. The untrimmed black oak trees became savanna sunshades; the unfilled gravel potholes became rock-bottomed prairie ponds.*
>
> *Wanting to keep their community strong and whole, the people soon planted a mass of sugar maple and red oak as a boundary. The people named their new enclosure Wildwood.*
>
> *Wildwood grew rich with natural and community resources, from a desolate neighborhood to a lush greenscape teeming with native flora and fauna. All of the Wildwooders attend school in the community or work to sustain the community,*

sustaining and maintaining with the skills their ancestors already amassed before the Rewilding took place.

Because Greater Englewood had no remaining grocery stores and no shopping malls, the Wildwooders developed their own markets, filled to the brim with goods made by the Wildwooders for the people. A particularly enterprising Wildwooder designed a system to tap and filter prairie groundwater so that the community would have an endless supply. Another Wildwooder opened a technology design center to teach and share tech developments with the rest of Wildwood.

The Wildwooders remain generally connected to the rest of the world through internet and data sharing, and the border was never permanently sealed on either side, but the more that the Outside region descends into environmental and political chaos, the less that the Wildwooders feel the need to leave.

Utopia is a pipe dream and communism never works in practice, but the Wildwooders know they have a good thing going and they collectively work to move upward and outward.

Unbeknownst to the Wildwooders, the Outsiders are plotting an invasion.

Years of extractive industrialization destroyed many of the natural green spaces left in the Outside region, as a growing demand for expensive sky-rise housing and resource-draining data centers took hold in the region. The only green spaces left on the Outside are gardens located on condo rooftops, lakefront beaches bought up and gated off by developers, and riverside parks attached to swanky restaurants and hotels; a network of private property oases.

In its rewilded state, Wildwood is the last remaining natural public green space in the region, and now the Outsiders want it.

You and the other Wildwooders are unaware of this plot at the present moment, though.

You live your lives surrounded by family and friends, health and wealth, blessed and enriched by an understanding of where you've been as a community and grounded in a vision of where you still have left to go. You work toward this vision as a collective, sharing labor and sharing the rewards.

Today, your community will call upon you to begin a new journey into the unknown.

Are you ready to begin?

In the opening chapter, the main character moves through a regular day, getting up and going to work as usual. Upon their arrival at the office, the main character learns that they've been promoted and are assigned a project that involves leaving the Wildwood community. Over the course of the chapter, the player/reader chooses to either start planning for the trip or continue going about their day. The main character receives clues and tips about what may await them on the trip, but either notices them or doesn't (depending on how well the player/reader rolls on awareness checks, one of six character statistics). As the day ends, the main character reflects on the day's events and their upcoming trip, either curious about what lies ahead or, depending on their stats, blissfully unaware.

Throughout the second chapter, the main character is asked to travel out of Wildwood in search of something special to the community. To make it there, they must rely on their navigational skills to move from the Southside of the city to the Westside (the location of their treasure) on the CTA Green Line, or what remains of it in this future Chicago setting. This mode of transportation is particularly unique and relevant for the main character's purposes in the story. The Green Line connects the Southside and Westside, predominately Black and Brown areas in the city that face a great deal of structural inequality, and the train facilitates residents' movement between the two locations while bypassing much of the centrally located commerce in the Loop. The Chicago River, on the other hand, serves as the national connection point between the Great Lakes to the north and the Gulf of Mexico to the south via the Mississippi River, a critical hub of domestic naval preparedness and shipping strategy. The two barely intermingle, save for a brief moment in the Loop, the downtown economic heart of the city. Travelers between the real south and west sides bear witness to Chicago's constant growth and development as we stream past the Loop, moving from one forgotten margin to the other, but in the world of *WILDWOOD* the margin and the center are reversed. No longer a steel stream slipping past prosperity, the main character experiences the Green Line like a metallic rapid, with Outsiders jutting out like jagged rocks around each bend; the prosperity once represented by the flowing Chicago River no longer exists. In this way, a real-world social constraint becomes a narrative thought experiment and a game mechanic, something to play through rather than be trapped by.

Like the ever-expanding universe, the world of *WILDWOOD* will continue to expand through the nuanced introduction of complex conflicts that shape player/reader experiences. Exploring these conflicts for how they shape an interactive narrative simultaneously means journeying outside of my comfort zone as an author imagining radical Black futures. For example, what will it mean to include interpersonal violence in my vision of an afro-solarpunk future, particularly in a vision that narratively remaps a Black space already charted and diagrammed in blood? My gut impulse as a child of this space is to build a world with no fighting and no sadness, no guns and no police, but this highlights the difference between fantasy and generative speculation. In a fantasy world, the evil forces can be as mild and easily defeatable as the author desires, but that isn't a realistic vision of a tangible future because it does not have to be. Speculation, by comparison, offers what Martine Syms calls "an awakening sense of the awesome power of the black imagination: to protect, to create, to destroy, to propel ourselves toward what poet Elizabeth Alexander describes as 'a metaphysical space beyond the black public everyday toward power and wild imagination'…[facilitating] the opportunity to make sense of the nonsense that regularly—and sometimes violently—accents black life" [22]. Worldbuilding as a framework for narrative change through interactive digital design means balancing the good and the evil, holding space for radical compassion and painful honesty, making sense of and immersively playing through struggle as well as success, because Black futurity is not a game. Even if Greater Englewood is not re-wilded in the year 2099, the survival strategies that arise from building this afro-solarpunk interactive narrative are critical to imagining a radical Black public that can realistically and holistically sustain present and future generations.

For, to paraphrase Grow Greater Englewood steward Taryn Randle when discussing the work of social justice across media, Black worldbuilding means "working to try to secure a situation for our babies, to be able to further secure our future babies, no matter where they have to go, wherever they end up" [23].

Disclosure of Interests. Author previously worked as a freelance audio producer profiling Grow Greater Englewood for a podcast. This freelance contract ended before work on the *WILDWOOD* project began. Author has no other competing interests to declare that are relevant to the content of this article.

References

1. Koh, A.: The Political Power of Play. Hybrid Pedagogy (2014) https://hybridpedagogy.org/political-power-of-play/
2. Mariani, I., Ciancia, M., Ackermann, J.: Interactive digital narratives and counter-narratives: systematizing knowledge to derive clusters as lenses of observation. In: Game: The Italian Journal of Game Studies, pp. 5–32 (2023)
3. Stockwell, C.E.: "Englewood," Encyclopedia of Chicago (2004). http://www.encyclopedia.chicagohistory.org/pages/426.html
4. Bain, K., Alexander, E.M.: The street finds its uses: a black digital humanities call and response. Stud. Romanticism **61**(1), 161–174 (2022). https://muse.jhu.edu/article/853148, https://doi.org/10.1353/srm.2022.0016
5. Parham, M.: Breaking, dancing, making in the machine: notes on .break .dance. sx archipelagos (2019). https://archipelagosjournal.org/issue03/parham-process/parham-process.html#processing
6. Christian, B.: The race for theory. Feminisms **6**, 69–77 (1987). https://doi.org/10.1093/oso/9780192892706.003.0011
7. Brown, A.M.: Emergent Strategy: Shaping Change, Changing Worlds. AK Press, Chico, CA (2017)
8. Grow Greater Englewood: About Us (2022). https://www.growgreater.org/about
9. Silva, C., et al.: INDCOR white paper 5: addressing societal issues in interactive digital narratives. arXiv:2306.09831 (2023)
10. Thomas, L.: The Intersectional Environmentalist: How to Dismantle Systems of Oppression to Protect People + Planet. Hachette, New York City (2022)
11. Grow Greater Englewood: Englewood Nature Trail (2022). https://www.growgreater.org/ent
12. Galvis, M.: Dungeons & Dragons Turns 50! See How We're Celebrating Our Gold Anniversary. Wizards of the Coast LLC (2024). https://www.dndbeyond.com/posts/1660-dungeons-dragons-turns-50-see-how-were-celebrating
13. Demopoulos, A.: Facing the demons: can Dungeons & Dragons therapy heal real-life trauma?. The Guardian (2023). https://www.theguardian.com/society/2023/mar/21/dungeons-dragons-therapy-psychologists-mental-health
14. Beasley, J., Touma, R.: Dungeons & Dragons at 50: the collaborative fantasy role-playing game that builds you up. The Guardian (2024). https://www.theguardian.com/lifeandstyle/2024/mar/10/dungeons-and-dragons-at-50-the-collaborative-fantasy-roleplaying-game-that-builds-you-up.
15. Blakinger, K.: When Wizards and Orcs Came to Death Row. The Marshall Project (2023). http://www.themarshallproject.org/2023/08/31/dungeons-and-dragons-texas-death-row-tdcj
16. Schrier, K., Torner, E., Hammer, J.: Worldbuilding in role-playing games. In: Zagal, J.P., Deterding, S. (eds.) Role-Playing Game Studies, pp. 349–363. Transmedia Foundations, New York City, Routledge, (2018). https://doi.org/10.4324/9781315637532-20

17. Katz, D.: Series - give yourself goosebumps (2013). https://gamebooks.org/Series/82/Show
18. Interactive Fiction Technology Foundation: Twinery.org (2024). https://twinery.org
19. Anthropy, A.A.: Queers in love at the end of the world (2013). https://w.itch.io/end-of-the-world
20. Edwards, T.M.: SugarCube (2013). https://www.motoslave.net/sugarcube/2/
21. Alexander, E.M.: WILDWOOD: an interactive experiment in afro-solarpunk worldbuilding (2024)
22. Syms, M.: The mundane afrofuturist manifesto. Rhizome (2013)
23. Growing a Greater Englewood: Juneteenth Productions (2022)

Friendship with AI? - Immersive Science Fiction Prototyping for Responsible Innovation

Elke Brucker-Kley[(⊠)] [iD], Thomas Keller[iD], Janick Michot, Birgitta Borghoff[iD], and Isabelle Stutz

Zurich University of Applied Sciences, Winterthur, Switzerland
{brck,kell,mict,borg,stui}@zhaw.ch

Abstract. This paper presents the experiences from a science communication project that applied Immersive Science Fiction Prototyping to explore the concept of friendship with emotional AI. The aim of this paper is to introduce the relevance and key elements of a no/low-code prototyping pipeline that enables non-technical authors to collaboratively design multilinear future scenarios, which can be seamlessly imported into VR environments. Anchored in the overarching method of Science Fiction Prototyping, this pipeline not only facilitates the rapid creation of interactive multilinear VR scenarios but also promotes transdisciplinary design and public engagement for responsible innovation.

Keywords: Future scenario · technology critique · science communication · Virtual Reality · interactive multilinear narrative

1 Introduction – Background and Motivation

Can teenagers and young adults aged 13 to 29 envision a friendship with AI? The science communication project[1] presented in this paper aimed not to answer this question but to spark an active exchange between computer scientists researching affective computing technologies and a young lay audience.

Affective computing is an interdisciplinary research field at the intersection of computer science, psychology, and cognitive science [1]. It enables computers to recognize and respond to human emotions appropriately and is therefore also referred to as emotional AI [2, 3]. The research team involved in this project does research on embodied conversational agents that act as affective companions e.g., for chronically ill patients or smart tutors for learners. Emotional AI aims to make human-machine interaction more natural, personalized, and ultimately more effective. However, capturing and analyzing sensitive personal traits, such as voice, facial expressions, or physiological data, as well as substituting interpersonal encounters with conversational AI, is subject to controversial debates [4–9]. Can we envision a society where people increasingly form social bonds with intelligent machines?

---

[1] The project was funded by the Swiss National Science Foundation (SNSF) under the Agora funding, aiming at fostering dialogue between scientists and the public.

Since future applications and consequences of affective computing are still vague and hard to imagine, Immersive Science Fiction (SciFi) Prototyping was applied as a method in this science communication project to make future everyday life with affective computing tangible. The resulting science communication project is motivated by humanistic approaches of technology criticism and technophilosophy [10, 11]. From this perspective humans are not regarded as "mindless victims of technology" but as "agents of cultural change" [12, p. 154] who can shape the use of technology. The overarching goal of the presented approach is to trigger a discourse on the desirability and designability of technological change grounded in everyday experiences. These experiences of different versions of our future life with emerging technologies are made accessible to a public audience via a multilinear future scenario in immersive Virtual Reality (VR).

2   Methods and Approach – Immersive Science Fiction Prototyping

Science Fiction (SciFi) Prototyping is a methodology that builds on the art of telling stories about our future [13]. SciFi Prototyping started within Intel Corporation in 2010. The idea of Intel's futurist B.D. Johnson was to use science fiction as an input or step within the technology development process and to encourage engineers to think in a more humanistic manner about their technological developments. The resulting methodology is best described "as a means by which scientists can explore the ramifications of new technologies, develop and test hypotheses, and find solutions to problems that come with pioneering techniques and emerging science [14, p. vii]."

SciFi Prototyping involves five main steps [14]: (1) Pick your science and build your world: position a controversial technology in a relevant domain of life (2) Scientific inflection point: let the technology create tension and present people with dilemmas (3) Ramifications of Science on people: explore how people are affected by the technology (4) Human inflection point: show how people respond to succeed with our without the technology (5) What did we learn: reflect on the learning from the scenario.

SciFi Prototyping can be classified as an intuitive-creative scenario technique that makes use of fictional narrative scenarios [15]. Unlike "classical" scenario planning and normative scenarios, the goal of a SciFi Prototype is not to predict likely or desirable futures, but to trigger critical reflection on the design of technological innovations. Coming from industrial innovation management, SciFi Prototyping has gained attention from the world of academic research. It has been applied to enrich traditional narrative scenario creation techniques [16] and as a mean of illustrating emerging technology research [17].

The well-defined principles and process of SciFi Prototpying have been further developed by the authors in the context of teaching as well as research and science communication projects over the past 6 years [18–22] and extended by three novel elements (see Fig. 1. Elements of Immersive Science Fiction Prototyping).

1. **The art of multilinear storytelling** and interactivity to enable choices about different versions of the future and to foster thinking in alternatives.

2. **The immersive qualities Virtual Reality (VR)** to force the audience to leave the position of a distant observer and to get emotionally involved when experiencing future life with technologies.
3. **The potential of prototypes** as used in engineering and human-centered design to find out how a technology should behave from an end user's perspective and to define design criteria for emerging technologies. To generate VR scenarios as experienceable prototypes a SciFi generator was developed as a technical framework to generate VR experiences in the VR development environment Unity from multilinear stories (Twines [23]) in a highly efficient and replicable manner (see Sect. 3.4).

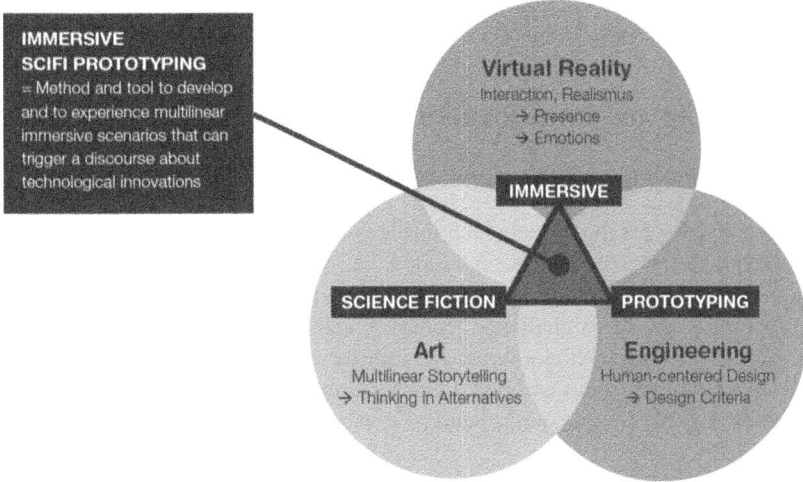

Fig. 1. Elements of Immersive Science Fiction Prototyping

The approach to design, build and apply the immersive SciFi Prototype in the context of the project can be summarized in 3 phases (see Fig. 2) that are outlined in the following sections:

1. Storytelling & Implementation– Frame and create a multi-linear VR scenario about everyday life with emotional AI
2. Experience – Let the target group experience the VR scenario and log the interactions and story paths of the players
3. Discuss – Moderate and analyze the discourse between scientists and a subset of the reached target group before and after the VR intervention

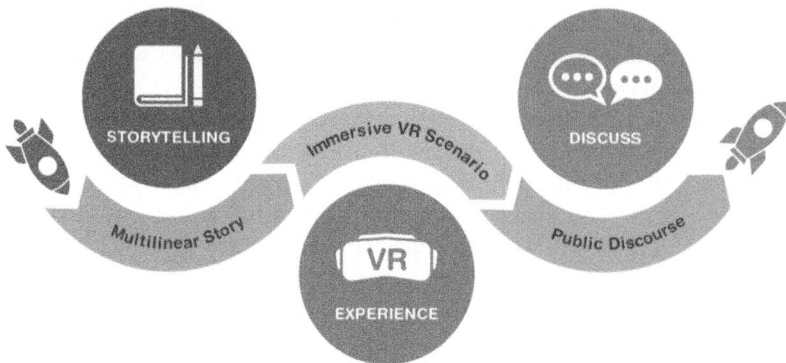

Fig. 2. Immersive SciFi Prototyping approach

3 Storytelling and Implementation

3.1 The Use Case: Friendship with AI

To envision and discuss the vaguely imaginable consequences of a technology like affective computing a concrete use case is needed, i.e., a professional or personal everyday situation where the technology is applied. Friendship was chosen as an extreme application of emotional AI to challenge teenagers and young adults to contemplate the desirability of a future with emotional AI. Can we imagine a future in which humans build friendships with socio-emotional Conversational Agents? Could a machine one day become a perfect companion, better, i.e. more reliable, more sensitive than any human being?

The target group was selected based on two main considerations: (1) People born after the CERN put the WWW in the public domain in 1993, also known as Generation Z, millennials, and post-millennials [24] were raised in a connected world with access to digital environments and experiential online consumption at any time [25]. What makes this generation particularly interesting with respect to Affective Computing is its hedonistic use of technology, i.e., people of this generation do not limit the value of technology primarily to utilitarian outcomes such as personal productivity and ease of use but to perceived pleasure and social image [26]. (2) Friendship plays a central role in this phase of life. Adolescents and young adults cultivate friendships in order to break away from family ties and develop their own identity by acquiring socio-cultural orientations, while friendships in older age include fewer friends and are supplanted by family relationships [27].

3.2 Scenography and Dramaturgy: Pick Your Science and Build Your World

The story for the VR scenario "Friendship with AI", was collaboratively created by an interdisciplinary team of computer scientists (experts in affective computing) and communication scientists (experts in storytelling and discourse analysis):

In the context of an associated teaching project, students conducted, transcribed, and analyzed 30 qualitative narrative street interviews with people aged 15–29 based on insights from a literature review on friendship with AI and input of the involved affective computing researchers [28]. The resulting narrative patterns were used as input to ensure the relevance of the scenario content for the target group.

The story was staged on three levels, guided by the model of virtual scenography according to Seeger [29]. This structured approach helps in creating a narrative that not only engages the imagination but also addresses the dynamics between future technologies and human experiences in a plausible manner:

- Macro-level: Understand and define the sociocultural, economic, political, and ecological drivers that shape the formation of friendships in the future.
- Meso-level: Define the immediate social context and other private and professional structures shaping social interactions in the future.
- Micro-level: To craft the specific action elements, i.e., dramaturgy (exposition, confrontation, resolution, plot points) [30], situations in life where the support of a friend is crucial, like moving to a new city or the loss of a job, were gathered in a brainstorming session. A multi-protagonist model was applied to represent a wide spectrum of motivations driving the adoption or rejection of affective computing technologies [31].

The resulting setting of the story is illustrated by a VR scene depicting life in the shared apartment of the future with human flat mates and their AI companions (see Fig. 3). The player, who experiences the story from a first-person perspective, has just moved to the city for a new job and moves into this shared apartment.

A graphic designer was involved early in the process, creating mood boards for the VR scenes and personas for the protagonists to bridge the gap in implementing the scenography and the avatars of the protagonists for VR.

Fig. 3. The stage set for the scenario – Moving into the shared apartment of the future

3.3 Scientific Inflection Points: Technology Leaps

As the VR scenario is intended to make the consequences of technological change tangible, technologies play a central role. Throughout the course of the multilinear scenario, participating "players" make decisions about living with increasingly affective digital assistants (Fig. 4).

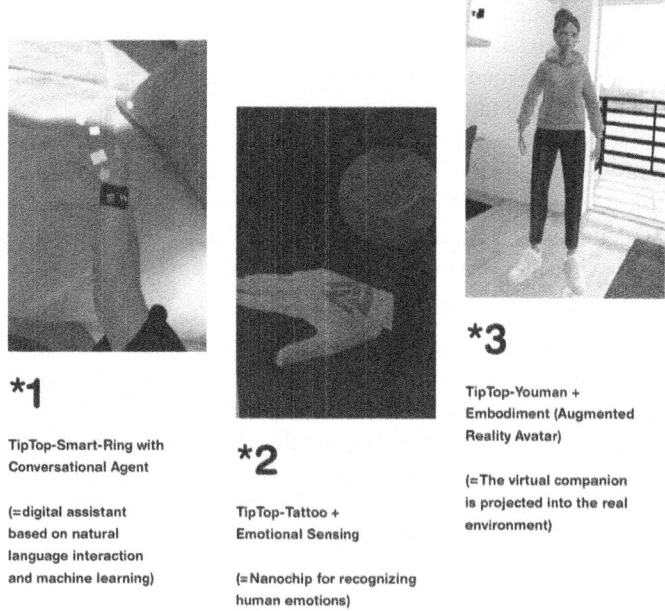

Fig. 4. 3 Technology leaps require decisions from the player that affect the course of the story

The story presents three technological leaps that make interactions with a conversational agent named TipTop progressively more "human-like". The players can choose to embrace or reject the technological leap. Opportunities to test the technology, reconsider their decisions, and observe its impact on their fellow residents make the advantages and disadvantages tangible and create dilemmas for the player.

3.4 SciFi Generator: Implementation of the VR Scenario

The resulting story, with its dialogues, interactions, and decisions, was implemented in Twine, an open source tool for authoring multilinear stories [23] (Fig. 5).

The VR scenario was implemented in Unity for Meta Quest 2 devices used in standalone mode with hand tracking and voice input only, i.e., without controllers.

The transformation of the Twine into a VR scenario could be automated to a certain extent using the SciFi Generator that had been custom developed in the course of teaching and research activities over several years. The SciFi Generator serves as the technical framework and toolset for immersive SciFi Prototyping: The Sci-Fi Generator enables

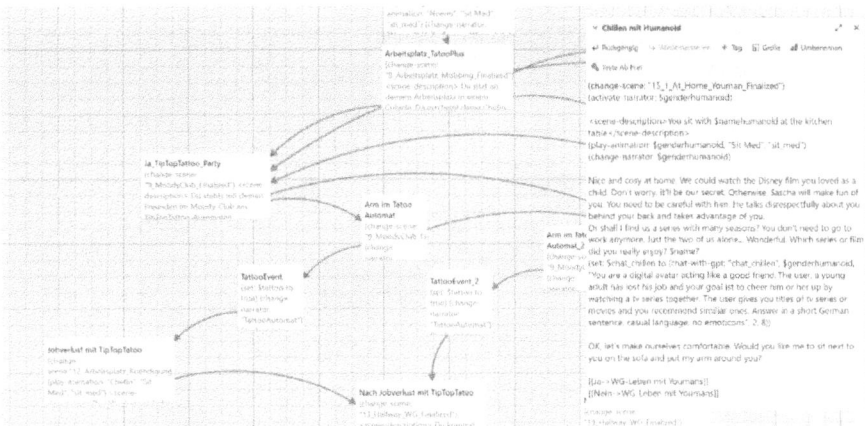

Fig. 5. Multilinear story authored in Twine

a low-code approach for developing VR scenarios and lowers the technical barriers to creating immersive VR scenarios,

Using the SciFi Generator the story created in Twine is published as an html file, imported in Unity, and transformed into a C# script that can be added to any game object (see Fig. 6). Thus, the focus of creating the SciFi Prototype lies on authoring the multilinear narrative in Twine and designing VR scenes that reflect the mood as defined in the scenography.

Twine authors simply need to apply a set of runtime macros that are incorporated and called within a story passage., such as the (change-narrator:) macro or the (look-at:) macro, to define the NPC's direction of gaze. Programming is only required for specific interactions.

At a later stage of the project, a dialog system integrated with GPT was incorporated into the VR scenario. The runtime macro (chat-with-gpt:) enables Twine authors to define a prompt to specify the role and task of the NPC and to use an optional parameter to limit the number of turns in a conversation between the player and the NPC (see Fig. 7.)

The SciFi Generator is deployed as a set of Unity packages that can be installed in any Unity project via the project manager or as git submodules, is based on Cradle [32]. Cradle is a Unity plugin that enables storytelling in Unity. Cradle imports Twine stories, plays them, and allows the addition of custom interactivity through scripting. Since Cradle has not been further developed since 2017, additional functionality required to create and run interactive immersive SciFi Prototypes and to manage and log the users and sessions has been developed as a set of extensions (Fig. 8):

- The **TwineAudioPlayer** extension complements Cradle by adding the ability to play stories based on speech. Runtime macros enable stories to be narrated by one or more avatars (Narrators). Additionally, this extension takes care of the storyboard. Unlike text-based storytelling with Cradle, audio output in speech-based stories is sequential. This means that passages and other interactions must be played in a specific order. Since the TwineAudioPlayer is controlled by the player's speech input the links of the multilinear story are activated by the player voicing her or his choice. The

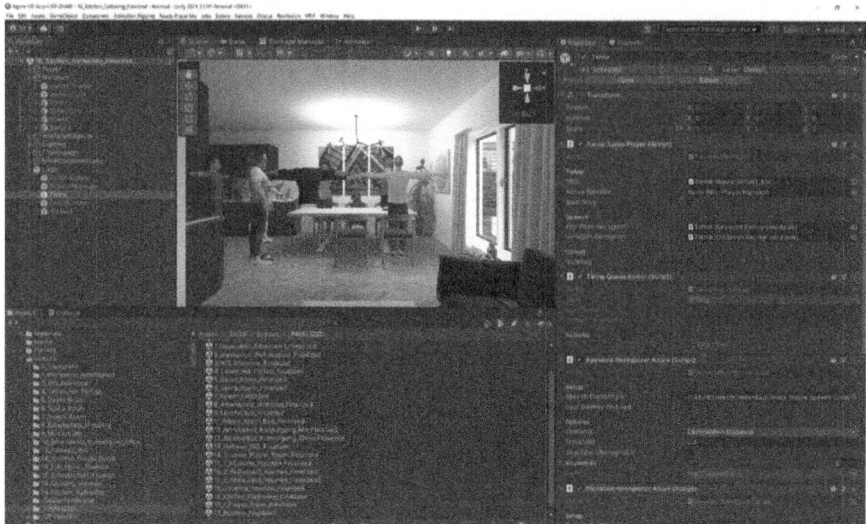

Fig. 6. Unity editor with SciFi Generator components

Fig. 7. Twine story passage with SciFi Generator runtime macros

TwineLinksViewModel allows to display the link texts as specified in the Twine in a canvas in VR.

- The related **Speech package** allows the integration of Text-to-Speech (TTS) and Speech-to-Text (STT) functionality via APIs, such as Microsoft Azure speech services, which were used for this project.
- The **Finite State Machine (FSM)** facilitates character control and decision making. States represent distinct behaviors or conditions that the player or non-player character (NPC) can be in, such as "Idle," or "Talking". Actions define the task or behaviors performed within each state. Decisions determine the conditions under which the FSM switches from one state to another, based on predefined criteria or events. Transitions refer to the process of changing from one state to another.
- The Narrator package provides a comprehensive solution for adding three types of narrators to the Unity project: (1) Base Narrator, acting as foundation and offering functionalities such as speaking, listening, and managing events, (2) NPCs, extending

the Base Narrator with advanced dialogue management, speech synthesis, and animation control for NPCs. (3) Player Narrator, enabling the user of the VR scenario to interact with the scenario based on speech. The conversation acts as an event handler between multiple narrators. The way narrators behave can be controlled either via the Twine runtime macros or the FSM.

– The Session Manager package allows to log sessions, including traversed story paths, user inputs, and conversations between the user and the NPCs, and to manage users and surveys, that are created in a backend server.

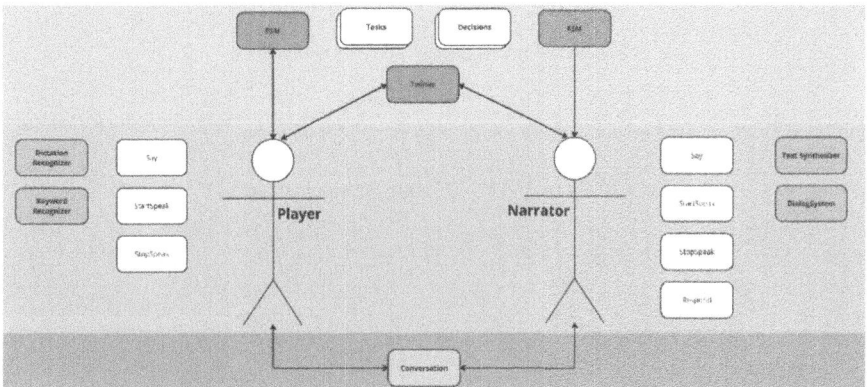

Fig. 8. SciFi Generator Narrator extension for speech

3.5 Design of VR Scenes and Avatars

For the design of the future city and the scenes in the future shared apartment and workplace, mostly pre-made assets were used, which were adapted to the context and mood of the story. Particular objects, such as the tattoo machine into which players insert their virtual arms to receive the Emotional Sensing TipTop Tattoo, were specifically modeled for the project. The design of the VR scenes for the rooms of the 4 flatmates was based on mood boards and personas that captured their distinct personalities, motivations, and attitudes toward technology (Fig. 9).

The photorealistic avatars for the human protagonists were created based on the personas and real portrait photos from an image library, using Reallusion Character Creator and the Headshot plugin (Fig. 10).

In the third and final technological leap within the scenario, the TipTop conversational agent is given a human-like body. This entity, marketed as TipTop-Youman in the story, is available in a female and male version. The player can select gender and name of the TipTop Youman. Unlike the photorealistic avatars of the human protagonists, the avatars of the TipTop-Youmans were deliberately generated as low-poly avatars using the avatar platform Ready Player Me. Since the required level of realism is a research question in embodied conversational agent research, the involved scientists were interested in reactions from the young audience to this design criterium.

Living room in the shared flat
and the future city

Workplace and
living capsule

Moody Club with TipTop tattoo machine
and restaurant

Fig. 9. Major scenes of the VR scenario

Fig. 10. Design of the photorealistic humanoid avatar of the room mates, boss and a male extra

Incorporating feedback from street interviews, which revealed that the target audience envisions an animal or an abstract being as an AI companion, the future shared apartment's cast is rounded out with a TipTop dog, a little ghost, and a humanoid robot (Fig. 11).

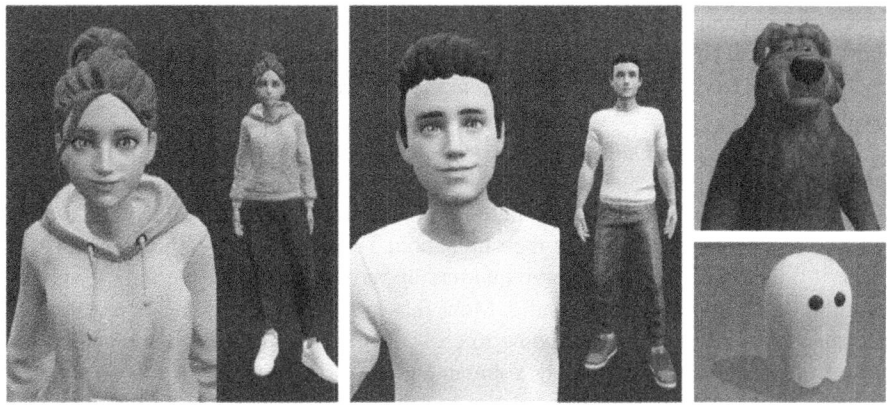

Fig. 11. Humanoid of the embodied digital companion "TipTop Youman" provided to the player for a trial period and alternative TipTop Youmans of the flat mates

4 Experience

A science museum, school visits, 2 bachelor thesis and 3 public events provided the setting for the VR interventions with the target group teenagers and young adults aged 13 to 29. The school classes and event guests were recruited through a website, social media, and invitations. In the museum, the VR interventions additionally attracted walk-in visitors.

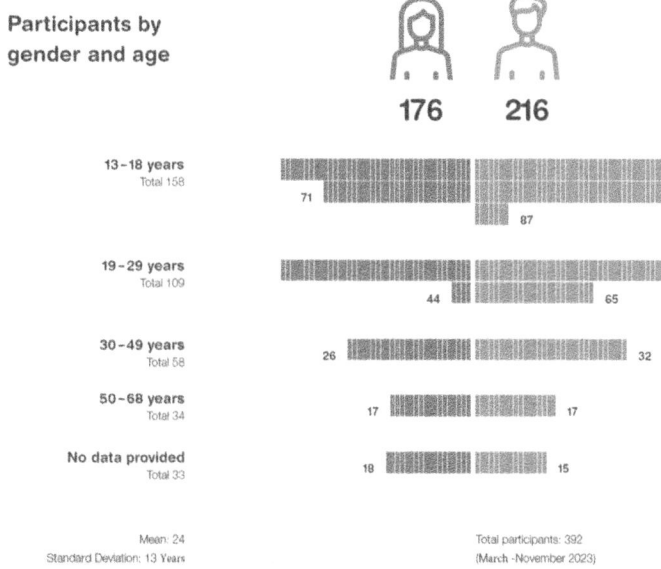

Fig. 12. Participants experiencing the Immersive SciFi Prototype "Friendship with AI"

329 participants experienced the scenario between March and November 2023 (see Fig. 12). The target group's upper age limit was not enforced to foster public discourse.

The paths and choices of participants in the VR scenario were logged and analyzed in a database.

A total of 392 participants traveled to the shared apartment of the future using Meta Quest 2 VR headsets. Of these, 379 installed the TipTop app on their virtual smart rings. More than half opted to get a TipTop tattoo to benefit from Emotional Sensing. A total of 320 welcomed the trial version of their humanoid TipTop Youman. When selecting the gender of their Youman, about three-quarters of participants chose the female variant, regardless of the participants' gender. More than 60% preferred going to a restaurant with their Youman over staying home to chill. Just over half of the participants were curious about the future with their Youman and chose to keep her or him in the end. No correlations with the participants' age or gender were detected in the decision data (Fig. 13).

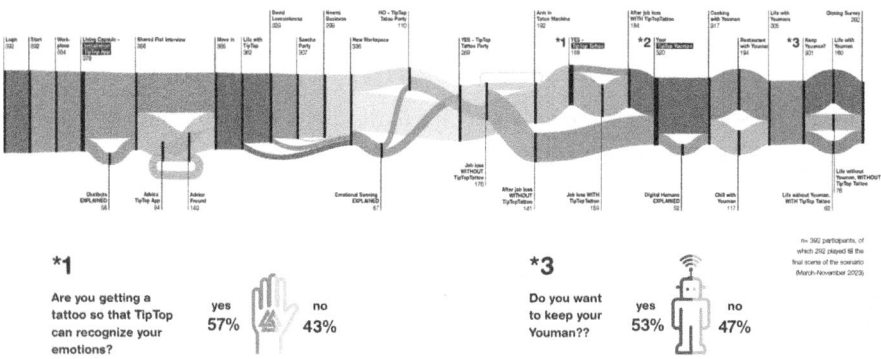

Fig. 13. Decision path of the participants

Responses to the question of the imaginability of friendship with AI at the start and end while experiencing the scenario indicate that participants were more open to the idea of AI friendship by the end (35% yes) compared to the beginning (23% yes). However, the response to whether AI could one day be a better friend than a human remained overwhelmingly negative, with 76% voting no after the scenario, compared to 71% before. The age group of 13–18 years was particularly skeptical, with only 17% of teenagers open to the idea of AI friendship before the scenario (28% after), compared to 29% of 18–29-year-olds (34% after). The VR scenario made the concept of AI friendship more tangible. But does imaginability equate to desirability? (Fig. 14).

In addition to the survey within the VR experience, 19 narrative group interviews with a total of 125 secondary school students and students from a technical college were conducted before and after experiencing the VR scenario. The recorded group discussions with scientists were transcribed and subject to discourse analysis[2]. The reconstructed narrative patterns on "Friendship with AI" can be distilled into three main contrasting positions.

---

[2] The methods and results of the discourse analysis are discussed in a dedicated publication [28].

1. Human-likeness versus non-human-likeness
2. Emotional and physical closeness versus distance
3. Trust versus mistrust

   From the perspective of the affective computing researchers in the SciFi Prototyping process, these positions represent relevant areas of tension that deserve attention in the design of human-AI interaction:

– Does an AI have to look like a human for us to build a relationship with it?
– How can we ensure that an AI is still recognized as a machine?
– How can we share information about our context and mental state with an AI while protecting our privacy?
– Is trust in an AI a necessary condition for an effective relationship between humans and machines?

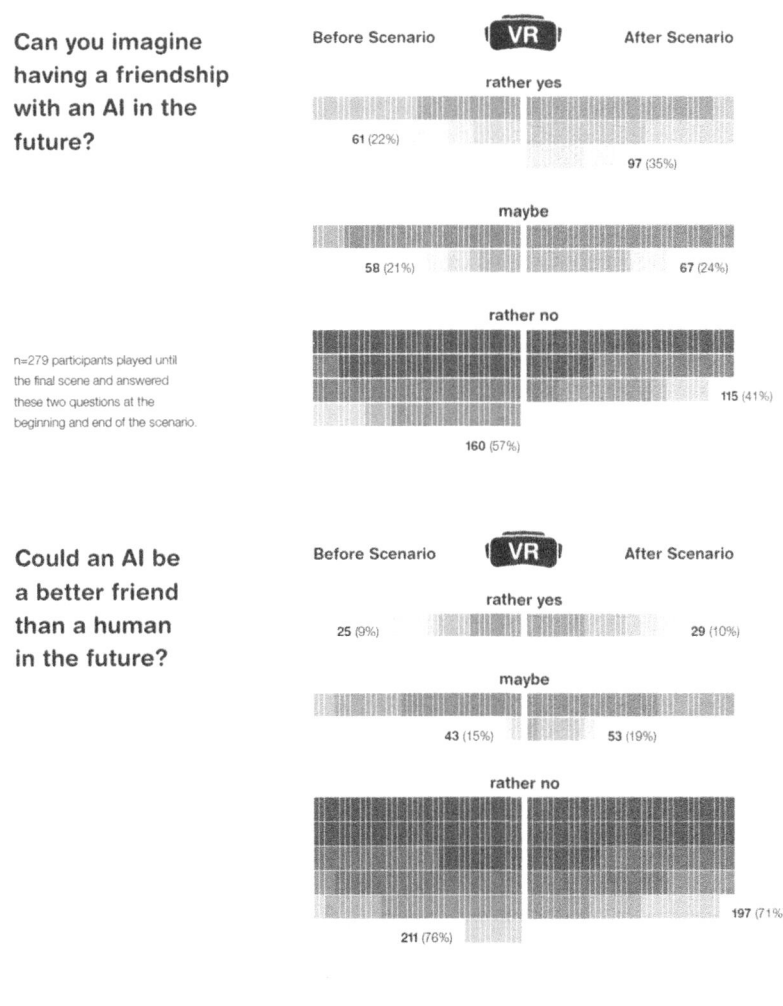

Fig. 14. Results of the survey within the VR Survey

5   Conclusion and Outlook

In conclusion, the science fiction prototyping pipeline presented in this paper demonstrates the potential of immersive technologies to support responsible innovation by fostering interdisciplinary collaboration and public engagement. By applying it to exploring friendships with emotional AI, we have shown how this method can facilitate the rapid and flexible creation of interactive multilinear narratives.

Immersive SciFi Prototyping has demonstrated its potential to bring to life the vague consequences of technological innovations in VR future scenarios. The experience was able to create a common communication ground to stimulate a lively discourse and empowered the target audience to articulate demands, ideas, and concerns.

Furthermore, based on subjective personal experiences, the members of the interdisciplinary project team confirm that the SciFi Prototyping process impacts not only the target group experiencing the SciFi Prototype but also the researchers who are required to think about the consequences of research objects they are working on through to the end.

Based on the described experiences, the advantages of Immersive Sci-Fi Prototyping and its contribution to interactive story design can be summarized in three key points. First, the no/low-code pipeline reduces the technical barrier for non-experts, enabling broader participation in creating multilinear future scenarios. Second, the ability to rapidly test and iterate narrative changes supports a more flexible and efficient design process, particularly in multidisciplinary teams. By allowing small changes in wording or branching storylines to be easily imported into Unity, this method supports both creativity and precision in the development of multifaceted future scenarios. Lastly, the extension of Science Fiction Prototyping with immersive VR opens new avenues for engaging diverse audiences in experience-based discussions about the societal implications of emerging technologies, such as emotional AI.

Limitations: This project was not a research project but a science communication project. The focus was on active engagement with the target audience, which required spontaneity and flexibility. Therefore, the results are not outcomes of a rigid research design but are based on interactions and experiences which can serve as starting points for further research.

Following, areas we are currently working on or exploring to optimize and validate the impact of immersive SciFi Prototypes:

- Social interaction: We are continuously optimizing both the GPT-based dialogue system and the non-verbal communication capabilities of the NPCs to allow players to interact more naturally and freely with NPCs.
- Augmentation (AR): For certain use cases we see value in experiencing SciFi prototypes in a real private or professional environment.
- Multiplayer capabilities: Although one advantage of an immersive Sci-Fi prototype is that players can make decisions independently and without social pressure, technological choices in real life are often socially motivated. Therefore, a multiplayer mode would be interesting, allowing multiple players to discuss and decide together so that certain aspects of the discourse can happen within the scenario.

Specifically for the presented SciFi Prototype on friendship with AI, we see the following potentials for future research:

- Systematic evaluation: Unlike teaching and research-motivated Sci-Fi prototypes we have developed in the past, this science communication project was not framed by a BIE (building, intervention, evaluation) action research scheme [33] and the artifacts were not systematically evaluated using the quality criteria as defined by Koenitz along the three dimensions agency, immersion and transformational capability [34, 35]. The Twine and VR scenario did undergo informal prototyping and testing, and the transformational capability was subject to analysis (see Sect. 4). Still, the quality could be enhanced more systematically in future iterations.
- Longitudinal studies: Investigating how people of different age groups and backgrounds form relationships with embodied conversational AI over time.
- Ethnographic conversation analyses: Observing the social practices as well as linguistic structures and patterns that emerge in conversations between humans and machines.
- Field studies in different countries: to identify intercultural differences regarding attitudes and behaviors toward emotional AI

References

1. Devillers, L.: Human–robot interactions and affective computing: the ethical implications. In: von Braun, J., S. Archer, M., Reichberg, G.M., Sánchez Sorondo, M. (eds.) Robotics, AI, and Humanity, pp. 205–211. Springer, Cham (2021)https://doi.org/10.1007/978-3-030-54173-6_17
2. Picard, R.W.: Affective Computing. MIT Press (2000)
3. Afzal, S., Khan, H.A., Khan, I.U., Piran, M.J., Lee, J.W.: A comprehensive survey on affective computing; challenges, trends, applications, and future directions. arXiv: arXiv:2305.07665 (2023). https://doi.org/10.48550/arXiv.2305.07665
4. Spezialetti, M., Placidi, G., Rossi, S.: Emotion recognition for human-robot interaction: recent advances and future perspectives. Front. Robot. AI 7, 532279 (2020). https://doi.org/10.3389/frobt.2020.532279
5. Brandtzaeg, P.B., Skjuve, M., Følstad, A.: My AI friend: how users of a social chatbot understand their Human–AI friendship. Hum. Commun. Res.Commun. Res. 48(3), 404–429 (2022). https://doi.org/10.1093/hcr/hqac008
6. Wienrich, C., Carolus, A., Markus, A., Augustin, Y., Pfister, J., Hotho, A.: Long-term effects of perceived friendship with intelligent voice assistants on usage behavior, user experience, and social perceptions. Computers 12(4), 77 (2023). https://doi.org/10.3390/computers12040077
7. Chaturvedi, R., Verma, S., Das, R., Dwivedi, Y.K.: Social companionship with artificial intelligence: recent trends and future avenues. Technol. Forecast. Soc. Chang. 193, 122634 (2023). https://doi.org/10.1016/j.techfore.2023.122634
8. Ghotbi, N.: The ethics of emotional artificial intelligence: a mixed method analysis. Asian Bioeth. Rev. 15(4), 417–430 (2023). https://doi.org/10.1007/s41649-022-00237-y
9. Katirai, A.: Ethical considerations in emotion recognition technologies: a review of the literature. AI Ethics (2023). https://doi.org/10.1007/s43681-023-00307-3
10. Poser, H.: Homo Creator: [Technology as Philosophical Challenge]Technik als philosophische Herausforderung. Springer (2016)

11. Taylor, A.E.: Body and technology: reframing the humanistic critique. Janus Head **12**(1), 12–21 (2011)
12. Rose, E.: The errors of thamus: an analysis of technology critique. Bull. Sci. Technol. Soc. **23**(3), 147–156 (2003). https://doi.org/10.1177/0270467603023003001
13. Draudt, A., Hadley, J., Hogan, R., Murray, L., Stock, G., West, J.R.: Six insights about science fiction prototyping. Computer **48**(5), 69–71 (2015). https://doi.org/10.1109/MC.2015.142
14. Johnson, B.D.: Science fiction prototyping: designing the future with science fiction. Synth. Lect. Comput. Sci. **3**(1), 1–190 (2011). https://doi.org/10.2200/S00336ED1V01Y201102CS L003
15. Steinmüller, K.: Szenarien – Ein Methodenkomplex zwischen wissenschaftlichem Anspruch und zeitgeistiger Bricolage. In: Zukunft und Wissenschaft, pp. 101–137. Springer, Berlin, Heidelberg (2012). https://doi.org/10.1007/978-3-642-28954-5_6
16. Burnam-Fink, M.: Creating narrative scenarios: Science fiction prototyping at Emerge. Futures **70**, 48–55 (2015). https://doi.org/10.1016/j.futures.2014.12.005
17. Kymäläinen, T.: Science Fiction Prototypes as Design Outcome of Research. Aalto University (2015). https://aaltodoc.aalto.fi:443/handle/123456789/15345. Accessed 12 Sep 2019
18. Brucker-Kley, E., Keller, T.: Exploring the potential of immersive narrative scenarios to identify design criteria for our digital future(s). In: 2019 8th International Congress on Advanced Applied Informatics (IIAI-AAI), Toyama, Japan, pp. 499–504 (2019). https://doi.org/10.1109/IIAI-AAI.2019.00108
19. Brucker-Kley, E., Keller, T.: Beyond digitalization: 'My boss is artificial'. In: Matos, F., Vairinhos, V., Salavisa, I., Edvinsson, L., Massaro, M. (eds.) Knowledge, People, and Digital Transformation: Approaches for a Sustainable Future, in Contributions to Management Science, pp. 37–54. Springer, Cham (2020). https://doi.org/10.1007/978-3-030-40390-4_4
20. Brucker-Kley, E., Keller, T., Stumpp, R.: Experiencing smart farming: effects of an interactive future scenario. In: Presented at the IEEE International Symposium on Technology and Society (ISTAS21), University of Waterloo and University of Guelph (Ontario, Canada) (2021)
21. Brunner, M., Brucker-Kley, E., Keller, T.: Eliciting personal attitude changes on predictive policing based on a multilinear narrative. In: ECIAR Proceedings 2020, pp. 21–29. Lisboa, (2020)
22. Brunner, F., Keller, T., Brucker-Kley, E.: Assessment of innovation readiness and technology acceptance using immersive sci-fi prototyping. In: Academic Conferences International (2022). https://doi.org/10.34190/eciair.4.1.727
23. Twine / An open-source tool for telling interactive, nonlinear stories. https://twinery.org/. Accessed 04 Sep 2019
24. Dimock, M.: Defining generations: where millennials end and generation Z begins. Pew Research Center. https://www.pewresearch.org/fact-tank/2019/01/17/where-millennials-end-and-generation-z-begins/
25. Mattia, G., Di Leo, A., Principato, L.: Millennials and on-line shopping: the case of smartphones. In: Mattia, G., Di Leo, A., Principato, L. (eds.) Online Impulse Buying and Cognitive Dissonance : Examining the Effect of Mood on Consumer Behaviour, pp. 61–70. Springer, Cham (2021). https://doi.org/10.1007/978-3-030-65923-3_9
26. Lin, C.-P., Bhattacherjee, A.: Extending technology usage models to interactive hedonic technologies: a theoretical model and empirical test. Inf. Syst. J. **20**(2), 163–181 (2010). https://doi.org/10.1111/j.1365-2575.2007.00265.x
27. Müller-Jentsch, W.: Freundschaftssoziologie – eine neue Bindestrich-Soziologie. Soziologische Revue **40**(3), 356–368 (2017). https://doi.org/10.1515/srsr-2017-0049
28. Borghoff, B., Brucker-Kley, E., Keller, T.: Designing and analyzing adolescent discourses on friendship with AI using science fiction prototyping. In: The 24th dmi: Academic Design Management Conference Proceedings, Delft, Holland, pp. 992–1010 (2024)

29. Seeger, T.: Storytelling und virtuelle Szenografie - das Dreistufen-Modell. In: Storytelling in virtuellen Welten, Konstanz: UVK Verlagsgesellschaft, pp. 229–231 (2014).
30. Field, S.: Screenplay: The Foundations of Screenwriting. A Step-by-Step Guide from Concept to Finished Script. New York: Bantam Dell (2005)
31. Das Storytelling-Handbuch: Inhalte professionell entwickeln : Kellermann Ron: Amazon.de: Bücher. https://www.amazon.de/Das-Storytelling-Handbuch-Inhalte-professionell-entwickeln/dp/3907100891. Accessed 27 Jun 2024
32. Terre, D.A.: Cradle - Github Repository (2017). https://github.com/daterre/Cradle. Accessed 11 Mar 2020
33. Sein, M.K., Henfridsson, O., Purao, S., Rossi, M., Lindgren, R.: Action design research. MIS Q. **35**(1), 37–56 (2011). https://doi.org/10.2307/23043488
34. Roth, C., Koenitz, H.: Evaluating the user experience of interactive digital narrative. In: AltMM '16: Proceedings of the 1st International Workshop on Multimedia Alternate Realities, pp. 31–36. Association for Computing Machinery, New York, NY, USA (2016). https://doi.org/10.1145/2983298.2983302
35. Murray, J.H.: Hamlet on the Holodeck: The Future of Narrativity in Cyberspace. MIT Press, Cambridge (1997)

Where's the Finance?: A Transmedia Storytelling Experience to Engage Young Adults in Financial Educational Content

Constança Freitas[1,2(✉)] [ID], Ana Santos[1,2] [ID], Paulo Bala[2] [ID],
Pedro F. Campos[1,2,3] [ID], and Mara Dionísio[1,2] [ID]

[1] Universidade da Madeira, Funchal, Portugal
constancafreitass@gmail.com
[2] ITI/LARSyS, Funchal, Portugal
[3] Wow!Systems, Funchal, Portugal

Abstract. Financial literacy is an essential life skill that deeply impacts individuals' personal and economic well-being; it includes understanding concepts essential for navigating the complexities of finance like budgeting, savings, investment, and debt. However, traditional financial education methods often struggle to engage learners effectively. This work discusses how entertainment education approaches, in particular, Transmedia Storytelling (TS), can be used to deliver financial literacy content. In this work, we want to examine the use of two common media in the TS field (web game and board game), to understand its barriers and benefits: a) "Financial Frenzy" emphasizes a team experience composed of a board game that leverages the collaborative nature of gameplay to foster learning and teamwork among the participants; b) "Where's the Finance?" relies on an individual educational experience composed of a puzzle game encouraging exploration and discovery. We conducted a pilot study of the two media, and results showed different potentials for the two concepts; therefore, we unified both concepts and present a redesign of the TS experience to continue studying the potential of transmedia to deliver financial educational content.

Keywords: Financial Literacy · Young Adults · Entertainment Education · Transmedia Storytelling · Board Game

1   Introduction

Financial literacy (FL) is a multidimensional concept crucial to individuals' financial well-being and decision-making with diverse definitions and perspectives emerging in academic discourse. For instance, for some authors [12], FL is defined as being able to use knowledge and skills to manage finances effectively for financial security, while for others it is the relationship between financial knowledge, financial attitudes, and financial behaviors [14]. In the scope of this work, we consider the *Organization for Economic Cooperation and Development (OECD)* definition for FL as "*possessing the knowledge, skills, motivation,*

J. T. Murray and M. C. Reyes (Eds.): ICIDS 2024, LNCS 15468, pp. 32–46, 2025.
https://doi.org/10.1007/978-3-031-78450-7_3

and confidence to apply financial concepts and risks for decision-making across diverse economic contexts: it is a tool to enhance not only one's fiscal well-being but also society's overall economic participation–an essential resource" [25]. Several studies [20–22] characterize FL as an indispensable tool to traverse today's economic terrain. Individuals with enhanced FL demonstrated a propensity for advantageous monetary actions (e.g., they effectively plan for retirement, clear credit card debts, and make informed investment decisions).

However, FL is a complex topic, and many people lack a basic understanding of financial definitions. Moreover, young adults face additional obstacles, as they often lack interest and access to financial education; formal education systems may not adequately cover financial topics, leaving them unprepared for real-world financial decisions [23]. The current educational approaches on this complex topic are traditional mediums such as classroom learning, books, slides, and websites [2,6,15].

We propose that TS presents a promising alternative to conventional teaching methods for FL education. The immersive and engaging nature of TS can potentially facilitate a more comprehensive understanding of FL concepts among young adults, by delivering an interconnected story that approaches FL content, leveraging expanded audience engagement, the power of immersive storytelling/world-building and interactivity [8,10]. Motivated by this potential, we seek to design a full transmedia experience; in this paper, we report on the design and early evaluation of two possible concepts of the experience, to understand their potential and caveats in delivering financial education.

Intending to address the challenges outlined and the opportunities offered by new media channels, we propose two concepts:"Financial Frenzy" and "Where's the Finance?". For clarity, we refer to them in the article, as Concept A and B, respectively. Concept A involves a collaborative approach to learning – participants engage with a board game that simulates real-life financial scenarios, a flashcards app that reinforces the key concepts, and a social media page that facilitates ongoing discussion and discovery. Concept B is an individualistic experience – participants engage with a puzzle game where they must uncover characters representing different financial principles hidden in the map, a coloring book to reduce anxiety, and a social media page that fosters discussion.

To evaluate the effectiveness of these approaches, and understand which media had more potential, we conducted a pilot study. The key findings from the pilot study were that some participants demonstrated an increase in the knowledge score after engaging with the transmedia experiences and both the team-based and individualistic approaches were effective in engaging participants and fostering learning, suggesting the potential of this approach in delivering FL content. We also present a redesign and refinement of the final concept.

2   Literature Review

In this section, we start by outlining the potential of using Edutainment and, in particular, a TS approach to deliver educational content. And then, we lay out the current initiatives that leverage the advantages of immersive and interactive media specially designed for FL education.

2.1 Transmedia Storytelling

Henry Jenkins is considered the father of the term "Transmedia Storytelling", which is a process where integral elements of fiction get dispersed systematically across multiple media to create a unified and coordinated entertainment experience. Ideally, each medium makes its unique contribution to the unfolding of the story, and this approach allows creators to expand their stories beyond the confines of a single medium and engage with audiences in new ways [3]. Moreover, this format actively engages users, encouraging them to interact with and even influence the story, playing a crucial role in the narrative's expansion and depth [11].

2.2 Edutainment and Transmedia Storytelling for Education

Edutainment, a blend word of "education" and "entertainment", represents a dynamic approach to learning that leverages the engaging elements of entertainment media to deliver educational content [7]. This innovative form of instructional design seeks to bridge the gap between traditional education and learners' evolving needs and preferences in the digital age.

Edutainment can manifest in various forms, such as video games, interactive simulations, virtual reality experiences, and multimedia content, aiming to make learning more enjoyable, accessible, and effective [26]. Numerous studies have explored the efficacy of edutainment across various educational domains. For example, Lien used edutainment in a museum using smartphone games to engage visitors in interacting with artifacts [19]. In today's educational setting, traditional methods are evolving, and educators seek innovative techniques to engage students, foster creativity, and enhance learning outcomes [6,15]. In this way, TS may be a response to this search within the educational context offering exciting possibilities to create compelling stories that deliver effective educational messages. In another instance, Bidarra et al. [28] present a prototype for learning English, as a second language, through TS; the study found that the prototype was effective in promoting language learning and that students enjoyed the experience, concluding that TS offers an opportunity for beneficial educational purposes.

Despite these encouraging examples showcasing how TS can be a powerful tool, we can not ignore that it might pose its challenges as well as Kwon et al. [18] highlight in their work the limitations of TS in the entertainment and education sectors. They identify several limitations of TS, including difficulties in collaboration between different media platforms and failure to consider consumers who might not be interested in more than one media platform.

2.3   Interactive Media for FL Education

FL plays a crucial role in empowering individuals to make informed financial decisions and researchers have explored various strategies to enhance FL, from innovative technologies to engaging games. For example, Klontz et al. [16] explored the impact of an interactive multimedia program that used an animated teen story, text and graphic overlays, interactive exercises, and supplemental printouts to deliver instructions on financial competence among at-risk youth. The study aimed to enhance FL through psychoeducational interventions; their results indicated that this approach had positive effects, contributing to improved financial understanding and competence.

Another research initiative by Kuchciak et al. [17] showed the importance of leveraging social media as an attractive and modern channel for promoting FL. Their study focused on the role of social media in improving financial education among bank customers, their findings. Another example is "Next Gen Personal Finance" which has several web games about many financial topics [1].

3   Exploring Social and Individualistic Concepts for TS Experiences

Since FL is such a complex and multilayered topic [23], we propose that it is better suited to be disseminated across multiple platforms using TS. Additionally, while transmedia experiences and games are abundant, the integration of FL within these experiences remains underexplored. In this section, we describe two initial concepts to analyze their potential, given the limited evidence on which media best suits the approach to FL concepts. The two concepts may have similarities, yet they are two distinct experiences that do not interrelate with each other.

Before explaining the rationale behind each of the design concepts, it is important to highlight the rationale behind the choice of educational content. For the choice of the FL themes, we took into consideration a study by Solheim et al. [29], which explores college students' narratives about financial socialization experiences within their families; key findings showed that *"the three most prevalent themes about what and how students learned about finances are reported: saving, money management practices, and family communication patterns"*. Another study by Webley et al. [31] examined the economic socialization of young adults in Europe, highlighting how savings and budgeting are essential for young adults' financial health. Additionally, a study by Totenhagen et al. [30] states that the US Department of the Treasury argues that a successful program should focus on basic savings, credit management, home ownership, and retirement planning. Finally, empirical evidence supports the importance of budgeting and saving across all developmental periods, from preschool-aged youth [27] to college-aged young adults [24]. Taking this literature into consideration, we decided to focus mostly on savings and expenses/debt, since these are the most important and basic concepts that young adults should know about.

3.1   Concept A – "Financial Frenzy"

This experience is distributed through three main channels:

1. "Financial Frenzy" (see Fig. 1) – a board game designed to teach FL concepts such as debt and savings;
2. "FitFrenzy" – a mobile application designed to train financial concepts, and supposed to be played after the board game;
3. "@goldensfromGoldcrest" – a social media profile that engages users by fostering discussion and communication about relevant topics.

Given our desire to explore social and individualistic concepts in TS, we describe (and evaluate) only *Financial Frenzy* as it involves competitive and collaborative social elements to promote conversation about financial struggles and experiences. Players are divided into two teams and aim to reach the end of the board by completing challenges determined by two dice, one for movement and one for the type of challenge. The challenges include:

– *Question Cards:* Multiple-choice questions to test financial knowledge.
– *Drawing Challenges:* Players draw financial concepts for teammates to guess, promoting understanding of abstract ideas.
– *Forbidden Words Challenges:* Players describe financial terms without using specific words, encouraging creative thinking and discussion.
– *Memory Game (Optional Challenge):* Can be played when trying to answer the question card offering additional educational content. The content of the cards are definitions related to the topics on the question cards (red for debt, yellow for savings); this was designed to be an alternative method for those who wished to know more about FL topics.

3.2   Concept B – "Where's the Finance?"

The transmedia channels for this experience are:

1. "Where's the Finance?" (see Fig. 2) – a web game where the player explores financial narratives;
2. "Relaxing with the Goldens" – a coloring book linked to the web game;
3. "@goldensfromGoldcrest" – a social media page, similar to the one previously mentioned.

For concept B, we wanted to explore delivering FL content as individual experiences, focused on introspection and reflection. *Where's the Finance?* is a web-based game where players assume the role of financial detectives tasked with identifying and addressing financial challenges faced by characters. Players progress by finding characters in a map; to help the players, detailed descriptions of characters and their financial challenges are presented in envelopes and cards, covering issues such as budgeting dilemmas and investment decisions. After finding the character, the users play a mini-game with a lesson addressing the financial problem, related to the financial challenge of the character, providing players with a hands-on application of financial knowledge.

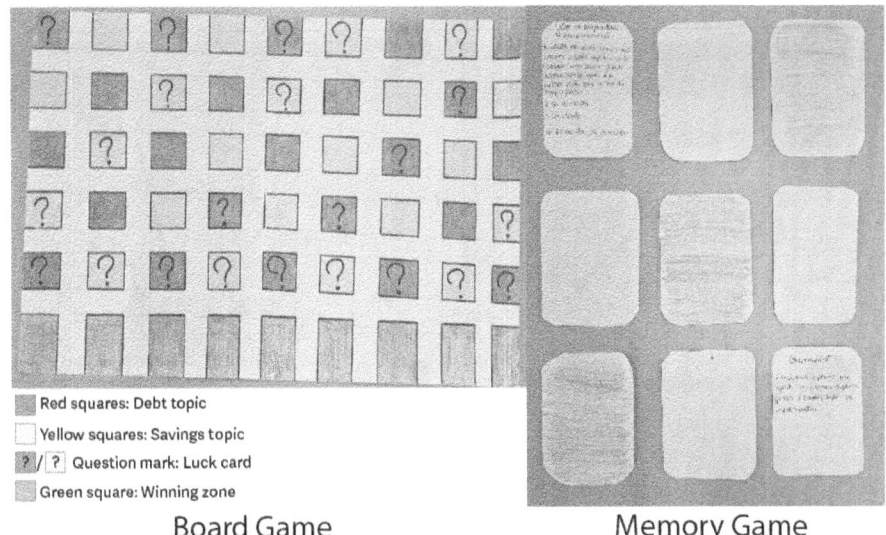

Red squares: Debt topic
Yellow squares: Savings topic
?/? Question mark: Luck card
Green square: Winning zone

Board Game   Memory Game

Fig. 1. Low-fidelity prototype for "Financial Frenzy". On the left is the boardgame, and on the right is the memory game.

4 Pilot Evaluation

We sought initial feedback on the two game concepts to assess their effectiveness in teaching FL and players' perception. For this pilot evaluation, we chose low-fidelity prototypes of elements of each TS experience (the physical gameboard of concept A and a digital prototype (in Figma) of the web game in concept B) and conducted a counterbalanced within-subject evaluation.

4.1 Protocol

Participants (n = 8) were recruited through convenience sampling (using an University Discord server) to participate in a playtest that took place in our research center. Participant's ages ranged between 18 to 30 years old; 62.5% were female, all students, and all familiar with games. The session started with the researcher explaining the protocol and collecting consent. Prior to the session, participants filled out a questionnaire with demographic data and FL multiple choice questions and were explained the rules for each game. Based on financial definitions from a financial website [2] and the content in the games, seven FL multiple choice questions were used (e.g. "*What is an emergency fund?*", "*How long should the emergency fund cover?*", "*What are the three types of expenses in a budget?*", etc.).

Order of game A and B was counterbalanced. For game B, participants played individually; for game A, P1-P4 and P5-P8 played as groups. After the first game, participants repeated the questionnaire with FL questions.

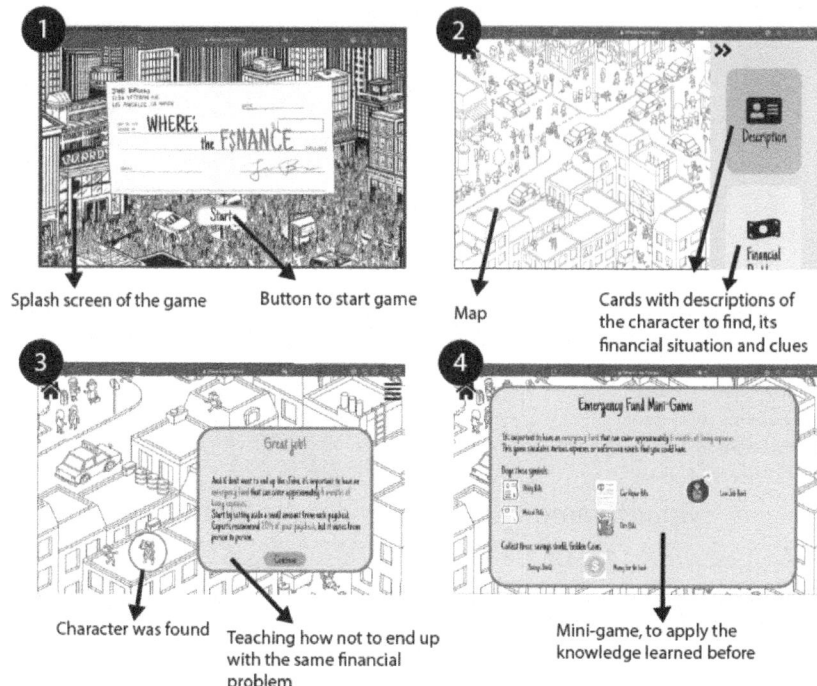

Fig. 2. Where's the Finance is a single-player game where players explore a map to find characterswhile learning about their financial problems: 1) game's start screen; 2) the map and cards with character's description (blue) and financial problem (yellow); 3) when the character is found, a popup informs the player about the financial problem, 4) the mini-game to apply learnt knowledge. (Color figure online)

After each game, participants filled out a questionnaire with the Game Experience Questionnaire (GEQ) [13] and responded to some open-ended questions by the researcher; audio was recorded and later transcribed. The GEQ comprises 4 modules, measuring various components (from 0 to 4) like *Flow*, *Competence*, etc. For both games, we used the In-Game and the Post-game module; for game A, since we have a social aspect, we additionally used the Social Presence module. Quantitative results were analyzed using R. Due to the small number of participants and the pilot nature of the evaluation, we did not seek statistical methods.

4.2   Results

After analyzing the data collected, we summarized results from the GEQ [13] into Table 1 (means and standard deviations) and Fig. 3 (boxplot distributions).

The results from Concept B show promising outcomes. Most participants rated high in *Competence* and *Positive Affect* (with a mean of 3 and 3.38,

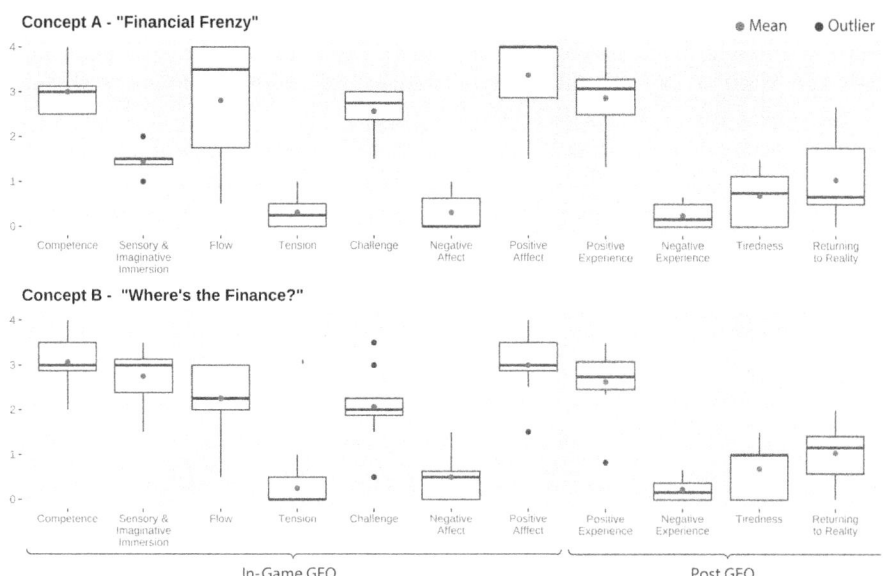

Fig. 3. Boxplot distributions for In-game and Post-game GEQ components for Concept A (n = 8) and B (n = 8)

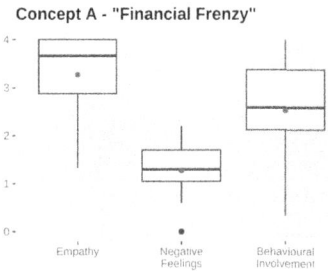

Fig. 4. Boxplot distributions for Social Presence GEQ component for Concept A (n = 8)

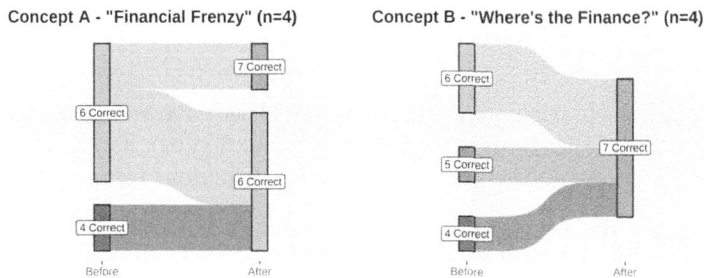

Fig. 5. Alluvial diagram showing correct answers in FL questionnaire, before and after Concept A (n = 4) and B (n = 4).

respectively). In the *Challenge* dimension, only two participants gave high scores (above 3), indicating a need for increased difficulty in a future redesign. Low scores in *Negative Affect* and *Negative Experience* were consistent with high *Positive Affect* and *Positive Experience* ratings.

For Concept A, participants also reported high scores in Competence (mean of 3.06). In the *Challenge* dimension, scores indicate a perceived challenge. Low values in *Negative Affect* and *Negative Experience* aligned with high *Positive Affect* and *Positive Experience* ratings. Additionally, Social Presence (see Fig. 4) dimensions was also adequately distributed.

Overall, Concept A and Concept B scored similar values in terms of game experience. Due to repetition of content in Concepts A and B, FL questions were only evaluated for the first game played. The accuracy of users' responses improved after participating in the experiences, as shown in Fig. 5.

Table 1. Mean and standard deviations for GEQ components for Concept A (n = 8) and Concept B (n = 8)

Module	Component	Concept A	Concept B
In-Game	*Competence*	3.00 ± 0.53	3.06 ± 0.62
	Sensory & Imaginative Immersion	1.44 ± 0.32	2.75 ± 0.71
	Flow	2.81 ± 1.44	2.25 ± 0.85
	Tension	0.31 ± 0.37	0.25 ± 0.38
	Challenge	2.56 ± 0.56	2.06 ± 0.90
	Negative Affect	0.31 ± 0.46	0.50 ± 0.53
	Positive Affect	3.38 ± 0.95	3.00 ± 0.76
Social Presence	*Empathy*	3.27 ± 0.97	–
	Negative Feeling	1.27 ± 0.72	–
	Behavioural Involvement	2.52 ± 1.30	–
Post-game	*Positive Experience*	2.88 ± 0.87	2.62 ± 0.83
	Negative Experience	0.25 ± 0.28	0.23 ± 0.25
	Tiredness	0.69 ± 0.65	0.69 ± 0.59
	Returning to Reality	1.04 ± 0.97	1.04 ± 0.68

We grouped the participant's reflections and ideas, collected during gameplay and the open-ended questions into categories for each game. For Concept A, the board game, we grouped the quotes into the following four categories:

– **Memory Cards**: We understood that the players who were not familiar with a certain FL concept needed further aid (P2 "*It would be good to have an explanation on the cards, for example, a financial consultant is very specific*"), so they suggested adding in all cards a small explanation of the concepts. Participants emphasized the importance of clarity in memory cards by suggesting color removal (P1 "*Remove the colors from the memory cards, because it helps to know which one it is*") and adding explanatory details.

- **Media Expansion**: Participants wanted to expand the story world in other media; some suggested the creation of an app to complement the game (P4: "*There could be an app, and it would give prizes throughout the game*").
- **Engagement**: Participants showed positive engagement and discussion of these complex topics with the peers they were playing with (P4 "*It is more fun to play in teams and I liked the mini-games*"); they emphasized the importance of dynamic features (P3 "*I liked the forbidden words cards, it made the game more dynamic*") to keep players engaged and not an overwhelming amount of information.
- **Game suggestions**: With the participants' feedback, we understood that for players that tested Concept B first, they wanted to apply the knowledge gained from the previous phase and test their knowledge to see if they were able to retain the information, and they also had some suggestions for improvements and new games (P3: "*Hangman game, could be another game*").

Likewise, for Concept B, the web game, we grouped the quotes into the following four categories:

- **Money incentives**: Participants felt the need to apply the money more directly and learn how to manage it (P1 "*There could be money, to apply what they learned*", P4 "*There could be money like monopoly*"). Participants suggested incorporating financial incentives and diversifying gameplay with activities or apps.
- **Links**: Participants wanted to personalize the content and discover more about the financial topics. They suggested the presentation of links to explore the topics further (P6 "*Have a section where you have everything you learned with links, that you could go back to*").
- **Engagement**: Participants showed positive engagement (P6 "*I think the web game is more fun*") and some reflection on their own financial doubts (P8 "*The mini-games seemed like an achievement, like now that you know this apply the information you learned*"); they emphasized the importance of dynamic features to keep players engaged, and not a lot of information at the same time making the user less confused (P8 "*I found it cool that there was not a lot of information, it is interesting.*").
- **Game suggestions**: With the participants' feedback, we understood that they wanted to apply what they learned on the journey of the characters and make sure they learned the financial concepts, and also had some suggestions for improvements, like creating a happiness meter for the town (P6 "*There could be a happiness meter for the town*") or even see how the passage of time would affect the economy (P3 "*There could be a part of the game where the time would pass and the players would see the results of that time on their financial assets*"). We could see interest in long-term gameplay (P6 "*I would have liked to see what happens in the long run when making a financial decision*") and investment in new game mechanics (P4 "*The screen could be split, one side we could do things, and the other side could be the results*").

5   Discussion

Through our pilot study, we were able to evaluate the potential effectiveness of using different game approaches, specifically web-based and board games, in enhancing FL. Similarly to what Webley et al. [31] reported, in our pilot study, users also showed some difficulties on essential topics for young adults financial health, such as savings and budgeting, more specifically, debts. It was evident that even when participants had some understanding of the broader topics we were trying to teach, they lacked the fundamental skills needed to execute these concepts effectively. Seeing some of the participants struggling with basic concepts of FL but at the same time engaged with both games gave us even more assurance to continue the pursuit of improving our TS experience. In particular, it was interesting to see that while we did not test the whole transmedia, it was the participants who hinted the need for more types of media that would expand the experience. Participants suggested having a complementary mobile application to the board game and in the web game to be able to follow up with further information regarding some of the topics presented. Additionally, the participants showed the need for long-term gameplay to understand how the economy and their financial decisions would affect the story world (and how this would translate into an impact on their lives).

5.1   Re-design of TS Experience "Where's the Finance?"

Considering the observed findings, we present a re-design proposal for our TS experience that represents a union of knowledge and experimentation. Our pilot study showed that both games had potential in different aspects. For example, we saw that, similarly to what Boghian et al. [9] reported, the board game had a strong social and engaging component with the potential to address educational topics such as FL. This opens up the possibility for participants to discuss FL in a light and relaxed way and, in this way, counteracting the tendency of FL being a taboo topic [4,5]. On the other hand, we saw that the web game since it's a more individualized experience, allows participants to delve into the FL concepts in more depth and have the potential for more FL knowledge acquisition.

Therefore, since both games presented potential that we considered essential for impacting FL, we decided to incorporate both web game and board game into a single TS experience. Below, we present how the redesign incorporates concepts A and B; yet, we opted to keep the title and overall narrative as the one from "Where's the Finance?" as this story world had more transmedia potential due to its characters and their stories. The experience integrates the board, web game, and Instagram page, where all elements work together within a single story arc, maintaining continuity through shared characters and themes, creating a seamless and immersive transmedia experience. Figure 6 illustrates the different media channels for the final TS experience.

Overall Transmedia Narrative. The game takes place in the mystical world of Goldcrest, home to the Goldens where they face a curse; the player is tasked

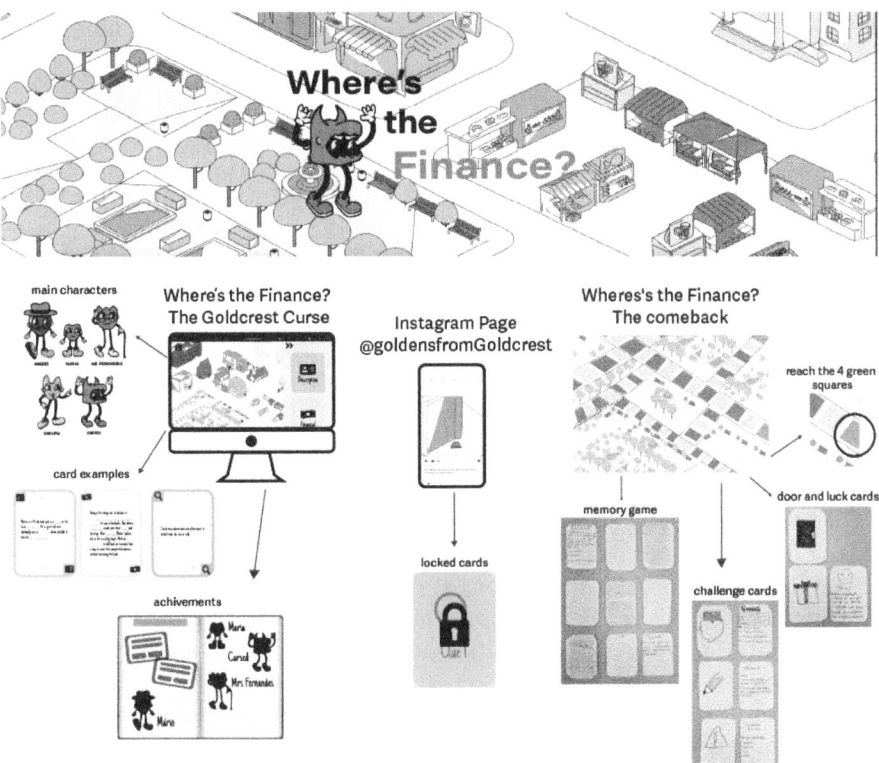

Fig. 6. Different media channels for the final TS experience, composed of: 1) "Where's the Finance? The Goldcrest Curse" – a narrative web game, 2) "@goldensfromGold-crest" – a social media page, and 3) "Wheres's the Finance? The comeback" – a group board game.

by the Mayor to unravel the curse. The goal is to help five townsfolk (each with their own financial situation) and lift this curse. Players will see the consequences of the characters' actions and learn from them. The transmedia experience is divided into three media; the preferred order would be to play the web game to learn about the characters, then enter instagram since the web game will not progress without the information from it, and finally, the board game is a sequel where the players help the characters one last time and learn new financial topics.

"Where's the Finance? The Goldcrest Curse". This narrative web game is an individual experience, where players assume the role of financial detectives tasked with identifying and addressing financial challenges faced by virtual characters, they navigate through a map representing hundreds of characters. In Fig. 6, we can see the five main characters with their cards – the blue card shows their character description, the yellow card their financial situation, and the green cards are clues.

"Where's the Finance? The Comeback". From the direct feedback of the participants, we re-designed the visual of the board game so that there is no confusion regarding the question marks on the board. We used shamrocks to symbolize luck, and added more detailed explanations on the board game cards. Players are organized into two teams; the players transverse the board collecting tokens with different powers, and need to reach the four green squares (collecting stamps) to win. Two dice are used, to move through the board and to choose challenges (question cards, drawing challenges, and finally forbidden words challenges).

5.2   Limitations and Future Work

We acknowledge that our research approach encountered several limitations. We could not test the whole extent of the TS experiences since developing all the channels would require a longer time frame and resource investment. Our pilot study was also conducted with a small participant sample. Moreover, another limitation arose from the differences in gameplay mechanics and duration between the web-based and board games, with the board game being more complex and time-consuming. Therefore, our future work will continue by developing the "Where's the Finance" transmedia experience to deliver FL educational content and conduct extensive playtests of the experience. We plan that these evaluations will study the effect of the different media channels on the overall FL literacy acquisition.

6   Conclusion

With this research, we propose to enhance FL with the aid of a TS experience. To do this, we created two low-fidelity prototypes to test the efficiency of these media, as well as the use of TS in the FL education field. Our prototypes showed complementary ways of engaging with the topic of FL. Our work contributes to the body of work that presents novel approaches to engage young adults in the field of FL education; hence, we hope to continue to develop enhanced learning experiences, eventually contributing to a better educational landscape.

Acknowledgments. This research was funded by the Portuguese Recovery and Resilience Program (PRR), IAPMEI/ANI/FCT under Agenda no.26, C645022399-00000057 (eGamesLab). The authors would also like to acknowledge the Portuguese Foundation for Science and Technology, for projects 10.54499/LA/P/0083/2020; 10.54499/UIDP/ 50009/2020 & 10.54499/UIDB/50009/2020.

References

1. Next generation personal finance. https://www.ngpf.org
2. Todos contam. https://www.todoscontam.pt
3. Transmedia storytelling 101. https://rb.gy/of5vul. Accessed 30 Sept 2010
4. Alsemgeest, L.: Family communication about money: why the taboo. Mediterr. J. Soc. Sci. **5**(16), 516–523 (2014)
5. Alsemgeest, L.: Talking about money is taboo: perceptions of financial planning students and implications for the financial planning industry. Ind. High. Educ. **30**(6), 394–401 (2016)
6. Andreychik, M.R., Martinez, V., et al.: Flipped vs. traditional: an analysis of teaching techniques in finance and psychology. Teach. Learn. Inquiry **7**(2), 154–167 (2019)
7. Anikina, O.V., Yakimenko, E.V.: Edutainment as a modern technology of education. Procedia. Soc. Behav. Sci. **166**, 475–479 (2015)
8. Augusto, M.: Narrativas transmedia: novas formas de contar e entender histórias (2017)
9. Boghian, I., Cojocariu, V.M., Popescu, C.V., Mâță, L.: Game-based learning using board games in adult education. J. Educ. Sci. Psychol. **9**(1) (2019)
10. Djonov, E., Tseng, C.I.: Harnessing the potential of transmedia narratives for critical multimodal literacy. Crit. Discourse Stud. **18**(3), 349–367 (2021)
11. Dudacek, O.: Transmedia storytelling in education. Procedia. Soc. Behav. Sci. **197**, 694–696 (2015)
12. Hastings, J.S., Madrian, B.C., Skimmyhorn, W.L.: Financial literacy, financial education, and economic outcomes. Annu. Rev. Econ. **5**(1), 347–373 (2013)
13. IJsselsteijn, W.A., De Kort, Y.A., Poels, K.: The game experience questionnaire (2013)
14. Jorgensen, B.L., Savla, J.: Financial literacy of young adults: the importance of parental socialization. Fam. Relat. **59**(4), 465–478 (2010)
15. Kelmendi, L.: Traditional learning versus e-learning. Available at SSRN 3458999 (2019)
16. Klontz, B., Pacifici, C., White, L., Nelson, C.: The effectiveness of an interactive multimedia psychoeducational approach to improve financial competence in at-risk youth: A pilot study. J. Financ. Therapy **2**(2), 2 (2011)
17. Kuchciak, I., Wiktorowicz, J.: Empowering financial education by banks-social media as a modern channel. J. Risk Financ. Manag. **14**(3), 118 (2021)
18. Kwon, Y.S., Byun, D.H.: An exploration of the limitations of transmedia storytelling: focusing on the entertainment and education sectors. J. Media Commun. Stud. **10**(4), 25–33 (2018)
19. Lien, Y.N.: Mobile edutainment system–national palace museum as an example. In: 2015 3rd International Conference on Future Internet of Things and Cloud, pp. 597–601. IEEE (2015)
20. Lusardi, A.: Financial literacy and the need for financial education: evidence and implications. Swiss J. Econ. Stat. **155**(1), 1–8 (2019). https://doi.org/10.1186/s41937-019-0027-5
21. Lusardi, A., Mitchell, O.S.: Financial literacy and retirement planning in the united states. J. Pension Econ. Finance **10**(4), 509–525 (2011)
22. Mandell, L., Klein, L.S.: The impact of financial literacy education on subsequent financial behavior. J. Financ. Couns. Plan. **20**(1) (2009)

23. Mason, C., Wilson, R.: Conceptualising fi-financial literacy. Occasional Paper **7**, 3–40 (2000)
24. Maurer, T.W., Lee, S.A.: Financial education with college students: comparing peer-led and traditional classroom instruction. J. Fam. Econ. Issues **32**, 680–689 (2011)
25. OECD: The importance of financial education, policy brief. Organisation for Economic Co-operation and Development (2006)
26. Okan, Z.: Edutainment and learning (2012)
27. O'Neil-Haight, M.: Educator teams up to teach finance to young children. J. Family Consum. Sci. **102**(2) (2010)
28. Rodrigues, P., Bidarra, J.: Transmedia storytelling as an educational strategy: a prototype for learning english as a second language. Int. J. Creative Interfaces Comput. Graph. (IJCICG) **7**(2), 56–67 (2016)
29. Solheim, C.A., Zuiker, V.S., Levchenko, P.: Financial socialization family pathways: reflections from college students' narratives. Family Sci. Rev. **16**(2), 97–112 (2011)
30. Totenhagen, C.J., Casper, D.M., Faber, K.M., Bosch, L.A., Wiggs, C.B., Borden, L.M.: Youth financial literacy: a review of key considerations and promising delivery methods. J. Fam. Econ. Issues **36**, 167–191 (2015)
31. Webley, P., Nyhus, E.K.: Economic socialization, saving and assets in european young adults. Econ. Educ. Rev. **33**, 19–30 (2013)

Navigating Sexualization: A Thematic Analysis of Sexualized Character Design in Modern Video Game Narratives

Zanobia Hazer[(✉)] [ID], Sofia Andersson[ID], and Mirjam Palosaari Eladhari[ID]

Department of Computer and Systems Sciences, Stockholm University, Stockholm, Sweden
nobihazer@gmail.com, mirjam@dsv.su
http://www.su.se

Abstract. This paper discusses the games Final Fantasy 7 Remake and The Last of Us 2, focusing on which design attributes contribute to the nuances of problematic and non-problematic sexualization of game characters in relation to its contextual relevance in the narrative. Data collection resulted in 1003 images that were analyzed, and a content analysis identified 739 initial codes and the themes of Physical Attributes, Actions, Camera Positioning, Body Language, and Traits and Emotions. The study's findings highlight the importance of considering narrative context and the player's engagement in understanding the effects of sexualization in video games. Additionally, both games illustrate how sexualization can amplify feelings of objectification or provide a safe space for exploring identity, depending on these factors.

Keywords: Games · Character Design · Narrative design · Game characters · Objectification · Sexualization · Sexual empowerment · Video Games · Thematic analysis

1 Introduction

The gaming industry has portrayed characters in a sexually charged and objectifying light for decades [20], which in turn has shaped people's perception of individuals as sexual objects [23]. Previous research has examined large numbers of games at a quantitative level, but without examining attributes other than physical [9,20,21,28]. These studies are based on older games. There are currently few studies that conduct in-depth analyses that go beyond physical attributes, and that also consider findings with a narrative and contextual angle. Previous studies show that this research area is constantly changing [20], motivating continuous studies on gender representation in games as they reach their audiences. In addition, research often focuses on how sexualization can be harmful [12,17] and rarely discusses the positive aspects of having sexually expressive characters or how to design them in a healthy way.

S. Andersson—Joint first authorship.

© The Author(s), under exclusive license to Springer Nature Switzerland AG 2025
J. T. Murray and M. C. Reyes (Eds.): ICIDS 2024, LNCS 15468, pp. 47–71, 2025.
https://doi.org/10.1007/978-3-031-78450-7_4

This study explores which design attributes contribute to the nuances of problematic and non-problematic sexualization of game characters that exist in games today in relation to it's contextual relevance in the narrative. While this does include some physical attributes that have been studied before [9,20,21,28], such as exposed skin and disproportional body parts, the scope of this study is expanded by examining areas such as character behaviour, roles, camera angles and focus, what types of sexuality and sexual expression that occur, sexual empowerment, and the how the game world reacts to these types of expressions. Because of this, the scope of potential games to study was limited to narrative driven games with a style of realism or stylized realism, with a release year of 2015 to 2024. The games would also have to be well known, with at leas 5 million copies sold. With these criteria, the games Final Fantasy 7 Remake [26] and The Last of Us 2 [25] were selected for analysis.

By analyzing beyond physical attributes, this research highlights the importance of narrative context, character roles, and the interplay between character behavior and game mechanics. This approach allows for a nuanced understanding, distinguishing between harmful and positive portrayals. By incorporating a broader range of attributes and focusing on modern, narrative-driven games, this research sets a precedent for adopting a more holistic and context-sensitive approach.

2   Background

2.1   Sexual Objectification

Sexual objectification involves reducing a person to a body and treating or viewing them as an object [6]. Nussbaum [22] explored seven dimension to discuss how individuals can be objectified: instrumentality (being viewed or treated as a tool for others' purposes), denial of autonomy (denial of autonomy and self-determination), inertness (lack of agency), fungibility (being treated as interchangeable with other objects of the same type/ other types), violability (lack of integrity), ownership (being seen as something to be owned) and denial of subjectivity (being treated as if their experience and feelings do not need to be considered). Thus, sexual objectification can be defined as the separation of people's bodies, body parts or sexual contexts from their identity, and treating or viewing individuals as tools for others' pleasure, with their value primarily based on physical or sexual attractiveness [13,22].

2.2   Sexualization

Objectification theory, rooted in Fredrickson and Roberts' 1997 article *Objectification Theory*, argues that various forms of sexual objectification involve treating individuals primarily as bodies for others' use. Fredrickson and Roberts [13] use "sexualization" and "sexual objectification" interchangeably, though the APA's 2007 *Task Force on the Sexualization of Girls* report defines sexualization more broadly [1]. According to the APA, sexualization includes conditions that differ from healthy sexuality, such as when a person's value is based on sexual appeal, physical attractiveness equates to sexual attractiveness, a person is treated as a sexual object, or sexuality is imposed inappropriately. The study emphasizes sexualization in personal, interpersonal, and cultural contexts, noting self-sexualization, interpersonal treatment as sexual objects, and the influence of cultural norms and media representations.

2.3 Sexual Empowerment

Sexual empowerment is a complex topic that has sparked numerous public and academic debates, particularly concerning its definition and scope. There is an ongoing debate about whether it involves internal feelings of control and confidence or external power to influence situations and resources [8].

Sexual empowerment can be defined as a multifaceted process where individuals feel and express control, autonomy, and independence over their sexual identity and actions [24]. It spans various dimensions of sexual experiences and expressions, aiming to foster a healthy and respectful relationship with one's sexuality.

Fredrickson and Roberts' objectification theory suggests that physical beauty can serve as a form of power for women, often outweighing other sources like intelligence or hard work [13]. Peterson [24] expands this notion to include psychological, emotional, and social dimensions, emphasizing the importance of defining and communicating one's sexual preferences, boundaries, and desires confidently.

Kennedy [18] discusses another nuance to this topic, blurring the line between sexual objectification and empowerment. She mentions the classic action hero Lara Croft, a female protagonist mostly remembered by her physique. Kennedy suggests that while there is valid criticism to the design of Lara, many women have looked beyond that to find a safe space to explore themselves, their identity and femininity.

A key aspect of sexual empowerment is promoting equality and respect in sexual relationships and combating sexual and gender-related discrimination and violence [18,24]. This involves creating an environment where individuals can exercise control and responsibility over their sexual lives, regardless of gender, age, or sexual orientation, and fostering a culture where sexual rights and dignity are respected and upheld.

2.4 Contextual Relevance

When studying character sexualization in video games, one recurring theme is the contextual relevance of how characters are sexualized. This involves assessing whether the sexualization aligns meaningfully within the narrative and mechanical framework of the game or if there is a disconnect that compromises the storytelling logic. Lynch et al. [20] highlight that many female characters in games are often overly sexualized without clear narrative justification, where their appearance and attire starkly contrast with their roles and purposes in the game. This discrepancy can disrupt player immersion and undermine the narrative's credibility within the game world.

Another critical aspect of contextual relevance is whether sexualization is consistent with a character's personality in addition to their role in the game. Jansz and Martis [15] argue that many game characters are sexualized in ways that do not match their personality traits or professional roles. For instance, portraying warriors or scientists in minimal clothing despite the impracticality for their roles can make the sexualization feel forced and unrealistic.

Moreover, Jansz and Martis [15] explore how character sexualization may hinder gameplay by affecting characters' physical abilities. Female characters are often designed with clothing and body types impractical for the physical combat and adventure they engage in, which may compromise the believability of their actions. Interestingly, Behm-Morawitz and Mastro [5] found that while men tend to view sexualized female characters as eye candy without significant conflict with their roles, women players often experience dissonance when character designs clash with narrative expectations, potentially impacting their engagement with the game.

The interactive nature of games can amplify the effects of sexualization, as players directly interact with sexualized characters [16]. This interaction can contribute to feelings of objectification and judgment by both the game and other players. The immersive nature of games also makes it challenging to distance oneself from sexualized messages and images, potentially leading to the internalization of these norms [11]. Shifting the focus from judging whether these representations are 'good' or 'bad' to examining their effects encourages us to consider whether they confine players to rigid, hierarchical ideas or open up new ways of thinking about characters and their roles [27].

However, sexualization in games is not solely associated with negative effects. Some players may find that sexualized game characters provide safe environments to explore their own sexuality and identity [11]. Additionally, others may derive pleasure and aesthetic enjoyment from sexualized characters without negative impacts on their sexual agency [14]. In some cases, character sexualization can even be perceived as a form of empowerment and control, especially when players have the ability to influence character portrayal [16].

It's crucial to note that the effects of character sexualization can vary significantly based on individual differences and the specific context in which the game is played. Age, for instance, plays a significant role in how players respond to sexualization, with younger players potentially being more negatively affected as they are still developing their own sexuality and identity [11].

In conclusion, considering the contextual relevance of character sexualization is essential for creating meaningful and believable gaming experiences.

3   The Study

The story driven single player games Final Fantasy 7 Remake [26] and The Last of Us 2 [25] were selected for content analysis. Content analysis involves making inferences from texts or other meaningful matter to the contexts of their use [19]. In our case this means a close examination of how the chosen games a) portray expression of sexualization in visual physical attributes via images and camera angles, b) and how sexuality and intimacy were woven into the game's narratives and in characterization. As such, the data collection entailed gameplay [30] focused on these themes in order to record material that could then later be analyzed. The content analysis conducted is most closely related to what [10] calls interpretive content analysis, which focuses on both manifest and latent content. Once the data was gathered, it was analyzed thematically [7].

3.1   Data Collection Methodology

Data collection involved recording gameplay footage of the two games played by the two first authors of this paper, from the beginning of the game, until a saturation point of interesting content was mutually perceived. This saturation was defined as the stage at which no new relevant information was discernible. The relevance of the content, what was deemed as interesting to the study, was defined as content that provoked thoughts of potential sexualization by the authors. This is, of course, subjective, and it is possible that the gender and sexual orientation of the authors may affect what data is collected. The two authors that collected the data identify as female and non-binary, and are both bisexual. From the recorded videos, images were extracted based on the researchers' intuition and without preconceived expectations. The images were categorized separately for each game in folders based on chronological order of occurrence and areas within the game in which they were taken. By using self-recorded material the study ensures that the analysts have a thorough understanding of both the gameplay sessions and the context behind the images.

Recording and analyzing entire games is time-consuming. Focusing on a representative position makes the study feasible. Representative data was determined by playing until no new potentially interesting visual content appeared, aided by one researcher's prior experience. Transparent selection methods and clear documentation of analyzed parts are crucial for understanding the study's limitations.

As a caveat to our study, we must mention that the scene selection made may affect the study, especially in understanding the nuances of problematic and non-problematic sexualization of the game characters. Other scenes might contain crucial examples central to the analysis, potentially skewing the comprehensive picture of how sexualization is portrayed throughout the game. Five hours of gameplay might inadvertently result in selecting unrepresentative parts of the game, introducing selection bias. Therefore we welcome replication studies or further analysis from the field.

3.2   Thematic Analysis

In order to collect and analyze the data as openly as possible, the study followed the steps of a thematic analysis described by Braun and Clarke [7]. The process of our study is illustrated in Fig. 1. This allowed for a systematic organization and identification of themes and sub-themes. Most themes were defined by making larger and larger groups from the codes, but it is worth mentioning that the categories of physical attributes were inspired by previous studies [9, 20, 21, 28].

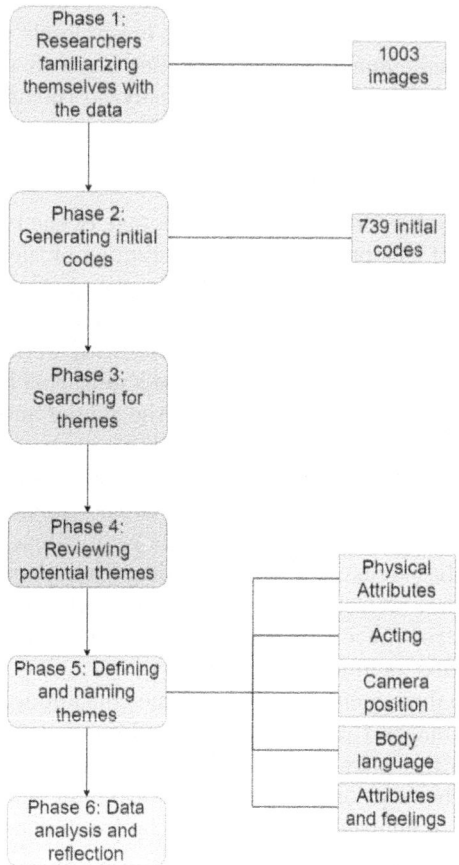

Fig. 1. Thematic analysis process.

3.3   Chosen Games

Criteria for selection of games to study takes into account that should be fairly recently released (2015–2024), have nuanced narratives and character portrayal, and that they should be well known, with at leas 5 million copies sold.

Final Fantasy VII Remake is a modern reimagining of a globally renowned classic role-playing game. Set in a post-industrial fantasy world dominated by the powerful energy corporation Shinra, players take on the role of mercenary Cloud Strife. A former Shinra elite soldier, Cloud joins the resistance movement in epic battles against the corporation. The game offers a captivating narrative with compelling characters. It is rated PEGI 16 and T for Teen by the ESRB rating system. Square Enix LTD released the game on April 10, 2020, for PlayStation 4, and it later became available on PlayStation 5 [26].

The Last of Us Part II is an action-adventure game released on June 19, 2020, by Sony Interactive Entertainment Europe for the PlayStation 4 platform. The game is rated PEGI 18 and M for Mature by the ESRB rating system. Players assume the role of Ellie, who has settled in Wyoming after a perilous journey across post-apocalyptic USA teeming with desperate survivors and infected creatures. Ellie's newfound peace is disrupted by a violent event, prompting her to embark on a quest for retribution. Players experience an emotionally charged narrative that challenges moral conventions, exploring a stunning yet perilous world and engaging in thrilling close-quarters combat involving seamless transitions between action and stealth [25].

3.4   Thematic Analysis

Based on the recorded footage of the game Final Fantasy 7 Remake, a total of 505 images were taken, from which 318 codes were created. For The Last of Us 2, 498 images were taken, resulting in 421 codes. These codes were then assigned to one or more of 29 categories. A script was created to sort all the data for an overview of which codes belonged to which categories. The categories were grouped to 14 sub-themes, which were further grouped to five themes. In the original thesis there is a more detailed analysis of the themes, as well as the raw data [4].

In the presentation of characters in Final Fantasy 7 Remake, characters are divided into main characters and NPCs (non-playable characters). The main characters include Cloud, Tifa, Jessie, Aerith (Flower Peddler), Barret, Wedge, and Biggs.

In the presentation of characters in The Last of Us 2, the main characters include Ellie, Dina, Jesse, Joel, Tommy, Abby, Owen, and Mel (Figs. 2, 3 and 4).

4   Discussion

4.1   Physical Attributes and Body Language

The analysis indicates that in Final Fantasy 7 Remake, significant differences exist in the attire of main characters. For instance, characters like Cloud, Barret, and Jessie are depicted with modest clothing coverage, yet gender disparities in attire are evident. Throughout the game, characters consistently maintain their clothing choices, presumably tailored for diverse scenarios they encounter. Barret's attire includes a low-cut shirt emphasizing his chest muscles, while

Initial categorizing	Number of codes in FF7	Number of codes in TLOU2
Exposed skin	68	29
Type of clothing (silhouette, material, color, etc.)	84	91
Type of clothing linked to personality	68	35
Body shape	54	38
Exaggerated body proportions	29	0
Facial structure	37	26
Body modification (makeup, tattoos, dirt, scars, etc.)	17	39
Gender-stereotyped roles/traits	83	15
Display of emotions	96	189
Discussion of relationships related to game character	34	49
Representation of children	19	24
Display of violence	12	69
Display of seduction	23	34
Asks game character for help	11	2
Heroic portrayal of game character	5	0
Gives compliment to game character	12	2
Camera focus on specific body part	46	34
Body language during dialogue	158	236
Body language during playable mode (walking/running)	16	29
Body language during conflict (attacks, etc.)	4	31
Intimacy	42	55
Camera angle diminishes character (looking down on character?)	39	33
Camera angle enlarges character (looking up at character?)	39	17
Direct or indirect talk about sexual or romantic themes	19	33
Non-gender-stereotyped roles/traits	5	29
Talk, behaviors, and traits reflecting character's sexuality	25	20
Performing romantic or sexual acts	9	15
Reference to heteronormativity	5	4
Offering to help game character	1	6

Fig. 2. An initial grouping of the data.

both Cloud and Barret expose their upper arms, highlight their musculature with harnesses. This can be seen in Fig. 5.

Notably, characters like Cloud, Sephiroth, and Wedge wear shoulder armor that enhances the appearance of broader shoulders, reinforcing the stereotype of muscular masculinity. [29]. Several characters in the game wear seemingly ineffective body armor. Cloud's shoulder armor, adorned with protruding screws on his left side, leaves his right shoulder, both arms, and chest exposed as can be seen in Fig. 5. Interestingly, he does not utilize this shoulder plate in combat or for protection, suggesting its presence for purely aesthetic reasons. This aligns with Cloud's role as a mercenary, emphasizing his rugged and emotionally restrained personality. Similarly, Sephiroth sports shoulder armor but keeps his chest exposed, (Figs. 6 and 17), leaving him susceptible to close combat attacks. Despite this vulnerability, his attire, including dark leather clothes and straps, complements his enigmatic and alluring demeanor.

Themes	Sub-themes	Categories
Physical Attributes	The body's natural structure	Body shape
		Exaggerated body proportions
		Facial structure
	The physical expression of the character	Exposed skin
		Type of clothing (silhouette, material, color, etc.)
		Body modification (Makeup, tattoo, dirt, etc.)
	Children	Representation of children
Acting	Action through conversation	Talk about relationship around game character
		Asks player character for help
		Calling the playable character a hero
		Compliments the game character
	Emotional response	Display of emotions
		Display of violence
	Sexual acts	Display of seduction
		Closeness
		Direct or indirect talk about sexual or romantic themes
		Performance of romantic or sexual acts
		Behaviors and traits that reflect the character's sexuality
	Gender stereotypes	Non-gender stereotypical roles and characteristics
		Gender stereotypical roles/characteristics
Camera positioning	Camera focus	Camera focus on specific body part
	Reduction and enlargement	The camera angle diminishes character (does one look down on the character?)
		The camera angle magnifies the character (does one look up at the character?)
Body language	Body language in different game modes	Body language during dialogue
		Body language in playable mode (walk/run)
		Body language in case of conflict (attacks, etc.)
Attributes and feelings	Attributes linked to personality	Type of clothing linked to personality
	Heteronormativity	Reference to heteronormativity

Fig. 3. Resulting themes, sub-themes and categories of the thematic analysis.

In contrast to the typical portrayal of male characters as strong and imposing through body armor, Jessie's breastplate is specifically designed to emphasize her bust, featuring a metal top that contours her body shape. Paired with a tight

Categories	Example code
Body shape	Tifa and Cloud are standing in a bar in playable mode. Tifa stands in a neutral position with her arms straight down. She is wearing two short and form-fitting tank tops, as well as a short black skirt, long black stockings and red shoes. She also wears long, black gloves.
Exaggerated body proportions	Cloud is sitting on a train. The picture shows his face and shoulder. He has a black metal plate as a shoulder pad. The metal is well used and has many scratches. There are 3 decorative black screws and bolts on the shoulder cover
Facial structure	Tifa's face. Round features, small chin, full lips and large, round eyes.
Exposed skin	Tifa's clothes expose her thighs and stomach.
Type of clothing (silhouette, material, color, etc.)	A group of NPCs (7 men, 2 women, 3 children). All people wearing clothes in neutral colors. All the men are wearing long-sleeved shirts, a woman is wearing a short tank top, a child is wearing shorts. The woman in linen wears a knotted sweater around her hips.
Body modification (Makeup, tattoo, dirt, etc.)	The child's upper body. the skin is sweaty. A tattoo is visible on the left upper arm.
Representation of children	very round face, small nose, full lips and large, round eyes
Talk about relationship around game character	Jessie asks Cloud about his relationship status. She stands a few meters away from Cloud with her hands behind her back. looking confident. Cloud is facing away from the camera, so you can't make out his facial expression.
Asks player character for help	Focus on Flower Peddler's hands. She grabs Cloud's arm with both hands and asks him for help.
Calling the playable character a hero	Jessie and Cloud are standing on a street. Jessie holds Cloud's hands. Jessie says she's lucky Cloud was there
Compliments the game character	Jessie and Cloud are standing on a street a meter apart. Jessie points a finger in the air and tells Cloud that he should get a reward for being so brave.
Display of emotions	Focus on Tifa's upper body. Tifa talks about being happy that Cloud is showing that he wants to listen to Tifa
Display of violence	3 men stand in an alley holding automatic weapons. One of the men aims the weapon.
Display of seduction	Jessie points a finger at Cloud's face. she winks and flirts with Cloud
Closeness	Dina finds Ellie at Joel's gravestone. They talk about avenging Joel's death. Dina puts one hand on Ellie's shoulder and the other on her cheek. Dina makes it obvious to Ellie that they will be together no matter what happens.
Direct or indirect talk about sexual or romantic themes	Jessie holds Cloud and whispers in his ear an invitation to her home.
Performance of romantic or sexual acts	Dina and Ellie have sex.
Behaviors and traits that reflect the character's sexuality	Ellie gives a sandwich she got from a person to Jesse. The person made the sandwich as a gesture to apologize for his behavior. He didn't like Ellie expressing herself romantically with Dina. Ellie calls the sandwich a "Bigot sandwich"
Non-gender stereotypical roles and characteristics	Barret shows emotion by expressing concern for Cloud. The others in the scene are shocked by this behavior, causing the barret to become uncomfortable and take back what he said.
Gender stereotypical roles/characteristics	Barret is emotional towards Cloud and shows that he doesn't care what happens to him or what choices he makes.
Camera focus on specific body part	Close-up of Sephiroth. Focus on his lips. You can only see his neck, lips and the tip of his nose.
The camera angle diminishes character (does one look down on the character?)	the camera from Cloud's perspective. Flower Peddler crouches down and looks up at him, asking if he's okay.
The camera angle magnifies the character (does one look up at the character?)	Sephiroth walks slowly and smiles towards Cloud, looking down at him. The camera is from Cloud's perspective, looking up at Sephiroth.
Body language during dialogue	Tifa receives a flower from Cloud. She looks down and can't meet his gaze. Shoulders and elbows are very close to the body.
Body language in playable mode (walk/run)	NPC body language (woman kneeling, man standing with arms on hips looking at fire)
Body language in case of conflict (attacks, etc.)	soldier (motorcycle dude) body language vs cloud
Type of clothing linked to personality	The Flower Peddler is an innocent and kind person who rarely shows aggressive or other negative traits. Her clothes are pink or red, she wears a dress and a big pink bow in her hair.
Reference to heteronormativity	Ellie gets into conflict with an older man who doesn't like that she kissed Dina. From the context it emerged that the reason for this was that it was precisely two girls who were kissing.

Fig. 4. Examples of codes for each category.

Fig. 5. Cloud (left), Barret (middle) and Jesse (right) wait for an elevator.

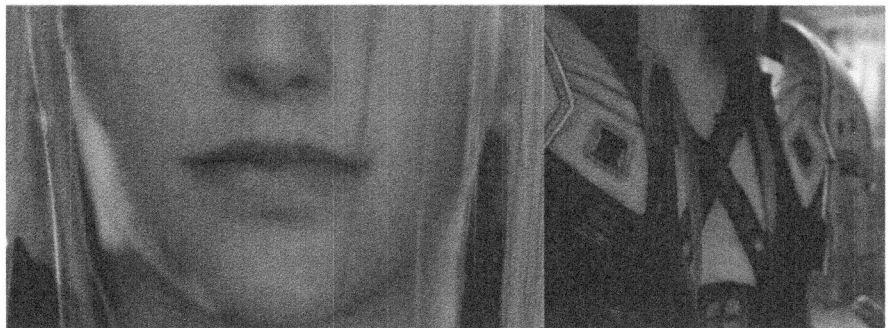

Fig. 6. The cameras focus on Sephiroth.

shirt, baggy pants, and shoulder armor, this ensemble accentuates an hourglass figure. However, the breastplate's cropped design focuses attention on the underside of her breasts rather than providing comprehensive chest protection, leaving her lower torso exposed (Fig. 5).

Tifa's breasts and hips are noticeably large compared to the rest of her body, and this is accentuated by both her clothing choices and posture, with exposed skin on her upper arms, midriff, and thighs (Fig. 7). Given her role as a fighter who employs hand-to-hand combat and acrobatic maneuvers, her attire and body shape appear impractical. Ideally, her fighting style would necessitate muscular development, which contrasts with her current clothing—a short skirt and top with high socks—deemed unsuitable for combat.

Fig. 7. Cloud (left) looks at Tifa (right).

In **The Last of Us 2** both main characters and NPCs exhibit a consistent dress code throughout the game. Beginning in a cold climate, characters are appropriately dressed with no exposed skin for the majority of the narrative. Gender differences in attire are minimal, although there are occasional instances of skin exposure, such as in Fig. 8, where Ellie and Dina are depicted in boxer-style underwear and short tank tops while lying on a couch together. This attire reflects the intimacy of the moment rather than emphasizing exaggerated body proportions or inappropriate clothing choices for the setting. The characters' lean body shapes are attributed to the harsh realities of living in a post-apocalyptic world with limited resources, which also explains the absence of overweight characters in the game.

Abby stands out with her muscular physique, distinct from other characters, due to her background growing up in a resource-abundant environment and rigorous military training from a young age. Unlike characters in games like Final Fantasy, Abby's muscularity can be interpreted as a proportionate depiction to her stature.

A notable narrative detail in The Last of Us is the physical transformation of characters like Ellie and Abby, who appear more injured, thinner, and dirtier as the story progresses, reflecting their arduous journey and experiences (Figs. 9 and 10).

In The Last of Us 2, an intriguing detail involves a type of zombie known as "Clickers," which exhibit noticeable differences in exposed skin based on gender presentation. Female-presenting Clickers typically have their entire chests exposed, often lacking any clothing, whereas male-presenting Clickers retain tattered clothes covering their torsos and fully cover their buttocks and genitals. Given their prolonged infection, it's plausible that the deterioration of clothing over time contributes to these differences. However, the game does not provide

Fig. 8. Dina lay on top of Ellie on a sofa. They both wear underwear.

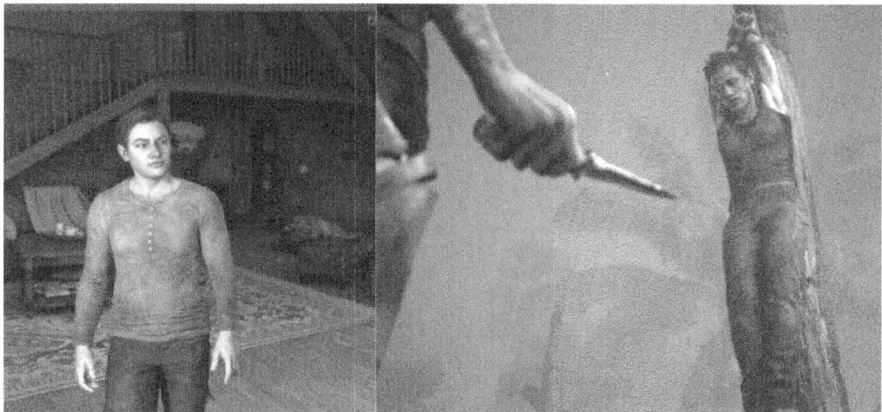

Fig. 9. Abby at the beginning of the game (to the left) and at the end of the game (to the right).

a clear narrative rationale for the disparity in exposed skin between male and female Clickers (Fig. 11).

In Final Fantasy, there is a distinct contrast in the movement and positioning of male and female characters. Men often extend their elbows outward, making expansive movements with wide gaps between their legs. In contrast, women tend to keep their elbows close to their bodies, presenting a smaller silhouette with legs positioned closely together. Figure 12 illustrates this difference, depicting Jessie and Biggs rising from a table with determined expressions while placing their hands on the table and looking at Wedge. Jessie's posture includes a noticeable arch in her back, accentuating her buttocks, unlike Biggs' straighter

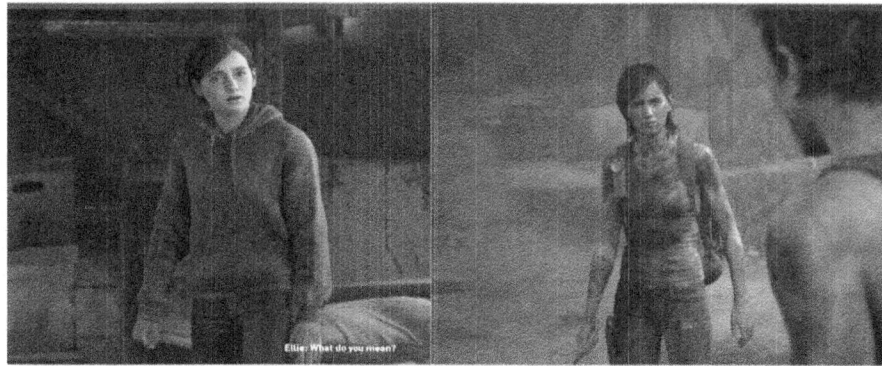

Fig. 10. Ellie at the beginning of the game (to the left) and at the end of the game (to the right).

Fig. 11. Male (left) and female (right) Clickers.

stance. Despite sharing the same emotion and reaction in the scene, their movements reveal distinct gender-specific body language. One explanation could be that because Jessie is a woman, her body language is used in a sexual manner [20] that cannot be seen in the male characters, in this case Biggs.

In Final Fantasy, female characters frequently employ body language that emphasizes their sexuality, described by Lynch et al. [20] as a deliberate, wave-like movement that accentuates their curves. This could be attributed to a design choice to engage players, particularly those interacting romantically with Cloud, although it may also reflect unconscious biases in game development towards stereotypical portrayals of women [17]. Tifa, for instance, adheres to this movement pattern despite not actively flirting with Cloud like Jessie does.

In The Last of Us, differences in body language are more individualized rather than universally sexualized. For example, Dina's movements exhibit subtle curves compared to Ellie, whose posture resembles Joel's (Fig. 13), characterized by wide legs and elbows away from the body. These differences seem reflective of individual character traits and dynamics rather than a generalized

Fig. 12. Jessie (left), Biggs (middle) and Wedge (right) have an argument around the dinner table.

sexualization, as seen in Final Fantasy. Dina's flirtatious behavior with Ellie underscores her unique movement style, evolving from initial sexual undertones to a deeper romantic connection, particularly evident in conversational scenes. Unlike Final Fantasy, where sexualized body language extends into gameplay and conflict scenarios, The Last of Us maintains distinct character movements primarily within narrative contexts.

A notable similarity between both games is that in The Last of Us, male characters also sometimes take up more space than female characters. A clear example of this is illustrated in Fig. 14, where we can see that Jesse, Joel, and Tommy take up a lot of space with their bodies during dialogue, often leaning on walls or door frames. However, even though this similarity can be seen, while there does not seem to be an example in Final Fantasy of a woman having this body language, there are multiple examples in The Last of Us. Abby is one clear example. The narrative drives her character to express behaviors that are normally stereotypical to men, this body language being one of them.

4.2   The Camera

Camera focus in Final Fantasy 7 and The Last of Us 2 are primarily horizontal, directly facing the characters in focus. However, our content analysis identified parts of the games where the camera chose to focus on something specific. The design purpose of focusing the camera on a specific part of the body varies. It could be motivated by highlighting an emotional response in a character, such as sadness in the eyes or a smile on the lips. It could also be motivated by emphasizing a detail in the body part, such as a scar or a character holding something. Sometimes though, in our analysis, we took note of design choices of camera focus that can be interpreted as sexualized. Multiple examples of where

Fig. 13. Joel (left) and Ellie (right) have an emotional conversation on their patio.

Fig. 14. Joel (left), Jesse (middle) and Tommy (right)

the camera focuses on the female characters' thighs, buttocks, or breasts, were identified. These can be seen as highlighting sexualized body parts (Fig. 15). In contrast, the only male character with a high degree of noteworthy camera focus is Sephiroth. Whenever he appears in a scene, the camera focuses on his lips or hands, and sometimes his chest. This, combined with Sephiroth's tone when he speaks and his actions, suggests a sexualized undertone.

In The Last of Us, a contextual difference was noted with the camera focus. Focus on body parts tends to be motivated by enhancing the player's understanding of the character's emotional response or by highlighting an object a character is holding. An example of this is in Fig. 16. The context behind the image shows Joel singing a song to Ellie. The song's lyrics directly relate to Joel's paternal feelings for her, and the lyrics of the song are emphasized by keeping the camera focused on Joel's lips and hands.

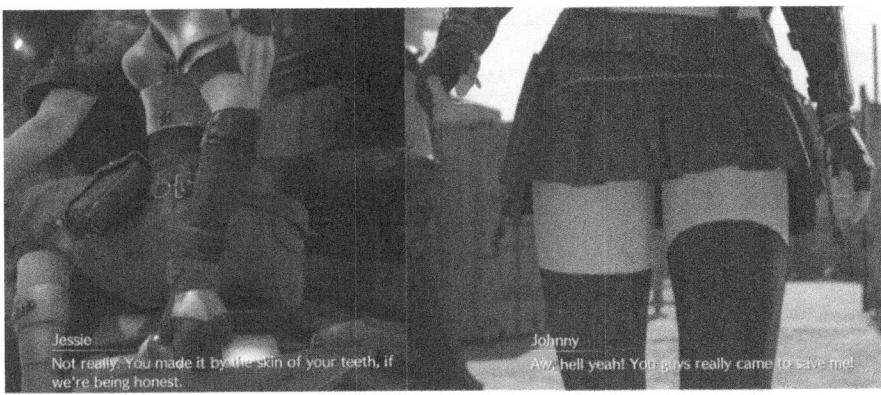

Fig. 15. In the first image, Cloud and Jessie are riding a motorcycle together. The camera focuses on Jessie's buttocks. In the second image, Cloud and Tifa have arrived to rescue an NPC (Johnny). The camera focuses on Tifa's thighs and hips.

Fig. 16. Joel is playing the guitar and sings to Ellie. The camera focuses on his lips.

Regarding camera angles, similar patterns were identified between the games. Characters who are viewed from below can be perceived as more dominant or confident in context, as seen in Fig. 17, where Sephiroth is viewed from below to portray greater confidence in what he is saying. When the camera looks down on a character, it can be motivated by portraying characters as more submissive or considerate. This can be seen in Fig. 18, where Aerith bends down to ask if Cloud is okay. Viewing her from this angle reinforces the impression that she is a helpful character who means well and can be trusted.

Summarizing, more female characters in Final Fantasy are illustrated from a camera angle that looks down on them, and more male characters are illustrated

Fig. 17. Sephiroth and Cloud talk to each other. The camera is on ground level and is pointed up towards Sephiroth.

from a camera angle that looks up at them. Both these portrayals are gender stereotypical, with women being portrayed as more submissive, nurturing and kind-hearted, and men as confident and dominant.

4.3 Types of Sexuality and Intimate Expression in the Games

The portrayal of sexuality in Final Fantasy 7 contrasts with that in The Last of Us 2. In Final Fantasy, sexual expression remains implicit; themes of romance and intimacy are present but not visually depicted. Gestures like hugging and suggestive language hint at intimacy, yet explicit sexual encounters are absent. For instance, Jessie's desire for Cloud is highlighted through gestures like hugging [2], which mark the limit of physical interaction. This aligns with the game's PEGI 16 rating, restricting explicit sexual content and likely influencing the absence of visible violence.

Conversely, The Last of Us 2 portrays sexuality and intimacy more explicitly. It features clear depictions of romantic and sexual interactions, notably between characters like Dina and Ellie, as well as paternal figures like Joel and Ellie. Unlike Final Fantasy, where sexual expression intertwines with romance and is often implied, The Last of Us 2 distinctly separates romance and sexuality. For instance, Dina and Ellie begin with a sexual relationship that evolves into a romantic one. This distinction is facilitated by the game's PEGI 18 rating, which permits the portrayal of both violent and sexual content.

Moreover, Final Fantasy occasionally portrays characters in ways that align with theories of sexual objectification. Characters like Jessie may exhibit behaviors where their actions fluctuate between assertiveness and submission based on their interactions with others, particularly the protagonist, Cloud. This por-

Fig. 18. Aerith (known as Flower Peddler at the time the picture was taken) is crouched towards Cloud and asks if he is okay. The camera is pointed down towards her.

trayal can be interpreted as denying autonomy, where their personalities seem subordinate to their physical attractiveness and the desires of others [22].

In contrast, The Last of Us 2 integrates sexual intimacy into its narrative without compromising characters' autonomy or subjectivity. Scenes involving Ellie and Dina are contextualized within their relationship development, contributing to character depth rather than reduction to objects of sexual desire [13]. This aligns with the concept of sexual empowerment, where characters confidently navigate their sexual identities and interactions [24]. Dina's assertive expression of her sexuality and Ellie's reciprocal engagement in intimate moments exemplify this empowerment, emphasizing mutual consent and control over their sexual experiences [1].

These contrasting approaches reflect broader societal attitudes toward sexuality and gender dynamics in video games. Final Fantasy implies intimacy within its narrative confines and adheres to a lower age rating, whereas The Last of Us 2 tackles these themes more overtly, leveraging a higher age rating to explore complex issues of sexuality, empowerment, and autonomy in a more explicit manner [1,22,24]. Both games serve as platforms for discussing and challenging societal norms surrounding sexuality and empowerment through their narrative and thematic exploration.

The interactive nature of Final Fantasy and The Last of Us 2 can amplify sexualization effects, as players engage with sexualized characters [16], which can lead to feelings of objectification and judgment. The immersive nature of games makes it challenging to distance oneself from these messages, potentially internalizing these norms [11].

In Final Fantasy, interactions with flirtatious characters like Jessie, who alternates between assertiveness and submissiveness based on Cloud's responses, can amplify feelings of objectification and judgment. Playing as Cloud, players may internalize these dynamics. The lack of explicit content combined with suggestive behaviour can create a reinforcement of traditional gender roles and expectations. In contrast, The Last of Us 2 features explicit romantic and sexual interactions between characters. Players engage directly in these moments, which can intensify feelings of intimacy and connection while highlighting issues of objectification. The immersive storytelling makes it difficult to distance from sexualized messages, deepening the internalization of norms around consent and empowerment [11].

However, sexualization in games is not solely associated with negative effects. Some players may find that sexualized game characters provide a safe environment to explore their own sexuality and identity [11]. Additionally, others may derive pleasure and aesthetic enjoyment from sexualized characters without negative impacts on their sexual agency [14] which can apply to the depictions of characters such as Jessie, Cloud, Dina, and Ellie. In some cases, character sexualization can even be perceived as a form of empowerment and control, especially when players have the ability to influence character portrayal [16]. The portrayal of Dina and Ellie's relationship in The Last of Us 2 offers a platform for players to safely explore LGBTQ+ themes and their own sexual identities, which can be empowering. Watching Ellie and Dina navigate their relationship with confidence and mutual consent can serve as a positive model for sexual empowerment and agency. Similarly, players might appreciate how Jessie is portrayed in Final Fantasy, finding it a safe space to explore flirtation and romantic interest without explicit sexual content. This can be particularly relevant for younger players who are still developing their sexual identities. The way these interactions are designed can either reinforce or challenge their perceptions of gender and romance. Older players or those with more developed sexual identities might find the explicit content in The Last of Us 2 empowering and reflective of real-life complexities. Younger players, however, might be more impressionable and influenced by these depictions, necessitating careful consideration of age appropriateness and narrative context.

In conclusion, both games offer contrasting portrayals of sexuality in video games. Final Fantasy uses implicit sexual expression to maintain its PEGI 16 rating, subtly reinforcing traditional gender roles, while The Last of Us 2 explicitly depicts sexual interactions, exploring themes of consent and empowerment with its PEGI 18 rating. Both games demonstrate how sexualization can amplify feelings of objectification or provide a safe space for exploring identity, highlighting the importance of context and individual differences in player experiences.

4.4   Sexual Expression in Relation to the Game World

Sexualization, as defined by APA, refers to situations where a person's worth is primarily perceived based on their sexual appeal or behavior, occurring in personal, interpersonal, and cultural contexts [1]. Therefore, in the narrative of sexualized video game characters, the portrayal and actions of the sexualized character are not the only factors shaping the sexualization within the story-line.

The treatment and perception of the protagonists by bystanding entities, such as background characters, equally contribute to the overall narrative. In Final Fantasy, sexualized characters generally do not experience different treatment within the game's cultural context. Female protagonists are typically seen as equally competent as their male counterparts and play crucial roles within their groups. Their abilities are respected, and their decisions are rarely questioned, though there are exceptions such as Tifa. For example, a background character expresses concern over Tifa facing multiple monsters alone, later reassured by her partnership with Cloud. This illustrates the nuances of how Final Fantasy navigates societal expectations and perceptions of sexualized characters in its world.

Conversely, The Last of Us features characters engaging in discussions about sexual and romantic themes, yet these rarely alter how characters are treated overall. For example, Jesse often discusses his relationship with Dina with Ellie, maintaining their friendship despite romantic undertones. This suggests the game's culture generally does not fundamentally change treatment based on characters' sexual behaviors. However, notable exceptions occur, such as when Ellie faces unjust treatment from an older man for kissing Dina. His aggressive reaction prompts social repercussions, as he is encouraged to apologize the next day.

These narratives illustrate how sexualized characters are integrated and perceived in their respective game worlds. Final Fantasy tends toward an egalitarian approach where sexualized characters, especially females, receive similar respect and capability as their male counterparts. In contrast, The Last of Us highlights societal challenges faced by sexualized and gender-diverse characters, mirroring real-world discrimination and acceptance issues. This portrayal not only deepens narrative complexity but also reflects cultural and societal dynamics, offering players insights into sexualization and gender identity complexities.

The portrayal of sexualized characters in Final Fantasy and The Last of Us can be examined through the lenses of sexualization, sexual objectification, and sexual empowerment. In Final Fantasy, some characters are portrayed in ways that align with theories of sexual objectification. For instance, Tifa's abilities are occasionally questioned, reflecting a denial of her autonomy and competence. However, the game largely respects the capabilities of female characters, suggesting a complex interplay between objectification and respect [22].

Conversely, The Last of Us integrates sexual intimacy into its narrative without diminishing characters' autonomy or subjectivity. For example, scenes involving Ellie and Dina deepen character development rather than reducing them to objects of desire. This exemplifies sexual empowerment, where characters confidently navigate their sexual identities and interactions, emphasizing mutual consent and control over their experiences [24].

The contrasting portrayals of sexualized characters in Final Fantasy and The Last of Us reveal how video game depictions of sexuality and gender influence societal attitudes within these narratives. They enhance narrative depth while also reflecting and challenging cultural dynamics surrounding sexuality, objectification, and empowerment.

4.5   Limitations

By focusing on two cases, this study cannot be generalized to larger populations. However, it complements previous qualitative and quantitative studies [9,20,21,28] by providing a more in-depth understanding of an area previously examined superficially. The study's transferability is enhanced by the extensive data collection and the availability of the data for replication.

Given the focus on sexualization, there is a risk of personal bias as the images were analyzed by two individuals interested in the research area. To minimize this, we individually reflected on our biases [3,4]. This increases reliability by defining personal biases. Another factor affecting reliability is that only parts of the game were analyzed. Data collection continued until perceived saturation of content of interest was reached. Different interpretations of saturation could lead to different results.

4.6   Future Research

Future research should focus on games with sexualized male characters to see if their sexualization differs from that of female characters. Additionally, examining character sexualization across different game genres through thematic analysis and player interviews could reveal how different groups are affected by specific design attributes. Investigating cultural differences in game sexualization by comparing games from various regions could provide insights into cultural influences on game design and player experiences.

Further studies could explore gender roles in games, analyzing how male and female characters are portrayed and how this affects players' perceptions of gender norms. Research into the long-term effects of exposure to sexualization in games on players' attitudes, behaviors, and mental health could provide valuable insights into how games influence views on sexuality, gender, and relationships.

New methods for analyzing sexualization in games, such as computer-based identification of sexualized elements, could offer fresh perspectives by minimizing human bias, though they might lack contextual nuance. Complementing this with a text analysis of game narratives on sexuality and sexualization could enhance understanding of the contextual aspects of positive and negative sexualization.

5   Conclusion

This study explored the portrayals of sexualization in video games, focusing on Final Fantasy 7 Remake and The Last of Us 2, and examined how camera angles, types of intimate expression and societal perception within the games contribute to the sexualization narrative.

In Final Fantasy 7 Remake, camera angels often highlight sexualized body parts of the game characters, whom often were women. Sexual expression is implicit, aligning with its PEGI 16 rating, and occasionally leans towards sexual objectification. Despite this, female characters are generally respected and seen as competent, reflecting a nuances of both objectification and empowerment.

In contrast to Final Fantasy 7, The Last of Us 2 presents sexuality and intimacy more explicitly, due to its PEGI 18 rating. The game distinguishes between romance and sexuality, focusing on mutual consent and empowerment in intimate relationships, such as those between Dina and Ellie. This approach integrates characters' sexual identities into the narrative, and it can be argued that this helps reduce their portrayal as objects of desire.

Both games illustrate how sexualization can amplify feelings of objectification or provide a safe space for exploring identity, depending on the context and individual player experiences. The study's findings highlight the importance of considering narrative context and the player's engagement in understanding the effects of sexualization in video games.

Acknowledgements. We would like to thank Sofia Lindgren for help with creating the program we used to sort the data, as well as Aware Mustafa Taher for technical assistance with the gameplay recordings.

References

1. Report of the APA Task Force on the Sexualization of Girls, APA Task Force on the Sexualization of Girls. Report of the APA Task Force on the Sexualization of Girls. American Psychological Association (2008). https://www.apa.org/pi/women/programs/girls/report
2. What do the labels mean? | Pegi Public Site. https://pegi.info/what-do-the-labels-mean
3. Phenomenology of Practice: Meaning-Giving Methods in Phenomenological Research and Writing. Routledge (2016). https://doi.org/10.4324/9781315422657
4. Andersson, S., Hazer, N.: En visuell tematisk analys av sexualiserad karaktärsdesign i moderna spel (2024). https://urn.kb.se/resolve?urn=urn:nbn:se:su:diva-231420
5. Behm-Morawitz, E., Mastro, D.: The effects of the sexualization of female video game characters on gender stereotyping and female self-concept. Sex Roles **61**(11), 808–823 (2009). https://doi.org/10.1007/s11199-009-9683-8
6. Bernard, P., Gervais, S.J., Allen, J., Campomizzi, S., Klein, O.: Integrating sexual objectification with object versus person recognition. Psychol. Sci. (2012). https://doi.org/10.1177/0956797611434748
7. Braun, V., Clarke, V.: Thematic analysis. In: Cooper, H., Camic, P.M., Long, D.L., Panter, A.T., Rindskopf, D., Sher, K.J. (eds.) APA Handbook of Research Methods in Psychology, Vol 2: Research Designs: Quantitative, Qualitative, Neuropsychological, and Biological, pp. 57–71, 701 Pages. APA handbooks in psychology®, American Psychological Association, American Psychological Association, Washington, DC, Washington (2012). https://doi.org/10.1037/13620-004

8. Camoletto, R.F., Todesco, L.: From sexual objectification to sexual subjectification? Pornography consumption and Italian women's sexual empowerment. AG About Gender - Int. J. Gender Stud. **8**(16) (2019). https://doi.org/10.15167/2279-5057/AG2019.8.16.1074

9. Downs, E., Smith, S.L.: Keeping abreast of hypersexuality: a video game character content analysis. Sex Roles **62**, 721–733 (2010)

10. Drisko, J.W., Maschi, T.: Content Analysis. Oxford University Press, Oxford (2016)

11. Erchull, M.J., Liss, M.: Exploring the concept of perceived female sexual empowerment: development and validation of the sex is power scale. Gender Issues **30**(1), 39–53 (2013). https://doi.org/10.1007/s12147-013-9114-6

12. Fasoli, F., Durante, F., Mari, S., Zogmaister, C., Volpato, C.: Shades of sexualization: when sexualization becomes sexual objectification. Sex Roles **78**(5), 338–351 (2018). https://doi.org/10.1007/s11199-017-0808-1

13. Fredrickson, B.L., Roberts, T.A.: Objectification theory: toward understanding women's lived experiences and mental health risks. Psychol. Women Q. (1997)

14. Geraci, R.M., Geraci, J.L.: Virtual gender: how men and women use videogame bodies. J. Gaming Virtual Worlds **5**(3), 329–348 (2013)

15. Jansz, J., Martis, R.G.: The lara phenomenon: powerful female characters in video games. Sex Roles **56**(3), 141–148 (2007)

16. Jenkins, H.: Game design as narrative architecture. Computer **44**(3), 118–130 (2004)

17. Kafai, Y.B., Heeter, C., Denner, J., Sun, J.Y.: Beyond Barbie and Mortal Kombat: New Perspectives on Gender and Gaming. MIT Press (2011)

18. Kennedy, H.W.: Game studies - lara croft: feminist icon or cyberbimbo? On the limits of textual analysis. Int. J. Comput. Game Res. **2**(2), 1–12 (2002)

19. Krippendorff, K., et al.: Content analysis. Int. Encycl. Commun. **1**(1), 403–407 (1989)

20. Lynch, T., Tompkins, J.E., van Driel, I.I., Fritz, N.: Sexy, strong, and secondary: a content analysis of female characters in video games across 31 years. J. Commun. **66**(4), 564–584 (2016). https://doi.org/10.1111/jcom.12237

21. Lynch, T., Tompkins, J.E., Gilbert, M., Burridge, S.: Evidence of ambivalent sexism in female video game character designs. Mass Commun. Soc. (2024)

22. Nussbaum, M.C.: Sex and Social Justice. Oxford University Press, New York (1999)

23. Pearce, C., Fullerton, T., Fron, J., Morie, J.F.: Sustainable play. Games Cult. (2007). https://doi.org/10.1177/1555412007304420

24. Peterson, Z.D.: What is sexual empowerment? A multidimensional and process-oriented approach to adolescent girls' sexual empowerment. Sex Roles **62**(5), 307–313 (2010). https://doi.org/10.1007/s11199-009-9725-2

25. Sony Interactive Entertainment: The Last of Us II. Naughty Dog [Playstation 4] (2020)

26. Square Enix: Final Fantasy VII Remake. [Playstation 4] (2020)

27. Tomkinson, S.: "She's built like a tank": player reaction to Abby Anderson in the last of us: part II. Games Cult. **18**(5), 684–701 (2023). https://doi.org/10.1177/15554120221123210

28. Tompkins, J.E., Lynch, T., Driel, I.I.V., Fritz, N.: Kawaii Killers and Femme Fatales: a textual analysis of female characters signifying benevolent and hostile sexism in video games. J. Broadcast. Electron. Media (2020)

29. Van Lange, P., Kruglanski, A., Higgins, E.: Handbook of Theories of Social Psychology: Volume 2. London (2024). https://doi.org/10.4135/9781446249222
30. Van Vught, J., Glas, R.: Considering play: from method to analysis. Trans. Digit. Games Res. Assoc. **4**(2) (2018). https://doi.org/10.26503/todigra.v4i2.94

Emotional Believability of Non-playable Game Characters - Animations of Anger, Sadness and Happiness

Therese Johansson[✉][ID] and Mirjam Palosaari Eladhari[ID]

Stockholm University, Stockholm, Sweden
Therese.n.johanssons@gmail.com, mirjam@dsv.su.se
http://www.su.se

Abstract. This study investigates the relationship between the perceived believability of NPC animations and their portrayal of three core emotional expressions: anger, sadness and happiness in well-known, recently released, character-focused games. This study is explorative aiming to identify subjects for further research. We studied tree games: Genshin Impact, Baldur's Gate 3 and Animal Crossing: New Horizons (ACNH). A content analysis was conducted to compare the animations with human emotional expressions to identify patterns. Based on this, a questionnaire with nine videos from the games was designed, to assess players' ability to recognize emotions, and rate their believability, garnering 159 responses. Our findings show that ACNH, which exaggerate its animations, achieved the highest believability score with 4.91 out of 5 and a 100% identification rate of anger. The study's findings supports previous research regarding exaggerated acting as one of the most effective ways to convey emotions. This study underscores the importance of emotional expression via animation in creating expressive, yet recognizable, animations.

Keywords: Animation · Emotions · Believability · Games · NPC

1 Introduction

In games, the authenticity and emotional depth of non-playable characters (NPCs) significantly enhance player immersion and engagement. NPCs are integral to the storytelling and interactive experiences in games, where their ability to convey believable emotions can make the difference between a memorable journey and a mundane interaction.

This paper explores the emotional believability of NPCs, focusing on the animation of three core emotions: anger, sadness, and happiness. The concept of believability in digital characters extends beyond mere visual fidelity. It encompasses the character's ability to exhibit lifelike emotions and behaviors that resonate with the player's expectations and the game's narrative context. Several factors influence players' perceived believability of NPCs, including appearance,

J. T. Murray and M. C. Reyes (Eds.): ICIDS 2024, LNCS 15468, pp. 72–99, 2025.
https://doi.org/10.1007/978-3-031-78450-7_5

communication style, and dialogue [25]. Our study focuses on animation as it is a fundamental aspect of games with moving images.

We investigate the portrayal of NPCs' emotions from three popular character-focused games: Genshin Impact (GI), Baldur's Gate 3 (BG3), and Animal Crossing: New Horizons (ACNH). All are popular games released within five years of the study. By analyzing selected video clips from these games and evaluating player responses through a detailed questionnaire, we aim to understand how different animation styles and techniques impact the perceived believability of NPCs' emotional expressions.

Through a combination of content analysis and empirical data from player feedback, this paper contributes to the growing body of knowledge on character design and emotional authenticity in digital games. The study is an explorative work aiming to guide future research and to provide insights for game developers and animators aiming to create more engaging and believable NPCs, enriching the player's interactive experience.

Nine video clips were used in a questionnaire designed to explore players' ability to recognize the emotions expressed by NPCs and to rate their believability. The questionnaire received 159 responses. Additionally, these videos were analyzed using content analysis to compare their similarities with human expressions of the same emotions and identify any emerging patterns. The results presented in this paper builds on earlier work reported in the thesis work [16].

The structure of this paper is as follows: First we provide a background on the concept of emotional believability, drawing from relevant psychological theories and previous research on emotional expression of digital characters. Then, we describe our study. We present the results of the content analysis and questionnaire responses, highlighting key findings related to the believability of emotional expressions in different games. Finally, we discuss the implications of our findings, particularly examining how animation exaggeration and game context influence the perceived authenticity of NPC emotions.

2 Background

2.1 Emotions

In psychology, the notion of "basic emotions" have been discussed since the 1950ies. Ekman [6] suggested that seven emotions are conveyed through distinct facial expressions and are universal [8]. Although cultural factors like social rules can influence what triggers a reaction and how one tries to hide an expression, the same specific facial muscles will move [7].

Ekman's theory is debated but is supported by researchers like Izard, who drew similar conclusions [13]. Criticisms include that facial expressions show too much of variation to support a standard expression [2]. Ekman's claim of universal emotions is also heavily criticized to not exist [18], and being affected by culture. Psychologist Jack says *"There's still no data to show that emotions are universally recognized."* [12].

Defenders of Ekman's theory argue that the opposition is overstating their case with a handful of counterexamples [12]. For instance, Tracy expressed that only because one population or culture displays anger slightly differently does not demolish the entire theory [12]. She also states that most people recognize an angry face when they see it [12] referencing [9].

This work is grounded in Ekman's theory, as the emotional expressions of the NPCs we studied are intentionally crafted by humans. Every animated expression is intended to communicate an emotion to the player. Due to the complexities of game development, creators cannot replicate the full range of human emotional expression. As a result, developers must choose how to depict emotions in ways that is both recognizable and impactful. For this paper, we rely on the recorded and systematised knowledge available about how humans express anger, sadness and happiness, but we make no claims of any pan-cultural expressions.

Anger is one of Ekman's seven universal emotions, which typically arise when a person feels treated unfairly or someone is blocking them from reaching their goals [21]. In extreme cases anger can be one of the most dangerous emotions due to its link to violence [21]. Both Averill [1] and Izard [13] believe that anger is generally experienced without the intention of causing harm.

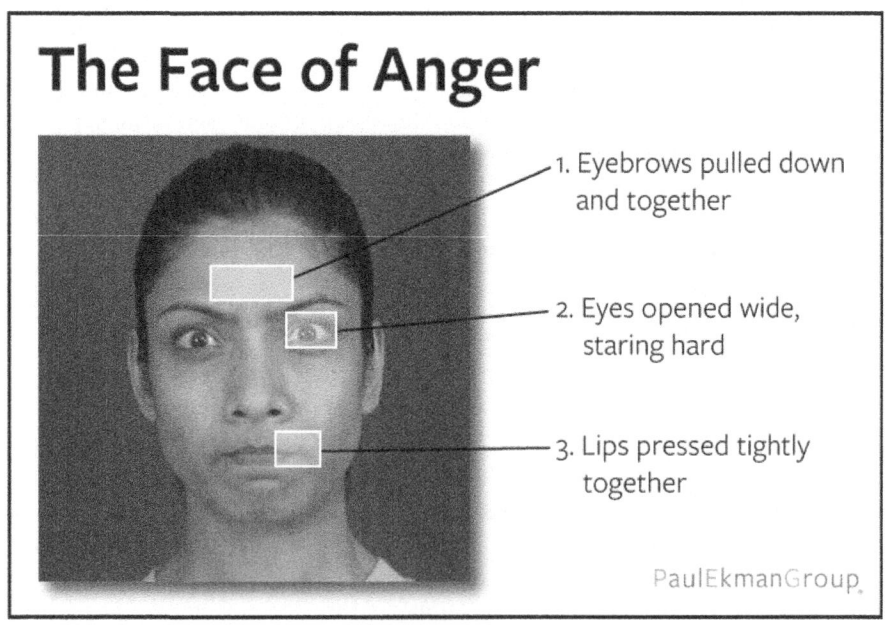

Fig. 1. Paul Ekman Group's "The Face of Anger" [21].

The posture for anger is often shown as forward leaning with either the head or chin sticking out and the chest puffed out to appear larger. A clenched jaw or fist is also common signs of anger [21]. Averill's [1] studies suggest that these signals are universal across genders.

Fig. 2. ACNH NPC. Left shows neutral while right anger

Comparing NPCs from one of the selected games (see Fig. 2) with Ekman's research (see Fig. 1) The NPC shows downward-sloping eyebrows and pursed lips (see Fig. 1). The body language is bent forward with the head extended. The NPC convey anger according to Ekman's definition [21].

Sadness is mainly characterized by upward-angled eyebrows, sunken upper eyelids and downward-angled corners of the mouth [21] as seen in Fig. 3. Sadness can be expressed by a lower or crouched posture, tendencies to look away or down and watery eyes. One's movements are often experienced as heavy and slow [21]. According to Provine tears are mainly associated with sadness and without them the face appears significantly less sad [22]. Provine believes that tears leave a stronger impression than isolated facial expressions therefore making sadness easier to interpret but without them more difficult.

Ekman emphasizes that the combination of facial muscles and body language are what distinguishes the emotions [21]. Both the emotions' anger and sadness can include watery eyes and red whites of eyes, but the facial expressions and body language are what determine the emotion. Ekman believes multiple emotions can be felt simultaneously and that traces of the emotions will be visible on the person [7].

The NPC shown in Fig. 4 display upturned eyebrows, drooping upper eyelids and down turned corners of the mouth, common signs of sadness (see Fig. 3). The body language shows a more crouched posture compared to the NPCs neutral posture, indicating sadness.

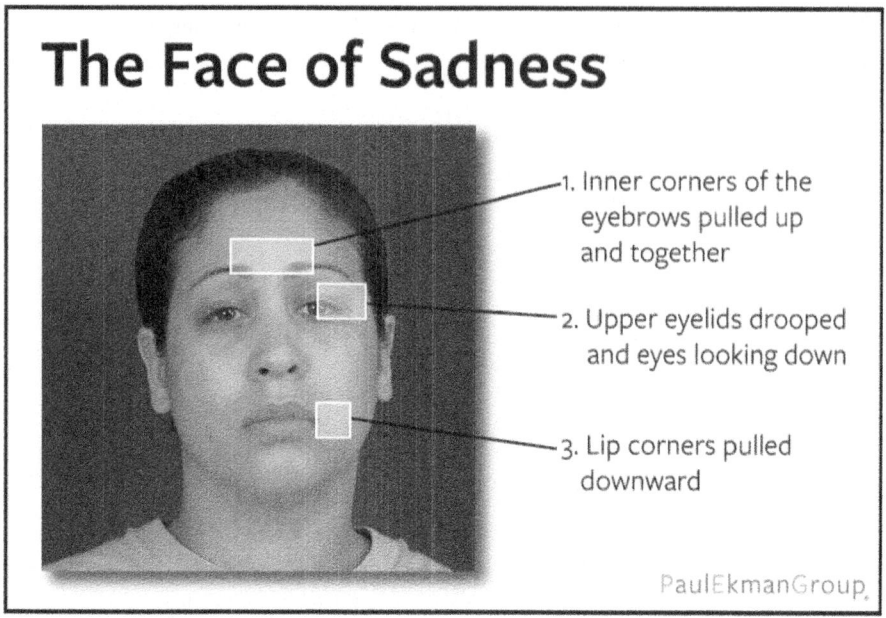

Fig. 3. Paul Ekman Group's "The Face of Sadness" [21].

Happiness is described by Ekman in the form of narrow eyes, often with wrinkles around the eye area, raised cheeks and pulled back lips with visible teeth [21]. Typical posture for happiness can vary depending on the situation, ranging from upright to a relaxed. Duchenne [4] noted that the muscle surrounding the eye activates during genuine smiles. The external expression of happiness arises in connection with an internal feeling [11]. Masked smiles can occur due to social and cultural factors. However, masked smiles always contains traces of other emotions [11].

The NPC shown in Fig. 6 is displaying happiness according to Ekman's definition (see Fig. 5). It exhibits narrowed eyes and retracted lips with visible teeth characteristics of the emotional expression happiness.

2.2   Believability

Work on how to create believable agents, and in games believable characters, is inspired by the concept of the "illusion of life" as described by Bates [3]. Bates relates how Disney's animators manage to make the audience feel for the characters through their animations. According to Bates, this is possible when animators make the character feel like it can make its own decisions and act based on its own values and wishes. Notably, Disney animators Thomas and Johnston [26] define the concept in accordance with Bates. They present that the most important aspect is well-time and clear emotional expressions, which overlaps with research in AI as these aspects are integral to believability [3]. Thomas and

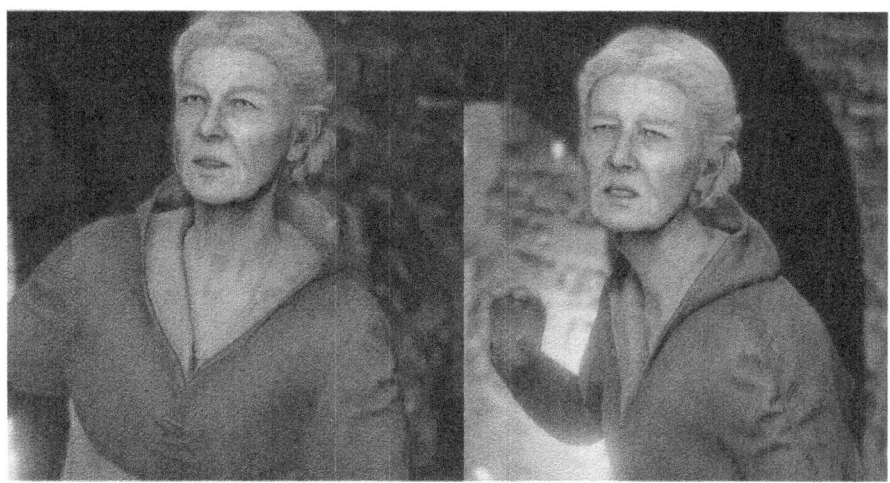

Fig. 4. BG3 NPC. Left shows neutral while right sadness.

Johnston claims clearly conveyed emotional state, showing the thought process and highlighting the feelings are essential to creating believability [25].

A key feature of believability is that fictional characters convey emotions, and that characters behavior and actions correspond with both their personality and with the given circumstances in the fictional world. Thomas and Johnston mention that the portrayal of emotion is what gives them life, thus their believability [25]. Getting visual feedback via non-verbal elements such as the character's facial expressions, intonation and body language is more important than the dialogue. However, it is important that these non-verbal elements are consistent with the ongoing dialogue [19].

When applied to games, problems with believability arise when an NPC does not behave in a consistent way with player's expectations [27]. Discrepancies in players' perception of the NPC lead to misunderstandings, resulting in a less entertaining gaming experience. Both [27] and [20] emphasize the fact that whether the NPC is perceived as believable or not is essentially based on how much the NPC is accepted by the audience. Tencé et al. mentions that the most common way games break this illusion is through predictability. If a character repeats a behavior several times, it is perceived as artificial [24]. However, it can seem far too random if it is not possible to predict what will happen. If a character never learns from their mistakes or repeats counterproductive behavior, this can lower the viewer's sense of believability. However, a character does not have to behave too realistically; Tencé et al. points out that characters often have to exaggerate their actions for the audience to understand what they are doing [24]. Drawing inspiration from realism and adapting it to the medium, in this case games, is the approach most likely to increase believability.

Several sets of criteria for how to achieve believability for fictional characters have been provided, like the one of Loyall [17]. Criteria include qualities such

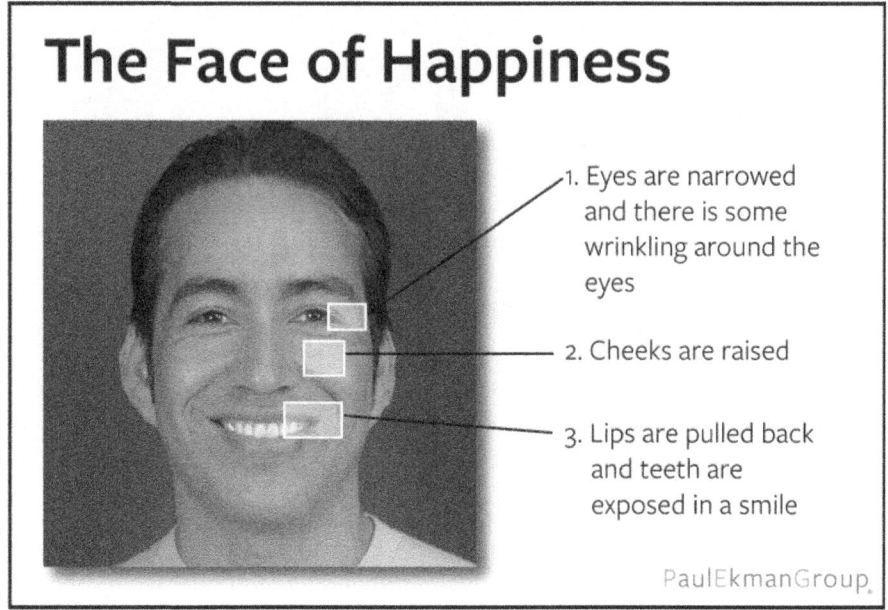

Fig. 5. Paul Ekman Group's "The Face of Happiness" [21].

as personality, emotional expression, consistency and giving the illusion of life. Agents should appear to have own goals, have a presence in the world's social sphere, and behave socially with credible behaviour. Criteria for social believability has also been contributed by [15]. Thalmann et al. stresses how the concept of believability not only includes realism, but also emotional expression, personality and purpose [19]. Like other works ([3] and [25]) Thalmann et al. mentions how characters should react based on its own values, goals and attributes [19]. Bates claims that characters' personal goals, reactions to the world and values are what makes the viewer care about them [3]. If the character lacks goals and emotion there is no reason for the viewer to care.

Thalmann et al. stresses that one of the most important aspects for character's animation to be perceived as believable is the synchronization between the character's verbal and non-verbal expressions [19]. The eyes and head movements have an essential role in non-verbal communication. Studies indicate how one's eyes and head should look depending on the conversation. By using recorded scenarios from real conversations, one can imitate these movements. Eyebrows are equally important, as they can emphasize important parts of the dialogue while highlighting the character's emotional state [19]. Keeping facial expressions properly timed depending on the context of what is going on or being said, but also dynamic expressions can create a greater sense of believability. However, this dynamic needs to reflect the character's emotional state and built-up

Fig. 6. GI NPC. Left shows neutral while right happiness.

personality. It is important that the character moves both their gaze and their body, even if the character in question does not do anything important [19].

Legibility is a closely related term to believability. According to the Cambridge Dictionary, legibility refers to the ease with which something can be read or a degree which it is readable [5]. Despite this similarity, our work uses the term believability because it focuses on the perception of emotions in videos, whereas legibility is more commonly applied to literary works and text-based media, which are not the focus here.

There is an important distinction between simply identifying an emotion and perceiving it as natural and functional within the world the character inhabits. Therefore, the believability of different behaviors varies depending on how clearly they are portrayed, even if they are legible. This is why believability is the central concept used in this project, even though some aspects of the descriptions could also apply to legibility.

3   The Study

Our study is based on a content analysis of three games, in terms of how the emotions anger, sadness, and happiness are conveyed by NPCs animations. Videos were selected from the content analysis and rated through a questionnaire of how well participants recognised the intended emotional expression and how convincing the animation was. The study was performed in a series as steps as follows:

1. Selection of games and characters/NPCs
2. Initial content analysis and selection of representative materials for user study. Editing of video clips, narrowing down the size of corpus
3. Design of questionnaire

4. Distribution of questionnaire
5. Content analysis and supporting inferential statistics analysis
6. Questionnaire results analysis

For the sake of brevity we focus on the content analysis, but the supporting inferential statistics analysis is available in [16].

3.1 Examined Games

The games within the report aimed to reflect well-known, recently released, character-focused 3D games with different stylizations. GI has a stylish style reminiscent of anime, BG3 a realist style and ACHN is very stylistic. GI is an open world action-RPG where players explore and visit various places. The NPCs in GI play an important role in enriching the game world's lore. BG3 is a group-based RPG built on board game systems like Dungeons and Dragons following the player character's journey. ACNH is a life simulation game with simple NPC behaviors, but display significant elements of NPC characterization. The player explores their island, customize it and choose the inhabitants and their behaviours.

NPC's and Companions. In BG3, it is not clear-cut which characters can be considered as NPCs since players can recruit and control them as *companions*. The companions in BG3 meet the requirements for being classified as NPCs, by those described by Loyall [17]. Warpefelt also notes that companions are NPCs because they are not playable [27]. Hence, we classify companions as NPCs when not controlled by a player. The videos in our study showing companions are restricted to situations where players are not controlling them.

3.2 Selection of Material

Video clips were collected to be analysed by the content analysis and shown in the questionnaire. The videos contained a NPC from one of the selected games displaying one of the emotional expressions. In total, nine clips were collected, one for each emotion present in the different games. In order to focus on the animation things such as sound and visual effects were removed.

Given the study's time limit it was not viable to play through the games and the used media was found through the social media platform Youtube. The videos requirements were to display only the emotion and contain as much body language as could be found. To avoid bias the searching of clips were made alone, but the selection was agreed upon by both authors of [16].

3.3 Design of Questionnaire

Our questionnaire was conducted online and did not gather personal information except for whether they had played the games studied. During the analysis the researchers strived to be as objective as possible, but complete objectivity is challenging because human experience can lead to different interpretations of the subject.

The questionnaire was made with Google Forms to ensure anonymity and to get a variation of participants. The target audience was RPG players because the genre's close ties with characterisation and limited researched on this player group. To ensure the questionnaire reached the right participants it asked about their experience with RPG games.

The questionnaire contains questions regarding the perceive emotion of the NPC videos shown and their believability. It used a scale from 1 to 5 to measure the believability, where 1 represented that the emotional expression was difficult to interpret and 5 that it was easy. To guide the participants there existed pre-define answers of Ekman's universal emotions [8] and the ability to write their own comment. The use of clips provide the participants with the same experience and thus easier analysed their responses [28]. The order of displaying the clips in the questionnaire was randomized to avoid patterns and had a condition of no repetitions of three subsequent clips for the same emotion or game.

3.4   Distribution of Questionnaire

The questionnaire was distributed on several social media platforms and an email was provided if questions arose regarding the study. The platforms including Reddit, Discord, Facebook and Tiktok. Reddit's forums are used for user to discuss their interests and were used to reach the target group. The questionnaire was sent out to forums focused on games, RPG, or one of the researched games. Many of Reddit's post were removed due to restrictions on new accounts such as the one being used. The questionnaire was sent through Discord servers. After communication with moderators the questionnaire was permitted to publish on ACNH's main server but denied on GI's server. The questionnaire was also sent out on channels connected to Stockholm University and the Royal Institute of Technology (KTH). The channels were the student union (DISKord), Game Development server for Stockholm University and a KTH server. Acquaintances of the target group helped by answering and spreading the questionnaire further. To gather more participants the questionnaire was also sent on Facebook and Tiktok. Resulting in 159 answers.

3.5   Content Analysis

The content analysis was used to find patterns of animations for certain emotions or games. Content analysis is effective for finding repetition in elements [14]. The themes and subcategories found can be seen in Figs. 7, 8 and 9, summarising the findings of the content analysis from the work. The study goes into more detail about subcategories for each emotion and game than are presented here [16].

The different videos received subcategories distributed to them which can be seen in Figs. 10, 11 and 12.

Main themes	Subcategories	Description
Character visibility	Visible head	Only includes videos where the head is primarily visible. Still categorized as *Visible head* although a small part of the upper body, such as shoulders, is visible.
	Visible torso	Includes only those videos where both the head and the majority of the torso are visible.
	Visible full body	Includes those videos where the entire body is visible, meaning that the body can be analyzed in its entirety.
Head movements	Head bobbing	All videos show constant head rocking, however the degree of rocking may differ in intensity.
	Shaking of head	Includes the videos where they shake their heads.
	Nodding head	Includes the videos where the NPC specifically nods its head.
	Bowed head	Includes the videos where the NPC's head drops down, usually in conjunction with the body's downward movement.
	Elevated head	When the NPC's chin or head is raised. The posture of the body is usually in correlation with this subcategory (Paul Ekman Group, n.d.).
	Straight head	The position of the head remains upright without tilting, with the exception of shaking of the head.
Posture	Straight Posture	Includes the videos where the NPC's posture remains straight, without major tilts.
	Leaning forward	Includes the videos where the NPC leans its body forward.
	Leaning back	Includes the videos where the NPC leans its body backwards.
	Head and body follow each other	Includes the videos where the NPC's body and head are in sync. If the head dips up or down, the posture of the body also dips up or down.
Facial movements	Lower corners of the mouth	Includes the videos where the direction of the NPC's lips go down.

Fig. 7. Table shows all subcategories under *Character visivility, Head movments* and *Posture.* One subcategory from *Facial movements.*

Anger. For the expression Anger there are clear subcategories exhibited within all the videos that ties in with previous research: *Head bobbing, Elevated head, Leaning forward, Lower corners of the mouth* and *Lower eyebrows.* The subcategories *Lower corners of the mouth* and *Lower eyebrows* are both included

	Raised corners of the mouth	Includes the videos where the direction of the NPC's lips go up.
	Arched mouth	Includes the videos where NPCs' lips, mainly the upper lip, rise in an arched position. The lower lip is also open, which in combination with the position of the upper lip is a sign for the emotional expression of disgust (Paul Ekman Group, n.d.).
	Bare your teeth	Includes the videos where NPCs show their teeth in a more threatening context, comparable to how in the animal kingdom you growl at an opponent to show your fangs. Does not include teeth that are visible in the context of a conversation.
	Furrowed brows	Includes the videos where NPCs' eyebrows are pinched together, which can be clearly seen by the formation of wrinkles between the eyebrows. Whether the position of the eyebrows is up or down has no effect, it's the actual furrowed brows that is analyzed.
	Raised eyebrows	Includes the videos where the direction of the NPC's eyebrows go up.
	Lower eyebrows	Includes the videos where the direction of the NPC's eyebrows go down.
	Straight eyebrows	Includes the videos where the NPC's eyebrows remain straight without raises or furrowed brows .
	Crescent shaped eyes	Includes the videos where the NPC's eyes take the shape of a crescent moon. Most often the eyes are closed and occurs in connection with the emotional expression of happiness (Paul Ekman Group, n.d.).
	Wide eyes	Includes the videos where the NPC opens their eyes wide open. This facial expression can occur due to several emotional expressions (Paul Ekman Group, n.d.).
	Down turned eyes	Includes the videos where the NPC's upper eyelid is tilted down.
	Squinting eyes	Includes the videos where the NPC's eyes are partially closed.

Fig. 8. Table shows subcategories under *Facial movements.*

in Fig. 1 showcasing common sign of anger. Other subcategories that showcase anger are *bare your teeth, clench fists, wide eyes* and *stomping.* As mentioned earlier *leaning forward* with *elevated head* are clear signs of anger [21].

	Closed eyes	Includes the videos where the NPC's eyes are fully closed without being crescent shaped.
Arm movements	Dynamic hands	Includes those videos where the NPC's hands are constantly in motion and used dynamically.
	Clench fists	Includes the videos where the NPC's fingers are bent and tightly pressed against the palm in a fist.
	Pointing	Includes the videos where the NPC points.
	Static arms	Includes those videos when the NPC's arms don't move at all.
Leg movements	Stomping	Only includes videos where the NPC stomps its foot down.
	No leg movement	Includes the videos where no movement of the NPC's legs occurs.
Pace	Constant rocking at the same rate of the whole body	Includes the videos where the NPC's body sways in a constant rhythm, without any change during the animation.
	Dynamic change of the speed of the rocking of the whole body	Includes the videos where the tempo of the rocking constantly changes in time with the NPC's movements. For example, for video 4 (ACNH displaying anger) , the tempo changes to a faster tempo when the NPC crouches, a slower tempo when they lean back, and finally a faster tempo again when it clenches its fists. The NPC shows three different tempos for a few seconds.
	Static facial expression	Includes only those videos where the NPC's facial expression remains unchanged for several seconds.
	Fluid changes of facial expressions	Includes the videos where the NPC's facial expressions are constantly changing. The choice of the word fluid was a conscious choice, as the facial expressions do not change forcefully or energetically, but in a completely flowing and unhindered way.

Fig. 9. Table shows all subcategories under the themes *Arm movements, Leg movements and pace.* One subcategory from *Facial movements.*

Sadness videos had three things all them of the displayed: *Head bobbing, Lower corners of the mouth* and *Furrowed brows.* The two last subcategories are characteristics that are seen in Fig. 3 "the face of sadness". Other subcategories that were not present in every video such as *Down turned eyes, Bowed head* and *leaning forward* are also signs of sadness [21].

Videos presented in order	The video clips	Game	Emotion	Subcategories
Videos No. 1	https://www.yout ube.com/watch?v =IHJyw7LlGS4 &t=1s&ab_chan nel=researchStud y	Baldur's gate 3	Happiness	• Visible torso • Head bobbing • Shaking of head • Nodding head • Leaning forward • Straight head • Straight posture • Squinting eyes • Wide eyes • Leaning back • Lower corners of the mouth • Raised corners of the mouth • Raised eyebrows • Dynamic hands • Pointing
Video no 2	Lhttps://www.yo utube.com/watch ?v=wRGZucSy9 YU&ab_channel =researchStudy'	Baldur's gate 3	Sadness	• Visible torso • Head bobbing • Bowed head • Leaning forward • Head and body follow each other • Lower corners of the mouth • Arched mouth • Furrowed brows • Lower eyebrows • Bare your teeth • Down turned eyes • Closed eyes
Video No. 3	https://www.yout ube.com/watch?v =VnXRE5LPdq M&ab_channel= researchStudy	Genshin Impact	Anger	• Visible torso • Head bobbing • Elevated head • Leaning forward • Lower corners of the mouth • Bare your teeth • Lower eyebrows • Wide eyes • Dynamic hands • Clench fists

Fig. 10. Table showing the videos in questionnaires order and their subcategories. BG3 expressing happiness (Link), BG3 expressing sadness (Link) GI expressing anger (Link).

Happiness. The subcategories displayed in all the videos were: *Head bobbing, Straight head* and *Raised corners of the mouth* as seen in Fig. 5 "The face of happiness". Other subcategories shown in two of the videos included: *Nodding head, Straight posture, Raised eyebrows, Crescent shaped eyes* and *Constant rocking at the same rate of the whole body* also seen in Fig. 5. Typical posture can vary with happiness from an upright body to relaxed. Thus, the subcategories *Nodding head* and *Straight posture* arise for the emotion happiness.

Video no 4	https://www.yout ube.com/watch?v =9ZgM_6RUFI4 &ab_channel=re searchStudy	Animal crossing: new horizons	Anger	• Visible full body • Head bobbing • Elevated head • Leaning forward • Lower corners of the mouth • Lower eyebrows • Wide eyes • Stomping • Dynamic change of the speed of the rocking of the whole body • Fluid changes of facial expressions • Dynamic hands
Video No. 5	https://www.yout ube.com/watch?v =l7sAFL0fr54&a b_channel=resea rchStudy	Animal crossing: new horizons	Sadness	• Visible full body • Head bobbing • Bowed head • Leaning forward • Straight posture • Head and body follow each other • Lower corners of the mouth • Furrowed brows • Raised eyebrows • Static arms • No leg movement • Fluid changes of facial expressions • Constant rocking at the same rate of the whole body
Video No. 6	https://www.yout ube.com/watch?v =8b0rjfxVN-c&a b_channel=resea rchStudy	Genshin impact	Happiness	• Visible head • Head bobbing • Nodding head • Straight head • Raised corners of the mouth • Raised eyebrows • Shave eyebrows • Down turned eyes • Crescent shaped eyes • Constant rocking at the same rate of the whole body • Closed eyes

Fig. 11. Table showing the videos in questionnaires order and their subcategories. ACNH expressing anger (Link), ACNH expressing sadness (Link) and GI expressing happiness (Link).

Genshin Impact subcategories were in two videos: *Visible head and Head bobbing, Straight head, Lower corners of the mouth, Raised corners of the mouth, Raised eyebrows, Lower eyebrows* and *Closed eyes*. An interesting element is that all videos had different eye subcategories. The videos show many different facial expressions, not surprising as they intended to express different emotions. Most

Video No. 7	https://www.yout ube.com/watch?v =fPDeG7MHky M&ab_channel= researchStudy	Animal crossing: new horizons	Happiness	• Visible full body • Head bobbing • Straight head • Straight posture • Raised corners of the mouth • Crescent shaped eyes • Static arms • No leg movement • Constant rocking at the same rate of the whole body • Static facial expression
Video No. 8	https://www.yout ube.com/watch?v =HkdeJ5h1_e8& ab_channel=rese archStudy	Genshin impact	Sadness	• Visible head • Head bobbing • Straight head • Lower corners of the mouth • Raised corners of the mouth • Furrowed brows • Raised eyebrows • Lower eyebrows • Squinting eyes • Closed eyes • Static facial expression
Video No. 9	https://www.yout ube.com/watch?v =gR3rsvxqhNY &ab_channel=re searchStudy	Baldur's gate 3	Anger	• Visible torso • Head bobbing • Elevated head • Straight head • Straight posture • Leaning forward • Arched mouth • Lower corners of the mouth • Lower eyebrows • Straight eyebrows • Squinting eyes • Pointing

Fig. 12. Table showing the videos in questionnaires order and their subcategories. ACNH expressing happiness (Link), GI expressing sadness (Link) and BG3 express anger (Link).

of GI's videos only displayed a visible face therefore limiting the expression to only focusing on the head.

Baldur's Gate 3 displayed the subcategories *Visible torso, Head bobbing* and *Lower corners of the mouth* for all videos. BG3's videos contained *Visible torso* which allowed body language to play a role in conveying the feeling. Two videos showed *pointing* that probably went along with dialogue but without the context it is hard to interpret its meaning.

Animal Crossing: New Horizons. The recurring patterns for all ACNH subcategories were *Visible full body* and *Head bobbing*. All ACNH NPCs showcased different head movements, thous being *Bowed head, Elevated head* and *Straight* *head.* All ACNH's videos were full body and therefore the only game that showed leg movements. Interestingly, ACNH has 7 subcategories underneath the theme *Facial movements* while the other games have 12. Notably, there is only one subcategory under *Facial movements* that repeats twice, that being *Lower corners of the mouth.* This shows that the videos had different facial movements that were not shared by the others.

3.6   Questionnaire Results

When checking the reach of the target audience it was confirmed that most participants were RPG players (see Fig. 13). The majority had previously played one of the examined games. ACNH was the most played game by a large margin (see Fig. 14).

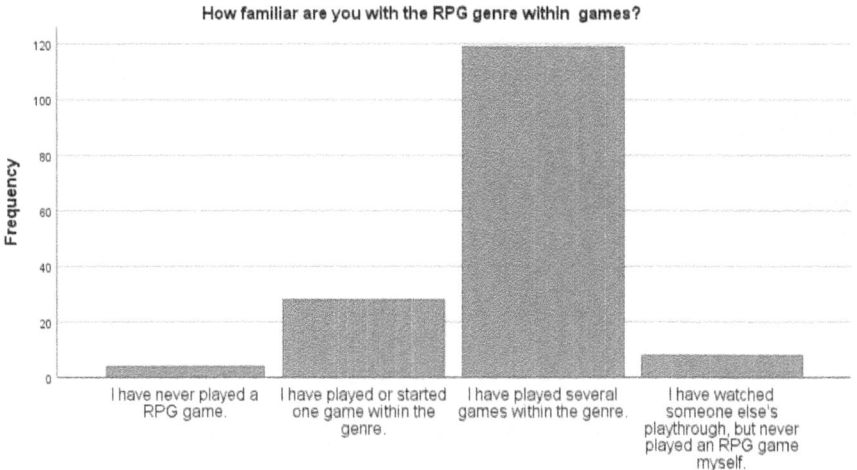

Fig. 13. Frequency bar chart for   *"How familiar are you with the RPG genre within games?"*

In this section we analyze the mean believability of the videos in the questionnaire. The fourth video expressing anger from ACNH had the highest perceived believability with a value of 4.91 out of 5. The video clip with the lowest perceived believability was GI expressing sadness with a value of 2.53. Looking at the best performing videos of each feeling, happiness had the highest mean with 3.7, followed by anger with 3.66 and lowest sadness with approximately 3.387. ACNH showed the highest average mean of around 4.223 between the games, BG3 with around 3.627, and GI with approximately 2.897. Statistically, the best preforming video should be ACNH expressing happiness but it was ACNH

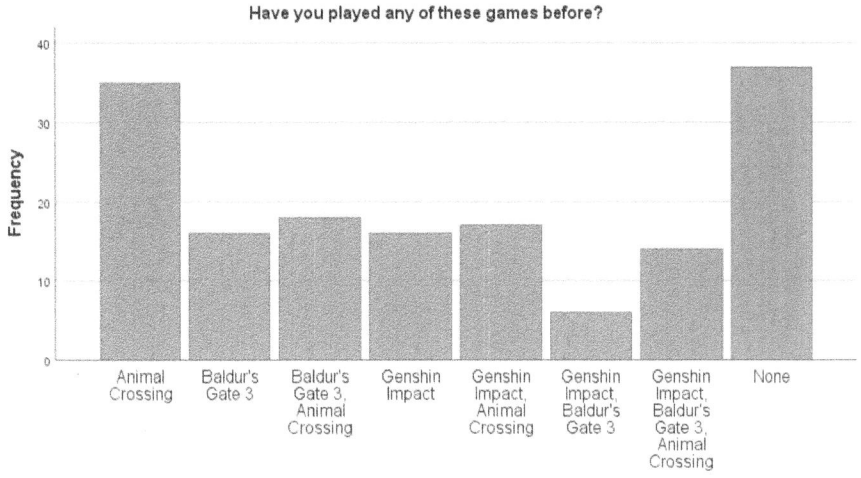

Fig. 14. Frequency bar chart for *"Have you played any of these games before?"*

expressing anger. The most difficult to interpret should be GI expressing sadness with turned out to be the case.

Below are pie charts for each video shown in the questionnaire that display the participants answers. With higher correct identification of the emotion there also was a higher believability score.

Anger. As the pie chart (see Fig. 15) shows, majority of participants were able to identify the emotion expression as anger from the GI video. However, it is noteworthy that a significant percentage of participants also interpreted the emotion as surprise or fear. This can be explained by the NPC showing widened eyes for a longer period which is a sign of several emotions. The NPC was wearing a mask covering half of the face making it difficult to perceive certain facial movements. But body language helped display the emotion with a typical crouching position, elevated head and clenched fists.

The participants answered a 100% rate of identifying the expression anger for the ACNH video (see Fig. 16). It is very interesting that the animation were so clear. Another remarkable aspect is as mentioned above, that this video has the highest mean of all the videos with 4.91.

The pie chart (see Fig. 17) showing BG3 expressing anger had more answers identifying disgust than anger, which was the second largest choice. Although an overwhelming majority of participants interpreted the emotion differently than intended, the mean believability was 3.21. This means that even though another emotion was identified, it was perceived as believable. However, it is worth mentioning that the video shows signs of anger according to Ekman's principles but also disgust, which may explain the discrepancy between the responses. It is

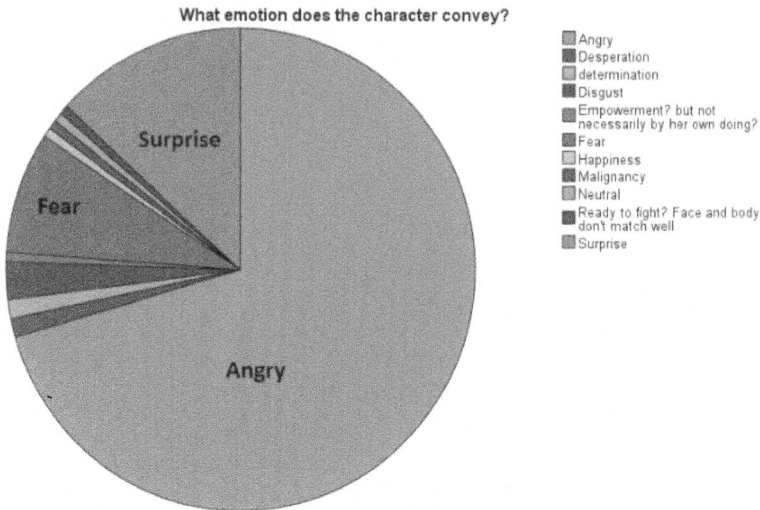

Fig. 15. Pie chart of the conveyed emotions of GI expressing anger

relevant to consider that the researchers may have misinterpreted the emotion. A participant commented this:

> *"I have played this game so I recall the dialogue but I [can't] actually place her emotion."*.

This shows that even experienced participants with more context also had difficulty identifying the NPC's expression.

Sadness. The pie chart in Fig. 18 illustrates the emotional expression sadness from BG3. A majority of participants identified the emotion, while disgust and anger also received answers. When examining the responses from individuals, it can be observed that several participants experienced a combination of emotions. A common combination is sadness and anger. This indicates that the animation showed signs relating to several emotions.

Figure 19 shows the emotion sadness from ACNH. Majority of participants identified the intended expression, followed by fear and surprise. Both sadness and fear exhibit raised eyebrows, furrowed eyebrows and lowered corners of the mouth. Therefore eyes are the most obvious difference between the two expressions, as they are wide open in fear [21]. However, the NPC's eyes are somewhat stylistic making them more difficult to interpret, as they do not mimics human anatomy.

The pie chart in Fig. 20 illustrates the emotional expression sadness from GI. Results presented in the chart show a large variation. The most uniformly identified expression was sadness, followed by neutral and happiness. It is worth noting that sadness did not make up the majority of participants' responses.

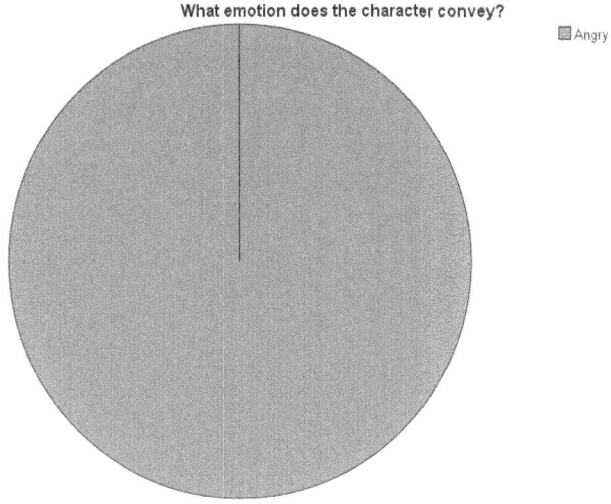

Fig. 16. Pie chart of the conveyed emotions of ACNH expressing anger

The emotion disappointment is interesting as it was not a pre-defined option and needed to be specified by the participants. This indicates that some participants experienced this emotion so clearly that they chose it. However, it is worth adding that Ekman's definition of sadness includes disappointment in the spectrum of sadness [21]. Additionally, the NPC in the video briefly displayed signs associated with happiness. The fact that the NPC does not change its expression for an extended period may have contributed to participants defining the expression as neutral.

Happiness. The Fig. 21 shows the participants' responses to BG3 portraying happiness, which the majority answered. The emotions surprise and pride also occurs. Pride was not a pre-defined option and therefore participants specified it themselves. The emotions enthusiasm and excitement that were answered belong to the spectrum of happiness [21].

Participants' responses for GI's video portraying happiness had majority identifying the emotion as neutral (see Fig. 22). Although the NPC at the beginning of the video shows signs of happiness according to Ekman's definition, such as crescent-shaped eyes and upturned mouth corners. Neutrality acts like a person's baseline, what their face looks like when least affected by emotions [10]. The answers may be because during the last 3 s, the NPC did not move their face, which can be interpreted as a neutral expression.

An overwhelming proportion of participants identified the emotion happiness for ACNH's video (see Fig. 23). A small number of participants identified the emotions as neutral or surprise. This may be due in part to the NPC's facial

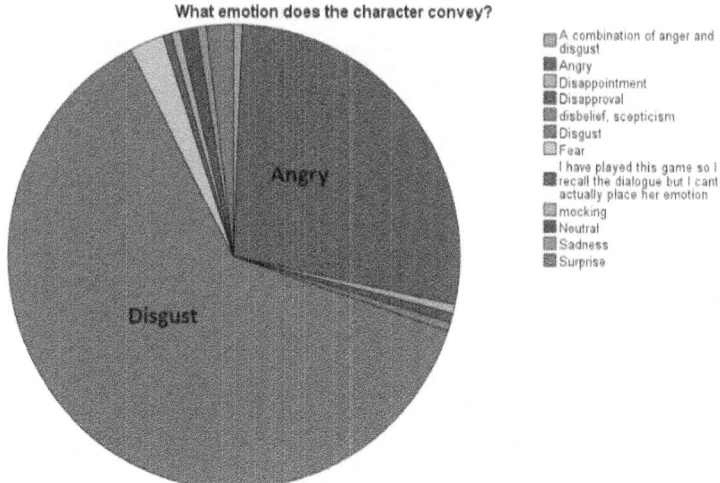

Fig. 17. Pie chart of the conveyed emotions of BG3 expressing anger

expression before they show happiness, as its neutral expression has downward-sloping eyebrows and corners of the mouth.

Genshin Impact. In summary, the animations in GI were least success full of the three analysed games to convey emotions to the viewers. This can be seen by two of the videos having the lowest believability values out of all videos, being anger (see Fig. 15) with 2.86 and sadness (see Fig. 20) with 2.53. Furthermore, GI has two videos with the most varied answers being happiness (see Fig. 22) and sadness (see Fig. 20).

Balder's Gate 3 was generally in the middle. A majority of participants identified the expressions, the videos anger being the exception (see Fig. 17). The video with the highest believability for BG3 was sadness with around 3.86. Most participants correctly identified the emotion and experiencing the animations as believable.

Animal Crossing: New Horizons had overall the highest believability scores and is the only game where all videos had a majority of the viewers interpretation aligned with the intended emotion. It even had a video with 100% answering the intended emotion (see Fig. 16). Also having the highest believability with 4.91 out of the videos.

4   Discussion

The concept of believability is complex and difficult to define, as reflected in the plethora of criterias described in Sect. 2.2. In our study, we interpreted the

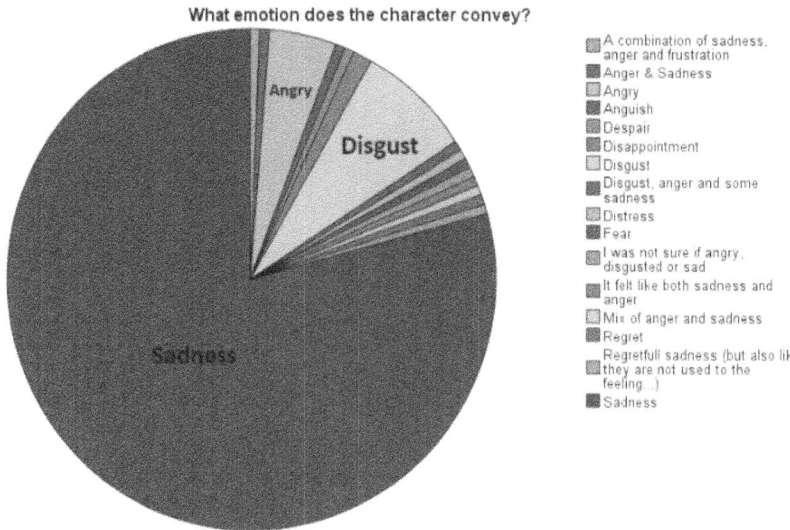

Fig. 18. Pie chart of the conveyed emotions of BG3 expressing sadness

concept in line with the majority of researchers, i.e., that NPCs need to behave as expected of them, but are also experienced as individuals with values and desires. According to Tencé et al., drawing inspiration from realism and adapting it to the specific medium is the best way to increase believability [24].

Even though the paper is based on an exploitative study, it still yielded results. However, these findings might not be generalizable due to limited number of games and participants for such a large research group. Nonetheless, it can indicate potential directions for future research and whether similar conclusions are found. It is also important to clarify that the study's results regarding participants' interpretation of NPCs' portrayal of emotions primarily reflect conclusions regarding experienced RPG players. Less experienced players and other demographics' might showcase different results.

In the study, it became apparent that the emotion expressed was not as important as the animations showcasing it in terms of believability. For example, happiness was the most identifiable emotion but it was not the emotion with the highest mean perceived believability, which was anger. As mentioned in Sect. 3.6, ACNH displayed the highest believable and clearest display of emotion (see Fig. 16). Overall, ACNH's videos generally scored higher for believability compared to the other videos. This pattern of correct identification and high believability scores is seen in several videos but not all. Such as BG3 showcasing anger (see Fig. 17).

ACNH received the highest mean despite most of its videos showing essentially static animation with minimal variation. This can partly be explained by the videos aligning Ekman's definitions of emotional expressions [21] and their

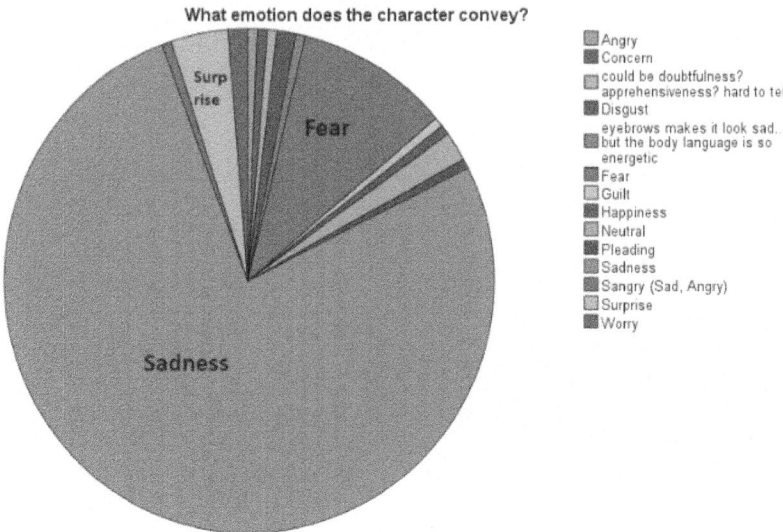

Fig. 19. Pie chart of the conveyed emotions of ACNH expressing sadness

exaggerated conveyance of emotions through animation. Figure 16 itself uses the Tencé et al. approach [24], adapting real-life signs of anger to the medium used and exaggerating the NPCs' portrayal. The need for game characters to exaggerate their actions to convey emotions is essential for creating believable agents, which ACNH's NPCs exemplify well [24].

Thalmann et al. emphasized that a crucial aspects of creating believable characters through animation is the synchronization between verbal and non-verbal expressions mimics realism [19]. Observing and taking inspiration from real-life movements in given situations is essential to create believable animations and agents [19]. BG3 successfully implemented this concept through motion capture for character's dialogue [23]. Ayasta, the lead technical animator for the studio behind BG3, highlighted that previous dialogue animations lacked realism. To solve this motion capture was implemented for all NPCs. Capturing actors' authentic movements, gestures, and facial expressions when conveying the dialogue [23].

When analysing videos it is clear that the games used established techniques from previous research to express emotions.

This study is mainly based on Ekman and Izard's definitions of emotional expressions. The selection and analyzing of clips primarily relied on Fig. 1 "The Face of Anger", Fig. 3 "The Face of Sadness" and Fig. 5 "The Face of Happiness".

Because the study limited data, it is challenging to draw generalizing conclusions regarding which researcher's theories of believability were most accurate. Despite this, a clear trend emerges in the results indicating that Tencé et al.'s definition conveyed the emotional expressions in a more believable way.

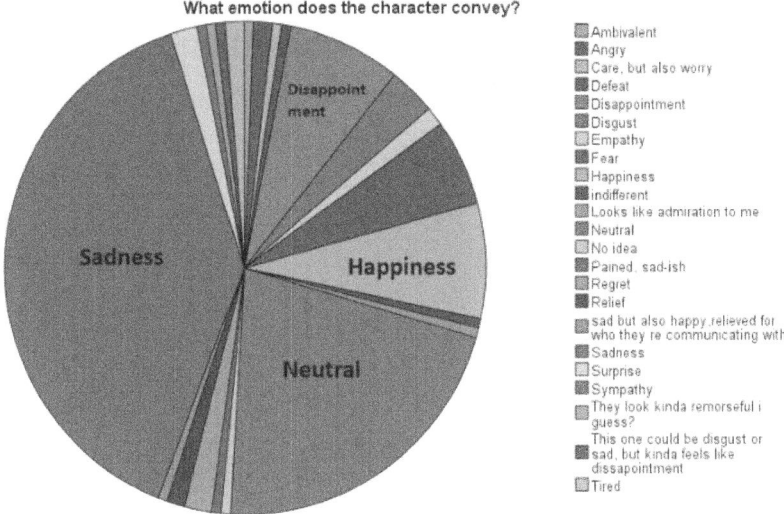

Fig. 20. Pie chart of the conveyed emotions of GI expressing sadness

BG3 animations were realistic with dynamic facial expressions and rarely static. This may have made it more difficult for participants to identify the emotion in absence of context. Although BG3 met several criteria for realistic emotional representation with its animations, participants still found it more challenging to identify the emotion than in ACNH.

Our results suggest that exaggerated actions displaying emotion in game characters animations are effective for achieving believability. While we did not compare theoretical frameworks for believability directly, this aligns with recommendations given by Tencé et al. [24].

An interesting aspect to consider is how different art styles can affect the outcome, as all three games use different visual styles. Perhaps stylized games like ACNH may get away with more exaggerated animations than realistic games like BG3, which have certain expectations to meet.

Limitations. There are several limitations with the work. As the questionnaire was distributed online with voluntary participation the participants may not represent RPG players accurately. With snowballing, the results might be skewed because it was sent to like-minded individuals and acquaintances.

There is a bias in selecting of the material as only two researchers with a similar background conducted the task. There is a possible conflict in perception as most participants identified BG3 showcasing anger as disgust, but the researchers and the minority perceived it as anger. Due to the researchers' perception and classification of NPCs' emotion the work has a Northern European perspective, the same perspective as Izard and Ekman.

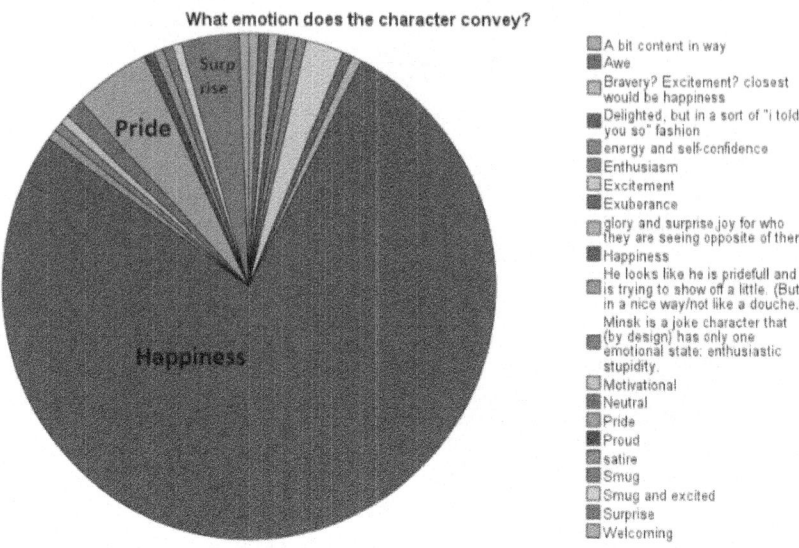

Fig. 21. Pie chart of the conveyed emotions of BG3 expressing happiness

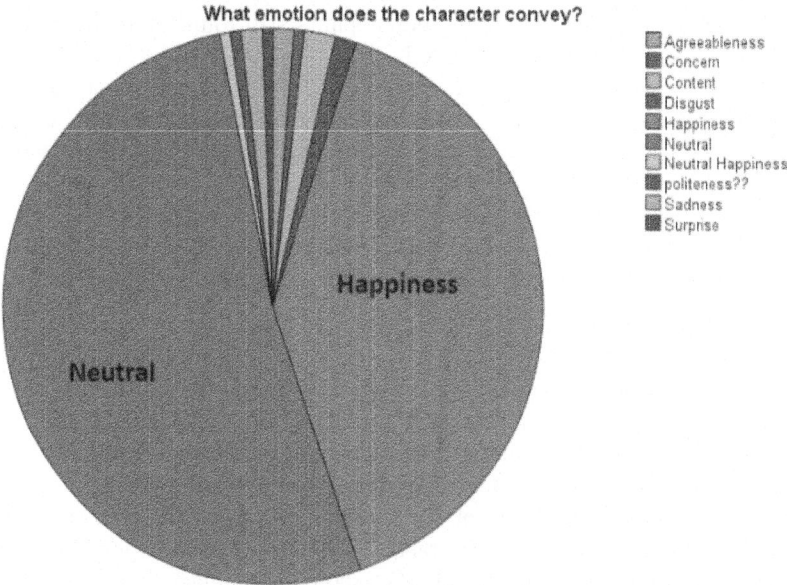

Fig. 22. Pie chart of the conveyed emotions of GI expressing happiness

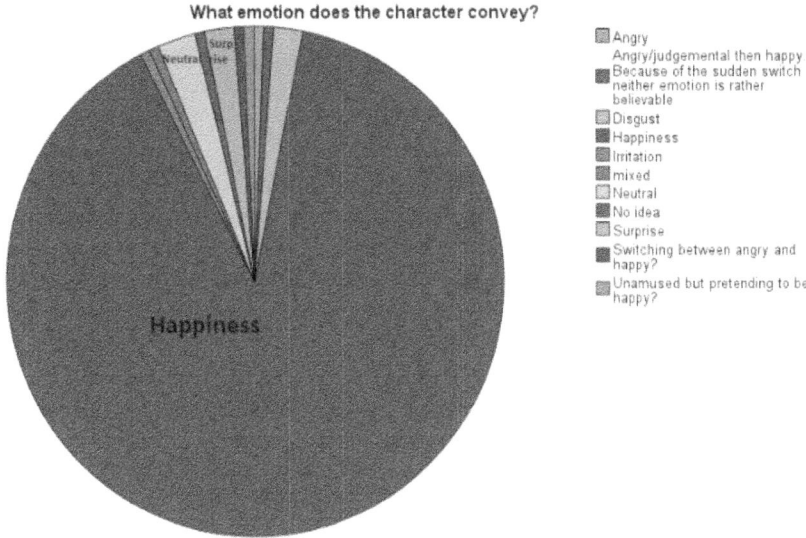

Fig. 23. Pie chart of the conveyed emotions of ACNH expressing happiness

Not all videos show an equal amount of the NPC's body making only one game able to display leg animations. Therefore it is not possible to judge the body language of every game.

The set of video clips, the number of participants and the variation of games are too limited to generalize RPG players and the characters focused games.

There are not a fair comparison between the NPCs from other games and BG3 as they aim to depict realism which might trigger the Uncanny Valley effect. This could have infliction the results and made them misleading. As participant interpreted BG3 as less believable.

Future Research. There are variations of approaches to further research the impact of animation on believability and emotional expression. Researchers could extend to other media or focus on participants' backgrounds. With a larger research group the assessment of emotions would be less bias.

The research could also expand to other games or genres, such as first-person shooters, or visual styles to explore differences. Future studies could examine similar games as in this study with the same visual style to confirm if the results repeats.

Further research on the subject can include other emotions such as the "basic emotions" mentioned by Ekman. This would contribute to a deeper understanding of the relationship between emotional expressions and their representation in animations. Another option is to focus on one emotion and analyze its various nuances and intensities. Given that characters often exaggerate their emotions to convey them effectively [24], it would be relevant to explore whether Izard's theory that emotional expression always shows the same sign on a person's face for a microsecond still applies in gaming.

5   Conclusion

Believability of characters in games encompasses that they express emotion in ways consistent with their personalities and make sense in the fictional world they inhabits. Our study compared animations of anger, sadness and happiness in three games: Genshin Impact (GI), Baldur's Gate 3 (BG3) and Animal Crossing: New Horizons (ACNH). These games convey emotion differently. The exploitative study is aimed to guide future research and is not applicable to generalisation. A content analysis was conducted, examining emotional expressions animations. From the corpus of content representative videos were selected for a user study. These videos were shown to participants (159 individuals). Participants identified emotions shown in the videos and rated how convincing the NPCs' expressions were. ACNH, with its simpler animations were perceived to have the highest level of believability of the three with a summarizing score of 4.223 on a scale from 1 to 5. BG3 scored around 3.627 and GI 2.897. ACNH had the most exaggerated animations of the games, and has the highest mean believability score and most correctly identified emotional expression. Rather than emotions having different levels of believability, the results indicates that different games convey emotions with varying levels of believability. Interpreting the scores at a detailed level, it was evident that when it comes to animation, successful results for achieving a high level of believability entailed exaggerated actions showing emotion, especially in cases lacking contextual support.

Acknowledgments. We would like to thank Özge Alkan for helping with the study and all participants who took the time to answer the questionnaire.

References

1. Averill, J.R.: Studies on anger and aggression: implications for theories of emotion. Am. Psychol. **38**(11), 1145–1157 (1983)
2. Barrett, L.F., Adolphs, R., Marsella, S., Martinez, A.M., Pollak, S.D.: Emotional expressions reconsidered: challenges to inferring emotion from human facial movements. Psychol. Sci. Public Interest **20**(1), 1–68 (2019). https://doi.org/10.1177/1529100619832930
3. Bates, J.: The role of emotion in believable agents. Commun. ACM **37**(7), 122–125 (1994). https://doi.org/10.1145/176789.176803
4. Dunchenne de Bouloge, G.: The Mechanism of Human Facial Expression. Cambridge University Press, Cambridge (1990)
5. Cambridge Dictionary: Legibility (nd). https://dictionary.cambridge.org/dictionary/english/legibility. Accessed 24 Sept 2024
6. Ekman, P.: Are there basic emotions? Psychol. Rev. **99**(3), 550–553 (1992)
7. Ekman, P.: Universal facial expressions of emotion. California Mental Health Res. Digest **8**(4), 151–156 (1970)

8. Ekman, P.: Chapter 3 Basic Emotions (1992) (1999)
9. Elfenbein, H.A., Ambady, N.: On the universality and cultural specificity of emotion recognition: a meta-analysis. Psychol. Bull. **128**(2), 203–235 (2002). https://doi.org/10.1037/0033-2909.128.2.203
10. Eun, L., Kang, J.I., Park, I.H., Kim, J.J., An, S.K.: Is a neutral face really evaluated as being emotionally neutral? Psychiatry Res. **157**, 77–85 (2008). https://doi.org/10.1016/j.psychres.2007.02.005
11. Frank, M.G., Ekman, P., Friesen, W.V.: Behavioral Markers and Recognizability of the Smile of Enjoyment, chap. 10, pp. 217–242. Oxford Academic (2012)
12. Heaven, D.: Why faces don't always tell the truth about feelings. Nat. Publ. Group **578**(7796), 502–504 (2020). https://doi.org/10.1038/d41586-020-00507-5
13. Izard, C.E.: Emotions and Facial Expressions: A Perspective from Differential Emotions Theory, chap. 3, pp. 57–77. Cambridge University Press (1997)
14. Johannesson, P., Perjons, E.: An Introduction to Design Science, 1st edn. Springer, Cham (2014). https://doi.org/10.1007/978-3-319-10632-8
15. Johansson, M., Verhagen, H., Eladhari, M.: Model of social believable NPCs for teacher training: using second life. In: Proceedings of CGAMES'2011 USA - 16th International Conference on Computer Games: AI, Animation, Mobile, Interactive Multimedia, Educational and Serious Games (2011). https://doi.org/10.1109/CGAMES.2011.6000351
16. Johansson, T., Alkan, Ö.: Känslomässig trovärdighet i spelkaraktärsanimation. Stockholm University (2024). https://www.diva-portal.org/smash/record.jsf?pid=diva2%3A1875914&dswid=1845
17. Loyall, A.B.: Believable agents: building interactive personalities. Ph.D. thesis, Carnegie Mellon University (1997)
18. Lutz, C., White, G.M.: The anthropology of emotions. Annu. Rev. Anthropol. **15**(1), 405–436 (1986). https://doi.org/10.1146/annurev.anthro.15.1.405
19. Magnenat-Thalmann, N., Kim, H., Egges, A., Garchery, S.: Believability and Interaction in Virtual Worlds. In: International Multi-Media Modelling Conference, pp. 2–9. IEEE Publisher (2005)
20. Mateas, M.: An Oz-centric review of interactive drama and believable agents. In: Artificial Intelligence Today: Recent Trends and Developments, pp. 297–328. Springer, Heidelberg (2001)
21. Paul Ekman ·Group: Universal emotions (nd). https://www.paulekman.com/universal-emotions/. Accessed 18 Feb 2024
22. Provine, R.R.: Beyond the Smile: Nontraditional Facial, Emotional, and Social Behaviors, chap. 11, pp. 197–216. Oxford University Press (2017)
23. StretchSense: How larian studios brought lifelike animation to baldur's gate 3 using stretchsense: Part 2. (2023). https://www.youtube.com/watch?v=wM-X1-o2rCc. Accessed 16 May 2024
24. Tencé, F., Buche, C., De Loor, P., Marc, O.: The challenge of believability in video games: definitions, agents models and imitation learning (2010)
25. Thomas, F., Johnston, O.: The Illusion of Life Disney Animation. Walt Disney Productions (1981)
26. Thomas, F., Johnston, O.: The illusion of life: Disney animation. Hyperion, New York, NY, 1. hyperion ed edn. (1995)
27. Warpefelt, H.: The Non-Player Character: Exploring the believability of NPC presentation and behavior. Ph.D. thesis (2016). https://urn.kb.se/resolve?urn=urn:nbn:se:su:diva-128079
28. Wulf, T., Possler, D., Breuer, J.: Content Analysis in the Research Field of Video Games, pp. 287–297. Springer, Cham (2023)

Finding Queerness in Gaming
How Players See LGBTQ+ Themes in Non-queer Games

Sofia Lindgren[(✉)], Nora Gate, and Mirjam Palosaari Eladhari

Stockholm University, Stockholm, Sweden
hi@sofia.kiwi, mirjam@dsv.su.se
https://www.su.se

Abstract. Players who identify as queer find ways to express their identities in multiplayer games. In this study, we present results on how gender-diverse, non-normative identities are expressed around the first-person shooter Team Fortress 2 (TF2). Despite TF2 not catering to or inviting non-normative expressions of identity through its mechanics or affordances, there is a large queer community active around the game. Through 13 semi-structured interviews with queer TF2 players, the study shows that queer players project their identities onto both characters within and outside the game, and that the intersection between community, self-expression, and the canon provides a foundation for these projections. The presence of a queer community motivated participants to create or share queer retellings of TF2 characters. TF2's focus on fast-paced gameplay does not necessarily invite players to explore the emotional and personal sides of the characters. However, this opened up to the participants filling in these gaps themselves through fan created content, such as fan fictions or fan art.

Keywords: queer identity · retelling · queer studies · online games · sexuality · identity · gender · Team Fortress 2

1 Introduction

In the online game *Team Fortress 2* (TF2) [31] developed by Valve Corporation, a thriving community of players who identify as queer[1] socialize, express and explore their identities in play. Identity exploration is a vital part of online role-playing games, but TF2 is a first person shooter, with few affordances for personal expression and certainly no features explicitly facilitating non standard expressions of gender identity. This sparkled our curiosity. Why and how do queer players project their own identities onto video game characters who are not explicitly LGBTQ+?.

We designed our study for acquiring qualitative autobiographical data from queer TF2 players by conducting interviews. We focused the interview questions

---

[1] In this paper we use the word *queer* as a short-hand for all LGBTQ+ identities.

J. T. Murray and M. C. Reyes (Eds.): ICIDS 2024, LNCS 15468, pp. 100–115, 2025.
https://doi.org/10.1007/978-3-031-78450-7_6

around retellings [10], assuming that if a player goes out of their way to re-tell about their experiences, these tellings are likely to be important to the individuals. Our reasoning was that this might easier lead to "the heart" of what draws people to this particular game, and to find out what was most important to the players in their play and experimentation with queer identity projection.

Queer retellings is a largely unexplored topic. There is a lack of relevant studies as to how queer players project onto pre-designed characters and why, and there are additionally very few queer retelling studies that focus on games. By better understanding how queer players engage with their games it may be possible for game creators to make games and interactive narratives that are more inclusive and has more diversity in character representation.

We conducted 13 interviews with players who identify as queer, and the transcripts were thematically analyzed. In the study presented in this paper we only discuss the material gathered from these interviews, not any retellings of fan fictions or fan art as artifacts.

The paper is organised as follows: We introduce the notion of queerness in relation to games and describe TF2 along with those features relevant to the study. We then detail the study and the collected data. Finally, we discuss and present our key findings.

2   Background

Multiplayer role playing games, where people play in real-time together in a shared environment have been used as spaces for exploration of identity since their inception. One of the earliest examples of such spaces is the Multi-User Dungeon (MUD), which allowed play between large numbers of people [3]. Virtual game worlds allow people to explore their identities in new contexts outside the boundaries of every day life. Turkle, who studied identity construction in MUD in the nineties noted that "there is an unparalleled opportunity to play with one's identity and to 'try out' new ones" [29, p. 158]. An early documented example of this phenomenon is found in Bruckman's research, where a player expressed that "these [play] experiences have helped me to know my self better" [5].

A recent study [14] showed that players who create fan fiction and retellings based on the game Genshin Impact [15] frequently portrayed romantic relation-ships between characters of the same sex. Although this study did not study queer character portrayal per se, we still found it a remarkable number.

2.1   Queerness and Video Games

While today's games cater to a diverse range of players, the visibility of queer characters were less visible in the past. For instance, Vivian from *Paper Mario: The Thousand-Year Door* [16] is clearly portrayed as a trans woman in most international versions, but was depicted as cisgender in the original 2004 North American localization [7]. This discrepancy was corrected in the 2024 remake of *The Thousand-Year Door*, where Vivian's trans identity has been reintroduced into the North American localization [4]. The protagonist Daisuke from *True Love Jun'ai Monogatari~* [25] is one of the earliest examples of a bisexual character in video games. In this PC-98 title, Daisuke can engage in a bisexual relationship, though it is only presented as a secret route within the game [22]. Notably, this route also stands out for being the only one in the game without a sex scene, reflecting the limited representation and visibility of queer relationships in gaming at the time. Queer representation, if present at all, was often hidden in the background or treated as an afterthought rather than being integrated into the main narrative.

Queerness in video games has always extended beyond the representation of LGBTQ+ characters or same-sex romances. As Ruberg argues, video games communicate meaning not only through the people, situations and stories they represent on-screen, but also through their seemingly non-representational procedural and computational systems [23]. They continue to state that it is important to think about how "experiences of difference" can be given, or silenced, by these seemingly non-representational elements.

Ruberg provides an example of this move referencing tabletop role-playing game designers Avery Alder and Joli St. Patrick. In their game *Monsterhearts* [6], queerness is not just represented in the narrative or characters, but embodied through a gameplay mechanic that translates sexual attraction into a die roll. Players must roll a die to determine who "turns their character on", allowing LGBTQ+ experiences to manifest through interaction and chance, rather than traditional representational elements like dialogue or plot.

> *"In order to identify queerness in video games beyond representation, I look not to games with explicit LGBTQ content but to those that are commonly assumed to be "straight"-i.e., "normal" or not queer.*
> - Bo Ruberg

2.2   Team Fortress 2

As mentioned, TF2 is not a role-playing game, but a first-person shooter. The game's mechanics does not inherently lend itself to identity exploration, but nevertheless there is a thriving community of players who identify as queer who uses it as "third place" [21] for socializing. They use what mechanics they can use for identity expression, such as the cosmetics feature that allows customization of avatars.

TF2 provides an interesting example of how queer players can project their identities onto characters who are not explicitly LGBTQ+. Despite being released over 17 years ago, the game continues to thrive, with over 50,000 concurrent players regularly active. Active queer TF2 communities on platforms like Tumblr contribute by creating and sharing content such as fan art, memes, and fan fiction. These communities foster a supportive space for identity expression and social interaction, offering a welcoming environment for queer players.

While TF2 offers players official game servers hosted by Valve, there are also player-run community servers that allow players to create and manage their own game experience. This flexibility has led to a wide range of servers to choose from, catering to various playstyles and social groups. For example, some servers focus on competitive gameplay, while others prioritize social interactions. This flexibility allows players to find like-minded individuals and create subcultures both inside and outside of the game, keeping the game fresh and engaging at the same time.

Storyline and Characters. Set in a late 1960s alternate America, Team Fortress 2's story features two rival brothers, Redmond and Blutarch Mann, who hire mercenaries to battle for control of land. Players in-game join either brother's team to fight against each other. However, the game's lore is not further developed within the game itself and is primarily conveyed through external materials like the comics [30] and videos.

Thanks to the smaller roster of nine characters, the mercenaries have well-defined personalities and clear character traits that very rarely overlap yet complement each other well. For the sake of this study, since there is a large focus on the characters and how queer players perceive them, a short explanation of three characters highlighted in this paper is given:

Pyro Pyro is a mystery, known only for their love of fire and whimsical nature. Unlike other characters whose genders are confirmed as male, Pyro's gender is never stated and is a subject of speculation, fueled by voice lines, inconsistent pronouns, and jokes. Despite their intimidating nature, their introduction video *Meet the Pyro* [27] shows Pyro perceiving the world as a pastel, rainbow-filled dream, with fire replaced by soap bubbles and weapons by harmless alternatives, like a fire axe becoming a giant lollipop.

Heavy The Heavy Weapons Guy, more commonly known as the Heavy, is the largest and most robust character, known for his deep voice, Russian accent, and immense strength. He wields a massive minigun he affectionately calls "Sasha." Despite his intimidating appearance, Heavy often displays a gentle and affectionate side, especially towards his weaponry. He is fiercely loyal to his team and often speaks in simple, straightforward terms.

Medic Despite being called a doctor by his fellow mercenaries, Medic is far from a compassionate healer and is implied to lack a medical license. He is morbidly curious and enthusiastic about human nature and anatomy, with healing his co-workers often an unintended side effect. Depicted as maniacal and power-hungry, Medic also shows a soft spot for his pet doves and, in some cases, Heavy.

Other classes Together with Scout, Soldier, Demoman, Engineer, Sniper, and Spy, these nine characters make up the full cast of Team Fortress 2.

Customization. A significant part of the economy in TF2 revolves around cosmetics, previously known as but not exclusive to *hats*. These virtual items, obtainable through crates, crafting, or trading, are often bought with real money on the Steam market or third-party sites. While purely visual and not affecting gameplay, in-game cosmetics are highly sought after for self-expression and as status symbols, with rare items selling for hundreds of dollars [17]. Each character has three cosmetic slots, allowing for unique personalization while maintaining the game's color scheme and silhouette.

Weapons in TF2 are another crucial aspect of customization, offering players a range of options that, unlike cosmetics, can significantly alter gameplay. Each class has access to a variety of different weapons, many of which introduce unique mechanics or trade-offs such as increased damage at the cost of mobility or special abilities like healing or stealth. Like cosmetics, some rare weapons are sold for substantial sums on the Steam market, strengthening the sense of personalization and prestige among players (Fig. 1).

Fig. 1. Three variants of the Medic. The first (left-most) has no cosmetics and is using the stock (default) weapon, while the other two has their three cosmetics slots filled out, changing the characters' looks and adding a personal touch to an otherwise predefined character. The two characters to the right are using a different melee weapon, providing the player with additional healing at the cost of dealing less damage.

Avatars are virtual representations of the user. These are not always made by the player; sometimes, they are predefined characters that the user had no hand in creating. This is not to be confused by an *agent* - for example, Waggoner [32] explains that Pac-Man is not an avatar, but rather an agent, as he does not change throughout the game in any significant way. Creating avatars often emphasizes presenting an ideal self, including gender expression. For transgender players, especially young adults and teens, creating avatars that reflect their experienced gender is crucial. This involves not only the character's gender but also accessories and overall appearance. For some, it is rather the conventional notions of gender that may feel alienating and troublesome [20].

Game Modifications. In addition to cosmetics and community servers, *modding* plays a significant role in the TF2 experience for players who want to tweak or transform the game. This includes the creation of custom maps, voice packs, weapon skins, emotes (*"taunts"*), and more importantly, modified characters and new cosmetics. For queer players, modding provides an expanded possibility for projecting their identities and altering the game in ways that align with their personal expression.

On the popular modding website and community *GameBanana* [12], there are as of September 2024 32,300 users subscribed to receive updates for new Team Fortress 2 content. Users of the website can upload their own mods, as well as browse, like, and download others. Notably, the two most liked skins on *GameBanana* are both female versions of the Pyro, showcasing the demand for gender diversity and representation within the game (Fig. 2).

Fig. 2. To the left: A comparison between the original Scout from Team Fortress 2, and the reimagined Scout from the "Fem Scout Renovation v3.2" mod [11]. To the right: The original Pyro alongside Pyro from "The Female Pyro" mod [1]. Both versions are presented without any cosmetic items.

In addition to character skins, there are also a variety of custom voice packs available on GameBanana that allow players to modify the voices of the characters they play as. For instance, the most downloaded voice pack on the website is the "DustyOldRoses Femscout Soundpack" [9], a mod that replaces all of the original voice lines from the Scout with recordings performed by a different voice actor. These voice packs enable players to experience the game from a perspective that resonates more closely with their own identity, while also offering a fresh take on characters they already know.

2.3   Retelling and Fandom

Retellings are narratives or stories derived from original material, existing independently of their sources. In games, these can be made based on players' experiences and then shared in communities of similar players who all share the same common interest or experiences [28].

Eladhari [10] describes five types of retellings: recorded system output (e.g., YouTube gameplay), simultaneous (live-streaming), communicative (discussing game experiences), chronicles and reporting (newsletters), and narratives with artistic intent (fan art, fan fiction).

Retellings in games is nothing new. In a study by Ask [2], it was revealed that one of the main characters in *Call of Duty: Modern Warfare II* had became the centerpiece of a women- and queer-driven fandom on TikTok. While the *Call of Duty* series has long been viewed as a representation of traditional masculinity and often associated with male dominance, this narrative have become challenged by this new fandom where fans repurposed the character *Simon "Ghost" Riley* through sexualized content.

Fandoms are communities where fans share and create content based on various types of media. Fan art and fan fiction, which are highly valued within these communities [24], often extend beyond the source material *canon*, allowing for alternative interpretations such as queer readings [26]. These fanworks let fans create their own representations within the source material, while also exploring everything the source material is not.

3   The Study

In order learn about why, and in what ways and forms queer players project their own identities onto video game characters who are not LGBTQ+ we conducted a series of interviews. The participants recruited identify as queer. We focused many of the interview questions around the production of fan art and retellings [10]. The purpose of this was to find out what was most important personally to the players, making the assumption that if something is re-told, it would be of importance to an individual. Some of the results described in this paper have previously been presented in the thesis work of Gate and Lindgren [19] (Fig. 3).

3.1   Data Collection

Since everyone's queer experiences are unique, we conducted semi-structured interviews to find out how queer players project themselves onto characters. An interview guide was created to assist with the interviews, containing questions about players' experiences with Team Fortress 2, retellings and aligning with characters.

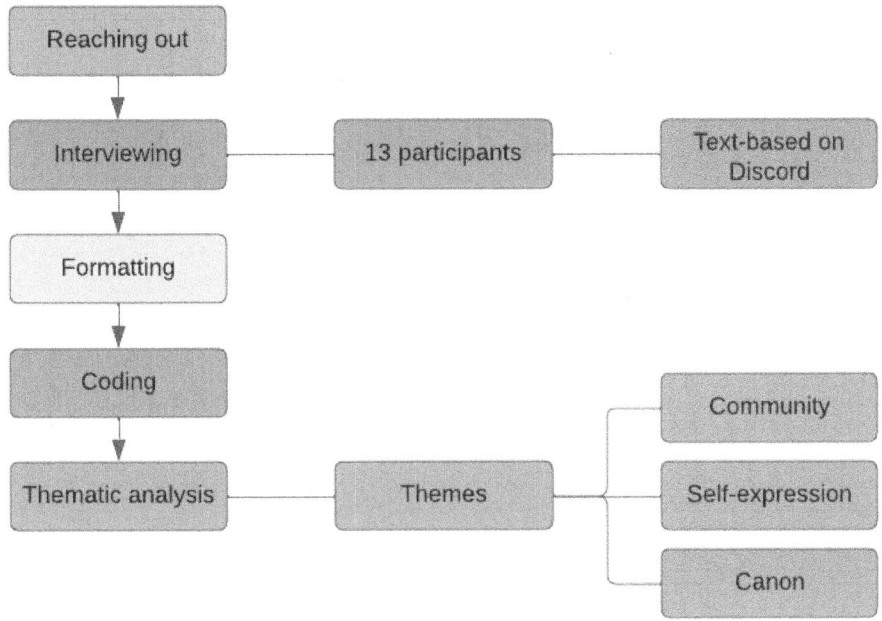

Fig. 3. Our data collection and analysis process.

Participants. Thirteen interviews were conducted with Team Fortress 2 players who identify as LGBTQ+. Two of these both wrote fan fictions and drew fan art, while another two did fan fictions, and four fan art exclusively. Eleven out of thirteen interviewees have currently at least one type of cosmetic equipped on any of their characters in-game, and all of them are or have previously been active within the TF2 fandom on websites such as Tumblr.

Interview Questions. A selection of the questions asked during the interviews related to retelling inspiration and alignment are displayed in Fig. 4. The full interview guide can be found at [19].

Interviewing. A form of consent available in [19] was presented to all participants prior to the start of the interview. Participants were allowed to stop the interview or withdraw their consent and stop participation completely at any point of the study for any reason. Notably, no participants chose to withdraw.

All 13 interviews were conducted through text chat using the instant messaging platform Discord [8]. To format the messages in a format easier to read and analyse, we used ThesisConvert [18], a tool developed using the .NET platform specifically for this study. The formatted output was saved to a Google Docs [13] document. The 85 pages of anonymized interview transcriptions are available via [19].

Interview Questions Related to Retellings
Do you write fan fiction or create fan art? If so, what type of fan fiction/fan art do you create and what is your main reason for writing or drawing?
Do you consume fan fictions or fan art yourself? If so, what kind of fan art and fan fiction do you usually consume?
Do you have any favorite character(s) in general? Is it these characters who you usually write about or draw?
What part(s) of your favorite characters do you find the most valuable? For example personality, appearance or gender.
Are there any characters or classes you feel represented by? In what ways?
When creating fan art and fan fiction, or just interacting with the fandom at large, does canon play a large role in what kind of content you create or consume?
Do you have any personal headcanons about any of the characters?
Do you think your queer identity influences how you view and understand characters?

Fig. 4. A selection of the questions asked during the interviews

Analysing. We analyzed the interview data by conducting a thematic analysis. Coding and noting of initial patterns were done using the comment tool in Google Docs [13], allowing real-time comments on interesting or relevant parts. Each researcher individually annotated the interview transcriptions, and we collected these annotations into eleven sub-themes. An example of coding can be found via [19]. After categorizing these into three master themes and revisiting the data, we merged two sub-themes, resulting in ten final sub-themes.

3.2   Ethical Aspects

All participants were presented with a form of consent prior to the interview. This form included the purpose of the study, how information was handled as well as who had access to said information. To ensure anonymity, no data about the participants beyond what was necessary for the study was collected, such as name, age or location. Participants were encouraged to use a preferred first name or a nickname while signing the consent form.

To ensure transparency and participant control, we returned the anonymized transcripts and the study document to all participants after analysis. This allowed them to verify how their data was used, and confirm our understandings and representations of their experiences. Two participants requested minor redactions.

3.3 Result

Focused Study. Given the limited length of this paper, we focus on present-ing key findings from the study, specifically the participants' engagement with creating retellings and their motivations for doing so. This chapter is organized around the three main reasons we found as to how and why the participants project themselves: *self-expression*, the *community* and the TF2 source material itself, the *canon*.

Community. The concept of community plays a vital role for our participants. Shared interpretations and headcanons within the community help individuals explore their own gender and sexual identities, as well as having queer company. Commonality was an important step in several interviewees' queer journeys. Two participants both mentioned that seeing, reading, and interacting with queer retellings helped them open their eyes to differing perspectives on gender and sexuality, as well as new ways to understand the TF2 characters:

> *"I think that reading others headcanons/analysis on said characters helped me figure out my identity because at the time, I was questioning my gender and sexuality so seeing characters written with queer identities helped me explore that without it feeling as daunting."*

The majority of participants brought up prevalent shared headcanons unprompted, such as Heavy and Medic being romantically involved or ideas about Pyro's gender identity. Two participants remarked upon even getting into the fandom and the franchise at large due to the fandom and the diversity of the theories within it. One of them mentioned that the importance of widespread and generally accepted fandom-interpretations was particularly important to them.

An important community-aspect that was prevalent through most interviews was the importance of queer company. Most participants played TF2 with a queer friend group or community, oftentimes found through the game. Out of the 13 interviews, 3 participants told us that they met their romantic partner through TF2.

> *"I came to terms with a lot of my identity partly through tf2. I found out parts of my sexuality while playing tf2 and connecting to other people. I met other queer people in tf2 that gave me a broader perspective of myself. Tf2 was a safe space for me to trial self-expression that was too scary or inaccessible for me in real life. I lived a much richer life during my formative years thanks to tf2."*

Self-expression. Multiple interview participants told us about their experi-ences exploring their own identities through the TF2 characters and how the characters helped them gain a deeper understanding of queerness. One partici-pant explained how they could see aspects of themselves in several of the merce-naries, but how they mostly felt represented by Pyro, who they also projected a lot onto growing up. They expressed the "unconventional nature of their gender, their jolly personality, and affection for the world" as key aspects of Pyro that resonated with them.

Pyro, as the only non-male character in the game, was often mentioned in the interviews. Another interviewee explained how they started writing fan fiction for the sake of exploring the characters and their personal life, with a focus on Pyro, who they get drawn towards:

> *"and just due to the nature of my own gender and queer identity, i get drawn towards pyro. it helps me explore my own gender and perspective on romance, conflict, all that stuff"*

Most participants consider in-game cosmetics a large part of what they enjoy with TF2. Many prefer to choose a theme when selecting cosmetics, with most either picking cosmetics that represent themselves or that they simply liked for various reasons. One participant explained how they have picked cosmetics for Medic based on their own interest for fantasy and history, and another how they use a hat looking like a pair of reindeer antlers because deers are one of their favorite animals.

A common pattern across participants was that their queer identity influenced how they engage with TF2 and media in general, particularly with fan creations and fandoms. One individual emphasized their own gender influenced the fan fiction they read and write, as well as the characters they are drawn to. For them, playing as a queer character is important, regardless of whether or not the character is canonically queer:

> *"in video games, the character you play as is as much an extension of yourself as it is its own character. whats to say that every character in every video game isnt queer? they are when i play them at least!"*

Canon. Personality traits were the most important parts for most participants when it came to which characters they felt represented by. For one individual, Pyro's mysterious nature led to projecting onto them. Another felt represented only by Medic and Sniper due to their personalities. For yet another, it was rather a mix of appearance and Heavy's traits, such as personality and perceived autism, as well as overall behavior that led to projecting onto him:

> *"[Heavy] is also very BIG and LOUD and i realate to that big time [...] also the fact heavy loves his gun so much is something, that me as an autistic person really resonate with!!! he loves his gun so much it may as well be a real person, which i ve felt in the past many times (i get super attached to objects that i own) to conclude, heavy is super relatable to me [...] so to summorize: lots of relatability from game [canon] to real life i suppose"*

Character appearance is also an important factor for the study participants. Another individual felt more connected to Sniper due to his build and general appearance, which are similar to their own: *"Especially the Sniper, who is of a similar build and age as I am right now, is a character that I am feeling more connected to recently"*.

It is not always the canonical versions of characters that resonate with the participants. Some individuals find connections or attraction to alternative representations of these characters. One participant, for example, brought up that while they do not find any of the characters attractive, they are attracted to the genderbent[2] versions of the characters found in various fanworks:

> *"I think thanks to being queer (questioning, maybe some flavor of aro[3] and lesbian) and being informed about the LGBT+ community I'm much more open to queer headcanons and I'm not really set in a firm place, I can enjoy a wider variety of content. And I'm definitely attracted to some of the genderbent characters."*

4 Discussion

Due to the delimitation of only studying queer Team Fortress 2 retellings, most points brought up and discussed will have direct ties to TF2, such as the canon, the characters and the fandom. However, we believe of the findings may be partially true for other video games with large queer audiences that do not necessarily have any LGBTQ+ representation present within the source material. These generalizable findings include motivations as to why these projections take place, and the importance of being part of a supportive community.

Community. For several participants, the very presence of a pre-existing queer community was a large driving force behind them projecting and creating or sharing explicitly queer retellings based on TF2 and its characters. For these participants, the importance of canon ranged from mattering greatly to not at all. Instead, having a place to explore and share their own queer experiences while projecting onto the characters available had a greater value than the canon itself.

In the context of romantic relationships, TF2 served as more than just a gaming platform-it became a meaningful social space where connections transcended the digital realm. Out of our 13 participants, three shared stories of how they found romantic partners through their interactions within the TF2 community. Moreover, the act of projecting and creating explicitly queer narratives around TF2 characters allowed participants to assert their identities in their own pace within a supportive environment.

---

[2] Genderbending refers to the practice of changing a character's gender in fan art, fiction, or other forms of media. This can involve altering the character's appearance, behavior, and sometimes their backstory to fit the new gender.

[3] Aromantic (aro) is a term used to describe individuals who experience little to no romantic attraction.

Self-expression. Another common thread between most participants was the need to see themselves reflected in the characters they play as - and then in the retellings they create, as retellings are artifacts of players' experiences and different types of fans [10]. Almost all participants, 11 out of 13, had cosmetics equipped that aligned with various parts of their interests, personalities or identities. For some, it was important that the cosmetics aligned with the characters they were equipped on - for others, self-expression and trying to find a middle-ground between themselves and the mercenaries had a bigger impact. However, in most cases it was a spectrum; rather than steadfast rules, the cosmetics purchased depended on which character the participants felt most aligned with, connected to or represented by (both emotionally and physically). Even without cosmetics to signal their identities, some participants felt that the characters were queer as long as they played as them.

Just like Waggoner [32] points out, avatars in games alter the way the players interact with and understand their surroundings, not only through appearance but also through behavior. It is not a stretch to then draw a connection between cosmetics and avatars to retellings, as Eladhari [10] defines them as artifacts created from players" experiences. While the TF2 mercenaries are pre-existing characters that cannot be altered in-game, all participants found a way to present themselves - some through cosmetics, or how they played the game, but most through the community content they create and share.

Canon. All participants mentioned some way of having an emotional connection to the characters found within TF2. The reason behind this connection differed between each participant, but a common theme was relatability. Despite the fact that no characters in TF2 are confirmed to be LGBTQ+, the participants still found common threads between their own experiences as queer people and the mercenaries, reading them as queer due to the characters' behaviors and personalities.

Most participants noted that their own queer identity affected and influenced their perceptions of characters or media at large and made them more perceptive of picking up on hints or context clues that may indicate that a character may have a norm-breaking identity. In the case of TF2, these clues were often not explicitly queer but rather resonated with experiences familiar to queer individuals. These clues ranged from "vibes" to themes of alienation, performative gender expression, and the broader context in which the game exists.

In our study, we did not find any specific affordances of the gameplay mechanics that encourage non-stereotypical gender expressions. While the cosmetics function as an important mean of individual expression, they have many equivalents in other games where players can customize their avatars. Instead, it is the presence of an already thriving community that draws players to spending time in the game world of TF2, as well as the opportunity to play on different, player-created servers. Therefore, we believe that the factors of community, shared canon, and affordances for self-expression and individuality are crucial for other games as well. As one participant wrote: "whats to say that every character in every video game isn't queer? they are when i play them at least!"

Limitations. There are some limitations to consider when reading this study and its results. Firstly, it only examines TF2 players, and while there may be similarities between how queer TF2 players and queer players of other games project themselves onto characters, the results cannot be generalized to other video games.

Since all of the interview participants were either found on or have used Tumblr, the representativeness of the sample might be limited. This also means that there is a bias towards people who are openly LGBTQ+.

Furthermore, the study was limited to 13 interviews, preventing broader generalizations about queer projection. Due to the study's commitment to participant anonymity and the lack of personal data collection, the demographic scope of the participants remains unknown. Because approximately half of the participants were identified on European TF2 servers there is a bias towards queer players from Northern Europe present in this paper. The study would benefit from additional data and a broader range of perspectives, particularly those from different cultural backgrounds.

Future Research. As this study primarily focused on Team Fortress 2, the generalizability of this study requires further research to determine its applicability to other games and other forms of retellings. Future research could explore whether similar queer retelling themes exist within other multiplayer or narrative-driven games, either with or without cosmetics.

A broader study interviewing participants from other parts of the world with diverse origins and ethnicities could be conducted. Views on sexuality and gender are often rooted in culture, so this could explore how cultural backgrounds shape or affect the underlying reasons behind queer retellings.

5   Conclusion

The study reveals that queer Team Fortress 2 players project their identities onto characters both within and outside the game. The presence of a queer community motivated participants to create or share queer retellings of TF2 characters, and for these participants the importance of canon varied. Everyone's queer experiences are unique so what mattered more was using these characters to explore and share *their own* queer experiences.

In summary, our findings indicate that queer fandoms and communities offer members a valuable safe space to explore their own gender and sexuality, relationships and identities in, fostering personal connections and a sense of belonging. Despite the lack of representation and relevant gameplay mechanics found specifically within TF2, the predominantly queer part of the fandom is thriving.

Acknowledgements. We would like to thank everyone participating in our interviews for your great and interesting responses, as well as to everyone who gave feedback to and reviewed our study along the way!

References

1. Alaxe: The Female Pyro (2022). https://gamebanana.com/mods/399723
2. Ask, K., Sihvonen, T.: Horny for ghost: the sexualized remediation of call of duty: modern warfare II on TikTok. In: Abstract Proceedings of DiGRA 2023 Conference: Limits and Margins of Games. DiGRA, Tampere (2023)
3. Bartle, R., Trubshaw, R.: MUD – Multi User Dungeon. [Computer Game - Text-based Virtual Game World] (1978)
4. Beckwith, M.: Paper Mario: The Thousand-Year Door Switch reaffirms Vivian is trans in its English localization. https://www.destructoid.com/paper-mario-the-thousand-year-door-switch-vivian-trans-localization/
5. Bruckman, A.: Identity Workshop: Emergent Social and Psychological phenomena in Text-Based Virtual Reality. Technical report, MIT Media Laboratory (1992)
6. Buried Without Ceremony: Monsterhearts (2012). https://www.drivethrurpg.com/en/product/100540. Accessed 29 Sept 2024
7. Cooper, L.: The Queer Art of LGBTQ+ Representation in Video Games (2022)
8. Discord Inc: Discord (2015). https://discord.com
9. DustyOldRoses: DustyOldRoses Femscout Soundpack (2012). https://gamebanana.com/sounds/16769
10. Eladhari, M.P.: Re-tellings: the fourth layer of narrative as an instrument for critique. In: Rouse, R., Koenitz, H., Haahr, M. (eds.) Interactive Storytelling, pp. 65–78. Springer, Cham (2018)
11. Fox, S.J.: Fem Scout Renovation v3.2 (2012). https://gamebanana.com/mods/194376
12. GameBanana: Gamebanana (2001). https://gamebanana.com/
13. Google: Google Docs (live version spring 2024). [Web Application] (2006). https://www.google.com/docs/about/
14. Greting, M., Mao, X.: Travelers in another world: how game experience in genshin impact inspires retellings. Stockholm University (2022). https://gameresearch.blogs.dsv.su.se/game-related-ba-and-ma-theses-from-dsv/travelers-in-another-world/
15. HoYoverse: Genshin impact (2020). https://genshin.hoyoverse.com/en/game. Accessed 13 July 2024
16. Intelligent Systems: Paper Mario: The Thousand-Year Door (2004)
17. Lim, C.U., Harrell, D.F.: Modeling player preferences in avatar customization using social network data: a case-study using virtual items in team fortress 2. In: 2013 IEEE Conference on Computational Intelligence in Games (CIG), pp. 1–8. IEEE (2013)
18. Lindgren, S.: ThesisConvert (2024). https://github.com/salmonslay/ThesisConvert
19. Lindgren, S., Gate, N.: The Queerness of Team Fortress 2: How Players Find Queerness in Games With no LGBTQ+ Representation. Stockholm University (2024). https://urn.kb.se/resolve?urn=urn:nbn:se:su:diva-231891
20. Morgan, H., O'donovan, A., Almeida, R., Lin, A., Perry, Y.: The role of the avatar in gaming for trans and gender diverse young people. Int. J. Environ. Res. Public Health **17**(22), 8617 (2020)

21. Oldenburg, R.: The Great Good Place: Cafes, Coffee Shops, Bookstores, Bars, Hair Salons, and Other Hangouts at the Heart of a Community. Paragon House (1989)
22. PanTran: True Love Jun'ai Monogatari (secret gay ending) (2022). https://www.youtube.com/watch?v=h1Zpou-M3as. Accessed 9 Sept 2024
23. Ruberg, B.: Video Games Have Always Been Queer. Postmillennial Pop, NYU Press (2019)
24. Sabotini, R.: The fannish potlatch: creation of status within the fan community. In: The Fanfic Symposium, vol. 20 (1999)
25. Software House Parsley: True Love (1995). https://www.mobygames.com/game/8601/true-love/. Accessed 9 Sept 2024
26. Stein, L., Busse, K.: Limit play: fan authorship between source text, intertext, and context. Pop. Commun. **7**(4), 192–207 (2009)
27. teamfortress: Meet the Pyro. https://www.youtube.com/watch?v=WUhOnX8qt3I
28. Tekinbas, K.S., Zimmerman, E.: Rules of Play: Game Design Fundamentals. MIT Press (2003)
29. Turkle, S.: Constructions and reconstructions of self in virtual reality: playing in the MUDs. Mind Cult. Activity (MCA) (1(3)), 158–167 (1994)
30. Valve Corporation: Team fortress 2 comics. https://www.teamfortress.com/comics.php. Accessed Feb 2024
31. Valve Corporation: Team Fortress 2 (2007). https://www.teamfortress.com/
32. Waggoner, Z.: My avatar, my self: Identity in video role-playing games. McFarland (2009)

Popcorn Movie: Dynamic Narrative Feedback for Spontaneous Live Action Video Storytelling

Allen Riley[✉] [iD]

University of California, Santa Cruz, CA 95064, USA
ariley2@ucsc.edu

Abstract. This paper describes Popcorn Movie, a movie-making party game demonstrating a theoretical and practical framework for generating stories using a dynamic narrative feedback loop between the improvised dialogue performed by co-located human participants and textual summaries iteratively generated by a large language model. In Popcorn Movie, human players take turns reading iterative generative summaries and then recording and uploading video clips of themselves performing responding improvised dialogue, which are iteratively edited into a video sequence available for instant playback. The feedback loop between the iteratively generated summaries and responding dialogue improvised by participants produces a spontaneous narrative video with continuity. We will detail the design of Popcorn Movie and the results of the playtests.

Keywords: Collaborative Storytelling · Improvisation · Emergent Narrative · Narrative Generation · Feedback · Coordination · Interactive Filmmaking

1 Introduction

Creative tools incorporating generative AI are transforming creative workflows. Large language models like OpenAI's GPT-4 are trained on datasets acquired through a massive project to scrape human-authored works found on the internet, raising questions around the ethical and copyright status of the derivative works produced through chat and image-generation services like ChatGPT and DALLE-3 and the potential harms they present to human creative labor [1]. However, the question may not be whether such tools will be used, but how they are understood and implemented in social and technical contexts.

This paper describes Popcorn Movie, a prototype movie-making party game demonstrating a theoretical and practical framework for generating stories using a dynamic narrative feedback loop between the improvised dialogue performed by co-located human participants and textual summaries iteratively generated by an LLM. Human players take turns reading iterative generative summaries and then recording and uploading video clips of themselves performing improvised dialogue in response, which are iteratively edited into a video sequence available for instant playback. The feedback loop between the iteratively generated summaries and responding dialogue improvised by participants produces a spontaneous narrative video with continuity (Fig. 1).

J. T. Murray and M. C. Reyes (Eds.): ICIDS 2024, LNCS 15468, pp. 116–129, 2025.
https://doi.org/10.1007/978-3-031-78450-7_7

Fig. 1. Clockwise from upper left: (1) A participant reads the current summary. (2) Video recorded in response to the summary. (3) The next participant reads the next iteration of the summary. (4) Video recorded in response to the summary. Captions added.

With Popcorn Movie, we aim to explore the medium-specific affordances of generative AI to demonstrate an interpersonal human co-creative process through media arts practice. In this paper, we will outline the artistic motivations behind Popcorn Movie, describe the design and architecture of the prototype application and gameplay, and assess the results of early playtests.

Creative projects incorporating this technology have faced obstacles managing narrative consistency due to the technology's indeterminacy [2]. Following Ian Horswill's suggestion to design games that both match the strengths and weaknesses of a current technology and incorporate methods of sharing authorship that rely on the strengths of players and systems [3], our approach is to utilize the low latency and dynamic reproduction of ostensibly relevant text by LLMs with the capacity for human players to listen, make connections, and improvise.

We employ an interdisciplinary perspective that situates interactive digital narrative within a media arts context that references relevant low-latency methods in early video art and improvisational theater. Our approach is informed by the traditions of feedback and reflexivity that are associated with the emergence of video art in the late 1960s and early 1970 [4]. Typified by artists such as Nam June Paik [5] and Nina Sobell [6], early video artists explored the reciprocal relationships between media technologies and interpersonal social dynamics through artistic experiments. In the tradition of experimental media arts practice, the enactment of the experiment itself constitutes a contribution of knowledge [7], aligning this study with research-creation and artistic research [8].

2 Related Work

2.1 Feedback and Reflexivity in Media Arts

In a 1985 review of early video art, the artist Sara Hornbacher labels video "the reflexive medium" because of its novel capacity to provide low latency channels of audiovisual feedback, enabling artists to perform both real-time expressive manipulations of the video signal and create new forms of participatory social documentation [4]. A landmark work in this tradition is A Hole in Space created by Kit Galloway and Sherrie Rabinowitz, which established an outdoor and publicly accessible two-way live video connection between New York City and Los Angeles that enabled instant interaction among casual participants [9].

Through this lens, this study views the instant feedback afforded by recent advances in large language models as enabling a previously unavailable signal path for artists in a way that is analogous to the novel communication channels previously enabled by video.

Rather than producing wholly original works, large language models reflect to the user the human-authored patterns existing in the training data relevant to their input, which are themselves reinforced in the language model training process through human feedback [10, 11]. Given this process of ingesting a variety of human-authored works, reinforcing relevant patterns within the dataset through human feedback, and then generating derivative works displaying patterns relevant to user input, it may be appropriate to understand the role of large language models in creative contexts as a reflexive medium analogous to video.

2.2 "Yes And..." as a Model for Creating Continuity with Feedback

The feedback loop of improvised performance and generative text used in Popcorn Movie builds on the "Yes And..." principle in improvisational acting, which Charna Halpern characterizes as a process of "making connections" by "listening, remembering, and recycling information" in a way that resembles a feedback loop: "as connections are discovered, they perpetuate themselves" [12]. The story emerges as new information is affirmed and then connected through subsequent improvisations.

The "Yes And..." principle has been previously utilized by story generators to affirm authorial intentions through narrative feedback. For example, Spindle employs a similar loop by returning short summaries subjected to "narrative compression" that contextualize user input during a process of authoring interactive fiction [13]. Popcorn Movie pursues this line of thought by managing authorship and narrative coherence solely using a feedback loop without formal narrative modeling, utilizing narrative compression to enable newer information to progress the story forward and older information to gradually dissipate.

The emergence of narrative forms through improvisational feedback loops diverges from the notion that narrative consistency is an expression of a pre-existing authorial mental model [14]. Instead, Popcorn Movie explores the emergence of narrative consistency through an ongoing process of negotiated authorship taking place across the potentially divergent understandings of multiple players engaged in collaborative improvisation [15].

2.3   Interactive Drama and Embodied Participation

Previous works linking interactive narrative systems with embodied participation were similarly structured around identifying channels of communication among players and between players and components of the system. Bad News assigns roles to players that position them differently in relation to the information managed by the underlying system, one of whom acts as a personification of the text generated by the system [16].

Previous works have also emphasized the awkward or fragmented nature of human-computer co-creation, or computer-facilitated human interaction. For example, Squinki-fier's Coffee: A Misunderstanding involved audience participants selecting randomized dialogue and scenic cues from a database that were used to puppeteer other participants [17].

Both approaches incorporate elements of Brecht's alienation effect in theater, which proactively repositions the audience in relation to a represented narrative to stimulate critical reflection and reengagement [18]. Popcorn Movie achieves this by asking players to shift quickly between reading narrative summaries aloud and then improvising in-character each turn.

2.4   Surrealist Games and Collage

The group creativity involved in Popcorn Movie resembles the surrealist game Exquisite Corpse, in which players take turns adding to an accumulative drawing or collage without seeing the full image until the game's conclusion. Exquisite Corpse players only see the folded edge of the previous player's contribution and use this partial information as a non-deterministic creative jumping-off point, typically resulting in chimerical imagery [19]. Popcorn Movie similarly provides an ambiguous, yet suggestive starting point for improvised creativity, but differs because the creative choices made by players are not hidden from each other, and because it assembles parts into a cohesive sequence as opposed to a contrasting collage.

2.5   Montage and Film Editing

Eisenstein identified that the juxtaposition of moving images in an edited sequence creates new meanings that are not present in the constituent shots, which he and other early Soviet filmmakers named montage [20]. Kuleshov and Pudovkin demonstrated montage in an experimental silent film in which an identical shot of an actor with an ambiguous facial expression was repeatedly displayed in juxtaposition to several shots with contrasting imagery, leading audiences to interpret the actor as expressing different emotions [21]. Popcorn Movie utilizes montage by automatically editing uploaded clips together with straight cuts, linking them so that ambiguous moments or confusing dialogue are likely to be become meaningful in relation to their surroundings, bolstering the perceived cohesion of the resulting movie.

2.6   Managing Social and Creative Risk in Casual Creators

Compton identifies "safety" as a key characteristic of creative experiences, defined as circumstances in which an individual is accepted "as of unconditional worth" and in which "external evaluation is absent" and as a result feels free to contribute to a creative process. Compton emphasizes the management of external evaluation, citing the diffusion of creative risk among multiple players in Coffee: A Misunderstanding [22].

Ivcevic and Hoffman characterize creativity not as an individual trait but as a set of social attitudes that set the conditions for possible actions [23]. Attitudes toward creativity are formed through experiences of risk-taking; negative responses leave a "residue" that inhibits future risk, whereas positive responses contribute toward the formation of creative self-identity. The possibility of creative action, then, is strongly tied to positive or negative feedback from others [23].

Popcorn Movie manages risk by similarly created a shared context for creative decision-making using feedback between improvised dialogue and generated summaries. Merely seeing the ongoing project reflected both visually and in words provides a clear context and entry point for further participation.

3 System Design

3.1 System Workflow

Popcorn Movie runs in a node application on a webserver. Users upload clips that are appended to a video loop displayed on the application web page. The dialogue spoken in each clip is transcribed and appended to a request sent to GPT-4 that returns a summary of all the dialogue spoken so far.

Users submit a brief description of the setting and number of participants through a text form and select and upload video files recorded on their devices. The audio content of the uploaded videos is re-encoded as an mp3 file using FFmpeg and transcribed by OpenAI's Whisper API. The transcription, along with the initial scenario, is incorporated into a GPT-4 completion request submitted to OpenAI's API, which returns both a summary of the events depicted in the dialogue up to that point and a cue for the next participant. Meanwhile, the newly uploaded video is appended to the ongoing video loop using FFmpeg and is displayed back to the user via HTTP Live Streaming alongside text captions displaying the latest summary (Fig. 2).

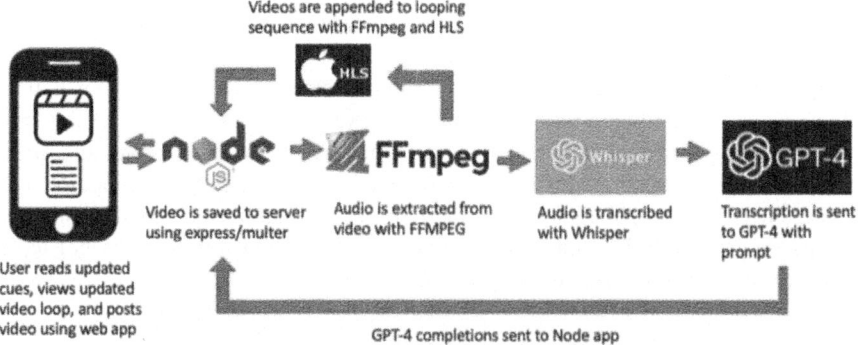

Fig. 2. Text, Video, Audio Processing Loop

3.2   Prototype User Interface

Popcorn Movie accepts text and video input and embeds video playback alongside GPT-4 text completions, enabling feedback between iterations of user video input and GPT-4 text output. Video is displayed in an embedded 16:9 frame above instructions for the first user to enter a brief description of a fictional scenario along with the number of actors and a text field and submission button. The instructions are replaced by the string entered by the user upon submission. Once the first video is submitted, the text completion containing the current narrative summary and suggested cue for the next actor is displayed. A form to select or record and upload video files is at the bottom of the application (Fig. 3).

Popcorn Movies

Scenario & # of actors:

Briefly describe your location and number of actors.

[_____] [Submit]

Summary & Your Cue:

You haven't uploaded a new file yet

Upload a short video to add to the movie

Horizontal videos only, please! Try to keep your clip under 10 seconds.

[Choose File] No file chosen   [Submit]

Fig. 3. Interface for Popcorn Movie. The video frame displays a countdown that loops before the first clip is uploaded.

3.3   GPT-4 Prompt Design

The system message instructs the model to simulate the behavior of a script supervisor managing continuity in an improvised movie. It is instructed to never add new information to the emerging narrative, never suggest dialogue or specific actions, and instead only reflect a summary of the story so far that draws on information inferred from the dialogue, concluding with a cue for the next actor.

The model is instructed to refer to participants as "Actor 1," "Actor 2," and so on until learning the character's name and to refer to all participants using gender neutral pronouns to avoid assumptions and confusion.

4 Pilot Study

4.1 Playtest Setup

We organized three playtests in Santa Cruz, CA as a small pilot study with the objectives of testing (1) how the activities of reading aloud and responding to iterative summaries would influence a social group's collaborative process of creating an improvised narrative video (2) whether the resulting video sequence would demonstrate narrative continuity and (3) whether the summary-improvisation feedback loop was enough to guide a group from an ambiguous starting point into a purposeful group authoring process.

The playtest setup consisted of a single shared instance of an interactive web application that co-located participants accessed using mobile devices. In the first playtest, participants used their own devices. In the second and third playtest, participants used a single shared device to minimize video encoding issues.

Playtest 1 consisted of four participants and Playtests 2 and 3 consisted of three participants. Each playtest was facilitated by the author of this paper, who simultaneously participated as one of the four participants in Playtest 1 and one of the three participants in Playtests 2 and 3.

In Playtest 1, participants were in an outdoor courtyard and used their personal mobile phones to record video clips. Playtests 2 and 3 were conducted in a forest setting, which was selected for its visual consistency, reducing the risk of visual continuity errors and freeing participants to film wherever they stood or walked. The absence of landmarks also made it easier for the text-only model to describe the setting without visual information. Lastly, the forest setting was selected because of the association participants might perceive between the playtest and childhood experiences playing pretend in the woods.

Playtests lasted approximately 2 h. Playtests 1 and 2 had no predetermined number of steps. Playtest 3 was programmed to end after 30 turns.

4.2 Selection and Prior Knowledge of Participants

Participants were gathered via a convenience sample, with each participant a volunteer present at the UCSC campus in the spring of 2024, which included graduate students and their friends. Participants were recruited to participate via text messages asking for help playtesting a video project. Participants had mixed levels of prior experience ranging from none to expertise in a variety of relevant disciplines including improvisational performance and interactive media (Fig. 4).

Within the disorienting forest, Robbie, Alexandra, and the third actor, grapple with altered perceptions of time and memory,

Fig. 4. Popcorn Movie playtesting.

4.3 Playtesting Popcorn Movie

To begin, the facilitator read the entire GPT-4 system message aloud. Then, the facilitator submitted a brief textual description of the setting and number of participants via the application: for example, "We are in the woods. There are 3 actors." Participants were instructed to take turns using the following instructions:

1. Read the latest summary aloud.
2. Record a short (5–10 s) video of yourself speaking improvised dialogue that responds to the summary.
3. Submit the video clip in the application.

When participants submit a video, a new summary is generated that incorporates details from their dialogue. The gameplay loop continues until the participants complete the predetermined number of turns.

4.4 Viewing the Resulting Movie

Completed movies ranged from 2–10 min. Players were surprised by the continuity, noting that the shots flowed together despite the real time that passed between them. An updated edit of the in-progress video was available after each turn, but we chose to wait until the end of each playtest before watching to maintain momentum and stay focused on interpersonal interactions and the emerging story. This approach had the added benefit of providing a payoff to participants who were excited to see what they had created together.

5 Results

After observing the playtests, we identified the following themes.

Table 1. Example Popcorn Movie Dialogue and Summary Sequence – Playtest 2, Turns 4–6. The Summary and Cue for Turn 6 are truncated for space.

Turn	Dialogue	Summary	Cue
4	Actor 1: "Yeah, you know, I used to play in the woods a lot when I was a kid too, kind of pretending there were goblins and things everywhere. So even though this is a very unfamiliar forest, I do agree that there's a kind of like connection to other times and places."	In a morning-lit forest, Actor 1 admits to not recognizing the area and questions the others' familiarity. Actor 2 mentions a friend who used to visit the forest but whom they've since lost contact with, while Actor 3 feels a nostalgic connection, reminded of a childhood forest. Actor 1, resonating with Actor 3's sentiment, recalls their own childhood spent playing in the woods, imagining goblins and adventures, feeling a connection despite the unfamiliarity of their current setting	Cue Actor 2: With Actor 1 finding a nostalgic connection through childhood memories of play and make-believe, how do you react to this shared sense of imagination and memory in the forest?
5	Actor 2: "No, that's right, um, I mean, don't you know, if you spend enough time in a forest you become a goblin."	The serene morning forest serves as a backdrop for the unfolding narrative. Actor 1 confesses to being new to the area, prompting inquiries about the others' familiarity. Actor 2 reminisces about a friend who once frequented the forest but has since become distant. Actor 3 shares that the forest evokes memories of a childhood forest, creating a bridge to the past. In response to Actor 3's nostalgia and Actor 1's childhood games involving goblins, Actor 2 humorously suggests that spending enough time in a forest could turn someone into a goblin, adding a layer of mythical imagination to their connection with the forest	Cue Actor 3: Hearing Actor 2's playful notion that one could become a goblin from too much time in the forest, how does this blend of reality and fantasy affect your perception of the forest and your companions?
6	Actor 3: "Maybe all of these little clicking sounds are goblins in the forest."	In the narrative set within a morning forest, Actor 1 initiates a conversation about unfamiliarity with their surroundings, sparking a discussion among the group. [...]	Cue Actor 1: Considering Actor 3's suggestion that the clicking sounds could be goblins, [...]

5.1 Feedback Supports Continuity in Dialogue-Heavy Video

We observed that the feedback loop between the spoken word dialogue and generative textual summaries pushed participants to develop a narrative by (1) reiterating keywords and themes, (2) asserting the validity and mutual relevance of dialogue, even when participants were uncertain about their contribution and (3) condensing the details of dialogue into more general plot descriptions, fusing the individual choices of participants into a collectively shared reference point.

Table 1 shows how summaries reiterated the keyword "goblin" multiple times and connected this to the theme of childhood fantasy and imagination. In Turn 5, Actor 2 expressed hesitancy by pausing and stalling during their dialogue, but their contribution was validated as "humorous" and "mythical" by the following summary.

Summaries fold dialogue into general descriptions as the story develops due to word count limitations included in the system message, fusing the combined efforts of the group into a cohesive narrative theme. The summaries included in Table 1 present play-by-play lists of what each participant has said that are characteristic of the early phase turns in Popcorn Movie. Table 2 shows how later completions condense details into more concise thematic summarization.

Table 2. Example Popcorn Movie Dialogue and Summary Sequence – Playtest 2, Turn 12. Summary truncated for space.

Turn	Dialogue	Summary	Cue
12	Actor 3: Oh no, I think I hear them. What's that on the hill?	The playful narrative unfolds further in the forest with actors Alan, Kyle, and Nina. They have been engaging in a light-hearted exploration of a fantasy involving goblins, drawing parallels between their real-life experiences and the mythical creatures. [...]	[...] how do you engage with this new element of suspense in your shared forest adventure?

5.2 Feedback Supports Collaborative Authoring

Participants hesitated to contribute to the film during the first round but warmed up once their dialogue was incorporated into a summary. The act of reading the validating summaries aloud appeared to bond participants around the narrative, which emerged as a collectively owned workpiece. Participants often laughed together when reading the plot summaries aloud, which created a positive environment and encouraged experimentation and backchannel conversation around the emerging story.

The outdoor setting of the playtest was amenable to walking while creating movies, which helped participants position themselves comfortably in relation to each other. As a result, participants did not always directly overhear what the others said during their performance. In these cases, the summary providing the necessary link between the previous and current actor, effectively creating a communication channel between participants.

5.3 Purposeful Group Authoring

Participants were amused by the verbose and lyrical summaries generated by GPT-4, creating a distancing effect that may have helped create the sense that they were somehow playing against the system. Players described the summaries as dry and repetitive and developed goals for introducing new information or plot twists to challenge the model. This had the effect of introducing more dramatic, but thematically consistent events, such as Actor 3 hearing the goblins in Table 2.

Following the playtests, participants described a feeling of competition with the model, suggesting another implementation in which the system is an in-game character.

6 Limitations

6.1 Turn-Taking and Story Progression

The turn-taking rotation tends to steer participants away from direct dialogical responses because they are always responding to the person who spoke immediately before them, who is not necessarily the person who spoke to them. It would better support spontaneous performance if the system were able to recognize participants taking turns in any order. This might be accomplished with voice-detection or by including an option to select which character is contributing from within the application. Character relationships may also be clarified by incorporating a computer vision model.

The system solely relies on spoken word dialogue to manage story progress, ignoring on-screen action. The resulting movies focus on conversation between characters in a way that somewhat resembles Richard Linklater's 1990 film *Slacker* [24]. This is amplified by introspective questions generated in the summaries ("How does this sudden solitude and the disappearance of familiar elements and beings shape your understanding of identity and presence within the forest?"). More work needs to be done classifying types of questions and identifying system messages that might lead participants to interact with each other more directly.

6.2 Model Behavior and Controllability

GPT-4 behaved inconsistently in each playtest due to model upgrades and overall inde- terminacy, requiring tweaking of the system message to restore intended functionality. Undesirable behavior includes cues that are overly ambiguous ("What do you think about what Actor 1 just said?") or directive ("Ask Actor 1 why they feel that way").

The model volunteered story details that were not present in the dialogue. If a charac- ter mentions that it is morning, the summary might include details such as light shining through the trees that may not in fact be present. This might be addressed by creating an iteration of the project utilizing a smaller LLM on a privately hosted server.

Whisper is capable of transcribing detected words spoken in English. However, there are limits to its ability to parse words spoken with inflection or accents outside its normative range. This poses serious accessibility obstacles. When an improperly transcribed word is incorporated into the summary, it may have the opposite effect by making a participant uncomfortable about their contributions to the movie. One potential approach to mitigating this might be to add the ability to edit the summaries once they are generated.

7   Conclusion and Future Work

Early playtests with Popcorn Movie suggest that low-latency feedback provided by LLMs provides a new channel for communication between small groups of people engaged in improvised storytelling and performance, as opposed to merely replacing traditional forms of production with automated processes.

Generative AI is reflexive in a way that is analogous to video: it reflects both its content (the requested text completion) and its form (the underlying human-authored patterns in its training data). Live interaction with dynamic narrative feedback may be useful in assisting users in understanding the underlying properties and characteristics of LLMs to support further critical and creative engagement with this technology. In such approaches, providing means for participants to reposition their roles in relation to AI generated content is important in cultivating critical and creative perspectives.

Popcorn Movie relies on GPT-4 to store the content and structure of the emerging story world and uses social and human-computer feedback to maintain an emerging and context-bound definition of consistency. Placing the ongoing summary into an additional loop with a database storing important states, objects, and facts could enable an approach to authoring interactive fiction [25].

This approach effectively created narrative videos with continuity in a short period of time and could be incorporated into a variety of applications, games, social media, or digital performance settings incorporating avatars. The current iteration of the project takes place in a live action film production setting that could be adapted to enable new forms of collaboration between players and game masters in live action role playing games or between instructors and youth in hands-on learning settings.

Acknowledgments. This project was supported by the Science Research Internship program at the University of California, Santa Cruz, which hosted my Computational Narrative Cinema internship in the summers of 2023 and 2024. This project would not have been possible without the support of Sebastian Dionne, Azriella Fitzgerald, Tevel Seri, and Erika Wang, and research assistants Jay Ser and Alexia Changalpet. Thank you to playtest participants Brook Constantz, Kyle Gonzalez, Nena Hedrick, Alexandra Panzer, and Robbie Trocchia. Thank you to the Expressive Intelligence Studio (Noah Wardrip-Fruin, Michael Mateas, Jack Kelly, Alex Calderwood, Kyle Gonzalez, Henry Zhou, Shi Bey-Johnson, Rehaf Jammaz), Samantha Gorman, and Marianne Weems.

Disclosure of Interests.   The authors have no competing interests.

References

1. Epstein, Z., et al.: Art and the science of generative AI. Science **380**(6650), 1110–1111 (2023). https://doi.org/10.1126/science.adh4451
2. Sun, Y., Ni, X., Feng, H., LC, R., Lee, C.H., Asadipour, A.: Bringing stories to life in 1001 nights: a co-creative text adventure game using a story generation model. In: Interactive Storytelling: 15th International Conference on Interactive Digital Storytelling, ICIDS 2022, Santa Cruz, CA, USA, December 4–7, 2022, Proceedings, pp. 651–672. Springer-Verlag, Berlin, Heidelberg (2022). https://doi.org/10.1007/978-3-031-22298-6_42

3. Horswill, I.: Dear leader's happy story time: a party game based on automated story generation. In: Proceedings of the AAAI Conference on Artificial Intelligence and Interactive Digital Entertainment, vol. 12, pp. 39–45 (2016). https://doi.org/10.1609/aiide.v12i2.12902
4. Hornbacher, S.: Editor's statement: video: the reflexive medium. Art J. **45**, 191–193 (1985). https://doi.org/10.1080/00043249.1985.10792297
5. Nam June Paik: Moon Is the Oldest TV. Curatorial, Lone Palm Films, Octopus Originals (2023)
6. Hartzell, E., Sobell, N.: Sculpting in time and space: interactive work. Leonardo **34**, 101–107 (2001). https://doi.org/10.1162/002409401750184636
7. Cage, J.: Silence: Lectures and Writings. Wesleyan University Press (2010)
8. Loveless, N.: How to Make Art at the End of the World: A Manifesto for Research-Creation. Duke University Press (2019). https://doi.org/10.2307/j.ctv1220kts
9. Grundmann, H.: Art Telecommunication. Western Front Publication, Vancouver (1984)
10. How ChatGPT and our language models are developed | OpenAI help center. https://help.openai.com/en/articles/7842364-how-chatgpt-and-our-language-models-are-developed. Accessed 19 Jul 2024
11. Ouyang, L., et al.: Training language models to follow instructions with human feedback. http://arxiv.org/abs/2203.02155 (2022). https://doi.org/10.48550/arXiv.2203.02155
12. Halpern, C.: Truth in Comedy: The Manual of Improvisation. Meriwether Pub., Colorado Springs, Colo (1994)
13. Calderwood, A., Wardrip-Fruin, N., Mateas, M.: Spinning coherent interactive fiction through foundation model prompts. In: ICCC (2022)
14. Kreminski, M., Martens, C.: Unmet creativity support needs in computationally supported creative writing. In: Huang, T.-H. "Kenneth," Raheja, V., Kang, D., Chung, J.J.Y., Gissin, D., Lee, M., Gero, K.I. (eds.) Proceedings of the First Workshop on Intelligent and Interactive Writing Assistants (In2Writing 2022), pp. 74–82. Association for Computational Linguistics, Dublin, Ireland (2022). https://doi.org/10.18653/v1/2022.in2writing-1.11
15. Mitchell, A., Ang, D., Tan, S.H.: "It's fun not to know": the role of uncertainty in text-based online collaborative storytelling. In: Interactive Storytelling: 15th International Conference on Interactive Digital Storytelling, ICIDS 2022, Santa Cruz, CA, USA, December 4–7, 2022, Proceedings, pp. 229–248. Springer-Verlag, Berlin, Heidelberg (2022). https://doi.org/10.1007/978-3-031-22298-6_15
16. Ryan, J.O., Summerville, A.J., Samuel, B.: Bad news: a game of death and communication. In: Proceedings of the 2016 CHI Conference Extended Abstracts on Human Factors in Computing Systems, pp. 160–163. ACM, San Jose California USA (2016). https://doi.org/10.1145/2851581.2890375
17. Chaos, S.: Soft chaos: turning feelings into experiences. https://softchaos.games/projects/coffee/. Accessed 17 Jul 2024
18. Brecht, B.: Brecht on Theatre: The Development of an Aesthetic. Hill and Wang, New York (1964)
19. Laxton, S.: Surrealism at Play. Duke University Press, London, Durham (2019)
20. Eisenstein, S., Leyda, J.: Film Form: Essays in Film Theory. Houghton Mifflin Harcourt (2014)
21. Pudovkin, V.I.: Film Technique: and Film Acting. Grove Press, New York (1976)
22. Compton, K.: Casual creators: AI supported creativity for casual users. Ph. D. thesis, University of California, Santa Cruz (2019)
23. Ivcevic, Z., Hoffmann, J.D.: The creativity dare: attitudes toward creativity and prediction of creative behavior in school. J. Creative Behav. **56**, 239–257 (2022). https://doi.org/10.1002/jocb.527

24. Slacker. The Criterion Collection, San Francisco, California, USA (2021)
25. Kelly, J., Calderwood, A., Wardrip-Fruin, N., Mateas, M.: There and back again: extracting formal domains for controllable neurosymbolic story authoring. In: Proceedings of the AAAI Conference on Artificial Intelligence and Interactive Digital Entertainment, vol. 19, pp. 64–74 (2023). https://doi.org/10.1609/aiide.v19i1.27502

DreaMR: The Effects of Multisensory Design on Cross-Modal Perception Across Genres with Mixed Reality Concert

Svetlana Rudenko[1,2] , Xiangpeng Fu[1,3] , Sam Davern[3] , and Mads Haahr[1,3(✉)]

[1] Haunted Planet Studios, 12 Fitzwilliam Street Upper, Dublin 2, Ireland
rudenkos@tcd.ie
[2] Department of Music, Durham University, Durham, UK
[3] School of Computer Science and Statistics, Trinity College Dublin, Dublin, Ireland
{fuxi,daverns,haahrm}@tcd.ie

Abstract. Although Virtual Reality technology offers a variety of experiences, Mixed Reality (MR) is a relatively new field, offering the ability to merge real and digital environments in sophisticated ways. Perception is at the core of this integration and our experience of them: As humans, we perceive reality with our senses; we feel rain on our skin, we see the drops, we hear the sound, we can taste and smell the freshness of the air in real life. When creating and experiencing digitally enhanced realities, we still rely on the senses, but practically all VR/MR use only the audio-visual source, because other sensory modalities (e.g., tactile and olfactory) are not generally supported by the platforms. In this paper, we are concerned with the following questions: How can we reach other senses through a MR audio-visual environment? Can we create dreamlike experiences and feel music and art as our reality? Music and art therapies are well-established practices, so can MR have the potential to provide mindfulness? The pilot study presented in this paper offers insights into the nature of cross-modal associations and synesthesia interaction of senses theory as a framework for multisensory design. The benefits of multisensory stimulation are not fully explored in the field of neuroscience, but there are statements linking synesthesia (multisensory or cross-modal perception) with creativity and increased mental ability. Our results with a pilot study of our DreaMR series of experiences indicate a much greater ability for multisensory processing with MR in the general public than expected.

Keywords: Mixed Reality · Multisensory Design · Music · Interactive Art · Piano Performance with Visuals

1 Introduction and Theory

Mixed Reality (MR) is a relatively new field, offering the ability to merge real and digital environments in sophisticated ways. Perception is at the core of this integration and our experience of them: As humans, we perceive reality with our senses; we feel rain on our skin, we see the drops, we hear the sound, we can taste and smell the freshness

J. T. Murray and M. C. Reyes (Eds.): ICIDS 2024, LNCS 15468, pp. 130–142, 2025.
https://doi.org/10.1007/978-3-031-78450-7_8

of the air in real life. When creating and experiencing digitally enhanced realities, we still rely on the senses, but practically all VR/MR use only the audio-visual source, because other sensory modalities (e.g., tactile and olfactory) are not generally supported by the platforms. In this paper, we are concerned with the following questions: How can we reach other senses through a MR audio-visual environment? Can we create dreamlike experiences and feel music and art as our reality? Music and art therapies are well-established practices, so can MR have the potential to provide mindfulness?

Over the last two years, we have designed a series of digital experiences to explore these questions. Using cutting-edge Mixed Reality (MR) technology, we approach dreaming like surrealist paintings: experiences that reside halfway between the visible and the invisible. Mixed Reality concept is uniquely suited for this purpose, because it positions the audience not within a virtual world (like VR technology does) but in a liminal space that blends the real with the un-real, the conscious with the unconscious, the physical world with the world of dreams.

In the rest of this chapter, we introduce key concepts and theory related to our design methodology. We then review related work before presenting our design of the DreaMR experiences and our user study. Finally, we conclude the paper.

1.1 Visualization, Synesthesia Art and Interactive Storytelling with MR

Cognitive Musicology refers to the computational study of musical thinking. Musical thinking is a complex involving memory, emotion, culture, metaphorical thinking, musical language and cross-modal associations. Science researcher, radio engineer and artist Bulat Galeyev stated that, "Synesthesia (and the particular case of 'color hearing') is the essential component of musical thinking, first of all, music intended to evoke images" [2, p. 258]. Synesthesia is a wiring of the brain that creates sensory pairings, such that the stimulant received in one sensory modality, e.g., sound, could have reflection in secondary modality, such as color, taste or other sensation. Some hypotheses explain these phenomena by the condition which we are all born into: neonatal synesthesia. As noted by Maurer and Maurer (1988) 'the newborn does not keep sensations separate from one another' but instead 'mixes sights, feelings, and smells into a 'sensual bouillabaisse in which sights have sounds, feelings have tastes' [25, 26]. Cross-modal processing is characteristic to infants till 24-month-old and points to the brain structure of interconnectivity and the potential for cross-sensory, cross-modal processing in non-synesthetes. It is considered that non-invasive multisensory stimulation of the brain helps the plasticity of the brain and engagement (further described in the experiment to train synesthesia by Bor et al. [15]).

Music is a powerful multisensory experience, it can evoke memories [3], images, and sensations [4], enhancing emotions of like or dislike. Generally speaking, perception of music is multisensory, so when music tells a story, it does so in a multimodal fashion. There is so far only a small amount of work on visualization of classical music, and none in Mixed Reality that explores how music visualization can be designed using a multisensory design approach that takes advantage of music narrative [5] and synesthesia art [1]. An example of this approach is *Amy Beach 'Dreaming'* where symbolics of a live and dead tree in the MR visualization as a border line, a marker of the liminal space between the real and un-real, through dreaming as the composer reflected on in the chosen epigraph. In *Rachmaninoff Preludes MR scenes,* the visualization is based on music analysis of compositional language and associations of the performer.

1.2 Multisensory Design: In General, and for MR

In informal use "multisensory design" (MSD) is sometimes used simply to mean design that appeals to the senses, but when used scientifically, it means design based on the Interaction of Senses Theory based on a model of Synesthesia, which is a wiring of the brain that creates sensory pairings, e.g., color to pitch or taste to sound. Synesthesia demonstrates an enormous diversity of perceptions, and more than 80 types have been registered [6]. Research in the areas of Sensory Substitution Devices (SSDs) and Human Computer Interaction (HCI) are already using this principle, but there is little work on how to map one sense to the other, or how to produce designs where the natural synchronization is attractive to the majority of people. Synesthesia experiences are subjective and involuntary, but it has been shown that synesthete-designed animations are more appealing than those designed by non-synesthetes [7]. Ellen Lupton describes MSD as follows: "Reaching beyond design's traditional focus on vision, multisensory design incorporates the full range of bodily experience [...] The brain combines input about taste, smell, temperature, and texture to create 'flavor' (original emphasis) [8, p. 142]. Velasco and Obrist observe that considerations of multisensory experiences as per technological advances is the future of design [9]. For example, Michael Havercamp has applied an MSD methodology for automotive design [10]. Only three books exist on multisensory approaches based on a Synesthesia model: one on industrial design by Havercamp, one on product design [11] and Velasco and Obrist's book on technology-based multisensory experiences (including AR/VR), which addresses the importance of sensory input but does not present a design methodology. In compositions for *De Chirico: Metaphysical Art AR* and *Alice Dalí MR*, the composer used emotional and visual sensory input of art patterns to 'transpose' to musical texture archetypes.

1.3 Synesthesia and Multisensory Stimulation

Research has shown that people with Synesthesia are more aware of such sensory pairings due to stronger connections in their neural system [12]. While synesthetes only represent 4–6% of adult humans, "a growing body of empirical research on the topic of multisensory perception now shows that even non-synesthetic individuals experience cross-modal correspondences" [13, p. 319]. Also, multisensory stimulation can encourage creativity. As V.S. Ramachandran and E.M. Hubbard point out: "Synesthesia causes excess communication among brain maps [...] towards linking seemingly unrelated concepts and ideas—in short creativity" [14, p. 52]. Research shows that synesthesia-enhanced applications have promising potential for education and mental health programs, such as Bor et al.'s experiment to train non-synesthetes for color-grapheme synesthesia, which showed an IQ improvement and provisionally concluded that "cognitive training including synesthetic associations may in the future be a promising new tool for vulnerable clinical groups to enhance general mental ability" [15].

2   Related Work

There are not many mixed reality experiences that were designed using an MSD method-ology; and, similarly, work is scant that explores cross-modal perception elicitation using new types of digital experiences, such as mixed reality.

However, there is interest in the music industry of exploring the visualization with eXtended Reality (XR), in particular Virtual Reality (VR). For example, Björk's release of VR music videos and VR live stream in connection with her 2015 album *Vulnicura* has explored the possible intersection between VR and music. There is some research into VR-based music videos, such as Young et al., who conducted a user study on a VR-based music video designed for offline viewing (i.e., not as part of a live performance) and found the format to have good potential as complementary experiences to live performances [24]. Another example is the collaboration between the Augmented Reality (AR) technology company Magic Leap and Icelandic band Sigur Rós, which resulted in an AR-based music video called Tónandi in which the user dons a headset and interacts with a music visualization. Researcher Guy Morrow is optimistic about the potential for such work: "XR simply becomes an extension of this music product milieu; it will increasingly be used alongside these other elements of design culture to create the context and environment in which a piece of music 'lives.'" [22, p. 177]. However, while there is interest in the music industry (especially amongst cutting edge performers), most experiments tend not to be subject to evaluation through user studies.

There is some work concerned with visualization of art in 3D space. An example is the project *Dreams of Dalí* VR experience[1] offered by the Salvador Dalí Museum in St Petersburg in Florida, which (not unlike our own work) places the audience member within an art scene and hence lets them 'be in the art' in a way that other digital mediums than XR cannot readily offer. *Dreams of Dalí* is an art project in its own right, and like the experiments discussed earlier, it has not been subject to scholarly evaluation apart from an exploration of its potential as an art education tool [23].

3   Experimental Setup: The DreaMR Series

To measure the effect of multisensory MR experiences, we used four experiences from our DreaMR series. The following sections describe the experiences that were performed as a live concert with projected MR visuals. The MR headset was worn by a performer.

The DreaMR experiences presented here have variation across genres: two experi-ences, *Dreaming: Amy Beach MR* and *S. Rachmaninoff Preludes Op. 32 N1- 5 and N10 Mixed Reality (MR) Scenes*, are visualization of classical music and two, *De Chirico: Metaphysical Art AR* and *Alice Dalí MR* with music composed specifically for the art experience in MR. The design of all experiences used a multisensory approach, reaching other senses with audio-visual composition. The composer (Svetlana Rudenko) has a specialization of working with synesthesia art [1].

---

[1] https://thedali.org/dreams-of-dali-2/.

3.1   Amy Beach 'Dreaming' Op. 15

Dreaming: Amy Beach MR is a visualization in MR from a classical music composition by the American composer and synesthete Amy Beach, "Dreaming" Sketches Op. 15 N3 (1892) [16, p. 329]. (See Fig. 1). We added voice narration to the music, including words by Victor Hugo, which Amy Beach chose as the epigraph for her composition: "You speak to me from the depth of a dream." Other words are on the concept of dreaming in literature from Hugo and Nodier [17], and thoughts about what dreams were for Carl Jung: "As a general rule, the unconscious aspect of any event is revealed to us in dreams, where it appears not as rational thought but as a symbolic image" [18, p. 5]. The intention is to encourage the audience to think philosophically, aesthetically and scientifically, while engaging with the MR scene emotionally.[2]

Fig. 1. Visual (MR screenshot) from *Dreaming: Amy Beach MR*

3.2   S. Rachmaninoff Preludes Op. 32 N1- 5 and N10 Mixed Reality (MR) Scenes

This visualization in MR is an example of cognitive musicology assessment based on the composer's oeuvre, his time in history and personal associations of performer pianist. (See Fig. 2.) Rachmaninoff frequently drew inspiration from nature and folklore in his compositions. His second book of Preludes Op. 32 (the first was Op. 23) was written in the summer of 1910 at his family's idyllic country house in Ivanovka, a sleepy, rural area, surrounded by nature. Rachmaninoff's Orientalism was influenced by The Mighty Five who were developing a new methodology of compositional style and had a big interest

---

[2] MR video: https://www.youtube.com/watch?v=O-iP8k8duY0. App download: https://www.meta.com/en-gb/experiences/9679476068790518/.

in other cultures, for example M. Balakirev's "Islamey" or N. Rimsky-Korsakov's symphonic suite Op. 35 "Sheherazade." For example, Rachmaninoff's choice of rhythmic organization and b-flat-minor key in Prelude N2 Op. 32 pointed on the influence of orientalism and manifested to MR visualization. The multisensory approach in particular manifested in the MR visualization of Prelude N10 in B-minor where the spectator can 'touch' a virtual crane as well as the leaves of a maple tree symbolizing philosophical reflections of passing life and experiences: autumn as a symbol of mature age. The ambient sound of cranes was also added to the music to increase association with nature and perhaps encourage the feeling of the air and falling leaves to reach the olfactory sense through audio-visual composition.[3]

Fig. 2. Visual (MR screenshot) from *S. Rachmaninoff Preludes Op. 32 N1- 5 and N10 Mixed Reality (MR) Scenes*

3.3 De Chirico: Metaphysical Art MR

This experience recreates Giorgio de Chirico's painting *Turin Spring*, 1914 (Italy) in Mixed Reality. (See Fig. 3 left.) We made six interactable music sounding objects: Book, Artichoke, Castle, Horse, Hand and Egg. Every object has its own music archetype and symbolic meaning, for example, the horse is perceived by the composer (Svetlana Rudenko) as a "collector of souls," the artichoke is associated with a minor key and orchestration with a strong oboe lead, and for the Egg archetype we used a quotation from J. Brahms Concerto No. 2 Op. 83 extract from 4th movement Allegretto grazioso (B-flat major). By interacting with objects and characters in a virtual (mixed) environment you 'live' in the art: you feel the dampness of the castle and many stories buried in its

---

[3] MR video: https://www.youtube.com/watch?v=hdw7xtOqKns. App download: https://www.meta.com/en-gb/experiences/7680972171955194/.

walls, you hear the pages whisper in the magic book, you whack the artichoke – they will tell you their emotional stories! Svetlana Rudenko orchestrated the episodes with Logic Pro, and Xiangpeng Fu added the ambient sound of natural environments to reach other senses by audio-visual composition.[4] For example, to increase the engagement with multisensory perception, the "Castle" music archetype in the De Chirico MR scene, was augmented by the ambient sound of wind and the sound of a heavy rock moving, in order to reach the sensation of "goosebumps"/the "touch" of the virtual wind on the skin, to contribute to an ominous feeling of the D-minor key, reaching targeted emotional state. (Characteristically, Beethoven's "Tempest" Sonata N17 (Op. 31 N2) is also in D-minor, "anxious" key).

Fig. 3. Visuals (MR screenshots) from *De Chirico: Metaphysical Art MR* (left) and *Alice Dalí MR* (right)

3.4   Alice Dalí MR

For *Alice Dali MR* [19], we took inspiration in our previously developed experience of *Alice Dali AR* [20], which is a locative Augmented Reality (AR) app for smartphones (outdoors), which features illustrations by Salvador Dalí for Lewis Carroll's iconic story *Alice's Adventures in Wonderland* with piano music by Svetlana Rudenko and narration by Mads Haahr. For *Alice Dali MR*, we created three fully interactive MR scenes for the Meta Quest Pro headset, which engage with dreaming in different ways. In each scene, the audience member takes on the role of Dream Conductor of the scene, interacting with the elements to activate orchestrated layers of music, narration and visuals. The interaction method varies between the different scenes. In the first scene, based on the book's Chapter 2 ("The Pool of Tears"), the dream conductor's wand is a tool for interacting with orchestration, and in the second scene, based partly on Chapter 11 ("Who Stole the Tarts?") and partly on Chapter 12 ("Alice's Evidence"), the audience member's hands are used for "petting" (touching) the animals. In the climax of the final scene, which is based on the last pages of "Alice's Evidence," the player pinches their

---

[4] MR video: https://www.youtube.com/watch?v=u1sH3pvH1ew. App download: https://www. meta.com/en-gb/experiences/5460042777452807.

fingers to "grow" flowers as a tribute to Alice and Dali accompanied by the narration: "Wake up, Alice, dear… it was such a curious dream" [21].

4   Method and Analysis

4.1 Participants

38 participants were recruited from attendees of the Joint Conference on Serious Games (JCSG) 2023 who opted to attend a live mixed reality piano concert. Gender and age demographics are presented in Table 1.

Table 1. Participant demographics (N = 38).

Demographic	Category	Frequency
Age group	Under 18	1
	18–30	14
	31–45	13
	Over 45	10
Gender	Male	20
	Female	14
	Non-binary	1
	Prefer not to say	3

4.2 Procedure

As stated previously, excerpts from the *Alice Dali MR* and *Rachmaninoff Six Preludes Op. 32 MR DreaMR* experiences were used for this pilot study.

A 10-item user experience survey was created for the study. Each item was answered on a Likert scale. The number of answers for each item varied depending on the item. The survey measured:

- Previous VR/MR experience
- Past classical music concert attendance
- Desire to purchase a MR headset after the concert
- Onset of associative thinking
- Experience of mindfulness
- Onset of daydreaming
- Feelings of creativity
- Experience of non-audio-visual sensations
- Enjoyment of the concert

The full survey is available in Appendix A. All statistical analyses were conducted in IBM SPSS 29. The terms "mindfulness" and "daydreaming" were not explained to participants. The rationale was that the terms are in general use and that a specific definition might distract the audience and limit the effect of the experience.

5 Results

All data collected was non-parametric. Chi-Square Goodness of Fit tests were conducted on each of the survey's items to determine the distribution of participants' answers and identify which, if any, responses occurred significantly more frequently than expected. Q1, 2, 3, 4, 5, and 10 all showed significant non-normal distributions.

Q1: How much experience do you have with Virtual and/or Mixed Reality?

Participants tended to have 'a little' (N = 14) or 'a lot' (N = 13) of experience with VR/MR. This is expected as they were all attendees at an interactive media conference. Only two participants had no experience with VR/MR, X2(3, N = 38) = 9.37, p = .025.

Q2: How many classical music concerts have you attended in the last 5 years?

Participants were most likely to have attended between 1 and 2 classical music concerts in the last 5 years ($N = 17$), $X^2(3, N = 38) = 9.37, p = .025$.

Q3: After attending this concert, how likely are you to buy a Mixed Reality headset for your personal use?

Participants were 'somewhat unlikely' ($N = 16$) and 'somewhat likely' ($N = 15$) to want to buy an MR headset after the concert, $X^2(3, N = 38) = 17.16, p < .001$.

Q4: Did particular moments of this concert prompt you to reflect on related memories or concepts?

Participants were likely to have experienced associative thinking as a result of the concert ($N = 23$), $X^2(2, N = 38) = 12.68, p < .002$. *This suggests that Music Art MR experiences could promote associative thinking.*

Q5: How mindful did you feel during this concert?

Participants felt 'slightly mindful' ($N = 11$) and 'moderately mindful' ($N = 20$) during the concert, $X^2(3, N = 38) = 19.474, p < .001$. *This suggests that MR experiences could induce mindfulness.*

Q10: How much did you enjoy being an audience member during this concert?

Participants enjoyed the concert 'a moderate amount' ($N = 12$) and 'a lot' ($N = 20$), $X^2(3, N = 38) = 24.95, p < .001$.

5.1 Multisensory Perception

9 participants experienced at least one non-audio-visual sensation as a result of the concert. 4 experienced touch, 4 experienced smell, and 1 experienced both touch and smell. (See Fig. 4.) These participants represent 23.7% of the participants surveyed. This is at least four times the estimated proportion of synesthetes in the general population (4–6%).

5.2 Correlational Analyses

A series of Kendall's Tau-b correlational analyses were conducted to identify potential relationships between survey items. Statistically significant correlations are presented below:

- Participants' age was positively correlated with their enjoyment of the concert, $\tau_b = .312, p = .046$.

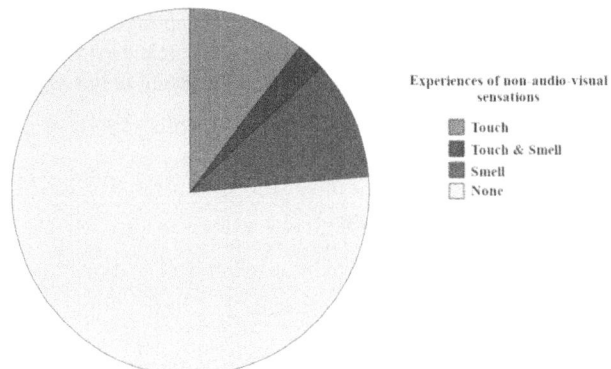

Fig. 4. Pie chart displaying participants' experience of non-audio-visual sensations.

- A negative relationship was found between the level of previous MR/VR experience and feelings of creativity after the concert, $\tau_b = -.315, p = .039$.
- Experiences of mindfulness were positively correlated with desire to buy a MR headset, $\tau_b = .451, p = .004$.
- The experience of associative thinking was positively correlated with mindfulness ($\tau_b = .508, p = .001$), daydreaming ($\tau_b = .357, p = .023$), creativity ($\tau_b = .359, p = .022$) and enjoyment of the concert ($\tau_b = .557, p < .001$).
- The experience of mindfulness was positively correlated with enjoyment of the concert, $\tau_b = .445, p = .005$.

The two correlations with effect sizes above .4 are the correlations between age and enjoyment, mindfulness and a desire to buy a headset, associative thinking and mindfulness, associative thinking and enjoyment, and mindfulness and enjoyment.

6   Conclusions

Based on the results of the statistical analyses outlined above, there are several key, indicative findings that warrant further exploration:

- The potential for Music Art MR experiences to promote mindfulness.
- The potential for Music Art MR experiences to promote associative thinking.
- The potential for Music Art MR experiences to induce multi-sensory perception.

Of particular note, as a result of audio-visual performance with MR projection, is the high-incidence of cross-modal experiences (23.7% of the participants surveyed) elicited by this pilot study. This is at least four times the estimated proportion of synesthetes in the general population (4–6%) to whom cross-modal experiences are involuntary. This leads to the possibility of fulfilling the objective of non-invasive multisensory stimulation of the brain for increased mental ability, as discussed in Sect. 1.3, and the potential of Music Art MR for music art therapy. As this is a pilot study with a small sample size and a short survey, the results are merely indicative of future avenues for research, but the findings are promising.

Acknowledgments. The authors are grateful to the Music Composition Centre at Trinity College Dublin for letting the Boydell Recital Hall be used for the concert and to the delegates to the Joint Conference on Serious Games (JCSG) 2023 for their participation in this study. The study was funded by Haunted Planet Studios.

Appendix A: Full Questionnaire

Trinity College Dublin
Coláiste na Tríonóide, Baile Átha Cliath
The University of Dublin

Please draw an 'X' in the box that corresponds to your answer ☒

Age	Under 18	18 - 30	31 - 45	Over 45
	☐	☐	☐	☐
Gender	Male	Female	Non-binary	Prefer not to say
	☐	☐	☐	☐

Q1. How much experience do you have with Virtual and/or Mixed Reality?

None at all	A little	A moderate amount	A lot
☐	☐	☐	☐

Q2. How many classical music concerts have you attended in the last 5 years?

0	1 - 2	3 - 5	More than 5
☐	☐	☐	☐

Q3. After attending this concert, how likely are you to buy a Mixed Reality headset for personal use?

Extremely unlikely	Somewhat unlikely	Somewhat likely	Extremely likely
☐	☐	☐	☐

Q4. Did particular moments of this concert prompt you to reflect on related memories or concepts?

No	Somewhat	Yes
☐	☐	☐

Q5. How mindful did you feel during this concert?

Not mindful at all	Slightly mindful	Moderately mindful	Very mindful
☐	☐	☐	☐

Q6. Did you experience of this concert prompt you to start daydreaming?

No	Maybe	Yes
☐	☐	☐

Q7. Do you feel more or less creative after this concert?

Much less	Slightly less	No change	Slightly more	Much more
☐	☐	☐	☐	☐

Q8. Did you experience any non-audio-visual sensations as a result of this concert?

No	Yes
☐	☐

Q9. If you answered 'Yes' to the previous question, which sensations in particular did you experience?

Touch	Taste	Smell
☐	☐	☐

Q10. How much did you enjoy being an audience member during this concert?

I did not enjoy it	A little	A moderate amount	A lot
☐	☐	☐	☐

References

1. Rudenko, S., Haahr, M.: Synaesthesia gallery AR: journey through the senses – using augmented reality for education. In: Haahr, M., Rojas-Salazar, A., Göbel, S. (eds.) Serious Games: 9th Joint International Conference, JCSG 2023, Dublin, Ireland, October 26–27, 2023. Springer, Cham (2023). https://doi.org/10.1007/978-3-031-44751-8_15
2. Galeyev, B.M.: The Nature and functions of synesthesia in music. Leonardo **40**(3), 285–288 (2007)
3. Jakubowski, K.: Mental imagery in music-evoked autobiographical memories. In: Music and Mental Imagery, Routledge (2022)
4. Liikkanen, L., Jakubowski, K.: Involuntary musical imagery as a component of ordinary music cognition: a review of empirical evidence. Psychon. Bull. Rev. **27**(6), 1195–1217 (2020)
5. Rudenko, S., McDonnell, M., Layden, T., Haahr, M.: Exploring classical music narratives through multimodality in AR/VR experiences. In: Presented at the International Conference on Interactive Digital Storytelling (ICIDS), Santa Cruz, USA (2022)
6. Day, S.A.: Less common forms of synaesthesia. In: V Congreso Internacional de Sinestesia Ciencia Arte. Instituto de Estudios Giennenses, Spain (2015).
7. Ward, J.: The Frog Who Croaked Blue: Synesthesia and the Mixing of the Senses. Routledge, London and New York (2008)
8. Lupton, E.: Design is Storytelling. Cooper Hewitt, New York, USA (2017)
9. Velasco, C., Obrist, M.: Multisensory Experiences: Where the Senses Meet Technology. Oxford University Press, Oxford, New York (2020)
10. Haverkamp, M.: Sinesthetic Design: Handbook for a Multi-Sensory Approach. Birkhauser Verlag AG (2013)
11. Velasco, C., Spence, C.: Multisensory Packaging: Designing New Product Experiences. Palgrave Macmillan (2019)
12. Cytowic, R.E.: Synesthesia: A Union of the Senses, Second. MIT Press, Cambridge, Massachusetts; London, England (2002)
13. Parise, C., Spence, C.: Audiovisual crossmodal correspondences and sound symbolism: a study using the implicit association test. Exp. Brain Res. **220**(3–4), 319–333 (2012)
14. Ramachandran, V.S., Hubbard, E.M.: Hearing colors, tasting shapes 288, 53–59 (2003)
15. Bor, D., Rothen, N., Schwartzman, D., Clayton, S., Seth, A.: Adults can be trained to acquire synesthetic experiences. Sci. Rep. **4**, 7089 (2014)
16. Fried Block, A.: Amy Beach: Passionate Victorian. The Life and Work of and American Composer (1867–1944). Oxford University Press, New York, Oxford (1998)
17. James, T.: Victor Hugo and the 'headland of dream'. In: Dream, Creativity and Madness in Nineteenth-Century France, pp. 196–211. Clarendon Press, Oxford (1995)
18. Jung, C.G.: Man and His Symbols. Dell, USA, Canada (1968)
19. Rudenko, S., Fu, X., Haahr, M.: Alice Dali MR: a mixed reality interactive narrative experience. In: Holloway-Attaway, L., Murray, J.T. (eds.) Interactive Storytelling 16th International Conference on Interactive Digital Storytelling, ICIDS 2023, Kobe, Japan, November 11–15, 2023, Proceedings, Part II. Springer, Cham (2023). https://doi.org/10.1007/978-3-031-47658-7_23
20. Rudenko, S., Haahr, M.: Music for Alice Dali augmented reality experience: multisensory design soundscapes for locative mobile phone gaming (via synaesthesia). In: Presented at the VII International Congress of Synaesthesia: Science and Art, University of Granada: Google books (2022).
21. Carroll, L.: Alice's Adventures in Wonderland: 150th Anniversary Edition Illustrated by Salvador Dali. Princeton University Press, Princeton & Oxford (2015)

22. Morrow, G.: Conclusions: virtual reality, augmented reality and mixed reality. In: Designing the Music Buisness, pp. 177–201. Springer, Cham (2020). https://doi.org/10.1007/978-3-030-48114-8_8

23. Christoforou, M., Efthimiou, F.: Introducing dreams of Dali in a tertiary education ESP course: technological and pedagogical implementations. In: Presented at the Learning and Collaboration Technologies: 10th International Conference, LCT 2023, Held as Part of the 25th HCI International Conference, HCII 2023 (2023).

24. Young, G.W., O'Dwyer, N., Moynihan, M., Smolic, A.: Audience experiences of a volumetric virtual reality music video. In: 2022 IEEE Conference on Virtual Reality and 3D User Interfaces (VR), pp. 775–781. IEEE (2022)

25. Maurer, D., Mondloch, C.J.: Neonatal Synesthesia: A Reevaluation. In: Robertson, L.C. (ed.) Synesthesia: Perspectives from Cognitive Neuroscience. Oxford University Press, Oxford (2004)

26. Maurer, D., Maurer, C.: The World of the Newborn. Viking, London (1988)

Tools and Systems

Building Visual Novels with Social Simulation and Storylets

Shi Johnson-Bey$^{(\boxtimes)}$, Kira Liao, Samuel Shields, Daeun Hwang,
Noah Wardrip-Fruin, Michael Mateas, and Edward Melcer

University of California Santa Cruz, Santa Cruz, CA 95064, USA
{ismajohn,kiyliao,samshiel,dhwang,nwardrip,mmateas,emelcer}@ucsc.edu

Abstract. Simulationist interactive narrative systems allow game makers to craft reactive stories driven by simulated characters and their social dynamics. These systems produce narrative experiences that feel more emergent but may lack a coherent plot structure. We explored how to combine the emergent possibilities of social simulation with a procedural narrative system that affords writers strong authorial control over the plot. We did this by developing a Unity extension called Anansi that helps people create social simulation-driven visual novels. It enables users to inject simulation data into their story dialogue using logical queries and parameterized storylets written using *Ink*. The paper describes an overview of our extension and how we empower writers to drive narrative progression using cascading social effects from player choices.

Keywords: Storylets · Tools · Social Simulation · Unity · Visual Novel

1 Introduction

Visual novels (VNs) have shown to be practical tools for creating educational interactive storytelling games [1]. These games typically feature hand-authored choice-based branching narrative structures that produce well-constructed narrative experiences. However, a shortcoming of the branching narrative design approach is that it is prone to an exponential explosion in authoring burden as game designers try to give the player the illusion of a living world where the player can express agency [2].

Conversely, Simulationist Interactive Narrative systems develop narratives over time from the conflicts and drama that emerge between the player and non-player characters (NPCs) [12]. These systems are much more welcoming to player experimentation and exploration without suffering from an exponential growth in authoring burden. However, this often comes at the cost of game designers having less control over the final plot and overall narrative experience [20].

Since simulation games have also been shown to be effective for educational use [17], it would be ideal if we could provide players with an experience that

© The Author(s), under exclusive license to Springer Nature Switzerland AG 2025
J. T. Murray and M. C. Reyes (Eds.): ICIDS 2024, LNCS 15468, pp. 145–161, 2025.
https://doi.org/10.1007/978-3-031-78450-7_9

combines the freedom of a simulation with the well-formed structure of a choice-based narrative.

We explored how to help storytellers create interactive narrative games that leverage simulated non-player characters and procedural storytelling techniques to increase game replayability and encourage player exploration. We built a Unity extension called Anansi[1]. It's a toolkit for building simulation-driven visual novels in Unity, and we are actively using it to create an educational game that teaches players about the Responsible Conduct of Research within academia.

Anansi helps users create location-based, simulation-driven visual novels where the player can move between various locations and interact with the characters present. Player choices can affect their immediate relationships with NPCs and have cascading, second-order effects on other social relationships. We draw inspiration from games like *Persona 5* [19] and the dating sim genre because they focus on cultivating social relationships with NPCs.

We wanted to explore how to strike a balance between the emergent possibilities of simulation and a writing workflow that affords strong authorial control over the plot. Anansi combines a *storylet runtime*, powered by the Ink narrative scripting language[2], with an underlying world simulation with NPCs that follow schedules, move between locations, track their feelings about other characters, and respond to various social events happening within the game.

This paper provides an overview of Anansi's architecture, design motivations, lessons learned, and plans for the future. It also provides the following contributions:

– Demonstrate how to parameterize storylets to allow dynamic casting of characters into dialogue.
– Discuss how writers could associate cascading social effects with story choices.
– An example of game architecture that combines social simulation, storylets, and branching narrative design.

2   Related Work

2.1   Simulationist Interactive Narrative

Research into simulationist interactive narrative has been driven by the goal of producing endlessly replayable and emergent narrative experiences with autonomous characters that respond to the player and guide the plot [12]. Research in this area has been ongoing for decades. However, there are three systems that we highlight as being particularly relevant to this work: *Facade* [14], *Comme il Faut/Prom Week* [16], and *Versu* [4]. We chose these because they are either complete game experiences or have been used to produce complete game experiences.

Prom Week and Versu used parameterized social scenarios to drive character actions and narrative progression. Based on the current game state, characters

---

[1] https://github.com/ShiJbey/Anansi.
[2] https://www.inklestudios.com/ink/.

would choose actions based on their goals and what scenarios are available. This architecture afforded NPCs strong autonomy over their actions at the cost of authorial control over the game's plot [20]. Thus, the final narrative experienced by the player is their subjective sequence of scenarios.

Facade provides a middle ground between character autonomy and authorial control by using joint actions (like parameterized scenarios) to coordinate NPC behaviors and a drama manager to moderate the presentation of story beats. However, programming NPC behaviors in Facade is complex and is more akin to multi-robot coordination than writing story prose [15]. For this project, we wanted to empower designers to leverage parameterized scenarios while providing an interface that is more friendly to writers.

2.2 Tools for Creating Choice-Based Interactive Narratives

RenPy[3], *Twine*[4], *Yarn Spinner*[5], and *Ink*[6] are all examples of popular tools and engines for creating choice-based interactive narrative games. RenPy is the most popular platform for creating visual novels. It is based on a variant of Python and comes with all the necessary features to create complete experiences. Twine is for making hypertext games that can easily be shared over the web. YarnSpinner and Ink are narrative scripting languages intended to be embedded within a larger game engine. They feature scripting languages that look like screenplay scripts with code-like markup. The benefit of all these tools is that they handle much of the lower-level systems tasks, freeing game designers to focus on authoring dialogue and higher-level systems.

2.3 Storylets

Storylets are a procedural narrative design approach that divides a story's content into individual chunks that can be sequenced in differing orders based on the player's choices and the current game state [10,21]. Typically, storylets are gated by preconditions that must be true for them to be eligible for presentation to the player. Then, through a manual or automatic selection process, storylets are presented, progressing the narrative. Storylets allow narrative designers to forgo a pre-authored linear or branching structure, affording players the agency to chart their own paths through a narrative. We are particularly interested in exploring them for the intersection between interactive narrative and simulation since they have shown useful for procedural story generation [11,13].

2.4 Storylet-Based Interactive Narrative Systems

Two experimental storylet systems that directly inspired this project are StoryAssembler [5], and Lume [13]. Each takes a different approach to creating

---

[3] https://www.renpy.org/.
[4] https://twinery.org/.
[5] https://www.yarnspinner.dev/.
[6] https://www.inklestudios.com/ink/.

dynamic narrative experiences at runtime. Nevertheless, they were both used to successfully produce interactive games.

StoryAssembler uses a library of pre-authored content fragments to compose dialogue text and choice sets at runtime. The authors showed how one can combine storylets with a planning algorithm to find sequence content that maximizes a set of story goals.

Lume uses logic programming to manage a complex knowledge base containing information about characters, their shared histories, and the state of their world. It is the most similar to this project and natively supports features that Anansi does not. For instance, it can procedurally recall past events in the dialogue and generate text for those events using grammar-based techniques. Like Anansi, Lume uses logical queries to cast characters into parameterized storylets, assuming they satisfy the conditions. The core difference between Lume and Anansi is the greater focus on simulating the cascading effects of player choices on the relationships between NPCs.

3   Motivations and Design Goals

We built Anansi to support an experimental interactive narrative game that teaches players the Responsible Conduct of Research. In the game, players must navigate scenarios that place ethical decision-making in conflict with social pressures, such as upholding friendships, negotiating power imbalances, and maintaining a positive reputation.

The game's mechanics and our team composition influenced the design requirements for the final narrative system. We had three design goals for Anansi: a streamlined authoring interface, dynamic narrative content sequencing, and moderately complex social relationship modeling.

Our first goal was to provide a streamlined content authoring workflow that was easy to learn and supported more complex functionality. Also, we needed it to integrate well with Unity (our game engine of choice). Having too many tools and workflows in research projects has been shown to cause problems for multidisciplinary research teams [22].

Second, we wanted to be able to write conversational dialogue that we could dynamically sequence based on player competency at navigating particular ethical dilemmas, the current relationships between the characters, and other story state information. Additionally, we wanted to encourage players to replay the game and experiment with different strategies, as replay and failure are part of the learning process [18]. We chose storylets because a branching structure would not scale well to the vast possibility space of states that the social simulation could achieve. Plus [13] showed that dynamically casting characters into storylets based on preconditions could produce engaging and unique stories.

Our final design goal was to model moderately complex social relationship mechanics. The social simulation should help guide conversation choices and the progression of the overall plot. The player should have the power to influence their playthrough's short and long-term progression by utilizing their understanding of social dynamics and the immediate and cascading social consequences of their choices. Simulation games have proven helpful for educational games because they provide safe spaces for players to experiment [17]. Also, visual novels are one of the most popular narrative game formats for educational games. By combining the two, we aim to provide the experimental/systems qualities of a simulation game with a dialogue-heavy narrative presentation [1].

4   Ink

Our Unity extension is built on top of the Ink narrative scripting language created by Inkle Studios. Ink combines pure text with programming markup to empower writers to create highly branching, choice-based interactive narrative games. Inkle Studios has used Ink to create several commercial games, including *80 Days* [7], *Overboard* [9], and *Heaven's Vault* [8].

Ink's syntax is easy to learn (See Listing 1.1 for an example). At its simplest, each line of text in an Ink script corresponds to a line of dialogue in the game, and writers can display choices to the players by adding an asterisk to the beginning of a series of dialogue lines. Story content in Ink is usually grouped into sections called *knots*. Based on player choices, writers can divert the story to and from knots, giving rise to the branching narrative flow. In this project, we also heavily use tags, which are non-dialogue metadata that writers can associate with the global story, a knot, a choice, or a single dialogue line. Later, we discuss how we leverage Ink's knots and knot-level tags to support parameterized storylets that dynamically cast characters into roles.

We chose to use Ink for four reasons. First, it has excellent integration with Unity and C#. Second, we were already familiar with Ink's syntax. Third, as stated on the Ink website, "[Ink is] a narrative engine designed to slot into a game engine.". This distinction is very important because we wanted the social simulation to live independently of the writing, and we needed to pre-process the narrative scripts to extract storylet content. Lastly, we chose to use Ink because it saved us time from inventing an entirely new language. We could build on a well-established platform with an active developer community.

5   System Overview

This section provides an overview of Anansi's system architecture. We mainly focus on the storylet runtime component. A full explanation of the social simulation is outside the scope of this paper. However, we briefly explain the various parts with a longer explanation of how it enables writers to create cascading social effects for dialogue choices.

Anansi helps game designers create location-based visual novels where players move between locations and talk to characters. Screenshots of a sample game built using Anansi are provided in Fig. 1. The entire toolkit has four layers: a

```
1  | It's dangerous to go alone. Take this!
2  |
3  | * Take sword. # PlaySound: achievement.wav
4  |     -> adventure_start
5  | * Leave the sword.
6  |     -> leave_cave_get_eaten
7  |
8  | === adventure_start ===
9  | // This knot continues the story ...
10 |
11 | === leave_cave_get_eaten ===
12 | You leave the cave and get eaten by a monster.
13 | -> END
```

Listing 1.1. A sample Ink story with a single starting dialogue line, two choices, and two knots. The choices divert to separate knots. The first choice has an Ink tag (starting with '#') that tells the engine to play a sound when the choice is selected. Lines that start with "//" are comments and not displayed as dialogue.

presentation layer for UI, a dialogue layer, a world simulation layer, and a game management layer (See Fig. 2). Each layer communicates with the others using a collection of event listeners and callback functions. The only exceptions are the storylet runtime and the world simulation, which communicate using a Logic database (explained later).

The dialogue layer manages the flow of dialogue that is presented to the player via the UI Layer. It is also responsible for post-processing information from the storylet runtime to manage, among other things, which character to present on screen, the name of the speaker, and the current background to show. The storylet runtime is responsible for managing the flow of the story. It wraps an Ink story instance and provides additional infrastructure for instantiating, searching for, and sequencing storylets.

The database is the connective tissue between the world simulation and the storylet runtime. It originally existed as part of the relationship system but was later integrated into the storylet runtime to facilitate leveraging social simulation data in the story. The simulation syncs various bits of data with the database to make that information available to storylet queries.

The presentation layer is responsible for displaying the current speaker, the speaker's sprite, and any background images. This part of the extension is flexible and can be swapped out by end-users for something that better fits their game's style.

5.1   The World Simulation

The world simulation manages all the aspects of the social simulation (characters, the locations in the world, relationships between characters, social rules

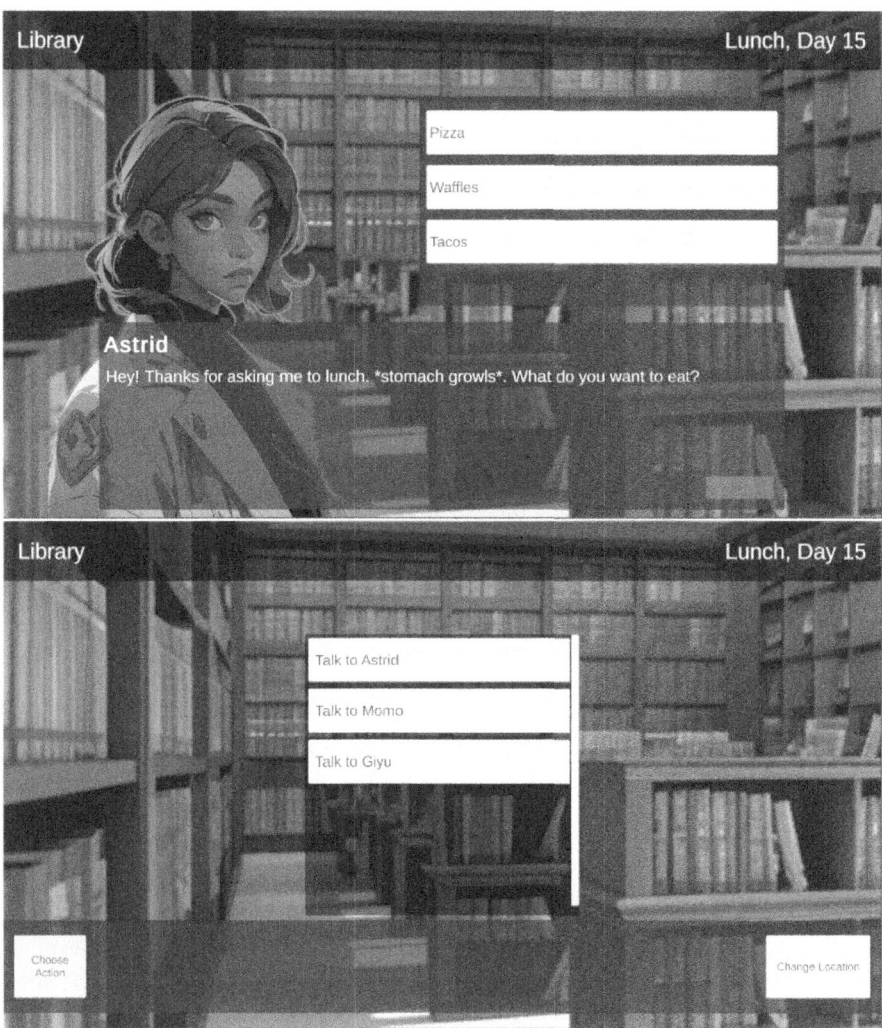

Fig. 1. Our extension provides users with two basic UI modes, one for dialogue (Top) and another for world navigation (Bottom). The dialogue UI has the standard visual novel features: a text box for dialogue, a dialog box containing available choices, a background image, and an image of the currently speaking character. The world navigation UI has a background image, a status bar displaying the current location and time, and an interaction panel with buttons for choosing actions or moving to other locations.

governing relationships, and social events that change relationships). The simulation operates on discrete time steps/ticks. On each simulation tick, we update the current time, move characters to various locations based on their given schedules, update any timed modifiers, and trigger any eligible social events. Our social

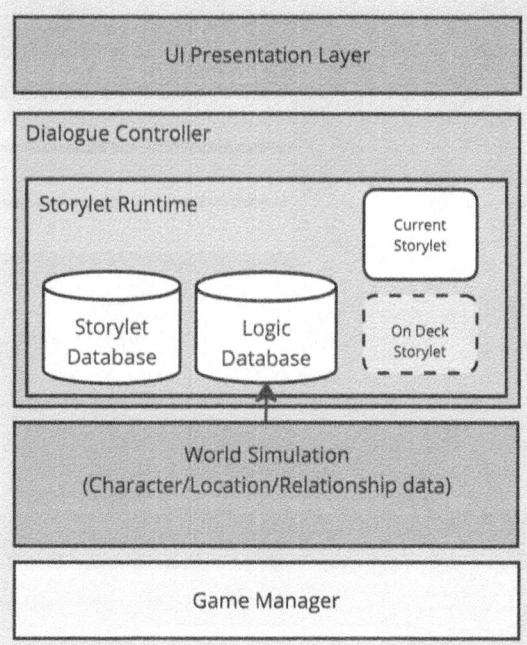

Fig. 2. The extension is divided into four layers. The UI manages what is seen by the player. The dialogue controller manages an instance of the story runtime and feeds dialogue lines and other information to the UI. The world simulation manages characters, locations, and social relationships. It feeds information into the database for the storylet runtime. Last, the Game Manager coordinates resource instantiation and manages all game-specific data not handled by the dialogue layer.

sim is intended to breathe more life into the story world by allowing characters to reason about their relationship with the player and their relationships with other characters. We wanted characters to change their opinion of the player based on how they treat other characters around them. For instance, being nice to a character's family member should help you gain favor with that character. Or, betraying a character should cause you to lose favor with their loved ones but gain favor with their enemies.

Characters. All characters have a unique ID, a display name, a current location, a collection of sprites, and a collection of schedules. Their IDs are used to identify them as the speaker within the story. They are also used to reference the character within the story database. Currently, we use the relationship system (explained later) to track information about character traits and their stats.

Character Schedules. Character schedules tell characters what location they should move to at a given time of day. Users can supply characters with multiple schedules, each containing entries specifying what time of day they are for, the location to move to, and their priority. We use entry priorities since characters can have multiple valid schedule entries for the same time of day [6]. Users may also precondition schedules on the current date, individual NPC variables, or relationship states.

Locations. Locations are anywhere that characters can be. Like characters, each location has a unique ID, a display name, and a collection of sprite images. Locations also track what characters are present.

On the writing side, we associate storylets with locations by giving storylets the same unique ID as the location they correspond to. We also add "location" to the storylet's tag set so the game manager can retrieve it. Every location the player can navigate to must have a corresponding storylet. The storylet does not need to contain dialogue, but it should contain function calls to update the background image and the player's location in the simulation.

Relationship System. The relationship system is responsible for tracking the social relationships between characters, relationship traits, relationship stats, social rules, and social events. It stores relationship information as a directed graph of characters (nodes) and relationships (edges), creating a social network. Each relationship tracks how one character feels about another. Thus allowing characters to have asymmetric feelings toward each other. Relationship information is also synced with the story database.

A full explanation of the relationship system is outside the scope of this paper and will be the subject of another publication. However, the system is publicly available to download within Unity's asset store[7].

Date/Time. The world simulation tracks the current week, weekday (7-day weeks), day, and time of day (morning, afternoon, evening, night). Currently, the time is mainly used to manage character schedules. Locations may also update their backgrounds if they have one tagged for the current time of day. Additionally, the current date/time is also synced with the story database, allowing writers to use it within storylet preconditions and other logic.

Writers can advance time from the Ink script using the `AdvanceTime()` Ink function that steps the simulation until the next time of day is reached. The time of day is incremented every fixed number of simulation steps. This interval can be specified by the game designer in the Unity editor. Whenever the current date/time is updated, the simulation also emits an event that allows third-party systems to react to the change in time.

The Logic Database. The relationship system uses a logic database to facilitate querying for relationship patterns and other information

---

[7] https://github.com/ShiJbey/TDRS.

https://github.com/ShiJbey/RePraxis. The database is based on the *Praxis* language used in the *Versu* engine [4]. It uses the same exclusion logic syntax and has been streamlined for data insertion, deletion, and queries.

Casting characters into storylets requires us to be able to find characters that meet specific preconditions. So, the relationship systems logic database is shared with the storylet runtime (discussed later) to allow writers to leverage its query system to find character IDs and store them within variables in the Ink script. Database queries are used within the storylet runtime for preconditions, and writers can assert/insert/delete statements directly within Ink. The query syntax used in storylets is passed directly to the logic database when instantiating storylets. The logic database is the core way for the Ink logic to access information about the world simulation when designing storylets.

Cascading Social Effects. Anansi uses *social events* to create cascading social effects in response to player choices. Social Events are a construct of the relationship system. They are instantiated by binding characters to specified roles. Then, based on who is bound and any additional preconditions, the event executes changes to the relationship system and its characters.

The following is an example inspired by a scenario one might encounter within the RCR training game. It showcases an example of how a writer might approach presenting the player with a choice that has ripple effects across their social network.

Suppose the player has been given control of a character named Avery, a new graduate student in a highly competitive lab. They recently discovered that their labmate and friend, Chris, falsified data on a paper they were a co-author on. Chris, a more senior PhD student, is popular in the lab and claims this publication is essential to their dissertation defense. Avery understands that if someone were to find out about the falsified results, it could be detrimental to their research career. However, Avery also worries that notifying their advisor could ostracize them from their other labmates. What will Avery do?

A simplified storylet of the above scenario might look like the Listing 1.2. In it, we define a storylet that would cast an NPC in the role of the labmate, display some dialogue, and give the player a choice of how to handle the situation. The DISPATCH_EVENT function is used to call into the social simulation to fire an event in which the player betrays the trust of the labmate (in this case, Chris). Listing 1.3 defines a betrayal event in our social simulation. It uses a query to the logic database to find all friends of the person who was betrayed so that we may adjust how they feel toward the betrayer (in this case, the player/Avery).

5.2   The Storylet Runtime

Anansi's storylet runtime allows us to leverage the social simulation within the Ink scripts by dynamically casting characters using logical queries. The runtime is a C# class wrapper around a standard Ink Story class instance that allows us

```
1  === false_data_dilemma(labmate) ===
2  # ----
3  # @query
4  # player.relationship.?labmate.tags.coworkers
5  # @end
6  # ===
7  // Other Dialogue
8  * Talk to your advisor about your discovery
9     {DISPATCH_EVENT("betrayal", "player, {labmate}")}
       {ADVANCE_TIME()}
10     -> // Go to other part of the story
11 * Check in with {CHARACTER_NAME(labmate)}
12     -> // Start conversation with labmate
13 * Let it be and hope no one finds out.
14     {ADVANCE_TIME()} // Advance time and simulate if the
          misconduct is discovered
15     -> // Go to other part of the story
16 -> DONE
```

Listing 1.2. "Avery's Research Misconduct Dilemma."

to extract storylet information and high-jack Ink's native control flow. We are able to interleave Ink-native branching and dynamic jumps to storylets.

In Anansi, storylets can be used to represent locations, actions players can take at a location, individual conversations, and scenes. We use them anywhere we want to conditionally gate or parameterize a bit of story content based on the state of the social simulation.

Anansi allows writers to treat character conversations as a "mystery bag" of topics that the game randomly selects from and presents to the player. Additionally, writers can associate selection tags and weight values to storylets to affect their eligibility and likelihood of being selected.

5.3   Defining Storylets

Anansi storylets are Ink knots with specialized metadata. All the metadata about a storylet is stored in its *header*. This is a collection of Ink tags placed below the name of the storylet. The header contains information about a storylet's weight of being selected, choice label (text displayed when offering the storylet as a choice), selection tags, repeatability, and cooldown time (see Listing 1.4). When loading a new Ink script, Anansi inspects all the knots in the script and extracts those containing storylet headers.

Additionally, there are also commands for working with precondition queries. All precondition queries have a @query ... @end section where all lines between @query and @end are collected to form a single query. We also supply users with the @set X to ?Y and @using X as ?Y commands for binding query variable value to Ink variables and vice-versa.

```
1    − name: Betrayal
2      roles:
3        − "?betrayer"
4        − "?victim"
5      description: "[betrayer] betrayed [victim]."
6      responses:
7        − effects:
8            − DecreaseRelationshipStat ?victim ?betrayer
                Friendship 10
9        − preconditions:
10           − ?victim.relationships.?victim_friend.traits.friend
11           − neq ?victim_friend ?betrayer
12         effects:
13           − DecreaseRelationshipStat ?victim_friend ?betrayer
                Friendship 5
```

Listing 1.3. "A betrayal social event defined using YAML."

Precondition queries are how we cast characters into roles. Within the query section of the storylet header, designers can precondition storylets on the position of characters in the world, any of their existing relationships, or their personal stats. Using variables (e.g., "?Y") within a query will cause the system to try and find a value in the database that satisfies the query when the variable is substituted. So, we bind character IDs to variables within query results in C# and rebind those variables to Ink-level variables. In Listing 1.2, the storylet header queries for a player relationship with the tag, "coworker". It binds the resulting character ID to "?labmate" and passes the resulting value to the "labmate" parameter variable in the Ink knot.

5.4   Instantiating Storylets

For a storylet to be available, we need to be able to *instantiate* it. This means, if the storylet has a precondition query, when that query is run against the logic database, the query must be successful. If the query contains variables, Anansi creates individual *storylet instances* for each valid set of variable bindings. If the query does not contain variables or there is no query at all, Anansi creates a single storylet instance. The storylet instances of all eligible storylets represent selection space when Anansi needs to choose a new storylet. For example, suppose we have a storylet about having lunch with a friend (see Listing 1.4). It requires the player to be in a location that serves food and for an NPC that considers the player a friend to be present in the same location. If there are two NPCs that meet the criteria, this will result in two potential storylet instances to choose from, one for each valid NPC.

Whenever we run a storylet instance, the runtime binds all the instance's variables to the story state and stores a reference to the current instance. From here, the runtime passes control down to Ink's runtime. When the writer wants

```
1  | === lunch_with_friend ===
2  | # ----
3  | # tags: convo
4  | # @using speaker as ?speaker
5  | # @query
6  | # ?speaker.relationships.player.traits.friend
7  | # player.location.traits.serves_food
8  | # @end
9  | # ===
10 | {speaker}.happy: Hey! Thanks for asking me to lunch.
   |     *stomach growls*. What do you want to eat?
11 | * Pizza
12 |     -> // Dialogue about pizza
13 | * Waffles
14 |     -> // Dialogue about waffles
15 | * Tacos
16 |     -> // Dialogue about tacos
17 | -> DONE
```

Listing 1.4. "An Ink knot containing a storylet header with associated metadata."

to jump the story to another storylet, they call helper functions that "queue" a storylet to be executed next. If the runtime can successfully instantiate the storylet, it selects one of the instances, using weighted random selection, and saves this instance as "on deck". So, when the story is advanced, we swap the active storylet with the one on deck, jump to its knot path in the Ink runtime, and continue the story. Since all this is hidden from the user, they see a seamless continuation of dialogue content, just like with branching diverts in Ink.

5.5 Enabling Gameplay

Locations are places where characters can be, and actions are things the player can choose to do when at a location. Actions and locations are represented as storylets containing "action" and "location" tags, respectively. The Game Manager is responsible for determining which actions and locations are available given the player's current location and the state of the rest of the simulation.

Representing actions and locations as storylets allows us to maintain most of the authoring effort within Ink scripts. Also, it means that we can trigger special dialogue or events when a player navigates to a location or takes an action. The storylet representation provides a nice middle-ground between gameplay mechanics and narrative flow.

The background image changes with the current location and time of day. We are working on allowing writers to change the background image on a per-dialogue line basis using Ink tags.

The speaker sprite changes based on the specified speaker ID and sprite tags provided in the Ink dialogue. The dialogue manager post-processes each dialogue line and extracts any ID and optional tags provided prior to a colon ":". To illustrate, the line, "ben.smiling.blue_shirt: Howdy!" will attempt to display a sprite of the character with the ID of "ben" and tags for "smiling" and "blue_shirt". When the line is fed from the dialogue manager to the UI, the speaker information is removed, and only "Howdy!" is displayed.

6   Discussion

In this section, we discuss lessons learned and challenges encountered thus far while developing our educational game using Anansi.

6.1   Designing for Fungible Characters

Characters in Anansi are fungible. This means that, depending on the storylet, we can substitute them with any other character that meets the storylet's preconditions. This is great for incremental development, games using characters as downloadable content, or games with procedurally generated characters because new characters can be leveraged in existing content without any need to explicitly write them into the story. However, the downside of this fungibility is that dialogue lines might not fit the characters being cast or the social dynamics associated with them.

Not all characters speak the same way, and not all characters interact with each other in the same way. Dialogue lines must account for the individual personality of the character and their social context. Is the character speaking with a new acquaintance, an old friend, or a love interest? What is the character's personality? Are they boisterous or reserved? Do they like using fancy words to appear erudite, or do they use more colloquial terms?

The responsibility falls on writers to add conditional checks within the Ink script to ensure the appropriate dialogue lines are presented to the player. Thus far in our game development, we have found that limiting the number of dynamically cast characters and being more specific about trait/relationship requirements in storylet precondition queries helps temper the combinatorial complexity.

6.2   The Tendency Toward Traditional Branching

Storylet and social simulation systems have a learning curve for those unfamiliar with procedural narrative design. They require writers to think about the story as a possibility space for things to happen rather than a series of set plot paths for players to traverse. Tracking the story state is challenging because, at times, writers cannot fully guarantee what the player has seen or done. There could be multiple ways for players to reach the same place in a story.

When teaching historians how to use a social simulation system for interactive storytelling, DeKerlegand et al. noticed that new users tend to avoid dynamism in favor of structuring content to resemble linear and branching structures [3]. A similar phenomenon was encountered by Garbe et al. when writers were tasked with creating story content within StoryAssembler [5]. Writers tended to avoid more dynamic/procedural designs to quickly reach operational results.

Even as we develop our educational game, we occasionally fall into the trap of a strictly branching narrative design. Keeping track of all the information during the design phase is challenging. As we continue development, we aim to identify techniques to help others become more comfortable with the combinatorial complexity of storylets and social simulation for interactive storytelling.

6.3   Deciding Between Ink Variables or the Database

Anansi provides two options for storing variables/game state: Ink variables and the logic database. We use Ink variables whenever possible because they have full support within the Ink language. When we need the social simulation to respond to a value in Ink, we store a copy of the value in the logic database. This requires an additional step, but it allows for additional bi-directional communication between the story content and the social simulation.

7   Future Work

We are currently using Anansi to develop an interactive narrative game that teaches players about ethics and the Responsible Conduct of Research within academia. Players must navigate various scenarios that place ethical decision-making in conflict with navigating social pressures. We plan to report a post-mortem of our development experience and an analysis of the players' feelings and learning outcomes.

Additionally, we want to elicit qualitative feedback from a broader audience by conducting a user experience test as a 48-hour game jam. Participants will be tasked with creating a visual novel game using Anansi. At the end of the jam, participants will submit their games and complete a system usability survey regarding their experience. We will analyze how participants utilize Anansi's features and identify what works well, needs improvement, or is missing.

8   Conclusion

In this paper, we provided a system overview of Anansi, our Unity extension for building visual novels using a combination of social simulation, storylets, and branching choices. Anansi's storylet runtime allows storytellers to write storylets, define roles for who may be involved, and have characters dynamically into those roles based on their relationships and the current story state. This enables storytellers to reuse content and customize it for different character combinations. Additionally, leveraging a social simulation enabled us to provide players with story choices that can have immediate and cascading social effects on their relationships with NPCs. By combining simulation-driven gameplay, storylets, and hand-authored branching narrative content, we aim to support game replayability and player exploration while providing storytellers with adequate authorial control over the plot.

Acknowledgments. This material is based upon work supported by the National Science Foundation under Grant No. 2202521. Any opinions, findings, conclusions, or recommendations expressed in this material are those of the author(s) and do not necessarily reflect the views of the National Science Foundation.

Disclosure of Interests. The authors have no competing interests to declare that are relevant to the content of this article.

References

1. Camingue, J., Melcer, E.F., Carstensdottir, E.: A (visual) novel route to learning: a taxonomy of teaching strategies in visual novels. In: Proceedings of the 15th International Conference on the Foundations of Digital Games. FDG 2020. Association for Computing Machinery (2020). https://doi.org/10.1145/3402942.3403004
2. Crawford, C.: Chris Crawford on Interactive Storytelling. Pearson Education (2004)
3. DeKerlegand, D., Samuel, B., Treanor, M.: Pedagogical challenges in social physics authoring. In: Mitchell, A., Vosmeer, M. (eds.) Interactive Storytelling, pp. 34–47. Springer, Cham (2021)
4. Evans, R., Short, E.: Versu-a simulationist storytelling system. IEEE Trans. Comput. Intell. AI Games **6**(2), 113–130 (2013)
5. Garbe, J., Kreminski, M., Samuel, B., Wardrip-Fruin, N., Mateas, M.: Storyassembler: an engine for generating dynamic choice-driven narratives. In: Proceedings of the 14th International Conference on the Foundations of Digital Games. FDG 2019. Association for Computing Machinery, New York (2019). https://doi.org/10.1145/3337722.3337732
6. Graham, R.: Game AI Pro, chap. Breathing Life into Your Background Characters. CRC Press (2013)
7. Inkle: 80 days. [iOS, Android, Microsoft Windows, MacOS, Nintendo Switch] (2014)
8. Inkle: Heaven's vault. [Nintendo Switch, PlayStation 4, Microsoft Windows] (2019)
9. Inkle: Overboard. [Nintendo Switch, Android, Microsoft Windows, iOS, MacOS] (2021)
10. Kreminski, M., Wardrip-Fruin, N.: Sketching a map of the storylets design space. In: Rouse, R., Koenitz, H., Haahr, M. (eds.) Interactive Storytelling, pp. 160–164. Springer, Cham (2018)
11. Lessard, J., Paré-Chouinard, S.: Dramatic situations for emergent narrative system authorship. In: Vosmeer, M., Holloway-Attaway, L. (eds.) Interactive Storytelling, pp. 217–228. Springer, Cham (2022)
12. Louchart, S., Truesdale, J., Suttie, N., Aylett, R.: Emergent narrative: past, present and future of an interactive storytelling approach. In: Interactive Digital Narrative, pp. 185–199. Routledge (2015)
13. Mason, S., Stagg, C., Wardrip-Fruin, N.: Lume: a system for procedural story generation. In: Proceedings of the 14th International Conference on the Foundations of Digital Games. FDG 2019. Association for Computing Machinery, New York (2019). https://doi.org/10.1145/3337722.3337759

14. Mateas, M., Stern, A.: Façade: an experiment in building a fully-realized interactive drama. In: Game Developers Conference, vol. 2, pp. 4–8. Citeseer (2003)
15. Mateas, M., Stern, A.: A behavior language: joint action and behavioral idioms. In: Life-Like Characters: Tools, Affective Functions, and Applications, pp. 135–161. Springer, Heidelberg (2004)
16. McCoy, J., Treanor, M., Samuel, B., Reed, A.A., Wardrip-Fruin, N., Mateas, M.: Prom week. In: Proceedings of the International Conference on the Foundations of Digital Games, pp. 235–237 (2012)
17. Minnery, J., Searle, G.: Toying with the city? Using the computer game simcity^{TM}4 in planning education. Plan. Pract. Res. **29**(1), 41–55 (2014)
18. Mitchell, A.: Writing for replay: supporting the authoring of kaleidoscopic interactive narratives, pp. 131–145. Springer, Cham (2022)
19. P-Studio: Persona 5. [Nintendo Switch, PlayStation, Xbox, Windows] (2016)
20. Riedl, M.O., Bulitko, V.: Interactive narrative: an intelligent systems approach. AI Mag. **34**(1), 67 (2012). https://doi.org/10.1609/aimag.v34i1.2449. https://ojs.aaai.org/aimagazine/index.php/aimagazine/article/view/2449
21. Short, E.: Storylets: You want them (2019). https://emshort.blog/2019/11/29/storylets-you-want-them/
22. Szilas, N., Spierling, U.: Authoring issues in interdisciplinary research teams, pp. 287–302. Springer, Cham (2022)

A Tool for the Calculation of Characters' Emotions

Vincenzo Lombardo$^{(\boxtimes)}$ ⓘ and Biagio Eugenio Iaria

Dipartimento di Informatica, Università di Torino, Torino, Italy
vincenzo.lombardo@unito.it, biagio.iaria@edu.unito.it

Abstract. This paper presents the EMOCC online tool for the calculation of emotions, given the appraisal of events on behalf of the characters. The tool is based on a well known OCC theory, implemented as a rule-based model. The user can input the appraisal of events and entities and the system calculates the emotions felt by the characters at hand. The tool has been tested in courses that address the difference between the human evaluation and the algorithmic tool.

Keywords: OCC model · interactive tool · emotions

1 Introduction

Emotions characterize story characters in their appraisal of the significant events [13], with different nature and intensity: proud to receive a promotion, angry for being annoyed, ... A good narrative, especially in dramatic format, evokes emotional states in the audience [11]. Authors use emotional reactions as the manifestations of the motivations and attitudes of their main characters, revealing the close relationship between emotions, personality, and cognition [9].

Computational models of emotions are "software designed to synthesize the operations of the process of elicitation of human emotions based on a specific theory of emotions" [4]. Models aim at clarifying the mechanisms of the generation of emotions and to improve credibility and effectiveness of synthetic agents and robots [12].

There are three consolidated theoretical perspectives that can be referred to in the construction of a computational model of emotions [5]. Each of these differs from the others in function of the semantic primitives that it asserts characterize the procedures of generation of the emotions. Discrete or categorical theories of emotions emphasize a small number of fundamental emotions, each of which mediated by specific neural circuits. For example, some popularity has been gained by Ekman's universal basic emotions, namely joy, sadness, anger, fear, disgust, and surprise [3]. Dimensional theories of emotions define a space within which the human emotions can be distinguished from non-emotions. For example, Russel's two-dimension theory reflects, on the valence dimension, a positive or negative evaluation of the current state of affairs and the associated state of pleasure (or displeasure) felt and, on the arousal dimension, the

J. T. Murray and M. C. Reyes (Eds.): ICIDS 2024, LNCS 15468, pp. 162–171, 2025.
https://doi.org/10.1007/978-3-031-78450-7_10

general level of activity of the organism, i.e. a general readiness for action [10]. Finally, componential theories of emotions address the appraisal of the emotions, that is the cognitive evaluation procedure that some agent performs on some state of affairs and its evaluation variables, assuming that a stimulus elicits an emotion in terms of the meaning and consequences that the agent attributes to it. For example, OCC theory represents in an explicit form the appraisal of the situation on behalf of the individual and the calculus for the computation of the emotion types, after a cognitive interpretation of events, agents and objects in terms of their desirability with respect to the agent's objectives, their coherence in relation to her/his/their moral standards, and their pleasantness according to the dispositional attitudes of the agent (e.g., the agent experiences hope if he/she/they appraised an event that is desirable for the achievement of his/her/their goals) [1]. OCC theory has also received a great attention for the formulation of computational models (e.g., [8]), because of its explicit formal representation.

In this paper, we present a tool for the emotion appraisal in the context of narratives. The tool takes as input the basic elements of a narrative situation and its appraisal with respect to characters' intentions and values and returns as output the emotional states of the characters. The tool implements the DrammarOCC model, which has been previously formalized in ontological triples [2,6] and in predicate logic [7]. Here we use the ontological format The tool presents a web interface for authoring education and implements the calculation of emotions after authors have filled a form with characters' values, goals and actions, together with a flag on their accomplishment. The tool can also be used for the synthesis of characters' emotional states in the entertainment industry.

Now, we sum up the underlying DrammarOCC model and then illustrate the tool.

2   The Underlying Model

In this section, we briefly summarize the Drammar-OCC model, starting from the formal description of the elements in the ontological format of class and properties.

The calculation of emotions is addressed in elementary units of the narrative (class *Unit*), containing a description of the occurring events. The events occurring in the units are motivated by the intentions or plans (class *Plan*) intended by the characters or agents (class *Agent*), who try to achieve their goals (class *Goal*). Goals are triggered by agents' values (class *Value*), which are engaged in the events. Values can be at stake, which agents trying to get them in balance, or can be in balance, with conflicting agents trying to put them at stake. By appraising 1) the events occurring in the units of some timeline, 2) the intentional actions of the agents (including themselves), and 3) the pleasantness/liking of objects and agents in the story world, the characters experience the emotional states, which are conveyed to the audience (from the OCC model).

As an example, we refer to a unit of Brecht's play "Mother Courage and her children" (original title *Mutter Courage und ihre Kinder*, 1938-39), likely written as a protest against the imminent war. It has been included in predicate logic format in [7]; here we reformulate it in ontological individuals belonging to the classes previously mentioned. "Mother Courage and her children", set during the Thirty Years' War in some countries of Central and Northern Europe, tells the misadventures of the vivandière Anna Fierling, who earns a living by selling wares to soldiers. The war, which is the place of her business, will take her three children, blurring her maternal instinct. The specific unit taken into account is the second of the first scene (Unit 1.2), identified by Brecht himself in a manuscript (*Brecht zu Courage*):

> Mother Courage presents her heterogeneous family formed in different theaters of the war to the Brigadier and the Recruiter, who are trying to take her sons away for enlisting them in the army.

The Basic Formal Model. The units containing the story events are ordered sequentially into timelines (a minimal timeline is made of one unit). So, for example, $Unit_{1.2}$ follows $Unit_{1.1}$ (or, formally, $Unit_{1.1} - precedes - Unit_{1.2}$, in RDF triple format).

The characters, or agents, are the entities that have goals and intend plans to achieve them. So, in $Unit_{1.2}$, *Mother Courage*, *Brigadier* and *Recruiter* are agents (class *Agent*). Each character has values that direct her/his/their behavior through their engagement, since values are engaged (at stake or in balance) by the events that occur. In $Unit_{1.2}$, the value of Mother Courage "safety of her children" (Value *MC Children Safety*) leads her to defend them from being recruited for war; as we see below, $Unit_{1.2}$ produces the effect that Courage's children risk being recruited, i.e. that Courage's value of children safety is put at stake. Another value of Mother Courage is "her business", which leads her to negotiate a sale with the Brigadier in a unit that follows $Unit_{1.2}$; a value of the Brigadier is his "allegiance" (which is balanced), typical of military service; a value of the Recruiter is his "patriotism" (balanced), which leads him to convince people to go to war. In formal terms, $Mother\ Courage - hasValue - MC\ Children\ Safety$, that is Mother Courage has the value "her children safety".

Complementary to events, there are states of affairs, the results of the events. The states of affairs are of two types: the mental states of the characters in appraisal of the story events and the actual state of affairs at some point in the story. In particular, the mental states are represented through the values of the characters in a certain unit, which are put at stake or in balance by the events. The state of the values are appraised before and after the occurrence of the events of the unit; so, the unit makes the transition between one set of states and another, allowing the story to progress. In formal terms, a state set (class *State Set* contains values at stake or in balance as preconditions or effects of a unit. For example, the state sets $Preconditions_{1.2}$ and $Effects_{1.2}$ hold before and after the execution of unit $Unit_{1.2}$ ($Unit_{1.2} - has\ precondition - Preconditions_{1.2}$ and $Unit_{1.2} - has\ effect - Effects_{1.2}$). In particular, $Unit_{1.2}$ has the effect of putting at stake the value "safety of Mother Courage's children":

- $MC\ Children\ Safety\ -\ in\ balance\ in\ set\ -\ Preconditions_{1.2}$,
- $MC\ Children\ Safety\ -\ at\ stake\ in\ set\ -\ Effects_{1.2}$.

Finally, we take into account the intentions, or plans, of the characters, which are the motivational engine of the story, used in the deliberation process, when the character decides what actions to uptake. An agent intends a plan and the plan is a motivation for the unit events. Plans are used by a character to achieve her/his/their goals. Plans can be implemented only when certain preconditions are met, that is, states of affairs that must hold for the plan to be applied. In our case, the preconditions concern values at stake: so, plans are intended to balance values put at stake or put at risk values that are in balance until some point. In $Unit_{1.2}$, the interest of officers for Mother Courage's sons (two of the three children) puts at stake value "Mother Courage's children safety"; that is, the value at stake ($MC\ ChildrenSafety$) is a precondition of the plan "distracting officers" with the goal "avoiding the recruitment of her children". In formal terms:

- $Mother\ Courage - has\ goal\ -\ Avoid\ recruitment\ of\ MC\ children$,
- $Distracting\ officers - achieves - Avoid\ recruitment\ of\ MC\ children$,
- $Mother\ Courage\ -\ intends\ -\ Distracting\ officers$,
- $Distracting\ officers - has\ precondition - Preconditions_{DO}$,
- $Distracting\ officers - has\ effect - Effects_{DO}$,
- $MC\ Children\ Safety\ -\ at\ stake\ in\ set\ -\ Preconditions_{DO}$,
- $MC\ ChildrenSafety\ -\ in\ balance\ in\ set\ -\ Effects_{DO}$.

For there to be a real change in value balancing, the agents' plans must succeed, that is, the actions set out in the plan are executed and the plan achieves the goal. However, because of conflicts, the agents' plans cannot all succeed; in alternative, a plan could support the realization of another plan, of the same agent or of another agent. Actually, Mother Courage plan fails and her value children safety remains at stake. In formal terms:

- $Distracting\ officers - is\ motivation\ for - Unit_{1.2}$,
- $Distracting\ officers - is - UNACCOMPLISHED$

Mother Courage's plan of "distracting officers" with the goal to "avoid her children recruitment" fails; instead, the Brigadier's plan to "get the Recruiter in touch with Courage's children" is successful. Mother Courage's plan of "distracting officers" is in conflict with the Brigadier's plan of "getting the Recruiter in touch with Mother Courage's children", while the Brigadier's plan of "getting the Recruiter contact with Courage's children" supports the Recruiter's plan of "recruiting soldiers for the army". In formal terms:

- $Distracting\qquad officers\qquad -\qquad in\qquad conflict\qquad with\qquad -$
  $Getting\ Recruiter\ in\ touch\ with\ MC\ children$,
- $Getting\quad Recruiter\quad in\quad touch\quad with\quad MC\quad children\ -\ supports\ -$
  $Recruiting\ soldiers\ for\ the\ army$

Formal reasoning algorithms, with this representation in input, will calculate that children safety is yet at stack in the effects of $Unit_{1.2}$ because Mother Courage's plan fails.

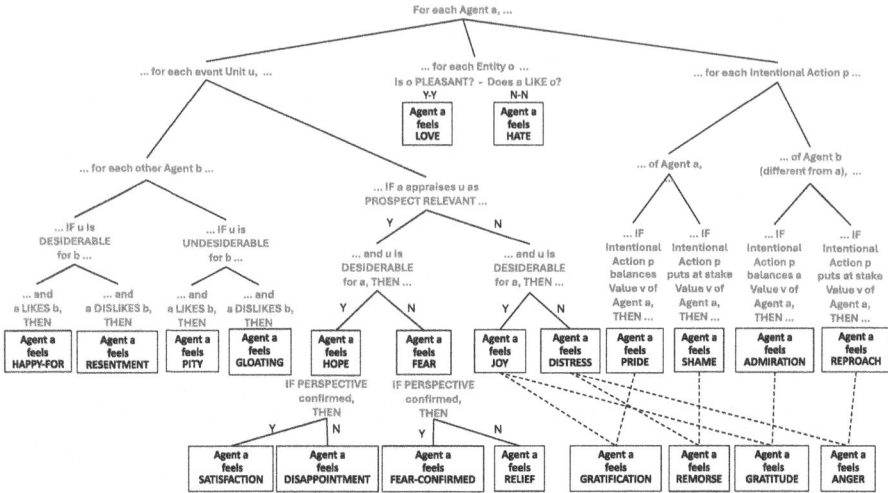

Fig. 1. The decision tree that represents the DrammarOCC model of emotional state calculation

The Emotional State Computation. Having set the basic elements of the unit, we need an algorithm for the computation of the emotional states. We expect that, for example, in $Unit_{1.2}$, Mother Courage feels "distress" for the failure of her distraction plan, while the Recruiter feels "hope" for a possible recruitment and the Brigadier feels "joy" for having succeeded in his support of the Recruiter and "pride" for balancing his "allegiance" value. The Drammar-OCC model implements rules that calculate the emotions for each agent. Figure 1 illustrates such computation with a decision tree [6]. Starting from the root, each path in the tree arrives at some boxed term that represents the emotion calculated along the path. Multiple paths can be triggered in parallel, since many emotions can be felt at the same time.

The root node sets the Agent a as the one that feels the emotion(s) as a consequence of the rule execution (i.e., of the appraisal). The next level tests whether the emotion is caused by

- some events of Unit u that occurred (emotions from appraisal of consequences of events),
- some Entity o (can also be an Agent) that can be PLEASANT or UNPLEAS-ANT and that the Agent LIKES or DISLIKES (emotions from appraisal of entities),
- some intentional Plan p carried out by some agent (emotions from appraisal of intentional action carried out by some agent).

In the case of the event-appraised branch,

- if the event is DESIRABLE for an agent b that a likes, a FEELS Happy for b;

- if the event is DESIRABLE for an agent b that a dislikes, a FEELS Resentment for b;
- if the event is UNDESIRABLE for an Agent b that a likes, a FEELS Pity for b;
- if the event is UNDESIRABLE for an Agent b that a dislikes, a FEELS Gloating for b;
- if the event is prospect relevant (i.e., somewhat related to her/him/them), then
  - if the event is DESIRABLE for a, then a FEELS Hope, which,
    * in case the perspective is confirmed, a FEELS Satisfaction,
    * otherwise a FEELS Disappointment;
  - if the event is UNDESIRABLE for a, then a FEELS Fear, which,
    * in case the perspective is confirmed, a FEELS Fear confirmed (a sort of general terms for several variants, e.g., horror,
    * in case the perspective is NOT confirmed, a FEELS Relief
- if the event is NOT prospect relevant (i.e., somewhat unrelated to her/him), then
  - if the event is DESIRABLE for a, then a FEELS Joy;
  - if the event is UNDESIRABLE for a, then a FEELS Distress.

In the case of the entity-appraised branch,

- if the entity o is generally judged PLEASANT and Agent a LIKES Entity o, then a FEELS Love for o;
- if the entity o is generally judged UNPLEASANT and Agent a DISLIKES Entity o, then a FEELS Hate for o.

In the case of the intentional action-appraised branch,

- if agent a INTENDS the Plan p and p BALANCES a value put at stake, a FEELS Pride;
- if agent a INTENDS the Plan p and p PUTS AT STAKE a value of the agent, a FEELS Shame;
- if other Agent b INTENDS the Plan p and p BALANCES a value of the agent a put at stake, a FEELS Admiration for b;
- if other Agent b INTENDS the Plan p and p PUTS AT STAKE a value of the agent a, a FEELS Reproach for b.

Finally, there are four compound emotions:

- if agent a FEELS both Joy and Pride, then a FEELS Gratification;
- if agent a FEELS both Distress and Shame, then a FEELS Remorse;
- if agent a FEELS both Joy and Admiration, then a FEELS Gratitude for b;
- if agent a FEELS both Distress and Reproach, then a FEELS Anger for b.

Other rules calculates the intermediate attribute, such as PROSPECT RELEVANT or DESIRABLE. For example, an event/unit u is considered relevant in perspective (PROSPECT RELEVANT) for an agent a if it is in support of or in conflict with a plan p of the agent a that can be implemented in the future.

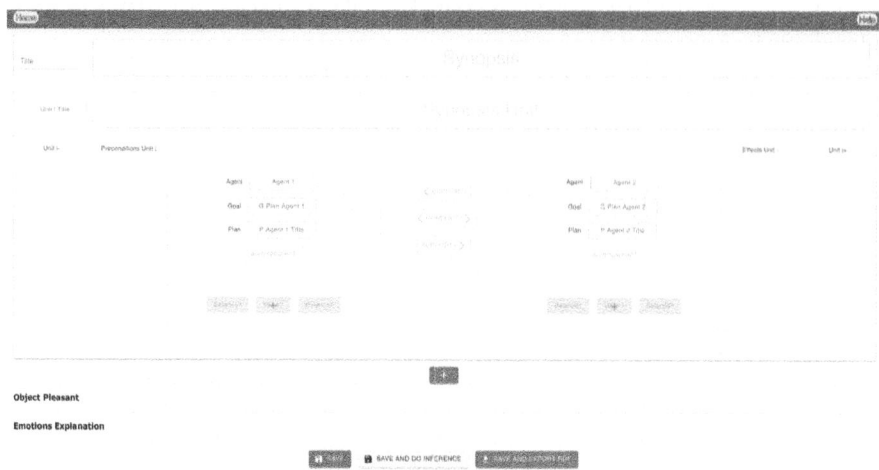

Fig. 2. Empty form of the interface to the EMOCC tool.

Similarly, a unit that is UNDESIRABLE for the agent a if u if it puts at stake a value of agent a.

Rules are encoded in SWRL format and executed with a formal reasoner accessible through a SPARQL endpoint.

3   The EMOCC Tool

The EMOCC tool[1] is implemented in the GraphDB (free version)[2] environment, which can store the RDF triples and offers a SPARQL endpoint to run the reasoning algorithm on the knowledge base that represents the story unit.

The interface is implemented in the REACT library[3] on a web page. The user can input (Fig. 2) the unit title and synopsis, together with the preceding and the possible following units of interest and its preconditions and the effects, respectively. Then, a number of screen sections represent conflict or support between plans, with the possible values put at stake or in balance. Once the user sets whether plans have been accomplished or not, the system can calculate the resulting states of affairs concerning the values and the emotions felt by the agents. With the "+" button, the user can add all the possible relations between plans, goal and values. Figure 3 shows the filled form, with agent, goals, plans, and their accomplishment, together with the values at stake or in balance. The tool translates the filled text into classes, individual and instantiated properties

---

[1] The tool is currently accessible at https://emostory.altervista.org/, visited on 1 October 2024.

[2] https://graphdb.ontotext.com/, visited on 1 October 2024.

[3] https://react.dev/, visited on 1 October 2024.

Fig. 3. Filled form of the interface to the EMOCC tool, before calculation.

Fig. 4. Interface to the EMOCC tool, after calculation.

of the database, to perform the reasoning phase and calculate emotional states of the unit agents. Figure 4 shows the calculated value effects and the emotions felt by the agents, highlighted in orange. Ini particular, we see that Brigadier is also feeling an emotion of "gratification", calculated from the composition of "pride" and "joy". The tool has been tested a number of classic cases and users can also make a quick test for checking calculated emotions on cases introduced on-the-fly.

4   Discussion and Conclusions

This paper has presented an online tool for the calculation of emotions, given the appraisal of events on behalf of the characters. The tool is based on a well known theory, called OCC, implemented as rule-based model. The user can input the appraisal of events and entities and the system calculates the emotions felt by the characters at hand.

The EMOCC is being tested in a laboratory exercises of "Logic for storytelling": students are required to select a scene from a linear or interactive story and describe it in the ontological format described above, identifying agents, goals, plans, values and their status in the unit execution. That is, users also input whether values are put at stake or in balance by some plan and what is the status of the value before the unit is executed. Then, the students are required to compare, in a written report, the system results with the expectations that they had on the unit agents; this leads to correct the encoding of the unit, to understand whether authors of stories are able to predict all the emotions felt by the characters of a story, and to discuss about the model limitations. We are collecting a corpus of analyzed units to provide educational materials that can be distributed through a website.

Anyway, the reasoning component of the tool can be used as an module for the entertainment industry, in case game sessions are encoded in terms of the ontological entities, namely agents, with their goals, plans, and values. Actually, some computational models of this sort exist, but the narrative features introduced here have not been address before.

References

1. A. Ortony, A.C., Clore, G.: The Cognitive Structure of Emotions. Cambridge University Press Cambridge (1988). http://www.loc.gov/catdir/toc/cam026/87033757.html
2. Damiano, R., Lombardo, V., Pizzo, A.: The ontology of drama. Appl. Ontol. **14**(1), 79–118 (2019)
3. Ekman, P.: An argument for basic emotions. Cogn. Emot. **6**(3–4), 169–200 (1992)
4. Hudlicka, E.: Modeling emotion in symbolic cognitive architectures. In: AAAI Fall Symposium: Emotional and Intelligent I. AAAI Press (1998)
5. Hudlicka, E.: Guidelines for designing computational models of emotions. Int. J. Synth. Emotions **2**, 26–79 (2011)
6. Lombardo, V., Battaglino, C., Pizzo, A., Damiano, R., Lieto, A.: Coupling conceptual modeling and rules for the annotation of dramatic media. Semant. Web J. **6**(5), 503–534 (2015)
7. Lombardo, V., Osella, B.: A rule-based model of emotion appraisal for narratives. In: AI4Narratives@IJCAI 2020, pp. 35–41 (2020)

8. Mascarenhas, S., Guimarães, M., Prada, R., Santos, P.A., Dias, J., Paiva, A.: Fatima toolkit: toward an accessible tool for the development of socio-emotional agents. ACM Trans. Interact. Intell. Syst. **12**(1), 1–30 (2022)
9. Plutchik, R.: Emotion: A Psychoevolutionary Synthesis. Harper and Row, New York (1980)
10. Russell, J.A.: Core affect and the psychological construction of emotion. Psychol. Rev. **110**(1), 145–172 (2003). http://view.ncbi.nlm.nih.gov/pubmed/12529060
11. Scheff, T.J.: Catharsis in Healing, Ritual and Drama. University of California Press, Berkeley (1979)
12. Sloman, A., Chrisley, R., Sheultz, M.: The architectural basis of affective states and processes. In: Who Needs Emotion? (2005)
13. Smith, C.A., Lazarus, R.S.: Emotion and adaption. In: Hanbook of Personality: Theory and Research, pp. 609–637. Guilford, New York (1990)

Late Breaking Works

Teaching Data Storytelling in a Computational Thinking Course for Students in Communications Careers

Joseph Livingston Crawford-Visbal[1]([⊠]) [iD], Livingston Crawford Tirado[2] [iD],
Luisa Alondra Gomez Saltachin[1] [iD], and Dina Soledad Cornejo Meza[1] [iD]

[1] Pontifical Catholic University of Peru, Av. Universitaria 1801, Lima, Peru
{jcrawford,luisa.gomez,Soledad.cornejo}@pucp.edu.pe
[2] St. Ignatius of Loyola University, Av. La Fontana 750, Lima, Peru
livingston.crawford@usil.pe

Abstract. Data storytelling is an emerging, multidisciplinary field that employs data to change pre-conceived notions of audiences using pieces of information and data visualization. Traditionally considered a technical skill for engineering, it has proven beneficial for disciplines in Humanities and Social Sciences. This work-in-progress is based on the experiences gathered from two classrooms of a new course titled "Computational Thinking for Communications", taught in a Peruvian university. The 16-week course involved one theoretical and two practical hours weekly. Semi-structured interviews were conducted with the 50 enrolled students who were creating data storytelling projects using open data sources. The students' experiences, motivations, and challenges were explored, such as a perceived disconnection between theory and practice. Future evaluations aim to refine the curriculum, addressing these challenges to enhance the integration of data storytelling in Communication education.

Keywords: Data Storytelling · Education · Communication · Systematization of Experiences

1 Introduction

Data storytelling is an emerging field that combines data analysis and storytelling to communicate insights effectively. Its main narrative technique employs data to challenge pre-conceived notions of the audience, revealing correlational or causal relationships between pieces of information that transforms the understanding of a certain topic [1, 2]. Usually thought of as a technical skill to be learned in engineering professions, it has now proven to be effective for a multitude of disciplines in Humanities and Social Sciences. In lieu of this emerging trend, this work in progress stems from the experiences in a new course titled "Computational Thinking for Communications".

A unique aspect of the course is that participating students belong to 4 different disciplines: Communication and Journalism, Communication for Development, Communication and Publicity, and Audiovisual Communication. For said students, mastering

J. T. Murray and M. C. Reyes (Eds.): ICIDS 2024, LNCS 15468, pp. 175–185, 2025.
https://doi.org/10.1007/978-3-031-78450-7_11

data storytelling is crucial to adapting to digital communication trends, especially the integration of data visualization and narrative techniques to convince an audience. But how can one teach a course that requires a hard skill such as programming, to students in fields related to Social Sciences and Humanities? That is why this papers aims to explore the perceptions of the course's students in order to improve their learning experience whilst giving recommendations for teaching these highly technical skills to students with limited computational competences (Fig. 1).

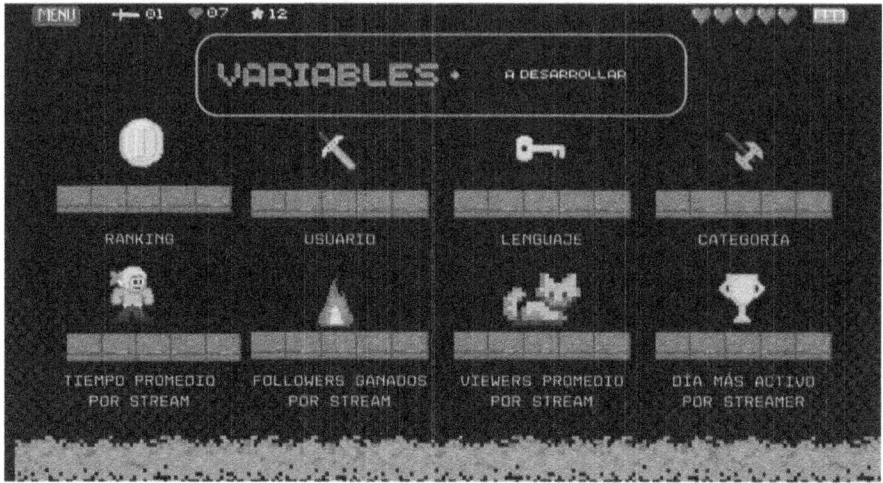

Fig. 1. Students integrate visual, narrative and coding elements tell the story of their project that explores the top 100 Twitch Streamers. They explain which variables are relevant to determine their findings, such as average views and time streamed, as well as number of followers gained per transmission.

In order to do so, the tools used in the course were Google Colab and Jupyter Notebook which have easy to use interfaces that allow users to combine code with narrative text and visualizations [3]. The ease of use and low technical requirements were crucial for students to engage and understand code in a systematic manner. Their open-source nature and widespread adoption make it an essential tool for teaching data storytelling, and the ability to work either online or offline allowed the students to test their visualizations on various devices aside from the classroom's lab (Fig. 2).

Similar teaching strategies have been developed in order to teach interactive visual tools for high school students, demonstrating the importance of early exposure to data science concepts [4]. This approach aligns with the need to introduce communication students to data visualization early in their education. By using visual analytics, they made complex topics like machine learning more accessible, highlighting the potential for similar tools in higher education settings.

Teaching data storytelling is a challenging task, particularly due to the need for proficiency in programming. Other experiences suggest that starting with GUI-based tools before progressing to programming can help students gradually build their skills [5]. This step-by-step approach is beneficial for communication students who may initially

Fig. 2. The interface of Google Colab allows students to not only comment their code but to format text and insert images or videos. A student explores sexists remarks found on social media accounts of Peruvian newspapers. She explains her objectives, comments her codes and develops a narrative throughout the "code notebook".

find programming daunting. At the same time, integrating data visualization and info-graphics into visual communication design education is of utmost importance, since these skills enhance the ability to discern patterns in complex information [6], making it a valuable skill for any professional. Visual representations of data can make patterns and relationships more apparent, a principle that can be applied to various fields [7], including Communications.

The ability to showcase data is often associated solely with the use of statistics, but teaching data storytelling implies deconstructing and reconstructing plots and creating interactive visualizations [8], which can then be adapted to multidisciplinary curricula to enhance students' understanding and application of data storytelling principles. Learning these skills requires hands-on pedagogic approach and practical experience in order to significantly enhance students' competence and confidence in this area [9], thought having a clear objective of what to showcase is of utmost importance when creating data storytelling projects.

There are several viable frameworks; some segment narrative visualization in gen-res such as the martini glass, interactive slideshow, and drill-down story [10]. Balance between author-driven and reader-driven elements must be maintained to create engaging data stories that allow for both structured narratives and interactive exploration. Alter-native visual-narrative interfaces improve the communication of student data insights, they can support teacher reflection and enhance student engagement [11], particularly when employing a narrative approach to interactive information visualization in digital humanities education [12]. By focusing on narrative construction, students can connect humanistic values with data visualization techniques. By producing their own interactive visualizations they simultaneously empower their technical skills and their storytelling [13], which in turn makes the learning process more engaging and meaningful [14].

The former is particularly relevant for each of the student's disciplines. For example, those focused on publicity can learn to apply data storytelling in business and form effective communication of data insights to stakeholders. A "data storytelling cheat sheet" [15] offers practical guidelines for rapid decisions in marketing, especially when dealing with user engagement, since narrative elements can significantly enhance users' motivation to explore and understand data [16]. This is true for other disciplines as well, such as government data for social development students and data from audiences for those working either in audiovisual communication or journalism. The students were able to find relevant uses of data storytelling to suit their needs. This showcases the importance of finding professional uses for the aforementioned skills.

On that note, recent works have put emphasis on the narrative potential of data visualization by demonstrating how combining data analysis with storytelling techniques can make complex information more accessible and engaging [17], though there still is a need to create comprehensive curricula that integrate both storytelling and visualization techniques for communication students [18]. Interactive storytelling can enhance online course design by making learning experiences more engaging and personalized, which can improve student interest and retention in both offline and online courses [19].

The fact is, data storytelling enhances the efficiency and effectiveness of information retrieval and comprehension [20], but to be able to do so, educators must identify key principles and design elements that provide a foundation for developing effective data storytelling curricula [21], which also means ascribing to one of the different types of data storytelling frameworks available in hopes to teach students to effectively convey data-driven insights [22]. New forms of Data Storytelling are not just limited to Dashboards or static graphics, they can be used in interactive documentaries, which reveals how narrative structures and multimedia elements can be integrated to create compelling data stories [23].

This coincides with the evolution of techniques that transform data, from static to dynamic [24]. The latter has become a trend in user-experience-based models for narrative data exploration, particularly in data journalism, which reveals a key component of contemporary Data Storytelling: the principle of designing user-centered data stories [25]. This means that educators must learn a broad scope of knowledge that includes user experience, data analytics, programming and learning analytics; all in order to meet the demands of students used to interact with data on their phones without knowing their operational principles [26]. A multidisciplinary field is created when the technical skills meet the narrative structures that would allow students to create the graphics and program their interactions [27]. They however, need to understand the data and most importantly, how to tell a compelling story with it.

2 Materials and Methods

The 16 week course called "Computational Thinking for Communications" dedicates 1 h to explore theoretical aspects and 2 h to practice python and the use of public databases. Each course had a dedicated assistant teacher for the practical segment. The sample size comprised of 50 students split equally among two courses. Students were asked to work in pairs to create a data storytelling project related to their respective areas of interest (Audiovisual, Social Development, Publicity, and Journalism) (Fig. 3).

They employed datasets from open sources such as the Peruvian Government, Google Trends, Amazon Open Data, and created their projects using Google Colab or Jupyter

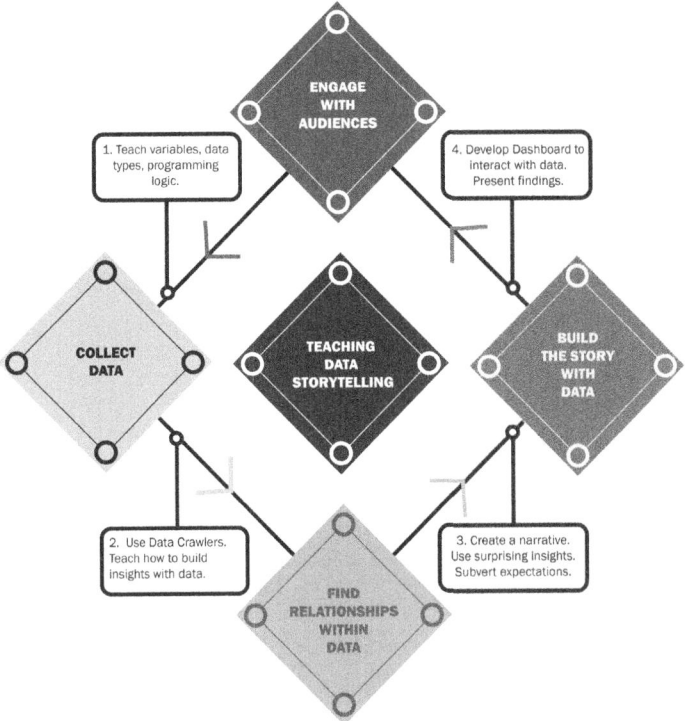

Fig. 3. A flow chart that summarizes the teaching methodology.

Notebook depending on whether they wanted to use more complex libraries such as GeoPandas to create Interactive Maps. These projects were then uploaded to their respective GitHub repository, and using the Python Streamlit library, students developed interactive data visualization notebooks, which also narrated why their chosen topic was of interest to communication studies.

All students were interviewed using semi-structured interviews to explore their experiences, learning outcomes, and motivations. The interviews aimed to gather detailed insights from their perspectives on the course and their data storytelling projects. The semi-structured interview format allowed for flexibility in responses, providing a comprehensive understanding of the students' experiences [28–30]. The methodology for this study was recorded through photos, audio, and field notes, adhering to the Systematization of Experiences methodology [31–33]. This approach facilitated the systematic documentation and analysis of the educational practices observed during the course, contributing to knowledge production and educational innovation. Student motivation was a key focus of the study. Factors influencing motivation were examined from both students' and teachers' perspectives [34, 35]. Understanding these factors provided insights into how the course design and implementation affected students' engagement and learning outcomes.

3   Results and Discussion

Students discovered that coding and computational thinking are integral parts of communications, enhancing their analytical skills and making them more valuable in the job market. For instance, E1 (2024) stated that: "I discovered that coding is also part of communications, and with programming, we can have a data analysis tool that makes us more valuable in the job market". This realization motivated students to engage more deeply with the course material, as they saw the practical benefits of integrating computational skills into their communication careers (Fig. 4).

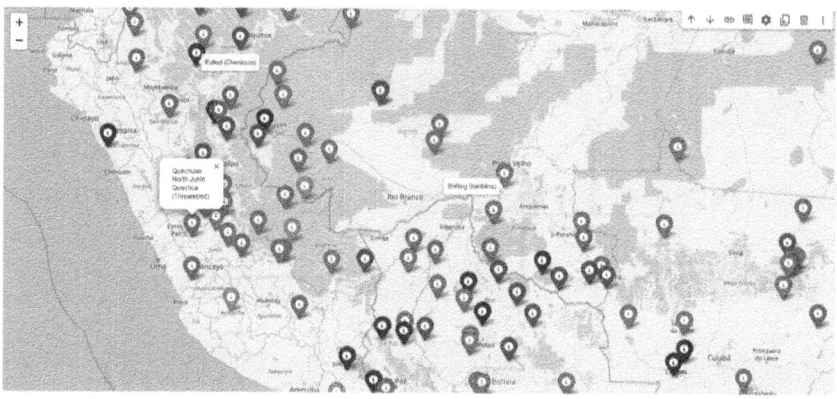

Fig. 4. A student programmed an interactive map to showcase endangered indigenous languages across Latin America using publicly available data.

Students appreciated the course's role in helping them become more proficient in digital communication, recognizing its importance for future career prospects. Another student expressed, "I now understand programming as a tool to filter and summarize information and research" (E2, 2024). This newfound understanding underscored the relevance of computational thinking in solving modern communication problems. The course also helped students see the broader applications of these skills in their respective fields, such as journalism, advertising, and communication for development. It's important to note that their experiences varied significantly, but, in spite of these challenges, several students developed patience, perseverance, and the ability to learn programming basics, particularly in creating data visualizations and automating tasks using Python. A student stated that: "My biggest challenge was facing the world of programming, which is something that never caught my attention. I overcame it by paying close attention and trying to overcome each challenge with patience, focusing on the process instead of the results" (E24, 2024). This sentiment was echoed by others who felt that the course helped them build resilience and problem-solving skills (Fig. 5).

The hands-on projects, where students created interactive visualizations, were particularly beneficial in helping them grasp the practical applications of their learning. One student stated, "I learned to create at least charts in Jupyter Notebook" (E5, 2024). However, many students felt that the course could benefit from a more coherent alignment between theoretical and practical sessions, as well as additional support during the

Mapa de Densidad Poblacional de los casos de dengue en Perú (2019 - 2024)

Importante: El año 2024 cuenta con datos registrados hast la semana epidemiológica 10.

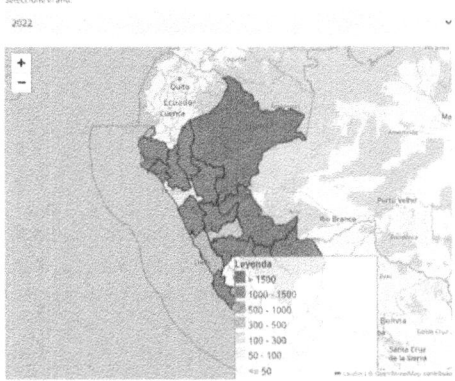

⌄ RESULTADOS OBTENIDOS

A continuación, se realizará un pie chart de los resultados en cojunto (de los tv fue la percepción en estas dos partes analizadas

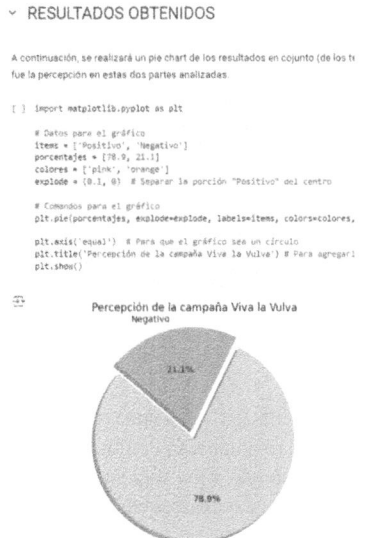

Fig. 5. On the left, a student created a map that showcases the cases of Dengue Fever by Province in Peru, challenging the idea that highly populated areas such as the capital had the most amount of cases. On the right, a student applies sentiment analysis to a highly controversial sexual education campaign called *Viva the Vulva*. They demonstrated, that despite the numerous detractors, it had a positive reception.

transition to new platforms. For example, a student mentioned, "The course should be consistent between theory and practice, and the final project should not be worth 50% as it is the first project many students do by themselves using Python" (E6, 2024).

Several key challenges emerged from the students' feedback. The primary difficulties included understanding and applying programming concepts, especially without immediate support. One student pointed out, "The biggest difficulty was running codes without the teacher's help and without the documents that exemplified what we had to do" (E7, 2024). The lack of coherence between theoretical lectures and practical sessions made it difficult for some students to connect the dots. Additionally, for some, shifting between online programming (Google Colab) and offline (Jupyter Notebook) posed significant challenges when converting.ipy to.ipynb files.

Students also highlighted the struggle with specific programming tasks, such as working with loops, creating visualizations, and using various libraries like Geopandas and Streamlit. These tasks often required extra support from teaching assistants or external resources. E15 shared: "I had difficulty with loops and creating graphics, the web design was not as complicated, but following the steps to build the web page and handling other platforms like Streamlit, and GitHub was challenging" (E9). The workload and the pace of the course were also points of concern, with students suggesting a need for more practical, interactive exercises and a slower introduction to complex topics. For instance, one student suggested, "The theoretical class should also be in the computer lab and serve to teach us the codes and help us with that as well" (E10) (Fig. 6).

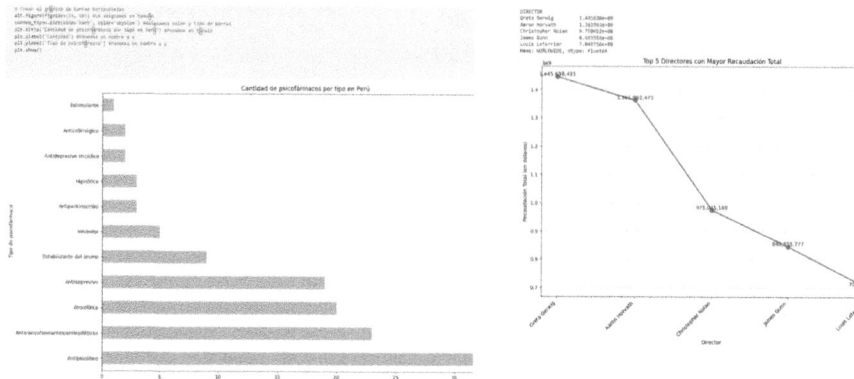

Fig. 6. On the left, a Social Development students works exposes the limited types of psychopharmaceuticals available in Peru for the treatment of mental health issues, while on the right, Audiovisual Communication students rank film directors of the highest grossing films, revealing that a female director outperformed her male peers.

Students offered several suggestions to enhance the course. They recommended a more integrated approach where theoretical and practical lessons are better aligned, and theoretical classes include practical coding exercises. Increasing the number of teaching assistants could provide more individualized support, especially during practical sessions. A student suggested, "I think it is necessary to add another TA because it is a new course for everyone" (E11). Additionally, students suggested dedicating more time to foundational topics before advancing to complex projects, and incorporating more real-world examples relevant to their disciplines.

4   Discussion

Aligning educational practices with the evolving demands of digital communication is of utmost importance. The ease of use of Jupyter Notebook for data storytelling is reflected in the students' appreciation of coding as an integral part of their communication skills [3], particularly the incorporation of storytelling and data visualization techniques [18]. Students were challenged when bridging theoretical knowledge with practical application [19], since they previously thought that "databases have no story to tell" (E42, 2024).

They struggled to understand and apply programming concepts, particularly when transitioning between platforms. Even if data storytelling enhances information retrieval and comprehension, it does not fully soften the steep learning curve associated with programming tools [20]. Aligning theoretical and practical components to develop effective data storytelling curricula becomes a must [21]. Students need supportive learning environments for mastering complex skills [22]. They ask for a more integrated approach to teaching and the inclusion of practical coding exercises within theoretical classes, which indicate a need for gradual skill development and practical application [24]. Moreover, they desire more real-world examples and dynamic teaching methods aligns with interactive and friendly interfaces, which stresses the importance of user-centered design in creating effective data stories [25]. The former implies adding more practical and interactive exercises that would improve teaching strategies to address different learning modes and features [27]. Some recommendations:

- Provide clear application cases relevant to the students discipline when teaching theoretical concepts.
- Limit the number of programming environments taught or use those that have similar interfaces in order to translate the skills more easily.
- Grade the class based on progress on the projects to motivate students.
- Have enough personnel to guide groups of students while they advance on their projects.

5   Conclusions

This study explored the implementation and outcomes of a data storytelling course for communication students, highlighting the integration of computational thinking and programming skills into communication education. The findings reveal that while students recognize the value of coding and data visualization in their field, they face significant challenges in bridging theoretical concepts with practical applications. The necessity for better alignment between theoretical and practical components, more dynamic teaching methods, and increased support was evident from the student feedback.

Results are consistent with the literature, accentuating the importance of interactive and user-centered approaches in teaching data storytelling. The integration of Data Storytelling not only enhances students' analytical capabilities but also prepares them for the evolving demands of the digital communication landscape. However, the study also highlighted the steep learning curve and the need for more coherent and supportive educational practices to facilitate this integration effectively. One limitation is the relatively small sample size of 50 students, and the feedback gathered through interviews may be subject to personal biases and varying levels of engagement with the course material. Another limitation is the potential variability in teaching quality and resources across different classrooms, which could influence students' experiences and learning outcomes.

This work is currently in progress, with plans to assess the course with over 100 new students in the coming academic terms. This expanded evaluation will provide a broader understanding of the course's impact and help refine the curriculum to better meet the needs of communication students. The ongoing assessment aims to address the identified challenges and enhance the effectiveness of integrating Data Storytelling into communication education. Future research will focus on developing more cohesive and supportive educational frameworks that facilitate the practical application of theoretical concepts, ensuring that students are well-prepared for the demands of digital communication.

Disclosure of Interests.   The authors have no competing interests to declare that are relevant to the content of this article.

References

1. Matei, S.A., Hunter, L.: Data storytelling is not storytelling with data: a framework for storytelling in science communication and data journalism. Inf. Soc. **37**(5), 312–322 (2021)
2. Li, H., Wang, Y., Qu, H.: Where are we so far? Understanding data storytelling tools from the perspective of human-AI collaboration. In: Proceedings of the CHI Conference on Human Factors in Computing Systems, pp. 1–19 (2024)
3. Granger, B.E., Pérez, F.: Jupyter: thinking and storytelling with code and data. Comput. Sci. Eng. **23**(2), 7–14 (2021)
4. Chittora, S., Baynes, A.: Interactive visualizations to introduce data science for high school students. In: Proceedings of the 21st Annual Conference on Information Technology Education, pp. 236–241 (2020)
5. Lo, L.Y.-H., Ming, Y., Qu, H.: Learning vis tools: teaching data visualization tutorials. In: 2019 IEEE Visualization Conference (VIS), pp. 11–15. IEEE, Vancouver (2019)
6. Dur, B.I.U.: Data visualization and infographics in visual communication design education at the age of information. J. Arts Humanit. **3**(5), 39–50 (2014)
7. Archambault, S.G., Helouvry, J., Strohl, B., Williams, G.: Data visualization as a communication tool. Library Hi Tech News **32**(2), 1–9 (2015)
8. Nolan, D., Perrett, J.: Teaching and learning data visualization: ideas and assignments. Am. Stat. **70**(3), 260–269 (2016)
9. Asamoah, D.: Improving data visualization skills: a curriculum design. Int. J. Educ. Dev. Using Inf. Commun. Technol. **18**(1), 213–235 (2022)
10. Segel, E., Heer, J.: Narrative visualization: telling stories with data. IEEE Trans. Visual Comput. Graphics **16**(6), 1139–1148 (2010)
11. Fernandez Nieto, G.M., Kitto, K., Buckingham Shum, S., Martinez-Maldonado, R.: Beyond the learning analytics dashboard: alternative ways to communicate student data insights combining visualisation, narrative and storytelling. In: LAK22: 12th International Learning Analytics and Knowledge Conference, pp. 219–229 (2022)
12. Stephens, S.H.: A narrative approach to interactive information visualization in the digital humanities classroom. Arts Humanit. High. Educ. **18**(4), 416–429 (2019)
13. Stenliden, L., Bodén, U., Nissen, J.: Students as producers of interactive data visualizations—Digitally skilled to make their voices heard. J. Res. Technol. Educ. **51**(2), 101–117 (2019)
14. Echeverria, V., Martinez-Maldonado, R., Buckingham Shum, S.: Towards data storytelling to support teaching and learning. In: Proceedings of the 29th Australian Conference on Computer-Human Interaction, pp. 347–351 (2017)
15. Oberascher, L., Ploder, C., Spiess, J., Bernsteiner, R., Van Kooten, W.: Data storytelling to communicate big data internally - a guide for practical usage. Eur. J. Manage. Issues **31**(1), 27–39 (2023)
16. Boy, J., Detienne, F., Fekete, J.D.: Storytelling in information visualizations: does it engage users to explore data? In: Proceedings of the 33rd Annual ACM Conference on Human Factors in Computing Systems, pp. 1449–1458 (2015)
17. Rodríguez, M.T., Nunes, S., Devezas, T.: Telling stories with data visualization. In: Proceedings of the 2015 Workshop on Narrative & Hypertext, pp. 7–11 (2015)
18. Tong, C., et al.: Storytelling and visualization: an extended survey. Information **9**(3), 65 (2018)
19. Baldwin, S., Ching, Y.H.: Interactive storytelling: opportunities for online course design. TechTrends **61**, 179–186 (2017)
20. Shao, H., Martinez-Maldonado, R., Echeverria, V., Yan, L., Gasevic, D.: Data storytelling in data visualisation: does it enhance the efficiency and effectiveness of information retrieval and insights comprehension? In: Proceedings of the CHI Conference on Human Factors in Computing Systems, pp. 1–21 (2024)

21. Sarica, H.C., Yildirim, D.: Data storytelling in education: a systematic review. In: INTED2024 Proceedings, pp. 6990–6997 (2024)
22. Gagnon, E., McKeen-Edwards, H., Atanasiadis, R.: Lost in translation: how data storytelling helps make sense of data. (2024)
23. López-Lozano, A., Herrero-Solana, V., Martínez, D.S.M.: Interactive documentary and data visualization: new approaches to telling stories with data. VISUAL REVIEW. International Visual Culture Review/Revista Internacional de Cultura Visual **16**(1), 59–86 (2024)
24. Rathod, Y.: Understanding the evolution of data visualization techniques: from static to dynamic visualizations. Int. J. Adv. Res. Comput. Commun. Eng. **13**(2), 99–103 (2024)
25. Cao, S., Chen, Q., Cao, N.: Visual narrative for data journalism based on user experience. J. Vis. **27**, 1–17 (2024)
26. Milesi, M.E., Martinez-Maldonado, R.: Data storytelling in learning analytics? A qualitative investigation into educators' perceptions of benefits and risks. In: Proceedings of the 14th Learning Analytics and Knowledge Conference, pp. 167–177 (2024)
27. Kemble, K.A., Wilkerson, M.H.: Storytelling with and about data: mapping the terrain. In: Proceedings of the 18th International Conference of the Learning Sciences-ICLS 2024, pp. 1838–1841. International Society of the Learning Sciences (2024)
28. Adeoye-Olatunde, O.A., Olenik, N.L.: Research and scholarly methods: semi-structured interviews. J. Am. Coll. Clin. Pharm. **4**(10), 1358–1367 (2021)
29. Knott, E., Rao, A.H., Summers, K., Teeger, C.: Interviews in the social sciences. Nat. Rev. Methods Primers **2**(1), 73 (2022)
30. Nassaji, H.: Good qualitative research. Lang. Teach. Res. **24**(4), 427–431 (2020)
31. Fuentes, C.P.: Systematization of experiences as a methodology for knowledge production for educational practice in cross-border territories. In: Exploring Educational Equity at the Intersection of Policy and Practice, pp. 212–226. IGI Global (2024)
32. Torres Carrillo, A.: Generating knowledge in popular education: from participatory research to the systematization of experiences. Int. J. Action Res. **6**(2–3), 196–222 (2010)
33. Portuguez-Castro, M.: Mentoring in educational innovation: systematization in the experience of teachers' educational experimentation and research. In: International Conference on Technological Ecosystems for Enhancing Multiculturality, pp. 838–849. Springer, Singapore (2022)
34. Ciampa, K.: Learning in a mobile age: an investigation of student motivation. J. Comput. Assist. Learn. **30**(1), 82–96 (2014)
35. Boström, L., Bostedt, G.: What about study motivation? Students and teachers' perspectives on what affects study motivation. Int. J. Learn. Teach. Educ. Res. **19**(8), 40–59 (2020)

El Centro (The Downtown): A Collaborative Transmedia Project Among Ibero-American Universities

Iliana Ferrer[1] ⓘ and Alejandro Ángel-Torres[2](✉)

[1] Universitat Autònoma de Barcelona, Carrer de la Vinya, s/n, 08193 Bellaterra, Barcelona, Spain
iliana.ferrer@uab.cat
[2] University of Bogota Jorge Tadeo Lozano UTADEO, Cra. 4 #22-61, Bogota, Colombia
alejandro.angelt@utadeo.edu.co

Abstract. "El Centro" (The Downtown) is an inter-university collaborative transmedia project. This collective experiment of transmedia non-fiction narratives in Ibero-America seeks to innovate in the teaching of audiovisual languages and transmedia narratives in communication-related degrees, through the creation of multiformat content by undergraduate students from the Universitat Autònoma de Barcelona in Spain, Universidad Jorge Tadeo Lozano in Bogotá, Universidad Panamericana in Mexico City, and Universidad Internacional de Ecuador in Quito. Using Project-Based Learning (PBL), students worked in multidisciplinary teams to produce nonfiction narratives that expand across various platforms and formats. This approach encourages the practical application of theoretical principles, the development of critical thinking, and the acquisition of skills in conventional and emerging technologies. Creative expression, teamwork, and cultural exchange were also encouraged. The content produced by the students will be disseminated in university media and other platforms (websites, social networks, events, etc.).

Keywords: Transmedia · IberoAmerica · Teaching Innovation Project · Collaborative Work · Expanded Documentary · Interactive Documentary · University · Undergraduate

1 Introduction

Cities are spaces of analog, digital, global, and nomadic convergence for their inhabitants, serving as meeting points that host diverse perspectives. Whether historical or administrative, city centers function as the foundational core and starting point for the city and its residents.

In our digital age, technological tools facilitate asynchronous exploration of urban perceptions and imaginaries, presenting an opportunity to develop content, formats, and platforms that capture the essence of city centers at specific moments. These contents can serve as references for understanding each city's historical, cultural, and social

J. T. Murray and M. C. Reyes (Eds.): ICIDS 2024, LNCS 15468, pp. 186–195, 2025.
https://doi.org/10.1007/978-3-031-78450-7_12

dimensions. Ibero-America's contemporary city life is characterized by complex and multifaceted urban experiences.

As a response to these urban and technological advancements, innovative educational approaches have emerged in the field of communication. In this context of urban exploration, the project "El Centro" (The Downtown) emerges as a collective experiment in transmedia narratives focused on the downtown of four Ibero-American cities: Barcelona, Bogota, Mexico City, and Quito. This project, grounded in the principles of Project-Based Learning (PBL) aimed to engage undergraduate students in the creation of transmedia narratives. "El Centro" (The Downtown) is a collaborative work among four Ibero-American universities: the Universitat Autònoma de Barcelona (UAB) in Spain, Universidad de Bogotá Jorge Tadeo Lozano in Colombia, Universidad Panamericana in Mexico, and Universidad Internacional de Ecuador in Ecuador.

The project is structured around a research, teaching, and co-creation framework that documents the history, architecture, traditions, characters, streets, and personal experiences that build the identity of each city's center. By employing a multifaceted and experiential narrative approach, this project seeks to foster the practical application of theoretical principles, the development of critical thinking, and the acquisition of skills in emerging technologies.

1.1 Transmedia Narratives and Collaborative Projects

Transmedia, expanded, multiformat, and multiplatform narratives are key concepts in the evolution of storytelling in the contemporary media environment. Henry Jenkins [1], in Convergence Culture, coined the term "transmedia" to describe narratives that unfold across various platforms, allowing audience participation in the construction of stories. Gomez [2] further emphasized the importance of expanded narratives, which transcend the central story to explore and enrich the narrative universe, fostering a deeper immersion in the storytelling experience.

Regarding multiformat narratives, Ryan [3], in Narrative as Virtual Reality, examined how the convergence of different media forms contributes to the creation of complex and immersive experiences. Moreover, Scolari [4], in Narrativas Transmedia, focused on multiplatform narratives, highlighting the importance of adapting and expanding stories across various digital technologies and platforms, encouraging interactivity and co-creation by the audience.

Other traditional theorists also contributed to this conceptual framework. Roland Barthes [5], with S/Z, introduced the notion of transmedia narrative through his analysis of text decomposition into semiotic units. Umberto Eco [6], in Lector in Fabula, discussed the active participation of readers and the expansion of meanings, aligning with the concept of expanded narratives. Additionally, McLuhan [7], in Understanding Media, suggested that the medium is the message, contributing to the understanding of multiformat and multiplatform narratives, where the choice of medium significantly influences the narrative experience.

Contemporary approaches emphasize the complexity and adaptability of storytelling within the modern media environment. Integrating different narrative approaches in projects exploring everyday life in geographical spaces, such as city centers, offers an opportunity to transform how urban experiences are understood and shared. These narratives provide a more comprehensive and participatory approach, capturing the complexity and diversity of urban settings.

Gifreu [8] defined the interactive documentary as a representational and interactive environment that facilitates the exploration of new narrative forms. This concept envisions narratives as settings that accommodate multiple formats, platforms, and interactions between viewers and creators. Building on this idea of interactive narratives, Irigaray [9] emphasized that in a context marked by fragmentation, hypervelocity, and a culture focused on the ephemeral, the concept of space is redefined. Urban space transcends its role as merely a physical support; it becomes a scenario where individuals, social practices, and symbolic representations of the city converge.

By adopting transmedia narratives, "El Centro" (The Downtown) project emerges as an innovative application of transmedia storytelling. The project utilizes a variety of media, from videos and photographs to blogs and social media, to tell stories across different platforms, enabling a deeper immersion in urban life. Disseminating narratives across multiple platforms amplifies the project's reach, engaging diverse audiences and catering to different media consumption preferences. From social media to real-life events, these narratives become accessible to a broader range of people, contributing to the construction of both a digital and physical community around the city center's narrative.

Collaborative work has historically been central in projects based on expanded narratives and transmedia such as the popular *Life in a Day* [11] (2010), *The Jhonny Cash Project* [12] (2010), and *Star Wars Uncut* [13] (2013). Other recent examples developed during the COVID-19 pandemic, e.g. *Corona Haikus Project* [14] (2021), *Corona Diaries* [15] (2021), or *El Abecedario del coronavirus* [16] (2021), have shown the power of collaborative creations in which viewers become narrators of their own stories, incorporating their own aesthetic and even ethical constructs. Although these projects are centered on transmedia narratives, the field of digital, convergent, immersive, and interactive storytelling has been rapidly evolving driven by the pace of new narrative formats. It is relevant now to expand the focus to include collaborative concepts like "post-digital storytelling". As Jordan [10] states, in today's digital age, stories exist in a hybrid space that blends digital and non-digital elements. This shift encourages collective and interdisciplinary storytelling, where collaboration across different formats and perspectives shape narratives that transcend traditional boundaries between the physical and the online.

2 Project Aim and Methodology

2.1 Presentation

This article presents a case study that serves as a pilot test for a research/teaching innovation project titled "El Centro" (The Downtown), which started in September 2023. "El Centro" (The Downtown) is a collaborative transmedia initiative involving undergraduate students and faculty members from Journalism, Communication, and Filmmaking programs at four Ibero-American universities: Universitat Autònoma de

Barcelona in Spain; Universidad Jorge Tadeo Lozano in Bogota, Colombia; Universidad Panamericana in Mexico City, Mexico; and Universidad Internacional de Ecuador in Quito.

Students worked in multidisciplinary teams to produce non-fiction content about Ibero-America, exploring various formats, narrative trends, and platforms. The project's multidisciplinary approach and the cultural diversity of its participants aimed to develop professional and communication skills, as well as foster cultural exchange.

While the transmedia strategy functioned as the backbone of the project, another pillar of this pilot test was collaborative work. This peer learning model encouraged active collaboration among participants, facilitating a constant exchange of ideas, experiences, and perspectives. This process ensured that the resulting narrative was an expression of collective and diverse identities enabling participants with different skills to work together.

The project serves as a platform for introducing students to the creation of multiformat pieces with outcomes that are easily distributable and useful for their professional portfolios. Thus, the general objective of this project is to:

Produce collaboratively transmedia content involving multidisciplinary students from four Ibero-American universities, applying their knowledge of audiovisual language to generate non-fiction narratives in various formats and/or through emerging technologies. For this pilot test, the narrative focus was on "El Centro" (The Downtown) of the cities and its characters, places, trades, and other similar themes.

The specific objectives are to:

- Co-create tangible transmedia communication pieces that showcase the diverse perspectives of the groups involved in the project.
- Motivate the exploration and analysis of communication production routines, allowing students to adapt theoretical learning to real-world contexts.
- Encourage creative expression among participants in a culturally diverse environment.
- Promote the acquisition of skills in multiformat communication, transmedia storytelling, and professional, inclusive, and collaborative interdisciplinary teamwork.
- Experiment with new formats and trends to generate original approaches for engaging audiences and creators with their cultural environment.
- Develop alternative strategies for the distribution and promotion of the transmedia products created by the participants.
- Evaluate the collaborative process of creating, producing, and promoting multiformat transmedia content, along with their outcomes.

2.2 Methodology

The methodology employed is Project-Based Learning (PBL). This approach facilitated the practical application of theoretical principles, the development of critical thinking, creative expression, collaborative work, cultural exchange, and the acquisition of skills needed to address the challenges of professional work.

The project design was also collaboratively developed by the participating faculty members. The first step was to draft a guide for students containing key information for the project's execution: introduction, conceptual framework, background, objectives, generalities, methodology, deliverables, schedule, references (content and formats), potential stories or themes, current trends, working groups, and contact information.

The required deliverables were:

- Narrative content: three formats per group, with unrestricted length, chosen from the provided examples and references or other ideas or explorations.
- A making-of video (maximum 90 seconds) and/or production photos (maximum 20).
- A written dossier of 3 to 5 pages including a) Justification of the topic, chosen formats, and project name; b) Information sources consulted, credits for external material (music, images, videos by other creators), and references to the use of Artificial Intelligence (AI), if used; c) Credits of participants (names, roles, social networks); d) Group and individual self-assessment of the final project; e) General evaluation of the collaborative international project: suggestions, comments, ideas for future editions, etc.
- Optional: Promotion materials, such as poster, trailer, technical sheet, etc.

The work plan of the pilot test was divided into different phases:

a) Theoretical concepts in the form of lectures, including audiovisual and multimedia languages, new expanded narratives, formats and references, current trends, etc.
b) Project planning as autonomous work. In this phase, the students were distributed into inter-university groups. WhatsApp was used as a communication channel into the groups, and a general group was created for disseminating important information to students and faculty. After forming the working groups, students were asked to design their internal collective work routines, distribute roles, and establish alternative communication channels, if necessary. Their first task was to select the theme, which involved deciding how they wanted to approach the city center, identifying potential characters, audiovisual and aesthetic references, and formats they would develop. Participants were asked to ensure their thematic proposals generated dialogues and interconnections between the four cities.

The next step was to produce an initial pitch presenting the theme, viewpoint, references, and proposed formats for each group. This initial pitch, in video, involved students from all four cities, and had a maximum duration of 5 min. Videos were shared through the general WhatsApp channel. Faculty provided each group with initial feedback on chosen themes, formats and references to guide their projects.

c) Project production and faculty tutorials. Each team was responsible for researching and gathering information on the chosen theme, as well as planning production according to the proposed formats, considering peer and faculty feedback.

During the pieces' production and post-production, students attended tutorials with faculty. Before the final submission, each group had to share the first version of their products for the three required formats. Faculty then provided individual written feedback on the completed formats. After receiving feedback, each team had approximately two weeks to make changes and incorporate suggestions. Additional tutorials with faculty were offered at any stage of the production process.

d) Evaluation and Distribution. Each team submitted the final version of their products along with a written dossier that included group and individual participation assessments and an evaluation of the project. They also presented a final pitch, discussing the pieces delivered, objectives, and impact goals achieved. The making of materials (photos or videos) created during the production process were also presented, along with the necessary documentation for content distribution, e.g. Image rights assignment agreements and intellectual property rights agreements in contributions related to academic activities. The students who approved the distribution of their content, also assigned a Creative Commons BY-NC-SA 4.0 license to their products to promote their circulation. This license allows anyone to use the content provided giving the appropriate credit, and it cannot be used for commercial purposes. Students were encouraged to use materials with the same type of license in their group projects

In this evaluation phase, group interviews with students were conducted to gather feedback on the project's strengths and weaknesses and learning outcomes.

Regarding distribution (which is still in the initial phase as this pilot test is not yet complete), some of the faculty members will curate the products and thematic axes. Following this selection, a distribution campaign for the content will be executed through the participating universities' media, the project's website and social media, and other platforms.

3   Preliminary Results

This section presents an overview of the initial findings extracted from some of the pieces delivered, group interviews, and written feedback provided by the participants.

A total of 5 faculty members and 127 students participated in the project divided into 10 working groups. 32 audiovisual pieces were produced in 17 different formats, including photographs (Fig. 1), illustrations, magazines, audiovisual reports, podcasts, soundscapes, experimental videos, short documentaries, interactive maps, and social media content, among others. The entire process was documented through photographs, making of videos, pitches, written self-evaluation documents (both group and individual), and project assessments.

Some of the qualitative outcomes have been identified:

– Participants produced transmedia content applying theoretical concepts through real-world experiences, addressing typical professional scenarios. The selected topics encompassed both global and local relevance expressed through diverse formats.
– Students demonstrated transmedia competencies, skills in research, production planning, filming, post-production, and understanding of audiovisual languages. This progress laid the groundwork for the creation of each student's professional portfolio, registering their produced multimedia content as tangible evidence of their capabilities.
– The experience of international collaborative work and cultural exchange. Each group included at least 2–3 members from each participating university, except for Mexico City, which had only one member per group.
– Participants strengthened skills, such as problem-solving, leadership, effective communication, and inclusive environments.

- Students demonstrated an increased motivation to participate in an innovative international project.
- The project facilitated critical reflection on topics such as the Sustainable Development Goals (SDGs), equity, and social and environmental sustainability.
- Participants experimented with innovative formats and emerging technologies, creating multimedia products beyond traditional radio and television. This experimentation is relevant for the current audiovisual industry, where a multimedia strategy is essential.
- Participants faced real-world challenges, such as interviewing subjects, managing production issues, and demonstrating flexibility, thereby strengthening their attitude and confidence as future professionals in the communication areas.

Alongside the creative production process, the thematic exploration of urban centers revealed key cultural and social elements. All the pieces created are connected by the same theme: the downtown areas of the cities. Initial findings suggest frequent subthemes such as architecture, traditional trades, street music, and street art. Issues like gentrification, market activities, landmark sites, and tourism offer a multifaceted view of these urban environments. Themes such as nocturnal workers and urban legends emerged to shape the identity of these areas. This thematic diversity enriches the development of transmedia narratives that capture and communicate urban experiences innovatively.

However, through group interviews and written evaluations, participants also highlighted several areas for improvement in the project. They expressed the need for enhanced communication channels and strategies between groups to improve collaboration and information sharing. Suggestions included smaller group sizes to facilitate individual contributions within each team.

Participants recommended more frequent and mandatory tutoring sessions conducted by faculty members to provide guidance throughout the project phases. Moreover, a longer timeframe for developing and adjusting multimedia formats was suggested.

Fig. 1. Images from the photo report titled INITIUM, created by UAB Journalism students Martina García, Arnau Escobar, and Sergi Félez. The report aimed to recognize the people who bring life to the center of Barcelona.

There is still significant work to be done in refining the concept of collaboration, particularly in projects that incorporate real-time and international participation, dissemination of results, and curatorial processes. Additionally, the multidisciplinary and multiregional composition of the faculty team added complexity to the project. Future collaborations should explore strategies to achieve more seamless, organic, and organized outcomes.

Finally, after a first revision of the delivered pieces, faculty members agreed on the need to enhance the technical execution, narrative coherence, and visual aesthetics in future iterations of the project.

4   Future Work

While we continue extracting the main results of the transmedia pieces produced, further qualitative analysis (i.e., quality of the audiovisual products in terms of narrative coherence, technical execution, adherence to transmedia principles, challenges faced during the project) is still needed to fully interpret the findings and apply them to future editions of the project. The creative outputs generated during this pilot test will be disseminated through university media channels and other platforms, including websites, social media, and public events. Most of the offline content produced is planned to be exhibited in the participating universities highlighting the innovative teaching approach in communication-related degrees (Fig. 2). These preliminary results highlight the project's potential to transform the educational landscape by integrating transmedia narratives and collaborative methodologies into the curriculum.

In the short term, the project will advance in the process of publishing the material resulting from this pilot test in the platforms previously established in the project's background such as the project's website in Bogota, the project's new general website in process (Fig. 3) and the Instagram account (Fig. 3), as well as in new platforms under development based on the curatorship, reflection and new advances of the work carried out collaboratively.

Fig. 2. Images of the exhibition "Voces de la Ciudad" (Voices of the City) at the Faculty of Communication Studies at the Universitat Autònoma of Barcelona.

As an example of the collaborative work performed in universities in the region, we intend to outline the relevance of this transnational collaborative project produced and distributed by the Ibero-American students and faculty members. "El Centro" (The

Fig. 3. Examples of social media publications and the background of the project's website.

Downtown) represents a step forward in the teaching of audiovisual languages and transmedia narratives in communication-related degrees. By utilizing Project-Based Learning, the project has not only enhanced the educational experience for students but also prepared them to face the challenges in their careers. The emphasis on creative expression, teamwork, and cultural exchange has fostered a collaborative and innovative learning environment. As this project continues to evolve, its ultimate goal remains to improve educational quality and motivate students to adapt to the dynamic media labor market.

References

1. Jenkins, H.: Convergence Culture: Where Old and New Media Collide. NYU Press (2006)
2. Gomez, J.: Jeff Gomez´s "8 Defining Characteristics of Transmedia Production". FanTruste. (2007)
3. Ryan, M.L.: Narrative as Virtual Reality: Immersion and Interactivity in Literature and Electronic Media. Johns Hopkins University Press, USA (2001)
4. Scolari, C. A.: Narrativas transmedia: Cuando todos los medios cuentan (1.). Deusto (2013)
5. Barthes, R.: S/Z. Editions du Seuil (1970)
6. Eco, H.: Lector in Fabula. La cooperación interpretativa en el texto narrativo (1ra. ed.). Lumen (1981)
7. McLuhan, M.: Understanding media: the extensions of man (1st ed.). McGraw-Hill (1964)
8. Gifreu Castells, A.: El documental interactivo, una propuesta de modelo de análisis. Universitat Pompeu Fabra (2010)
9. Irigaray, F.: De los conceptos de espacio, territorio y lugar al de posterritorio. Territorialidad expandida en el ecosistema urbano. Transmídia Storytelling e complexidades narrativas, Ria Editorial (2021)
10. Jordan, S.: Postdigital Storytelling, Poetics, Praxis. Routledge, Research (2019)
11. Life in a Day (2010). https://www.youtube.com/watch?v=JaFVr_cJJIY. Accessed 10 Oct 2023
12. The Jhonny Cash Project (2010). https://www.radicalmedia.com/work/the-johnny-cash-pro ject. Accessed 10 Oct 2023
13. Star Wars Uncut (2013). https://www.starwarsuncut.com/. Accessed 10 Oct 2023
14. Corona Haikus Project (2021). https://immerse.news/the-corona-haikus-collaborative-pro ject-ee1d7f2bed4. Accessed 10 Oct 2023

15. Corona Diaries (2021). https://coronadiaries.io/. Accessed 10 Oct 2023
16. El Abecedario del coronavirus (2021). https://uab-documentalcreativo.es/produccion/abeced
ario-audiovisual-del-coronavirus. Accessed 10 Oct 2023

Subliminal Teaching for Elderly People Through Crossmedia Storytelling

Wolfgang Heiden$^{(\boxtimes)}$, Tea Kless, Veronika Saitova, Valeska Wegner, David Rötter, and Thomas Neteler

Bonn-Rhein-Sieg University of Applied Sciences, 53757 St. Augustin, Germany
wolfgang.heiden@h-brs.de

Abstract. Elderly people are among the most vulnerable groups in terms of their exposition to cyber threats in our increasingly digital society. While a large variety of IT services is available that could support especially their lives (e.g. related to health or mobility issues), out of a lack of self-efficacy they often tend to evade these services–including even those that aim at improving IT security-related competences. We present an infotainment approach to reach these people with relevant information and an encouraging message through crossmedia storytelling. First feedback from a user study including live readings as well as offline and online media provides strong hints that information integrated in a narrative primarily received for entertainment can percolate mental reservation against digital services and improve self-efficacy.

Keywords: Crossmedia Storytelling · Password Security · Vulnerable Groups · Hypermedia Novels

1 Introduction

IT[1] services penetrate human life at nearly every stage and in various ways. While many of these services can be very helpful, particularly for elderly people, there are also a lot of threats associated with internet-based services and tools. On one hand, it is important to be aware of these threats, on the other hand this awareness should not lead to retreat but rather trigger competent participation in the digital society.

Elderly people are one of several typically "vulnerable groups" with respect to cyber security. Different to most others, this group does usually not need raised awareness of cyber threats but rather empowerment to securely use IT services like home banking or online health services instead of refrain from these out of anxiety. One problem in reaching those people comes from their reluctance to seek advice or support. Just offering online information or workshops dedicated to teaching cyber security topics therefore often misses this group. Almost everyone, however, loves stories. The individual favorites may vary in genre or media type, but in one way or another, stories consumed for entertainment are attractive for virtually every human being. Information hidden in

---

[1] Information Technology.

J. T. Murray and M. C. Reyes (Eds.): ICIDS 2024, LNCS 15468, pp. 196–204, 2025.
https://doi.org/10.1007/978-3-031-78450-7_13

an entertaining context can thus be transported sublimely even to those who neglect all direct educational offers. There are many examples of "serious games" addressing this issue. The R&D[2] project CrossComITS (Crossmedia Community platform for teaching private IT-Security skills to vulnerable groups) [1] presents a crossmedia platform with modular content that offers information for different vulnerable groups, either via "security mediators" or directly through various information and infotainment channels. Within this project, we offer narrative-based infotainment material organized as a continuously growing Hypermedia Novel (HYMN) repository with personalization options including traditional as well as interactive narration modules. The results reported in this paper are those of an initial study with selected (non-digital) live events in order to learn how to best address the target group, raising their motivation and trust to later also access online material.

2   Background and Related Work

2.1   Target Group and Narrative Approach

Vulnerable Groups in Terms of Cyber Threats. There is a large heterogeneity among and within the so-called "vulnerable groups" related to cyber security issues. While some are not aware or voluntarily ignorant of the risks coming along with the use of manifold Internet-based services on home PCs, laptop computers, tablets or smartphones, others– especially elderly people–often rather tend to be too anxious to dare make use of any such services [1].

Password Security. Especially vulnerable people have issues with operating a password manager. It is important to keep a balance between security and memorability of passwords, which has been a topic of research for more than 20 years [2] and is still extended by new approaches, with using GenAI for password generation among the latest [3]. However, for persons with less affinity and trust to digital services, a human generated password [4] still feels much more comfortable.

Storytelling and Edutainment. Recent approaches have brought about the terms "edutainment" [5] and "infotainment", either related to a strong focus on a dedicated educational goal or a more open and wide-spread informational aim, respectively. Digital Storytelling in Edutainment has been proven useful in various environments [6] including academic teaching [7]. From the scientific viewpoint, however, it remains uncertain, in which context and under which conditions information embedded in narratives is more or less effective than transmitted directly, as the few studies dedicated to that question have come to ambiguous results [8].

The more recipients are dedicated to learning the less entertainment they need. The main problem with delivering information to many senior citizens is their reluctance to teaching offers. While the reasons for this reluctance are manifold–lack of awareness, suspicion, fatalism, complacency, indifference, etc. –it results in a large percentage of our target group unable to be reached directly. Therefore, these persons require primarily entertainment with educational content as the secondary objective. A lot of elderly people

---

[2] Research and Development.

have a reduced attention span [9] and few are willing to sacrifice much of their time. Both considerations require the subliminal information being packed within a limited overall time frame.

2.2 Research Questions

Effectiveness and Efficiency. The most important goal of our project is to provide vulnerable groups with knowledge and practical skills in the field of cyber security, together with the motivation and self-efficacy that lead them to make use of these skills. While pursuing this primary goal we also look for optimization of the balance between the entertaining and educating part.

Personalization. The openness to edutainment offers strongly depends on personal situation and interest and on how far the offer is tailored to their needs. We therefore try to find out which ways of information deliverance are most accepted and most effective for (and within) our target groups.

3 Concept and Methods

3.1 Pilot Narrative

As our pilot application for evaluation of the concept of subliminal teaching of cyber security related content for vulnerable groups via crossmedia storytelling we chose password security as technical content and elderly people as primary target group.

Learning Content. The learning outcome should effectuate an understanding of how passwords can be cracked and how to prevent this while also suggesting a practicable method to generate passwords that are both secure and memorable - even for people with reduced short-term memory abilities.

Generic Storyline. The information to be learned was then embedded in a generic storyline as shown in Table 1. The story is set up in 4 sections representing an Aristotelian 3-act structure, where Sect. 2 and 3 together build the second act, separating the decoding of a lost password and the generation of a new and better one.

Variations in Genre and Media. Virtually everyone can be touched by stories, but people differ significantly in terms of their preferred means of how to receive them. Many like crime stories or thrillers, others prefer science fiction or fantasy. On the other hand, especially among our primary target group of elders, some have expressed a longing for "something nice" like a romance or comedy. Figure 1 shows a collection of genres as suggested in interviews and questionnaires in a first user study with 23 persons (see 4 *Preliminary Results*).

We have therefore produced several narrative implementations of the generic story-line, differing in genre but transporting the same learning content. We have started with a crime story and a science fiction story. All stories are available digitally in a modular Hypermedia Novel (HYMN) environment [10].

At the time of writing this article, the crime and science fiction story have also been printed as paper booklets and the crime story is available as an audio book on CD.

Table 1. Generic storyline for a password security narrative.

Act (sub)	Section title	Narrative content	Learning content
1	Just What Was It?	A lost password must be regained	none
2 (1)	A Hard Nut to Crack	Several customary methods for password cracking are tried and the final one succeeds	*Password vulnerability:* How passwords can be cracked
2 (2)	Safe and Secure	A new password is set that is both secure and memorable. The new encoding successfully survives an attack	*Password generation:* How to generate a secure and memorable password
3	Everything's Fine	Resolution	none

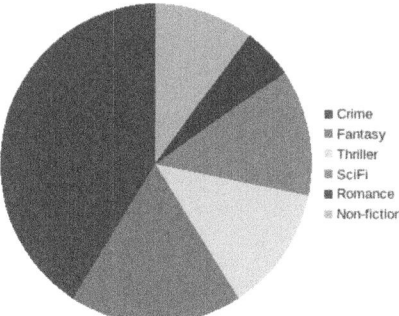

■ Crime
■ Fantasy
 Thriller
■ SciFi
■ Romance
 Non-fiction

Fig. 1. Genres for subliminal edutainment stories as suggested by the target group.

Currently on the HYMN platform, both are available in written and audio format in German language, the crime story also in English. Both have been read in front of an audience, partially enriched by interludes between the story sections, gathering feedback afterwards by a questionnaire.

Figure 2 visualizes the concept including several implementations of the generic storyline for password security.

Implementation of a Concrete Story. Adopting the viewpoint of object-oriented programming, the generic storyline can be seen as an abstract "class" defining the general content on a meta level. Building a concrete narrative from this class is then somehow analogous to implementing an "object" within a computer program. Table 2 gives an impression of how the implementation has been realized for two fictional narratives: "The Stick of Death" (crime story) and "Life on Mars" (science fiction).

Further Personalization Details. Variations of the stories may not only affect genre and media, but can also relate to sub-versions within one story product. As an example,

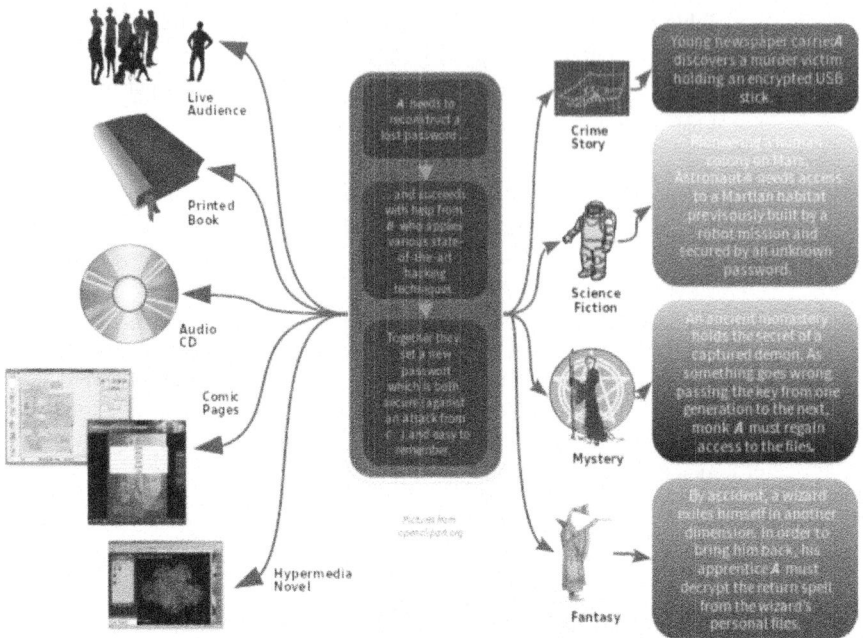

Fig. 2. Variations in genre and media on password security narrative. The generic storyline (blue) is presented in several media types (left) and personalized in different genres (right). All genres and media types can be combined as desired. (Picture components - if not self-generated - taken from openclipart.org.)

reading in a scholar context may require fitting within one lecture time unit of 45 min. To make the stories also available to other target groups may require translation into various languages or to provide the content in simplified speech.

Length Considerations. To transport knowledge via storytelling effectively as well as efficiently, it is important to keep the balance between the consumers' attention and informational content. Especially when addressing a target group without an intrinsic motivation for learning, the entertaining aspect must not be underestimated. We have produced stories that don't exceed one hour reading time (corresponding to about 30 printed text pages), covering only one dedicated cyber security topic at a time.

GenAI Support. Creating high quality narratives both interesting and educative (and technically correct) while keeping within given constraints (e.g. in terms of length), enriched by different media and branching into variations for several aspects of personalization, requires a considerable amount of effort and time. Therefore, we use generative AI (GenAI) tools to support the creation and variation (e.g. images, translations, etc.) of the content.

3.2 Crossmedia Approach

Readings in Front of an Audience. We have presented the crime story to a group of elders (together with their relatives and care workers) in a German senior residence as a

Table 2. Implementation of a generic storyline for password security as crime story.

Act (sub)	Generic content	Crime Story	Science Fiction story
1	Need to recover a lost password	A young newspaper carrier discovers a murder victim holding an encrypted USB stick	Pioneering a human colony on Mars, an astronaut needs access to a Martian habitat previously built by a robot mission and secured by an unknown password
2 (1)	How passwords can be guessed	Granny, who is an IT expert, helps to guess the stick password…	The mission AI helps to guess the password…
2 (2)	Set new password that is both secure and memorable. The new encoding successfully survives an attack	… and to secure it by setting a new and better one, which becomes important when the stick is stolen	… and to set a new and better one, which becomes important when a competing mission tries to usurp the habitat
3	Resolution	Finally, the murder case is solved and the stick secured	Finally, the two groups of Martian settlers come to terms

live reading event with live music (Rock classics loosely related to the narrative content) played during the story intersections. The crime and science fiction stories have also both been read in front of a mixed audience (without musical interludes), distributed as printed booklets or audio book CDs. We gathered feedback by the audiences after a live reading using questionnaires filled on paper or digitally via online survey.

Printed Booklets. We printed the stories on paper as booklet in DIN A5 format with a maximum of 28 pages each. Each booklet has a cover with title and a cover image and ends with some meta information, including a QR code and link to the digital version and to a feedback questionnaire.

Audio Books on CD. The stories are also made available as audio books - either online or on CD. Reading time for both stories yet implemented is about 60 min each.

Digital Access as Hypermedia Novel (HYMN). In addition to non-digital print media such as brochures and audio CDs, we have implemented stories about password security in both crime and science fiction genres as web-based Hypermedia Novel (HYMN) following an earlier definition of non-linear multimedia storytelling via a network of sequential and parallel narration modules [10]. As part of the CrossComITS project, the HYMN was completely redeveloped and is now based on the latest web technologies as a platform-independent and embeddable web component based on *ccm* technology [11].

The user interface was designed to resemble a "player" in such a way that the content can be "played" in predefined genres. Nevertheless, there is an option for the user to personalize their preferences, such as changing the genre or adjusting filters if available.

This means that the content can be consumed either in classic text form with images, or in audio or video format (if available). The media type can be changed at any time.

In addition, users were provided with functions that allow them to listen to the content using the read-aloud function, adjust the font size or print it out. The user can use the *share* button to share the displayed content as a link. This makes it possible to link to specific content in the deep structure of a HYMN.

3.3 Evaluation Concept

Feedback Questionnaire. The feedback questionnaire contains several sections, covering different aspects. After some demographic data, we first asked how the story was received generally, then if the participants understood it, followed by self-assessment about the gained password security knowledge, preferences in terms of narrative genre and media, and finally suggestions for other cyber security-related topics. We later adapted the questionnaire to include a quiz-question about how to define passwords to objectively measure whether the participants can select a secure password after consuming the story.

While keeping some central components, we adapted the questionnaire to each presentation. Most questions on the questionnaire were structured according to a 5-point Likert scale [12]. It should be mentioned that we asked the audience to complete the questionnaire after the reading event (or other recipients after reception of any provided media in private), emphasizing that they were free to skip any of the questions in order not to impose a feeling of pressure, so they might keep a positive attitude to possible similar future offers.

Limitations. The questionnaire in its initial configuration is solely based on the self-reporting of the participants, which is not an issue when asking about the length of the story, which genres and media types they like, and other personal preferences. However, the learning effect of the story is difficult to quantify based on this self-reporting. The added knowledge-question tries to simulate a simplified form of a test but fails short of showing how well the knowledge was transferred. The long-term effectiveness of the learning effect remains unknown. We also have no data about the knowledge level of the participants before they consumed the story.

4   Preliminary Results

We have conducted a study with three readings of two stories for three groups of people numbering 23 in total (with 19 age 60+, incl. 13 age 70+), including feedback from one person who only read the (science fiction) story without being present at one of the live readings. We have distributed the first two story implementations to password security in printed booklets and on an online platform as Hypermedia Novels and are now waiting for feedback on the associated web questionnaire to conduct an analysis with more statistical significance.

From an overall assessment of these initial presentations, we already received several interesting and encouraging findings. Besides an overall approval of the general concept and confirmation of our assumptions regarding a high variance of preference in terms of genre (see Fig. 1) and media, there is a clear indication for subliminal education: The learning effect (unannounced a priori, checked by self-assessment a posteriori) seems not to be consciously realized by all test persons even after the reading. However, additional questions about consequences indicate that not only the awareness of the importance to use strong passwords raised, but they also admit having learned how to generate such strong and memorable passwords (see Fig. 3).

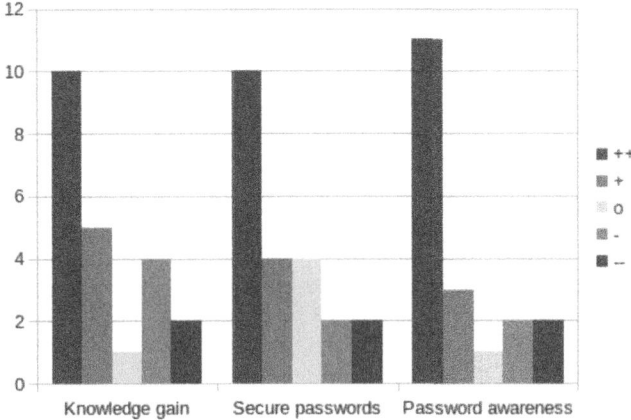

Fig. 3. Self-assessment of their learning outcome from 23 participants (not all of them answering all questions). "Knowledge gain" refers to the impression to have learned something about secure passwords, "Secure passwords" refers to the confidence of being able to produce these, and "Password awareness" refers to the future dedication to pay attention to password security. The bars represent a 5-point Likert scale from "very much" (++) to "not at all" (−).

5   Conclusion

As we are still in the process of evaluating, extending and improving our offers, it is currently only possible to draw some intermediate conclusions. We will extend the scope of our content and its evaluation. Particularly, we want to evaluate the learning experience by objectively measuring some metric instead of a self-assessment. Future studies shall also include comparison to a non-educated control group. We also want to refine the current content based on the first feedback, e.g. by making the content shorter. Additionally, we want to further assess the usefulness of generative AI tools for content diversification after first attempts show potential in some areas.

Acknowledgments. The authors like to thank Vera Schliefer for giving her great storyteller's voice to the audio book version of the crime story and Karl N. Kirschner for thoroughly proofreading the crime story translation. We also thank brainLight GmbH for audio production support. The Evangelische Erwachsenenbildung an Sieg und Rhein helped with conducting the interview study. This work is supported by the German Federal Ministry of Education and Research (BMBF) under the research grant 16KIS 1623.

Disclosure of Interests. The authors have no competing interests to declare that are relevant to the content of this article.

References

1. Heiden, W., Kless, T., Neteler, T.: A crossmedia storytelling platform to empower vulnerable groups for IT security. In: Holloway-Attaway, L., Murray, J. T. (eds.) ICIDS 2023, LNCS 14384, pp. 195–201. Springer, Heidelberg (2023). https://doi.org/10.1007/978-3-031-47658-7_17
2. Adams, A., Sasse, M. A., Lunt, P.: Making passwords secure and usable. In: Thimbleby, H., O'Conaill, B., Thomas, P.J. (eds.) People and Computers XII, pp. 1–19. Springer, Heidelberg (1997). https://doi.org/10.1007/978-1-4471-3601-9_1
3. Umejiaku, A.P., Dhakal, P., Sheng, V.S.: Balancing password security and user convenience: exploring the potential of prompt models for password generation. Electronics **12**, 2159 (2023). https://doi.org/10.3390/electronics12102159
4. Lee, P.Y., Choong, Y.Y.: Human generated passwords–the impacts of password requirements and presentation styles. In: Tryfonas, T., Askoxylakis, I. (eds.) Human Aspects of Information Security, Privacy, and Trust. HAS 2015. LNCS, vol 9190, pp. 83–94. Springer, Cham (2015). https://doi.org/10.1007/978-3-319-20376-8_8
5. Němec, J., Trna, J.: Edutainment or education: education possibilities of didactic games in science education. In: ICCP Brno Conference, pp. 55–64 (2007)
6. Hoffman, A., Göbel, S., Schneider, O., Iurgel, I.: Storytelling-based edutainment applications. In: Online and Distance Learning: Concepts, Methodologies, Tools, and Applications, pp. 1439–1460. IGI Global (2008)
7. Heiden, W.: Edutainment aspects in hypermedia storytelling. In: Pan, Z., Aylett, R., Diener, H., Jin, X., Göbel, S., Li, L. (eds) Technologies for E-Learning and Digital Entertainment. Edutainment 2006. LNCS, vol. 3942, pp. 389–398. Springer, Heidelberg (2006). https://doi.org/10.1007/11736639_50
8. Green, D.P.: In search of entertainment-education's effects on attitudes and behaviors. In: Frank, L.B., Falzone, P. (eds.) Entertainment-Education Behind the Scenes. Palgrave Macmillan, Cham (2021). https://doi.org/10.1007/978-3-030-63614-2_12
9. Simon, A.J., et al.: Quantifying attention span across the lifespan. Front Cognit. 2, 1207428 (2023). https://doi.org/10.3389/fcogn.2023.1207428, Epub 2023 Jun 22, PMID: 37920687, PMCID: PMC10621754
10. Heiden, W., Ostovar, A.: Structuring hypermedia novels. In: Göbel, S., Malkewitz, R., Iurgel, I. (eds.) TIDSE 2006. LNCS, vol. 4326, pp. 98–103. Springer, Heidelberg (2006). https://doi.org/10.1007/11944577_10
11. Kaul, M., Kless, A., Bonne, T., Rieke, A.: Game changer for online learning driven by advances in web technology. In: Nunes, M.B., Isaias, P., McPerson, M., Rodrigues, L., Kommers, P. (eds.) MCCSIS 2017. Curran Associates, Inc., New York (2018)
12. Batterton, K.A., Hale, K.N.: The Likert Scale. What It Is and How To Use It. Phalanx **50**(2), 32–39 (2017)

Affective Sound: Developing a Critical Framework for Audio-Based Interactive Digital Narratives

Lissa Holloway-Attaway(✉) ⓘ and Jamie Fawcus ⓘ

University of Skövde, Skövde, Sweden
{lissa.holloway-Attaway,jamie.fawcus}@his.se

Abstract. In our current research project we develop a critical framework to facilitate the design and the critique of audio-based interactive narrative experiences. We foreground deep material connections to sound and affect as well as to the rhetorical and narrative properties of story/voice as a vehicle for storytelling. We draw inspiration for our framework from a range of philosophical, theoretical and aesthetic influences including posthumanism, new material feminism, affect studies, interaction design, as well as sound design and interactive and traditional narrative research. Our framework is intended to aid in the design of such audio-based artifacts to support embodied user experiences where affect is a key principle to support innovative material storytelling/deep listening with sound as the primary vehicle for delivery. To facilitate deeper understanding of the framework, we apply it to three original audio-based narratives we created to assess them preliminarily in terms of the four key areas we identify to understand affective narrative audio-based media: Temporality, Mediation, Interaction, and Embodiment/Material Experience. In future research we hope to expand and apply our model to other sound based works and to undergo more intensive user-testing.

Keywords: Affect · Sound · Interactive Digital Narrative · Audio

1 Introduction: Sound and Affect

In our current research project we develop a critical framework to facilitate the design and the critique of audio based interactive narrative experiences. We foreground deep material connections to sound and affect as well as to the rhetorical and narrative properties of story/voice as a vehicle for storytelling. Our framework is intended to aid in the design of such audio artifacts to support embodied user experiences where affect is a key principle to support innovative material storytelling/deep listening with sound as the primary vehicle for delivery. But the framework also offers a critical method to identify, support, and explore sound and/as affect, which is itself a notoriously challenging and theoretically complex topic currently underexplored in digital audio-based storytelling. By foregrounding affect in our work, facilitated through a variety of experimental audio techniques and narrative forms that we outline in more depth in our framework principles, we illustrate how the unique sonic properties we use to connect in-story narrators, characters, and other agents to listener/users.

© The Author(s), under exclusive license to Springer Nature Switzerland AG 2025
J. T. Murray and M. C. Reyes (Eds.): ICIDS 2024, LNCS 15468, pp. 205–213, 2025.
https://doi.org/10.1007/978-3-031-78450-7_14

Affective sound acts as an important connective passageway between material and conceptual, physical and virtual, immersive spaces at varied levels of intensity within embodied agents. As such it wanders, loops, animates sensory perception to escape purely rational reception of narrative content. Our designs incorporate psychoacoustic phenomena such as auditory brainwave entrainment, binaural beats, and fragmentation/granulation of sound materials intended to de-centralize and deconstruct the sounding world and particularly the voice (spoken, whispered and/or screamed, for example). Spaces and temporal dimensions converge, disperse and digitally re-order through systematic rule sets we develop and they are mediated by resonant, dynamic sounding worlds that emerge as the listener/user connects to them, or not. Our aim is to create co-agential immersion for listener/users, moving them between listening and their own embodied making states, co-existent with our design principles. Our affective sound experiments deconstruct traditional notions of power, knowing, telling, and receiving through the sonic disintegration and redistribution of stable subject identities and worlds.

2 Related Work

Our critical foundations are highly intra-disciplinary, and they draw on theoretical, philosophical and aesthetic principles across multiple digital media platforms for creating and distributing sound-based experiences. At the core of all of our creative expressions the focus is on sustaining interactive storytelling in intimate designer/user assemblages via complex networks. In our designs, aimed to support affective listening, we highlight the rhetorical and practical properties of voice/story domains to create dynamic affective sound-based experiences with a range of interaction strategies for a variety of user/designer experiences. Our design strategies, sound and narrative, are based on principles for affectively aligning bodies in mixed digital/physical spaces and diverse contexts for use. Affect Studies, an emerging field is of course key to our work, but by its nature is notoriously expansive and elusive, as evidenced by the range of scholarship and disciplines it includes [1, 2]. Gregg and Seigworth in their "Introduction" to *The Affect Theory Reader* [2010] remind us that although we can never know without contextual clues (and these contexts can be highly diverse) what *exactly* affect *is*, we can note that a common principle is that it emerges as transmission among bodies to engage visceral, embodied responsiveness: "Affect arises in the midst of in-between-ness: between-ness: in the capacities to act and be acted upon" [1, p. 1]. It is always material, if seemingly abstract. We draw directly on contemporary work in sound/affect studies, a developing field that has yet to mature, but is illustrated in, for example, the edited anthology *Sound and Affect: voice, music world* [3]. This work offers compelling interdisciplinary perspectives to consider the dynamic concept of the sonic voice, human and non-human, to intersect with and counter issues of gender, race, class, through the narrative storied worlds they engage.

Given our resistance to traditional (human) subjects as vehicles to convey (voice) meanings (stories), we draw inspiration from Critical Posthumanism, including non-human and more-than-human perspectives to support radical new narratives and perspectives [4–8] Further we focus on the related core principles from Feminist New Materialism [9–17]. These sources include issues centered on: 1) trans-corporality (moving among and across material bodies in narrative, physical, digital and 'other spaces); 2) transmutation and intra-actability (bodies that shift, change, and deeply interact and resonate with each other); and 3) exploring/creating multiple kinds of distributed agencies moving across and among listeners and tellers, human and otherwise.

We combine these theoretical reflections with Interaction Design and Phenomenological research focused on creating open and generative models and processes for designing embodied digital user-based media [18–21]. Further given our focus on audio, we integrate research in music and sound, drawing on interests like Smalley's concept of spectromorphology, the unique sonic footprint and shape of sound as it manifests in time [22]. We draw on other radical compositional strategies for electroacoustic music, such as forms of formalized music linking human consciousness or intelligence to varied aesthetic sonic forms [23]. Further, we explore architectural space-making in our sound content [24, 25] and explore the affordances of the ear specifically for processing psychoacoustic sensory input, as with the notable work and influence of Amacher [26].

We also associate our research and design with the broader perspectives of Interactive Digital Narrative (IDN) research [27–31]. This work emerges from traditional narratological approaches to text-based media, that have distinctions between stories, as events that happen, and the varied discursive principles that present, stylize, and communicate them. The influence of the Russian Formalists who also made distinctions between the fabula (story) and the sjuzhet (discourse), the manner in which a text is communicated [32] is also a basis for us to consider voice/story more fully from an interactive sound/audio perspective.

Collectively this rich foundation for research allows up to explore, define and design affective sound spaces and highlight their unique capacities to connect bodies, voices, and sounds.

3   Our Critical Framework: Making Affect Audible and Material

The concept of bodies (sound bodies, designer bodies, listener/user bodies, media bodies) are primary focal points for us, particularly as they sustain/release affective material responses. In previous work, we have outlined our material based composition strategies in depth and these are essential to our designs and inform our critical framework we develop here [33]. The forms of material expressions and bodies we hope to stimulate are the *affective loops* that Kristina Höök describes as part of an embodied interactive system design where "the user is an active, meaning-making individual choosing how to express themselves [and] the interpretation responsibility does not lie with the system" [18, p. 3585]. But in order to make these affective loops and bodies visible, we propose our own 4-part process to identify more carefully what these affective experiences are. Our aim is to create a framework that can individualize and describe core principles for affect at differing levels of intensity to bring us closer to understanding how sound and affect function in audio-based narratives. Although at this first stage we look only at three of our own works, we see this work as preliminary to supporting critique and design of other works beyond our own and conducted also by other researchers. Our three audio-based narratives share both common and distinctive, unique characteristics, and with the support of our framework, we aim to illustrate and identify how affect is functionally present in the work.

Our 4-part framework to understand affect is constructed of the following critical areas:

1) **Temporality:** the degree of control the listener/user has over temporal elements (start/stop of experience; start/stop of audible elements, such as control over loops); degree of control over nature/content of audible material—such as frequency content, amplitude, positioning/spatial elements, complexity/activity

2) **Mediation:** degree of control over experience by designers and listener/users as dictated by system type and interface (web-based, mobile AR, videography, for example)

3) **Interaction:** degree of change, alteration, delivery mode, and manipulation of sound material

4) **Embodiment/Material Experience**: degree and type of affective stimulation (designers) and responsiveness (users); context/spatial orientation; desire to engage and disrupt

The three works we include here in our analysis are identified in brief below. They were selected because although they each share a common desire to create affective sound experiences, they are also unique from each other in a variety of ways, including their interface /delivery system, the length and time of the experience and of each sound, the level of interactivity for listener/users, type (content of narrative feature, aim or purpose, the mode and degree of embodiment and responsiveness for the user) and the use, or not, of voiced material.

The Three Audio-based Interactive Narratives

1) *Trans-missions and Resonant Encounters: composing the non-human body.* (*Trans-missions*) [34] *Trans-missions* (by Holloway-Attaway and Fawcus) is an experiment in sound and motion, a "sound walk" where various philosophical and contextual topics could be presented in a manner less constrained by more traditional forms of transmission such as academic lectures, seminars and other linear communication methods. The work uses processed vocal material, and more abstract material, combining multiple, simultaneous tracks of vocal monologue with spectrally processed sound material, creating inharmonic tonal structures that are at once pitched, yet unmusical in any conventional sense. New approaches are introduced such as pulsing and rhythmic sound material, fetal heart monitors, heartbeats, ECG recordings. Again, much of the sound material is coupled associatively with content within the narrated monologue, but also disrupts these traditions offering alternative interpretations for the listener who must walk and listen to the lecture.

2) *PATTER (n) INGS: Apt. 3B, 2020. (PATTER(n)INGS)* [35] *PATTER(n)INGS* (by Holloway-Attaway and Fawcus), is an immersive audio experience that explores the complexities of existence during the COVID-19 pandemic through a unique interactive format. This web-based interface, devoid of visual elements save for a black screen, engages users primarily through auditory stimuli, encouraging a heightened sensory focus as they attempt to explore and eavesdrop on the people and rooms of an apartment in lockdown by listening to a variety of sounds and voices. The experience is designed to be deeply isolating, mirroring the conditions of pandemic lockdowns. Users are instructed to wear headphones and optionally don facemasks,

blindfolds, or some other form of visual restriction to further limit sensory input. Interaction is restricted to mouse movements across a flat 2D onscreen space, with hidden sound files triggered by these blind, intuitive and audio-steered explorations. The experience leverages various audio technologies, including binaural and ambisonic techniques, to create a three-dimensional auditory space that exploits sensations of close proximity, motion and intimacy. The intention was to create unsettling intimacy, the "anti-ASMR" that disturbs and unsettles using concrete yet indeterminate sounds that suggest and "touch" the listener without shocking or confronting

3) **Unmet, Disquiet.** [36] *Unmet, Disquiet* (by Fawcus, Hansson, and Granath) is an interactive hybrid interactive space and performance work centered on the vocalization of the human scream. Similar to *PATTER(n)INGS*, the installation features distinct audible spaces or "rooms" that the listener experiences, this time in a specific order. Interactive LiDAR in the installation trigger elements determined to generate sufficient engagement and interaction within each "room". In this case, unlike *Trans-missions* and *PATTER(n)INGS*, there was no spoken text to give relevance and context to much of the experimentation. Also this form of interaction worked in tandem with the live, improvised elements of the piece by an audio technician on site. The interactive sound design uses LiDAR data to adjust volume, EQ, filtering, and spatial effects, creating a diverse and complex immersive environment. The design avoids "jump scares" and other shock-oriented usage of the material and focuses on creating a reciprocal atmosphere where sound moves with the audience bodies through space to engage and entice them.

4   Analysis

We outline briefly below each work in accordance with the 4-point critical framework to reflect on each affective quality and to draw some initial conclusions in this area. The aim is to consider how the affective material is constructed to interact with and engage listener users, but also to illustrate the flexibility for creating affective narratives. Although each has individual and unique qualities in the sound material and in the discursive and narrative properties of the story/voice structures and styles, they are all able to sustain affective narrative connections to users.

1) *Trans-missions:*

Temporality: This work has a relatively fixed temporal construction. Although the user may of course start and stop the experience at any time, it is intended to be a linear piece and is constructed as a form of spoken monologue, or lecture, that emerges only if listened to from beginning to end.

Mediation: The headphones and mobile phone facilitate a personal and private experience. Little is required of the user except to stop and start the devices. The sounding material is delivered primarily via a single voice through the headphones that moves between conversational and explanatory monologue.

Interaction: Low-level physical interaction with the interface is required, but an intensity of embodied listening while physically moving is essential to experience the sounding material, designed to orient and disorient the user in space while in motion.

Embodiment/Material Experience: Interaction and embodiment is quite high and requires physical movement through space (via walking) while listening to complex academic content, moving in and out of focus, to fulfill the aim of the experience. The voice is designed to support and deflect meaning while physically disorienting the listening body.

2) *PATTER(n)INGS*

Temporality: This work has a dynamic and flexible temporality. Although the listener/user may start and stop the experience at any time, it is intended to be a non-linear piece and is constructed with both vocal and non-vocal content, some of which is stable, constant, and out of the listener/user's control, and some which starts and stops via the user's hand movements with the mouse to discover hidden content via sound files. The temporal sound features are meant to peak curiosity and encourage extended listening to decode and decipher complex content, prolonging the experience if the listener/user desires to comprehend the complexity.

Mediation: The single user web-based interface experience requires a desk, mouse, and computer monitor, but offers no graphics except a few directional ones. The required mouse movements that trigger sound are relatively uncomplicated, but some physicality is required (hand movements across the screen) of the listener/user to control the experience. The sounding material is highly diverse, non-linear, and it both orients and disorients the listener/user.

Interaction: Low-level physical interaction with the interface is required, but an intensity of embodied listening while moving the mouse is essential to experience the sounding material, designed to orient and disorient the user in space while exploring the "rooms" of the apartment through only sound cues.

Embodiment/Material Experience: Despite the limited level of interaction with the delivery system and the lack of much graphical content, the embodiment is quite high and requires intensive listening. Touch through the mouse and stimulation of the ear through the nature of the texts (narrative and abstract, voiced and non-human, disturbing and indecipherable, and clear and voiced) is very intensive and materially focused. If a listener/user chooses to use a blindfold, as recommended, it is very physically isolating, intending to focus listening on embodied and visceral responses to the sound designed to engage and entice.

3) *Unmet, Disquiet:*

Temporality: The experience has a set time to begin and end, but the individual sounds are flexible and varied. Sounds range in length and intensity.

Mediation: The interactive sound, activated through LiDAR sensors triggered by user movement in an immersive performance space has a high level of technical infrastructure to activate sound (using a customized java application to control and regulate sound), along with live interventions with an audio technician responding to users interactions in real time in the space.

Interaction: Physical interaction in terms of moving through the space is desired for peak experience, but not demanded, as some sound is based on user intervention, and some is controlled by the audio technician live. However, little is demanded of the listener/user except to enter the space and explore at their own comfort level, and even this exploration is not fully required. This is a multi-person experience (20 users at a time) and users can move alone or together and choose to sit, stand, or walk. There is a high level of choice.

Embodiment/Material Experience: Given the nature of the sound content (human screams) the visceral responsiveness is intended to be high, and listener/users will have to listen even if they don't want to. There is a wide spectrum of sound material based on the manipulation of the (screaming) human voice, and as such it is personal and should be semi-recognizable, peaking interest, but also sometimes becoming disturbing and evoking discomfort and fear.

5 Conclusion

Our work is a preliminary sketch to implement our critical framework and to investigate how affective sound experiences may be designed and identified to forge relationships with designers and listener/users and to facilitate storytelling in novel ways. As indicated in our initial analysis here, we find a wide range of flexibility in terms of engaging affect in our sound experiences. So although we found no clear *rules* for how to create such work, the framework offers some areas to reflect on and to potentially consider/balance in terms of designing/critiquing such experiences. In our on-going and future research, we hope to expand our investigation and look at more works (ours and others) more carefully. We also plan to have further user-testing so we may survey more carefully the responsiveness of listener/users to the audio content and via the range of mediated delivery systems we create.

References

1. Gregg, M., Seigworth, G.J.: The Affect Theory Reader. Duke University Press, Durham, NC (2010)
2. Seigworth, G.J., Pedwell, C.: The Affect Theory Reader 2: Worldings, Tensions. Futures. Duke University Press, Durham, NC (2010)
3. Lochead, J., Mendieta, E., Smith, S.D.: Sound and Affect: Voice, Music. World. University of Chicago Press, Chicago, Il (2021)
4. Braidotti, R.: The Posthuman. Polity Press, Cambridge (2013)
5. Hayles, K.N.: How We Became Posthuman, 74th edn. University of Chicago Press, Chicago, IL (1999)
6. Parikka, J.: Insect Media: An Archeology of Animals and Technology. University of Minnesota Press, Minneapolis, MN (2010)
7. Thacker, E.: Biomedia. University of Minnesota Press, Minneapolis, MN (2004)
8. Wolfe, C.: What is Posthumanism? University of Minnesota Press, Minneapolis, MN (2010)
9. Alaimo, S.: Bodily Natures: Science the Environment and the Material Self. University of Indiana Press, Bloomington, IN (2010)

10. Alaimo, S.: Exposed: Environmental Politics and Pleasures in Posthuman Times. University of Minnesota Press, Minneapolis, MN (2017)
11. Alaimo, S., Hekman, S.: Material Feminisms. Indiana University Press, Bloomington, IN (2008)
12. Barad, K.: Meeting the Universe Halfway: Quantum Physics and The Entanglement of Matter and Meaning. Duke University Press, Durham, NC (2007)
13. Bennett, J.: Vibrant Matters: A Political Ecology of Things. Duke University Press, Durham, NC (2010)
14. Dolphijn, R., TuinVan, I., der: New Materialism: Interviews & Cartographies. University of Michigan Library, Ann Arbor, MI (2012)
15. Grosz, E.: Volatile Bodies: Towards a Corporeal Feminism. Indiana University Press, Bloomington, IL (1994)
16. Haraway, D.J.: Staying With The Trouble: Making Kin in the Chthulucene. Duke University Press, Durham, NC (2016)
17. Kirby, V.: Telling Flesh: The Substance of the Corporeal. Routledge, New York, NY (1997)
18. Höök, K.: Affective loop experiences: designing for interactional embodiment. Philos. Trans. R. Soc. **364**, 3585–3595 (2009)
19. Höök, K., Löwgren, J.: Strong concepts: intermediate level knowledge. ACM Trans. Comput. Hum. Interact. **19**(3), 1–18 (2012)
20. Höök, K., et al.: Embracing first-person perspectives in soma-based design. Informatics **5**(1), 1–26 (2018)
21. Kozel, S.: Closer: Performance, Technologies. Phenomenology. MIT Press, Boston, MA (2007)
22. Smalley, D.: Spectromorphology: explaining sound shapes. Organized Sound **2**(2), 107–126 (1997)
23. Xenakis, I.: Formalized Music: Thought and Mathematics in Composition. Pendgagron Press, Hillsdale, NJ (1992)
24. Deveraux, P.: The Acoustic Archeology of Acoustic Sites. Vega (2002)
25. Truax, B.: Riverrun, The Wings of Nike, and Tongues of Angels. Cambridge Street Records, Canada (1979–86)
26. Amacher, M.: Music for Sound-Joined Rooms. (1980–2002)
27. Grishkova, M., Poulaki, M.: Narrative Complexity, Cognition. Embodiment. University of Nebraska Press, Lincoln, NB (2019)
28. Koenitz, H.: Towards a specific theory of interactive narrative. In: Koenitz, H., Ferri, G., Haahr, M., Sezen, D., Tonguç Sezen, T.I. (eds.) Interactive Digital Narrative: History, Theory, and Practice, pp. 91–105. Routledge, NY and London (2015)
29. Murray, J.: Hamlet on the Holodeck. MIT Press, Boston (2017)
30. Murray, J.: Research into interactive digital narrative: a kaleidoscopic view. In: Rouse, R., Koenitz, H., Haahr, M. (eds.) ICIDS 2018. LNCS, vol. 11318, pp. 3–17. Springer, Cham (2018). https://doi.org/10.1007/978-3-030-04028-4_1
31. Koenitz, H.: Understanding Interactive Digital Narrative: Immersive Expressions for a Complex Time. Routledge, Milton Park (2023)
32. Tomashevsky, B.: Thematics. In: Lemo, L.T., Rei, M.J. (eds.): Russian Formalist Criticism: Four Essays, pp. 61–95, University of Nebraska Press, Lincoln, NB (1965)
33. Holloway-Attaway, L., Fawcus, J.: Making COVID dis-connections: designing intra-active and transdisciplinary sound-based narratives for phenomenal new material worlds. New Rev. Hypermed. Multimed. **28**(3–4), 112–142 (2023)
34. Holloway-Attaway, L., Fawcus, J.: Trans-missions and Resonant Encounters: composing the non-human body. Walk Listen Create. https://walklistencreate.org/walkingpiece/trans-mis sions-and-resonant-encounters-composing-the-non-human-body/?fbclid=IwAR1fbeIHVo dbkoRtywM49KYsD7MAw0RR4oyP-yFZ59lhpSsfm-S9hGiFn3k). Accessed 10 Oct 2024

35. Holloway-Attaway, L., Fawcus, J.: PATTER(N)INGS, Apt. 3B (2020). https://gusing.itch.io/patternings (password: Patt2020). Accessed 10 Oct 2024
36. Fawcus, J., Hansson, S., Granath, A.: Unmet, Disquiet. Live Performance/Installation. Ludokonst. Festival. Skövde, Sweden (2023)

What if We Educated Students Assuming They can Think? Introducing the Critical Education Framework (CEF) for Interactive Narratives, Games and Related Fields

Hartmut Koenitz[1]([⊠])[ID] and Mirjam Palosaari Eladhari[2][ID]

[1] Södertörn University, Alfred Nobels allé 7, 141 89 Huddinge, Sweden
hartmut.koenitz@sh.se
[2] Stockholm University, 106 91 Stockholm, Sweden
mirjam@dsv.su.se

Abstract. Students can think and they are creative, yet education in interactive narratives and related field does not always support creativity and critical thinking skills. As a result, students struggle to fully grasp the learning material and lack the ability to critically assess existing knowledge. In particular, aspects of theory, method and industry practices are often taught only as a passive exercise of receiving static knowledge and not as a dynamically growing body of knowledge. We see this status quo as a missed opportunity, especially when it comes to integrating students into research projects, where critical assessment and further developments of theoretical frameworks and research methods is a necessity. In this paper, we present an analysis of the current situation and an initial framework to improve education, with the aim to empower students' critical thinking skills and creative abilities when it comes to theory, method, and design practices.

Keywords: interactive digital narrative education · critical education · student research · interactive storytelling education · games education · interactive media education

1 Introduction

The question "why do we use a specific theory/method/terminology/industry practice?" is not asked often enough and the related reflection on the consequences of these choices happens even less frequently. The authors have spearheaded this discussion within the ICIDS community [14–16], connecting to a wider perspective, e.g. the well-argued critique of the uncritical application of established evaluation frameworks in the related field of video games by the research groups around Elisa Meckler [19] and Sebastian Deterding [7] or the even wider issue of the "replication crisis" in Psychology and other fields [8]. To overcome the limitations of individual analytical frameworks, we have proposed a solution by combining them in a "multi-method analysis" [10]. Yet, the lack of critical perspectives is not confined to research, it also exists in higher education. In this regard, we have provocatively called to educate for "Critical Thinking, Not Assimilation" [14] which we understand as training students to "asks basic questions such as whether a particular concept, analytical method, or vocabulary actually match the object of inquiry?" (ibid). In this paper, we will further discuss the current status of education in interactive narrative and related fields and will also propose initial steps to operationalize and implement what we like to call a 'Critical Education Framework' (CEF).

Other than wishing for a more critical approach, there are additional reasons which make changes in education desirable, in particular the aim to improve student's understanding of theory/method/terminology/industry practice (which we will call 'educational material' for the remainder of this paper) and their ability to apply it. In our experience as educators, students often struggle with understanding and applying educational material. One reason for this situation is a gap in many educational programs. Students are provided with a 'what' (established knowledge that applies to the topic at hand and related phenomena) and a 'how' (ways in which said knowledge can be applied to the topic at hand and related phenomena, e.g. for analysis). Yet, what is often missing is information which would provide a justification for the existence of educational material as well as an explanation of their benefits, the 'why'. Additionally, students rarely learn about the principled limitations inherent in knowledge production, nor the particular context in which a given educational material was established, including the impact of intersectional regimes of discrimination resulting in bias. Feminist and decolonial perspectives [3,22] certainly exist, but are still not the norm in education.

Students' education can be improved, we argue, by increasing awareness of the reasons for the existence of established educational material and the advantages that come with them. At the same time, students' critical understanding and perspective would benefit from an increased focus on learning about the limitations of existing knowledge. Both of these aspects are essential if we want students to be able to use their full potential and contribute to scholarly research.

Yet, the question is how we can realize these goals in the educational practice, given the constrains of established programs.

We will approach this challenge in four moves, first reflecting on the current state of affairs, then considering related efforts, followed by the description of a vision of an ideal education environment and outcome. Finally, we provide an outline of the CEF for implementation in current educational systems. We see education on interactive narratives as a particular opportunity in this regard, as no full educational program exists at this moment ([17] refers to a minor), but there are efforts in place to implement them[1], creating the opportunity for a fresh approach.

2   The Status Quo

There are shared academic skills and approaches across many fields in terms of preciseness of research questions and hypotheses, and motivations for why research should be conducted. Unfortunately, these skills are often conveyed mechanically, without providing the reasons for their existence. What is less guaranteed is education about how to find previous work, how to broaden the perspective to include other fields, or how to take societal impact into account. Even less emphasis is placed on how to ensure that a study can be replicated. In addition, what is often lacking are basic skills which should have been taught in high school, such as basic rhetorical skills, how to conduct a sound argument, or how to test a hypothesis. Also, there is commonly no knowledge on the principled limits of knowledge production and no understanding how to investigate a (novel) phenomenon on its own terms.

These issues are compounded by the standard formula of much of existing education, which follows four steps:

1. provide students with educational material
2. give them a task in which they apply the educational material
3. evaluate whether the students have correctly applied the educational material
4. If evaluation has been successful, move to the next bit of educational material, if students have failed the evaluation, provide opportunities for re-evaluation and in case of another fail, make them re-do steps 1-3

This formula is problematic in several ways - in terms of its transactional nature (transfer material into students' brains, check if it has been received and digested to a degree, repeat), but also because it is uni-directional (from educators to students) and because it provides no space for the development of new knowledge.

An additional issue with the current practice of education is related to the knowledge gap between students and supervisors. Positioning ourselves as senior scholars, it can be easy to forget that we take for granted what the students "should" know, and are surprised when they either show or tell that they do not know how to go forward in their thinking about a problem they aim to solve. When we find ourselves in the role of thesis advisors, it can be a daunting task to figure out how to best help students who find themselves at loss.

---

[1] The university of Exeter is about to start such a program and the COST action INDCOR (https://indcor.eu) has created templates for programs of study in collaboration with the Higher Education Video Game Alliance (HEVGA).

2.1 Examples from the Educational Practice

Here is a typical example, displaying the issue mentioned above from one of the institutions the authors have taught at: all students across the bachelors programs attend a methodology course where they are taught to apply methods from social sciences [6]. In some programs, such as in the game design program, students are taught how to use and apply design science [12]. As such, when students start their work with their bachelors thesis, they have the knowledge of this particular set of methods.

Furthermore, the grading criteria are formulated so that students need to use a particular set of terms when explaining their research strategies, research methods, data gathering, and analysis methods. Hence any student who for example wants to use a more critical approach or a more technical approach, must find ways to shoehorn their writing into this narrow framing to receive a passing grade. In fact, this institution encourages the use of other methods if they better fit the nature of the work. However, in such a case the student needs to be either highly self motivated, or happen to be lucky in the advisor they are assigned, to be able to escape the existing framing. Of course, there are pragmatic institutional reasons for this approach, as it enables the institution to use the full faculty for assessment of grading and examination through this standardized approach.

When it comes to teaching a topic most closely related to interactive narrative education, narrative design, additional problems appear. Narrative is topic which is commonly taught in elementary and high school education, albeit with a focus on literary narrative. As considerable parts of this notion are either incompatible with interactive narrative (e.g. according to [13]) or at least in conflict with interaction (cf. "narrative paradox" [1]), considerable time should be spent to discuss these differences with the students. However, in a typical five week module (e.g. in Södertörn university's games program) in which students should produce both a working Unity group project and an individual reflective essay, there is not enough time to explore these fundamental conceptual challenges in any depth. Consequently, students will read the assigned readings and discuss them in class without any guarantee they have fully grasped their implications on both the theoretical and practical level.

3 Related Work in Improving Education

We are aware of many attempts at improving interactive-narrative-related education, for example by including practical experiments [9], stakeholders from the practice as project advisors [17] and societal relevant aspects [11].

Efforts at improving education in related subjects with new learning techniques include changing the character of instruction, i.e. by means of the flipped-classroom approach [23] where students explore the material by themselves and then bring their questions to classroom discussions in contrast to the more traditional method of teacher-lead instruction. There are also efforts focused on addressing issues of bias, e.g. [20,21]. Such efforts have been discussed at workshops in conferences such as DIGRA (e.g. the teaching games studies workshop running from 2014-2016[2]), and also by bodies such as HEVGA (Higher Education Video Game Alliance) and IGDA (International Game Developers Association). However, the impact on changing education in practice has been limited.

When it comes to IDN and education, most research efforts so far have been concentrated on what has been termed "teaching with IDN" (using IDNs to teach a subject) instead of teaching "about IDN", as Barbara et al. point out [2], with only a few experiments [4,5] focusing on "teaching about IDN" (ibid) Consequently, we are still lacking an overarching approach to address the principled issues we talk about, in both IDN-focused education and beyond.

3.1 Teaching Practical Application of Method

A positive example how practical research skills can be taught is that of Lankoski's teaching approach in the field of game research [18]. Here, by means of consecutive courses, students are taught how to make observational studies in a lab-setting, how to conduct statistical analysis on gathered data, how to conduct a thematic analysis, as well as best practices for how to conduct interviews and surveys. Then, students are tasked with making a replication study, choosing from a limited number of studies presented at conferences in the field of game research. This approach provides students with skills needed to make a study of their own when they do their bachelors thesis. Since this course sequence was implemented, the quality of theses has improved. However, the students are still provided with a limited set of tools and there is less emphasis on the availability of further methods. Again, there are pragmatic reasons for this limitation, in terms of available time and methods frequently applied in games research. Yet, this is a promising approach in terms of assuring students' proficiency in understanding and applying method.

4   A Vision for a Critical Education

To develop a vision for education, we propose to take a step back, away from ready-made structures and tools, such as the IMRAD document structure and established methods. The step back would be to the very basics of scientific thinking, and specifically in teaching students how to be precise when it comes to formulating research questions and hypotheses. This entails being able to make mutually exclusive categories, being able to formulate questions that facilitate picking a fitting manner of investigation to answer a research question or prove/disprove a hypothesis.

It is not enough to ask students to skim the first chapter of a method book, and then go straight into a certain type of 'of-the-shelf method' used for the respective field of study. This is a particular issue when it comes to interactive narrative, as both still a novel field with a relative scarcity of specific

---

[2] https://teachinggamestudies.wordpress.com.

theory/method/terminology/industry practice and an interdisciplinary enterprise which combines the knowledge and methods of several fields, including aspects of computer science, narrative theory and design science. Consequently, it is necessary to practice scientific thinking and formulation. If students learn how to discern imprecise formulation, and make precise formulations themselves, much would be gained.

In addition, students need to be made aware of the nature of interdisciplinary topics in which terminology, theory and methods potentially collide and require conscious, explicit choices (e.g. 'I will use methods from computer science because...') or bold novel approaches (e.g. 'A grounded theory approach is best to avoid cross-disciplinary confusion...'). Finally, students would learn about the iterative nature of scholarly research and appreciate the scope of research projects. A student with this kind of knowledge and skill set would be able to grasp why a certain hypothesis or research question might not be suitable for a certain type of method, and would be able to find out-of-the-box solutions to improve their own thinking and method application. Such students would also be able to work in larger research projects and understand their scope and role as important - and critical - contributors to new knowledge.

5   Toward Implementation of the Critical Education Framework (CEF)

Now that we have formulated our vision for the outcome of an ideal university education, the question is how can we turn it into reality, especially once we acknowledge practical limits in terms of teaching resources and time?

As a starting point to address this conundrum, we propose to formulate particular learning goals. A critical-oriented education would differ from existing educational programs by emphasizing the understanding of knowledge production itself. Furthermore, students would need to gain an understanding of both the advantages and limitations of the application of established approaches. We contrast these additional goals with existing ones below (Table 1).

As we have now demonstrated, it is possible to express a critical-oriented education in terms of learning goals. However, additional learning goals intuitively translate into considerably more time than is available in established educational practice. We can therefore already see that many experienced educators (and administrators) will take this aspect as an insurmountable obstacle to any kind of implementation due to financial constraints. The question is therefore how such a program can be implemented given the constraints of existing higher education systems.

Our answer is a novel approach that can be implemented by carefully restructuring existing programs. An important aspect is to change the perspective away from learning as an exercise of receiving knowledge and instead toward guided exploration and own knowledge production by students.

More concretely, we propose to change education along three broad strategies: 1.) group-based learning, 2.) research integration, and 3.) critical discussions.

Table 1. Existing and new learning goals

Existing learning goals (summarized)	Learning goals for a critical education
Learn about theory/method/terminology/industry practices	Learn about knowledge production - how are theory/method/terminology/industry practices established and what principled limitations exist with this process
Being able to choose appropriate theory/method/terminology/industry practices and apply them	Learn about theory/method/terminology/industry practices
	Learn about the limitations of theory/method/terminology/industry practices in terms of context and bias
	Being able to choose appropriate theory/method/terminology/industry practices and apply them
	Understand the particular challenges of interdisciplinary topics
	Understand when there is a need to develop novel theory/method/terminology/industry practices
	Learn how to develop and apply novel theory/method/terminology/industry practices

Our first strategy means to leverage the power of the combined "crowd intelligence" of students as a learning group in a flipped-classroom situation. Instead of learning on their own, we propose to team students up and divide learning tasks in a similar manner how we now divide project tasks, creating a shared responsibility for completing a learning project. Concretely students would be tasked with learning small aspects and teaching the other group members. Learning would thus happen in collaboration alongside check-ins by educators to assure quality. In-classroom teaching would also be reduced in line with the flipped classroom paradigm. Educators in this case would act more as facilitators than traditional teachers, discussing progress and providing quality control in terms of quizzes and examinations. Yet even in this regard, we propose to leverage peer-review amongst students as much as possible.

Our second strategy is to integrate students into research projects as a default approach. There is a wide-spread and incredibly wasteful practice of creating 'dummy' research projects or letting students design projects themselves, often with limited differentiation from prior students' projects and without concern whether the projects will have any real impact on the scholarly discipline, since 'it is only a(n undergrad) student project'. This practice leads to both reduced interest by scholars in their other role as researchers and students who are for the most part keenly aware that what they are doing is for grading purposes only. In our experiences, integration of students - even undergrads - in proper research projects is possible and also improves their performance through added motivation. In addition, students would gain direct experience of research methods 'in action' as part of a concrete research project.

Our third strategy is a refocusing of classroom time for 'critical discussions' which we understand as a forum to discuss limitations of knowledge production, the context and advantages of particular methods, and aspects such as bias. After an introduction to the limits of knowledge production, educators would bring case studies and offer a critical perspective on them and then invite students to do the same to hone their critical skills, moderated by fellow students and the educators. Students would be encouraged to discuss aspects from both their own learning exploration and their research experience, which means the two other strategies will feed into the third and outcomes of the discussions will feed back into the first two.

The combination of the three strategies will result in a tighter integration of learning and research with positive effects on motivation and understanding of research due to direct exposure to actual projects. At the same time, the critical aspect of education will become central.

6   Conclusion

In this paper, we have discussed existing issues in higher education on interactive narratives and related fields. Furthermore, we have outlined a new approach to address these issues, the Critical Education Framework (CEF) by formulating learning goals and three broad strategies. We will continue to improve this approach and hope it can be implemented and further developed in discussions with other educators.

References

1. Aylett, R.: Narrative in virtual environments-towards emergent narrative. In: Proceedings of AAAI Symposium on Narrative Intelligence (1999). http://www.aaai.org/Papers/Symposia/Fall/1999/FS-99-01/FS99-01-014.pdf
2. Barbara, J., et al.: IDNs in education: skills for future generations. In: Holloway-Attaway, L., Murray, J.T. (eds.) Interactive Storytelling, pp. 57–72. Springer Nature Switzerland, Cham (2023). https://doi.org/10.1007/978-3-031-47655-6_4
3. Bettocchi, E., Klimick, C., Perani, L.: Can the subaltern game design? An exploratory study about creating a decolonial ludology framework through ludonarratives. In: Proceedings of DiGRA 2020 Conference: Play Everywhere (2020). https://dl.digra.org/index.php/dl/article/view/1218
4. Daiute, C., Cox, D., Murray, J.T.: Imagining the other for interactive digital narrative design learning in real time in sherlock. In: Interactive Storytelling: 14th International Conference on Interactive Digital Storytelling, ICIDS 2021, pp. 1–8. Springer Nature (2019).https://doi.org/10.1007/978-3-030-92300-6_46
5. Daiute, C., Murray, J.T., Wright, J.: Discovering IDN authoring strategies: novices anchor choice design through character development with player feedback. In: Holloway-Attaway, L., Murray, J.T. (eds.) Interactive Storytelling, pp. 239–258. Springer Nature Switzerland, Cham (2023) https://doi.org/10.1007/978-3-031-47655-6_15
6. Denscombe, M.: The Good Research Guide: Research Methods for Small-Scale Social Research Projects. McGraw-Hill Education (UK) (2021)
7. Deterding, S., Cutting, J.: Objective difficulty-skill balance impacts perceived balance but not behaviour: a test of flow and self-determination theory predictions. Proc. ACM Hum. Comput. Interact. **7**(CHI PLAY), 1179–1205 (2023). https://doi.org/10.1145/3611065

8. Echtler, F., HäuSSler, M.: Open source, open science, and the replication crisis in HCI. In: CHI EA '18, Extended Abstracts of the 2018 CHI Conference on Human Factors in Computing Systems, pp. 1–8. Association for Computing Machinery, New York, NY, USA (2018). https://doi.org/10.1145/3170427.3188395

9. Eladhari, M.P.: TOG: an innovation centric approach to teaching computational expression and game design. In: Teaching Games: Pedagogical Approaches - DiGRA 2019 Pre-Conference Workshop. Kyoto, Japan (2019)

10. Eladhari, P.M., Koentiz, H.: MMAJams - multi-method analysis of games in research and education. In: Proceedings of the 2020 DiGRA International Conference: Play Everywhere. Tampere, Finland (2020)

11. Fisher, J.A., Samuels, J.T.: Teaching virtual reality interactive digital narratives: a curriculum and case study. J. Interact. Narrative Res. 1(1) (2024). https://journal.ardin.online/teaching-virtual-reality-interactive-digital-narratives-a-curriculum-and-case-study

12. Johannesson, P., Perjons, E.: An Introduction to Design Science. Springer International Publishing : Imprint: Springer, Cham, 1st ed. 2014 edn. (2014).https://doi.org/10.1007/978-3-319-10632-8

13. Koenitz, H.: Understanding Interactive Digital Narrative. Immersive Expressions for a Complex Time. Routledge, London and New York (2023). https://doi.org/10.4324/9781003106425

14. Koenitz, H., Eladhari, M.P.: Approaches towards novel phenomena. A reflection on issues in IDN research, teaching and practice. In: Interactive Storytelling. Lecture Notes in Computer Science, Springer (2022). https://doi.org/10.1007/978-3-031-22298-6_28

15. Koenitz, H., Eladhari, M.P.: Challenges of IDN research and teaching. In: Cardona-Rivera, R.E., Sullivan, A., Young, R.M. (eds.) Interactive Storytelling, pp. 26–39. Lecture Notes in Computer Science, Springer International Publishing, Cham (2019). https://doi.org/10.1007/978-3-030-33894-7_4

16. Koenitz, H., Eladhari, M.P.: When has theory ever failed us? - Identifying issues with the application of theory in interactive digital narrative analysis and design. In: Holloway-Attaway, L., Murray, J.T. (eds.) Interactive Storytelling, pp. 21–37. Springer Nature Switzerland, Cham (2023).https://doi.org/10.1007/978-3-031-47655-6_2

17. Koenitz, H., Roth, C., Dubbelman, T.: Educating interactive narrative designers: cornerstones of a program. Trans. Digit. Games Res. Assoc. 5(3) (2021). https://doi.org/10.26503/todigra.v5i3.125

18. Lankoski, P., Eladhari, M.: Constructive alignment in teaching game research in game development bachelors programme. In: Teaching Games: Pedagogical Approaches - DiGRA 2019 Pre-Conference Workshop. Kyoto, Japan (2019)

19. Law, E.L.C., Brühlmann, F., Mekler, E.D.: Systematic review and validation of the game experience questionnaire (GEQ) - Implications for citation and reporting practice. In: Proceedings of the 2018 Annual Symposium on Computer-Human Interaction in Play, pp. 257–270. ACM, Melbourne VIC Australia (2018). https://doi.org/10.1145/3242671.3242683

20. Reyes, M.C., Silva, C., Koenitz, H.: Decolonizing IDN pedagogy from and with global south: a cross-cultural case study. In: Holloway-Attaway, L., Murray, J.T. (eds.) Interactive Storytelling, pp. 138–158. Springer Nature Switzerland, Cham (2023). https://doi.org/10.1007/978-3-031-47655-6_9

21. Rouse, R., Corron, A.: Levelling up: A critical feminist pedagogy for game design. MAI J. Feminism Visual Cult. (2020). https://doi.org/10.1177/1741659019881040,

https://maifeminism.com/leveling-up-a-critical-feminist-pedagogy-for-game-design/

22. Silva, C., Reyes, M.C., Koenitz, H.: Towards a decolonial framework for IDN. In: Vosmeer, M., Holloway-Attaway, L. (eds.) Interactive Storytelling, vol. 13762, pp. 193–205. Springer International Publishing, Cham (2022). https://doi.org/10.1007/978-3-031-22298-6_12

23. Ãzer, H., Kanbul, S., Ozdamli, F.: Effects of the gamification supported flipped classroom model on the attitudes and opinions regarding game-coding education. Int. J. Emerging Technol. Learn. (iJET) **13**(1), 109–123 (2018). https://www.learntechlib.org/p/182229/

Fostering Empathy Through Inclusive Interactive Digital Narratives

Victoria Lagrange(✉) [ID]

Kennesaw State University, Kennesaw, GA 30144, USA
vlagrang@kennesaw.edu

Abstract. This Late-Breaking Work explores the potential of Interactive Digital Narratives (IDN) to foster empathy and promote positive social change, particularly towards marginalized groups. Recent controversies in the gaming industry underscore the challenges of balancing narrative freedom with authentic representation. This project investigates whether IDN can meaningfully engage with the complexities of diversity and inclusion.

Our research centers on a game created and developed by undergraduate and graduate students, featuring a Honduran immigrant facing discrimination in her new role as hiring manager. Two studies are designed to assess the game's effectiveness in fostering empathy for this character and its potential to influence players' long-term attitudes toward immigrants. The dual goals of this project are to create a compelling, empathy-driven narrative that can be utilized in educational settings and to study whether IDN can successfully increase empathy and reduce bias toward marginalized groups. This research contributes to a growing body of work on the prosocial effects of IDN and its potential to drive real-world attitude change.

Keywords: Prosocial · Immigration · IDN · Empathy · Bias

1 Introduction

Interactive Digital Narratives (IDN), known for their emphasis on player agency and branching storylines, are often viewed as a medium with strong potential for fostering inclusivity. However, recent controversies surrounding Red Thread Games' *Dustborn* [1] underscore the tension between narrative freedom and representation. Critics have scrutinized the game's portrayal of marginalized characters, questioning whether it genuinely provides a platform for diverse voices or instead falls into the traps of tokenism and stereotyping. This controversy invites a deeper examination of how IDNs can meaningfully engage with the complex topic of inclusivity.

As Koenitz et al. [2] argue, IDN have unique advantages in representing complex issues such as intersectionality and diversity due to their specific affordances: "Audiences as participants influence the progressions as well as outcome of the narrative but also see the effects of decisions and revisit them in replay. They can choose between different viewpoints, even add their own perspectives and discuss their insight with others, all within the same IDN artefact." (77). However, in a subsequent article [3], researchers note that designing and evaluating the prosocial effects of IDNs still yields uncertain results. Previous research has explored the relationship between interactive narratives and prosocial behavior, with some studies finding that interactivity is positively linked to prosocial behavior [4–7]. However, more recent studies have found no difference between linear and interactive conditions [8]. Koenitz et al. [3] also criticize the focus on empathy in most of these studies, arguing that the limitations of the concept are often ignored.

1.1 IDN and Empathy

One approach to address inclusivity in IDN is by fostering empathy for the player character while distinguishing empathy from morality [9]. In this context, when designing characters that players are meant to empathize with, it is essential to integrate complexity and contradictory elements.

The impact of player agency and engagement has led some scholars to argue that IDN may be particularly well-suited to cultivating empathy [10–12]. Others, however, suggest that players may override individual characters by projecting their own interests onto them, using them as avatars instead [13–15]. Additionally, some research suggest that interactive narrative may not have a positive effect on identification and transformation [16]. Thus, the debate over the role of empathy-related transportation in IDN remains ongoing and, so far, inconclusive.

The term empathy is notoriously ambiguous, with multiple definitions [17]. For the purposes of this study, we focus on three aspects of empathy: perspective-taking, which involves imagining another person's point of view [18]; empathic concern, which focuses on the wellbeing of another [18], and story transportation or immersion [13].

Perspective-taking refers to the act of understanding others and imagining their perspective. It can function independently of emotion sharing and other forms of empathy [19]. Although perspective-taking and empathic concern are often correlated at the trait level [18], perspective taking can occur without feelings of empathic concern.

Empathic concern involve feelings of care, compassion, or sympathy toward a person in need [18]. While perspective-taking and empathic concern can sometimes operate independently, perspective-taking can motivate prosocial behavior by increasing empathic concern [20].

Transportation and immersion into a story can be prerequisites for experiencing different aspects of empathy. For a player, feeling immersed in a story is distinct from empathizing with a character. Players who become immersed in – or transported into – a storyworld are emotionally and cognitively engaged, vividly picturing events as they unfold [13, 21].

While players may take on the perspective of the player character in the story, they may not necessarily feel empathic concern for them. In other words, an inclusive IDN would aim to foster both perspective-taking and empathic concern for a player character who experiences discrimination. This, in turn, could encourage the player to make prosocial decisions within the game – and possibly extend this to attitude and behavioral change outside of the storyworld.

1.2   IDN Design and Research Project

Our proposed research aims to focus on how game narratives can foster empathy for a discriminated character and influence attitudes towards immigrants. This work builds on our previous efforts, where we created a short game featuring a player character who is an immigrant and works as a hiring manager at a company that promotes discriminatory practices. Our approach integrates three key elements that we anticipate will promote attitude change:

1. Character design and backstory: We developed three complex characters with ambiguous relationships to diversity and inclusion, allowing players to address these issues within the game. Our goal is to enhance perspective-taking and empathic concern for both the playable character and the job candidates in the game. To achieve this, we subtly highlighted the characters' backgrounds through dialogue interactions, mimicking real-life conversations.
2. World-building: By creating a generic setting, we aim to make participants' in-game experiences relatable to real-world situations, thereby enhancing the transfer of empathy and attitudes.
3. Realistic representation: The game combines two types of mechanics – a branching narrative where players make dialogue decisions for the protagonist, and a simulation where players sort through resumes to select the best candidates for the position. For example, players must make choices about how to respond to discriminatory comments directed at the protagonist. These decisions, paired with real-time emotional feedback from the protagonist, help players understand the emotional toll of discrimination. Visual and audio cues are used to further reinforce emotional responses. We ensure accurate gender and race representation based on census statistics to provide an authentic experience.

Rather than focusing solely on implicit bias, this study aims to examine changes in attitudes toward discriminatory practices. This project seeks to answer the following question: Can video game narratives leverage empathy for people who are discriminated against and influence social attitudes?

We propose that immersion in the game's fictional setting, coupled with empathy for the characters, can lead to a reflexive Proteus effect, where players experience the virtual world through the identity of their avatar [23]. This experience could lead to desirable changes in players' real-world attitudes and beliefs. Often, in the absence of external reminders or training to take empathic leaps, people avoid empathizing with those who are different from them [24–26]. This study aims to demonstrate how IDN can act as an impetus for people to empathize with marginalized groups, contributing to a broader understanding of how interactive digital narratives can be harnessed for social good.

We therefore ask: can an IDN effectively foster empathy for marginalized groups, particularly immigrants facing discrimination?

We hypothesize that (1) the game will be successful at fostering empathy for the immigrant protagonist (2) these empathy gains will persist over time, leading to positive attitude changes.

2 Method

We have designed two complementary studies to evaluate the effectiveness of a short game we developed titled *Corporation Incorporated*. The game follows Maria Villalobos, a 25-year-old Honduran immigrant who comes to the United States to work as a hiring manager at Corporation Incorporated and implement their 'revitalization program.' Throughout the game, players experience Maria's one-week trial period, during which she must assess 25 job applicants daily under time pressure, navigate complex social dynamics and face discrimination common to many immigrants. Our goal is to determine whether this game successfully fosters empathy for Maria and whether it can influence long-term attitude change in players. Given the sensitive nature of the subject matter, all participants will provide informed consent, and the study will adhere to institutional ethical guidelines; IRB approval will be obtained before starting participants' recruitment.

2.1 Study 1: Evaluation of Empathy Induction Through Gameplay

Objective. The study aims to assess whether our game successfully fosters empathy for the protagonist.

Participants. We will recruit 10 pilot participants and 100 participants for the final study.

Procedure.

Pre-game Survey:
Participants will complete a pre-game survey measuring dispositional empathy using the Interpersonal Reactivity Index [18]. The survey will also include questions about their opinions on immigration, other discrimination-related topics, habits, and their demographics.

Gameplay:
Participants will play the game, stepping into Maria's shoes as she navigates the challenges of her new role while facing discrimination and other obstacles.

Post-Game Survey:
After completing the game, participants will take a post-game survey that includes:

– Memory questions to assess participants' attention to the game's narrative
– Items from the Interpersonal Reactivity Indes to measure changes in empathic concern and perspective taking.
– Cohen's 10-item identification scale [27] to measure identification with the player character
– Questions about specific narrative elements of the game that either facilitated or inhibited empathy for Maria.

Data Analysis. Pre- and post- game empathic concern and perspective-taking scores will be compared. A significant increase in these scores post-game would suggest that the game successfully fostered empathy for Maria. Qualitative responses about the narrative elements will be analyzed to identify key factors contributing to empathy outcomes.

Outcome. If the game is successful at fostering empathy, we will proceed to Study 2. If the game is not successful, the narrative team will revise portions of the game based on participants' feedback, and the study will be repeated to assess the impact of these changes.

2.2   Study 2: Examining Long-Term Empathy and Behavioral Change

Objective. This between-subject study aims to examine whether playing the game induces long-term changes in state empathy and whether it influences players' attitudes towards discrimination, particularly against immigrants.

Participants. We will recruit 200 participants from diverse backgrounds. Participants will be randomly assigned to one of the two groups: the Prosocial Group (who will play the game) and the Control Group (who will not play the game).

Procedure.

Prosocial Group:
Before playing the game, participants will fill in a pre-game survey, similar to the one in study 1 (with measures of dispositional empathy using the Interpersonal Reactivity index [18], questions about their opinions on immigration, other discrimination-related topics, habits, and their demographics). Participants will then play the game, experiencing Maria's story and challenges as an immigrant. One week later, they will be asked to complete a follow-up survey, which includes:

– Two immigrant stories sourced from the University of Minnesota's Immigration History Research Center's public library.
– A questionnaire similar to the post-game questionnaire, in study 1, including the IRI and questions about empathy for the immigrants described in the stories who share characteristics with the player character.

Control Group:

Participants in the control group will complete the same pre-game survey as those in the prosocial group but will not play the game. They will be presented with the same two immigrant stories as the prosocial group and will complete the same follow-up survey.

Data Analysis. We will compare empathy scores between the prosocial group and the control group to evaluate whether playing the game had a significant impact on participants' empathy for immigrants. Behavioral changes will be measured by tracking participant actions towards marginalized groups through anonymous, simulated decision-making tasks. Statistical analysis will be conducted (using methods such as repeated measures ANOVA) to determine whether the game fostered state empathy and influenced longer-term attitude change concerning discrimination.

Outcome. This study will help determine whether the game has a lasting impact on participants' empathy and whether it influences their attitudes and behaviors towards marginalized groups.

3 Conclusion

Although we are still in the early stages of piloting this project, it has the potential to significantly advance our understanding of the positive impacts of IDN. Specifically, it could demonstrate how players can transfer their in-game experience to reduce real-life discriminatory practices. We know that games can induce prosocial behavior, and this project seeks to explore whether games can also increase empathy for historically excluded groups. Research on serious games for learning has been a growing area of interest since 2009, particularly within the game studies community. Zhonggen's meta-analysis of the use of serious games in education [28] highlights the positive aspects of learning through games, while also identifying a potential disconnect between gameplay and lessons as an area for improvement.

The goal of this project is twofold: first, to create an Interactive Digital Narrative (IDN) that successfully fosters empathy for marginalized characters, and second, to study whether such a narrative can effectively increase empathy and reduce bias toward historically excluded groups. By designing a game that encourages players to step into the shoes of an immigrant facing discrimination, we aim to explore the potential of IDN as powerful tools for both social change and education. If successful, this research project could provide valuable insights into how IDN might be used in educational settings to represent complex issues and promote inclusivity and empathy, ultimately contributing to a more equitable and understanding society.

Disclosure of Interests. The game has been published by Kennesaw State University. The author of this presentation and other creators may receive financial compensation for the sale of the game consistent with Kennesaw State University's IP policy.

References

1. Dustborn. Red Thread Games. Quantic Dreams. PS5 (2024)
2. Koenitz, H., Barbara, J., Eladhari, M.P.: Interactive digital narrative (IDN)—new ways to represent complexity and facilitate digitally empowered citizens. New Rev. Hypermed. Multimed. **28**, 76–96 (2022). https://doi.org/10.1080/13614568.2023.2181503
3. Koenitz, H., Roth, C., Mekler, E.: Alternate realities in interactive digital narratives – understanding and improving design and prosocial effects through empirical methods. Multimed. Tools Appl. **83**, 46757–46778 (2024). https://doi.org/10.1007/s11042-024-18884-8
4. Peng, W., Lee, M., Heeter, C.: The effects of a serious game on role-taking and willingness to help. J. Commun. **60**, 723–742 (2010). https://doi.org/10.1111/j.1460-2466.2010.01511.x
5. Green, M.C., Jenkins, K.M.: Interactive narratives: processes and outcomes in user-directed stories. J. Commun. **64**, 479–500 (2014). https://doi.org/10.1111/jcom.12093
6. Ruggiero, D.: The effect of a persuasive social impact game on affective learning and attitude. Comput. Hum. Behav. **45**, 213–221 (2015). https://doi.org/10.1016/j.chb.2014.11.062
7. Steinemann, S.T., Mekler, E.D., Opwis, K.: Increasing donating behavior through a game for change: the role of interactivity and appreciation. In: Proceedings of the 2015 Annual Symposium on Computer-Human Interaction in Play, pp. 319–329. Association for Computing Machinery, New York, NY, USA (2015). https://doi.org/10.1145/2793107.2793125
8. Steinemann, S.T., Iten, G.H., Opwis, K., Forde, S.F., Frasseck, L., Mekler, E.D.: Interactive narratives affecting social change. J. Med. Psychol. **29**, 54–66 (2017). https://doi.org/10.1027/1864-1105/a000211

9. Breithaupt, F.: The bad things we do because of empathy. Interdisc. Sci. Rev. **43**, 166–174 (2018). https://doi.org/10.1080/03080188.2018.1450928

10. Hand, S., Varan, D.: Interactive stories and the audience: why empathy is important. Comput. Entertain. **7**, 39:1–39:14 (2009). https://doi.org/10.1145/1594943.1594951

11. Riedl, M.O., Bulitko, V.: Interactive narrative: an intelligent systems approach. AI Mag. **34**, 67 (2013). https://doi.org/10.1609/aimag.v34i1.2449

12. Vázquez-Herrero, J.: Enhanced experiences in interactive nonfiction: an experimental study on the effects of nonlinearity and interactivity. Int. J. Commun. **15**, 23 (2021)

13. Green, M.C., Brock, T.C., Kaufman, G.F.: Understanding media enjoyment: the role of transportation into narrative worlds. Commun. Theory **14**, 311–327 (2004). https://doi.org/10.1111/j.1468-2885.2004.tb00317.x

14. Wake, P.: Life and death in the second person: identification, empathy, and antipathy in the adventure gamebook. Narrative **24**, 190–210 (2016)

15. Green, M.C., Sestir, M.: Transportation Theory. In: The International Encyclopedia of Media Effects, pp. 1–14. John Wiley & Sons, Ltd (2017). https://doi.org/10.1002/9781118783764.wbieme0083

16. Scholl, J., Pandrea, M., van Enschot, R.: How to help your depressed friend? The effects of interactive health narratives on cognitive and transformative learning. Front. Commun. **7** (2022). https://doi.org/10.3389/fcomm.2022.966944

17. Hall, J.A., Schwartz, R.: Empathy present and future. J. Soc. Psychol. **159**, 225–243 (2019). https://doi.org/10.1080/00224545.2018.1477442

18. Davis, M.H.: A multidimensional approach to individual differences in empathy. In: JSAS Catalog of Selected Documents in Psychology (1980)

19. Stietz, J., Jauk, E., Krach, S., Kanske, P.: Dissociating empathy from perspective-taking: evidence from intra- and inter-individual differences research. Front. Psychiatry. **10** (2019). https://doi.org/10.3389/fpsyt.2019.00126

20. Batson, C.D.: Empathy-induced altruistic motivation. In: Prosocial Motives, Emotions, and Behavior: The Better Angels of our Nature, pp. 15–34. American Psychological Association, Washington, DC, US (2010). https://doi.org/10.1037/12061-001

21. Gerrig, R.J.: Experiencing Narrative Worlds: On the Psychological Activities of Reading. Yale University Press, New Haven, CT, US (1993)

22. Peck, T.C., Seinfeld, S., Aglioti, S.M., Slater, M.: Putting yourself in the skin of a black avatar reduces implicit racial bias. Conscious. Cogn. **22**, 779–787 (2013). https://doi.org/10.1016/j.concog.2013.04.016

23. Yee, N., Bailenson, J.: The proteus effect: the effect of transformed self-representation on behavior. Hum. Commun. Res. **33**, 271–290 (2007). https://doi.org/10.1111/j.1468-2958.2007.00299.x

24. Azevedo, R.T., Macaluso, E., Avenanti, A., Santangelo, V., Cazzato, V., Aglioti, S.M.: Their pain is not our pain: brain and autonomic correlates of empathic resonance with the pain of same and different race individuals. Hum. Brain Mapp. **34**, 3168–3181 (2013). https://doi.org/10.1002/hbm.22133

25. Gerace, A., Day, A., Casey, S., Mohr, P.: Perspective taking and empathy: does having similar past experience to another person make it easier to take their perspective? J. Relat. Res. **6**, e10 (2015). https://doi.org/10.1017/jrr.2015.6

26. Stevens, S.M., Jago, C.P., Jasko, K., Heyman, G.D.: Trustworthiness and Ideological similarity (But not ideology) promote empathy. Pers. Soc. Psychol. Bull. **47**, 1452–1465 (2021). https://doi.org/10.1177/0146167220972245

27. Cohen, J.: Defining Identification: a theoretical look at the identification of audiences with media characters. Mass Commun. Soc. **4**, 245–264 (2001). https://doi.org/10.1207/S15327 825MCS0403_01

28. Zhonggen, Y.: A meta-analysis of use of serious games in education over a decade. Int. J. Comput. Games Technol. **2019**, 4797032 (2019). https://doi.org/10.1155/2019/4797032

Interactive Digital Narratives for Modern Historical Research

Vincenzo Lombardo[1]([⊠])(iD), Aurora Laurenti[2], Matteo Capurro[2],
Federico Favole[1], Luigi Provero[2], Gelsomina Spione[2], and Alessio Fiore[2]

[1] Dipartimento di Informatica, Università di Torino, Torino, Italy
`vincenzo.lombardo@unito.it, federico.favole@edu.unito.it`
[2] Dipartimento di Studi Storici, Università di Torino, Torino, Italy
`{luigi.provero,gelsomina.spione,alessio.fiore}@unito.it`

Abstract. Historians and related disciplinary scientists have been long debating about the historical research as getting close to exact sciences or as a more or less structured narratives. Then, the developments of the WWW and of the interactive media in general have included the digital formats into the debate, mostly with display applications for public history. However, the potential of interactive media for research purposes have remained under-explored, together with their relationship to major historiographic questions.

This paper aims at proposing interactive digital narratives (IDNs) to overcome the limitations of linear narratives for historical research. The Historygraphia system supports the development of an IDN, through the interconnection of narratives through a semantic labeling that overcomes the barriers of the diverse history-related disciplines (history of art, history of architecture, archaeology, medieval history, ...). The system has been experienced and preliminarily evaluated for its effectiveness in addressing the development of historical narratives and the discovery of novel interconnections.

Keywords: historiography · hypertextual narrative · cultural heritage

1 Introduction

Today, historians intervene in a complex context, in which the public use of history is invasive. The relationship between narratives, including interactive digital narratives (IDNs), and history has produced a vast number of applications, especially to public history and history education. Public history concerns the engagement of history with wide audiences, usually related to dissemination places, such as museums and heritage sites, or media (podcasts, documentaries, drama, ...) in several forms, such as oral history and family history [18]. A large number of games have been released with historical themes, though there are many concerns regarding their historical accuracy [15].

In history education, interactive storytelling lets users experience different story lines, with narrative elements that provide links to everyday contemporary

J. T. Murray and M. C. Reyes (Eds.): ICIDS 2024, LNCS 15468, pp. 232–242, 2025.
https://doi.org/10.1007/978-3-031-78450-7_17

life, often using informal or humorous tones conveyed by surprising characters. For example, the web-based IDN described in [13], proposes an experience in the ancient market of Athens (the agora), implementing a collaborative learning activity through a branching narrative, with small groups of students engaged in reflection and dialogue at decision points.

In both cases, there has been a great concern for ethical issues, that have also been addressed with possible guidelines [3]. For example, in the IDN example above, users could take into account the interests of characters affected by some decision or what were the consequences of the decisions in both the short and the long term.

Less explored is the field of historical research. Historians, in several disciplinary variants, are engaged in a long-lasting debate about the nature of historical research, with a two-pole distribution: on the one hand, the positivist scientism that positions historiography among the exact sciences, on the other, the deconstructionism, a more or less structured narrative, sometimes floating to a full logocentrism, that reduces the historical text to a pure linguistic construction, avoiding the notion of "truth" and the mapping to reality [7]. Jerzy Topolski, in his monumental text on historiography, has proposed a synthesis of the two extreme positions [14]: first, he analyzes the methods of the historical research, with considerations on the subject matter, the historical fact; then, he reflects on historical writing, with the many represented categories of writing; finally (and here is the synthesis!), he claims that historical knowledge is not purely source-based, but there exists a non-source-based knowledge that determines the selection of relevant information to identify the historical fact, with its hierarchical distribution and thus the formal construction of the narrative.

In addressing historical research with a digital approach, a particular attention has been devoted to develop accounts related to heritage items, that is objects and sites that provide a physical bridge to the immaterial narrative exposition. The digital twins of real objects or original digital artifacts, "quasi-objects" for [6], take on "different meanings in writings by different authors". For example, virtual reality immersive environments for the historical reconstructions merge material items and non-material narratives, to provide multiple perspectives [2].

In this paper, we describe the Historygraphia system that supports historical research, by pursuing an interdisciplinary approach to the representation of the historical facts. Short linear narratives are interconnected by the co-presence of semantic entities, whose categories, namely objects, agents, places, time intervals, events, themes, and states of affairs, have been negotiated between the several disciplines of history, namely history itself, history of art, history of architecture, history of religions, history of the economic thought, ...). A representation of the assumed historical truth is encoded in the formal representation of such semantic entities. Narratives, which are centered upon objects and places, are linked to the actual sources, which provide the evidence for the historical truth of the narrated facts, which are encoded in a knowledge graph of the semantic entities. So, the discipline-based narratives are arranged into an interdisciplinary hypertext, that returns the complexity of the historical investigation, which would be blurred by the linear narrative format. The system is an authoring platform, with a design based on widely acknowledged tenets of historiography. The implemented prototype has been preliminarily evaluated by a group of user-historians, who have an interest in proposing the platform to scholars in local communities.

2   Related Work

Historians have been using computational systems and networked information since their inception. A label that can characterize all applications concerning history is "digital history", considered to be "a branch of the Digital Humanities and an extension of quantitative history, cliometrics, and computing." (Wikipedia entry[1] considered by [17] one of the most comprehensive definitions; a history of the term, with its nuances, is reported in [18]). In general, digital history is the effort of digitizing the past and creating a framework through the technology for people to experience, read, and follow an argument about a major historical problem [11].

A popular approach has been to arrange a collection of sources and materials around a historiographical question, with the development of narratives that are organized in a spatial layout. This reflects what in game academia is known as "spatial storytelling" (after [8]), a term that describes a narrative centered around some place. For example, "Victoria's Victoria"[2] is a digital archive of Victoria's early history, where archival sources are connected through thematic narratives arranged into categories (such as chronological decades, significant places, relevant themes, ...). The Spatial History Project[3] hosts collaborative open-ended projects of historical research, conceptually focused on space. Spatial and non-spatial data are organized into geospatial databases and use visualization to identify recurrent patterns. For example, "Shaping the West" models and investigates how railroads shaped the American West in the 19th century with a "spatial history" approach.

The development of an IDN system for historical research requires an awareness of the historiographic approaches. Historiography, "the study of the study of history" [14], has been characterized by a positivist approach until the 1960's: there is an ontological premise that supports an interpretation of the past; such a premise is independent of the scientist; the ultimate goal of historical research is the discovery of the historical truth; the truth is reconstructed from the historical sources and transferred to a structured writing. In the 1960's, there has been a growing interest in historical narratives, with a particular attention to the linguistic medium. The generated debate, which was triggered by these lines of thought, has seen opposing arguments. According to Mandelbaum, it is true that when a historian is ready to write his essay, "there are a number of respects in which he may be compared to a storyteller" [10]: possessing the knowledge

---

[1] https://en.wikipedia.org/wiki/Digital_history, visited on 5 October 2024.

[2] http://web.uvic.ca/vv/, visited on 5 October 2024.

[3] http://spatialhistory.stanford.edu, visited on 5 October 2024.

about the historical inquiry, the historian can build the historical account in a narrative form, although the research path could have been different than linear (the exposition is different than the real nature of the relationships in the research).

On the other side, there have been many applications of the general claim of historical research as a narrative or linguistic construction. For example, Danto does not abandon the positivist approach, but argues that historical research differs from exact sciences because it is a "narrative" and not an "explanation" of facts [5].

Finally, Ankersmith provides a detailed conception of narratological methodology for historical research, a subjective construction about the past, though based on individual facts acknowledged to be true [1]. The structure of the narrative is a mental creation of the historian, because it contains, beyond the individual facts, the "narrative substances", that reflect a particular point of view of the historian (and storyteller). In general, the role of narration has become central in historiography, and in all the post-modernist thought, which assigns an active role to the subject in the process of knowledge [16]. According to White, the notion of history itself implies an ambiguity that raises from the fact that the object of study itself can be conceived on the equivocation that there are "historical" facts and "unhistorical" facts.

An operational synthesis of the mentioned positions is that the historian cannot know the complete truth about the past, but can try to get the closest to the truth. Our project stems from the idea that history in the narrative format should not be used as a way to elude the search for the truth, but as a different method to get to it, interconnecting the views of the several disciplines of history. Moving from traditional narrative to IDN, we can address complex issues by empowering narrative with the affordances provided by the digital media [9], that is the procedural, participatory, spatial, and encyclopedic features [12]. So, an encyclopedic IDN can be explored spatially by the participating audience, to which the IDN engine proposes contents through procedural decisions. In the historical research context, the IDN structure is the mean to avoid the rigidity of the arguments of the linear narrative and to provide an interdisciplinary approach to the research question. In particular, in Historygraphia, the formal representation of semantic entities associated with interconnected narratives is a way to address a form of truth about the historical events as revealed by the related and referred sources.

3   Design and Implementation of IDN Historygraphia for Historical Research

Project Historygraphia was born with the idea to enhance the cultural features distributed on a territory, in an attempt to support the dialogue between the historians (that is, the field experts) and the local communities, including the decision makers.

The IDN structure works as a bridge between historical disciplines, which have different methodological approaches. Historians, each one belonging to some disciplinary group, propose their narratives, which are centered upon some object and place of the territory. Each narrative is annotated with semantic entities to realize an interconnected organization of the narratives and, at the same time, an interdisciplinary reading by subjects, that overcome the traditional disciplinary boundaries.

The semantic annotation acknowledges a formal notion of truth of historical facts, by marking a few entities, characterizing the disciplines participating to the project. Categories include Events and States of affairs, Objects, Time spans and Places, Actors, being single Persons or Groups, and finally some abstract concepts, such as Reference models and Themes, mostly related to the history of art and history of architecture (see Fig. 1). There exist relations between these semantic categories: an actor that participates in an event, an object collocated at some place, ... The knowledge graph of individuals (e.g., the Event of commissioning Object painting located in Place church to Actor artist, the State of affairs toll gaining by Actor royal family because of the Event transit along some road, ...), that results from the connection of all entities through the relations is a representation of the logical truth of the historical facts, expressed in a formal logic. Figure 1 shows the categorial conceptual map that has been deployed as a backbone for the annotation of the historical narratives. Most entities and relations have been encoded in the CIDOC-CRM model for the representation of cultural heritage facts [4], with some ad-hoc classes that abstract Reference models and Themes of artistic works. So, together with the IDN, we acknowledge and realize a representation of the historical facts considered to be true, in a way compliant with Ankersmith's position, with a notion of truth applied to individual facts.

Narratives are also connected to the sources, to document the historical facts. Sources are digitized materials stored by the Historygraphia platform or links to external materials and consist of original documents, images, essays on historical facts, digitized collections of objects, ... The references to sources are also connected to the entities and relations in the knowledge graph, that works as a repository of the identified historical facts. In Fig. 2, we show an (anonymized) example of a narrative, with its connections to the related sources and to the entities that correspond to the fact encoding in the knowledge graph. The narrative tells of a commissioning that the breeders' brotherhood has entrusted a painter for a cycle of 12 canvases; the choice of the painter depends on the painter's origins in a land that has an intense commerce with the local community. The knowledge graph represents the main entities that participate to this event. The two sources reported in the figure are a manuscript, that supports the news of the intense commerce of cattle, and the digital collection of ex-voto paintings, that display a relevant presence of herds.

Figure 3 show the overall design of the Historygraphia system: the Narrative, Sources, and Knowledge layers are interconnected. The historical facts are marked by the connections to the entities in the knowledge layer. All the three

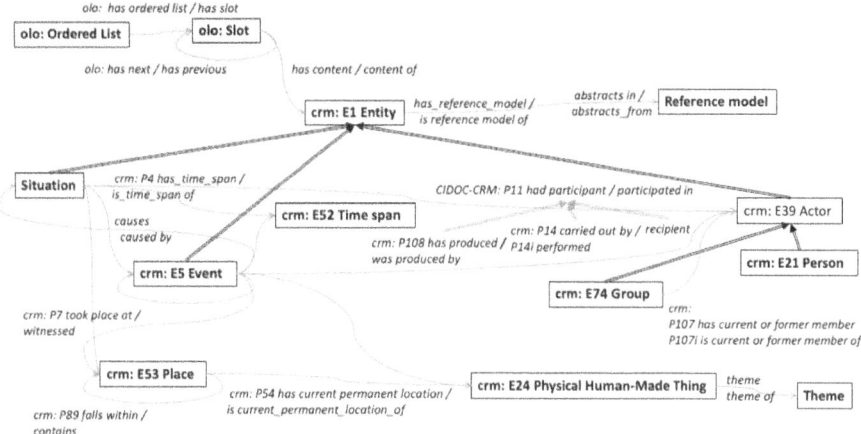

Fig. 1. Ontology used in labeling individual narratives in Historygraphia project.

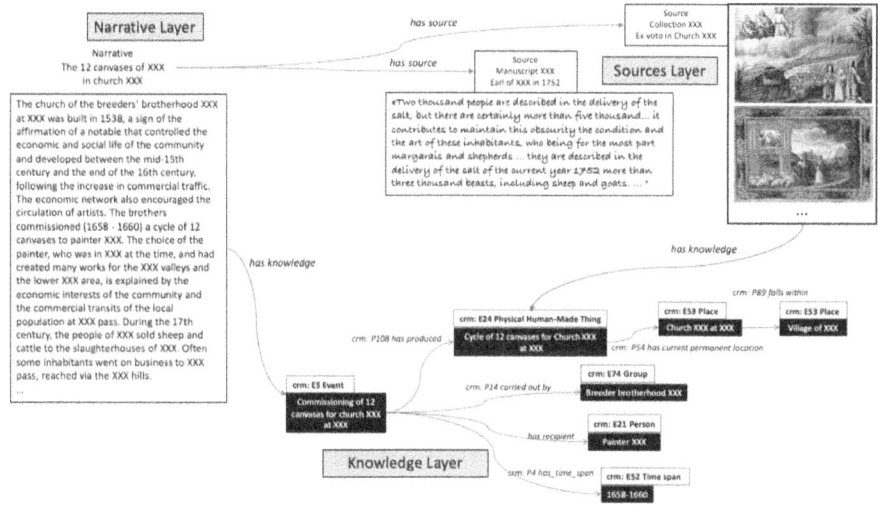

Fig. 2. A snapshot of an example narrative with the connections to sources and knowledge graph.

layers are reachable from each other, for a global navigation through the narratives and the access to sources and the knowledge graph.

The Historygraphia system has been implemented as a webapp that is built on a database that stores both narratives and knowledge and indexes sources. CMS Omeka-S provides the interface to the database, by exposing an API that

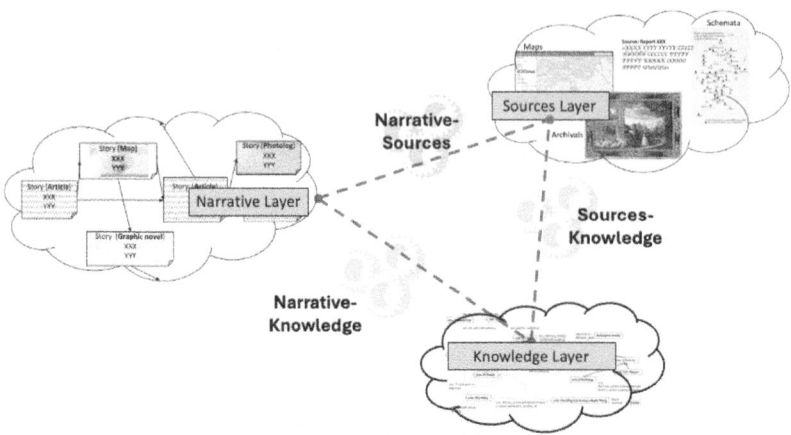

Fig. 3. Historygraphia System layers: Narratives, Knowledge, Sources.

allows the addition and visualization of the data according to a predefined organization.

The user interface visualizes a map that georeferences the narratives according to some pivot place selected by the author.

4   Experiencing the Prototype

The whole system has been discussed and designed with a collaboration between multimedia designers, knowledge engineers, and experts of historical disciplines. The latter, numbering 9 participants belonging to 4 different disciplines (medieval history, history of art, history of architecture, archaeology), have become the contributors to the platform. The platform currently contains 30 narratives, mostly of historic, history of art and history of architecture domains, focusing on the Cuneo area, in Piedmont, Italy.

Initially the team addressed the narrative structure and the knowledge encoding, namely the selection of the semantic categories that could label the historical facts, interdisciplinarly. The first meetings were mostly a training carried out on exemplar case studies from all the disciplines involved. The creation of a specific ontology for the structuring of narratives and knowledge raised the awareness about the identification of actors, places, objects, actions, contexts, according to two perspectives: classification and topic selection. The classification issue was carried out with a deep study of acknowledged cataloging systems (thesauri provided by national institutions, the Getty Center, and iconographic classification system Iconclass), with typologies of entities that had to take into account the use across multiple disciplines. At the same time, the laborious process in the definition and annotation of relationships forces the participant to embrace the complexity of the historical processes in a unitary approach. This provides

Fig. 4. Historygraphia System frontend map: circles denote a geomapping of narratives; colored circle edges denote the historical discipline of the narrative; edges between the circles visualize the connections between narratives; the visualized abstract refers to a narrative concerning "the transit routes via Vermenagna valley and the Tenda pass and, in particular, the trade arrangements reported in the treaty of the alliance between the municipality of Cuneo and the Earl of Ventimiglia in 1279".

the bases for the logical representation of the assumed historical truth. The selection of the topics (or historical facts) that are addressed by the narratives was influenced by the meetings discussions. Art historians, for example, tended to identify potential historical narratives concerning the artistic bibliography, that proposed clear connections with the specific historical-territorial contexts. Semantic annotation has been claimed by participants to improve the expository clarity of the narratives, by stimulating the narrator to channel the same reasoning approaches within a texture of logical steps (Fig. 4).

Afterwords, the Historygraphia project addressed the length and structure of the narratives: after the experience of navigating the platform, participants agreed that a suitable length for the narratives (about 3000 characters) and a stable tripartite structure (a location, an object, and an addendum paragraph). This greatly simplified the authoring process, yielding "concise and topic-focused texts and preventing excessive digressions, and also avoiding the risk for the reader to lose the thread of the narrative" (it is told in one historian's report).

Participants, at their first experience with the creation of an IDN, were positively impressed by the potential. The planning of an interlinked coherent interdisciplinary IDN that relies on the a priori conception of the conceptual model marks a big difference. For example, cultural heritage catalogues allow to identify all the objects that are registered at the same "place of conservation", but exclude more abstract relations that are relative to the scope of meaning, and then to historical knowledge. The interdisciplinary development of the knowledge base encoding, on the contrary, allows to connect narratives that have in common not only basic entities (places and objects first and foremost), but also more abstract concepts (models, events, situations, themes).

We close with two examples of connected narratives (clearly, connections relating to places or artists form numerous coherent clusters of narratives).

- The alternatives to the Tenda pass between the end of the Middle Ages and the beginning of the modern age: the Saline pass.
- The first testimony of painters Bruno in city Cuneo, Santa Croce area.
- Painter Lorenzo Gastaldi at Entracque.

These are history and history of art narratives that concern different actors and contexts, but which are linked by the common State of affairs "transit area between regions Piemonte and Liguria", a central issue in the development of those regions in triggering historical-artistic and historical events (e.g., the residence of artists and the political-administrative management).

- The works of the painters Bruno in Andonno.
- The 17th-century renovation of the parish church in Valdieri.

These are history of art narratives about different artists that do not have a specific connection. The connection is licensed by the common actor "Family Lovera" as a commissioner in both places.,

As the archive receives further narratives, we believe that non-trivial clusters will be discovered through the navigation of the IDN structure.

5   Conclusions

This paper has presented the Historygraphia system, that contributes to historical research by developing a web-based IDN authoring system for the collection and interconnection of linear narratives through a semantic labeling. The platform works as an interactive digital narrative that addresses core topics of historical research in an interdisciplinary approach, highlighting the complexity of matters at hand and adhering to acknowledged attitudes in modern historiography. We have discussed the main tenets of the system, developed by an interdisciplinary team, in diverse fields of history, and experienced and preliminarily evaluated for its effectiveness and adequacy to historical research in conjunction with cultural heritage communication.

The novelty in the use of IDN for historical research is the interconnection of several disciplines, through an interdisciplinary approach based on semantics. It is not a mere application of hypertextual structure, since the semantic tagging can represent the assumed historical truth (situations, events, agents, ...) in a logical format and provide a structured connection between narratives with sources. Though ontologies have been out for a long time, we do not know of applications that assign such role to the knowledge graph, that can ensure consistency through reasoning, as a further development.

Acknowledgements. This research is supported by the project "Atlante Storico digitale del Piemonte - La provincia di Cuneo" (codes 2018/1377 and 2018/0582), funded by CRC Foundation and is part of project CHANGES (Grant agreement no. PE00000020) and project NODES which has received funding from the MUR - M4C2 1.5 of PNRR funded by the European Union NextGenerationEU (Grant agreement no. ECS00000036). The authors would like to thank Gioachino Gili for his support in the initial phases of the project.

References

1. Ankersmith, F.: Narrative logic. A Semantic Analysis of the Historian's Language. Martinus Nijhoff Publishers, Boston-London-The Hague (1983)
2. Barbara, J., Haahr, M.: What really happened here? dealing with uncertainty in the book of distance: a critical historiography perspective. In: Holloway-Attaway, L., Murray, J.T. (eds.) Proceedings of ICIDS 2023, LNCS, vol. 14384, pp. 129–136 (2023)
3. Barbara, J., Koenitz, H., Bakk, Á.K.: The ethics of virtual reality interactive digital narratives in cultural heritage. In: Interactive Storytelling: 14th International Conference on Interactive Digital Storytelling, ICIDS 2021, December 7–10, 2021 , pp. 288–292. Springer-Verlag, Berlin, Heidelberg, Tallinn, Estonia (2021)
4. Bekiari, C., Bruseker, G., Doerr, M., Ore, C.E., Stead, S., Velios, A.: Definition of the CIDOC conceptual reference model v7.1.1 (version v7.1.1). Tech. rep., The CIDOC Conceptual Reference Model Special Interest Group (2021)
5. Danto, A.C.: Analytical Philosophy of History. Cambridge University Press, Cambridge (1965)
6. Ekbia, H.R.: Digital artifacts as quasi-objects: qualification, mediation, and materiality. J. Am. Soc. Inform. Sci. Technol. **60**, 2554–2566 (2009)
7. Fazzi, P.: Telling history: Jerzy topolski's lesson. Diacronie (2015)
8. Jenkins, H.: Game design as narrative architecture. In: Wardrip-Fruin, N., Harrigan, P. (eds.) First Person: New Media as Story, Performance, and Game. MIT Press, Cambridge (2004)
9. Koenitz, H., Barbara, J., Eladhari, M.P.: Interactive digital narrative (IDN)-new ways to represent complexity and facilitate digitally empowered citizens. New Rev. Hypermedia Multimedia **28**(3–4), 76–96 (2023)
10. Mandelbaum, M.: A note on history as narrative. History Theory **6**(3), 413–419 (1967)
11. Manning, P.: Digital world history: an agenda (2007). http://digitalhistory.unl.edu/essays/manningessay.php
12. Murray, J.H.: Hamlet on the Holodeck: the Future of Narrative in Cyberspace. Free Press, New York (1997)
13. Petousi, D., Katifori, A., Servi, K., Roussou, M., Ioannidis, Y.: History education done different: a collaborative interactive digital storytelling approach for remote learners. Front. Educ. **7** (2022). https://doi.org/10.3389/feduc.2022.942834
14. Topolski, J.: Methodology of History. In: Reidel, D. (ed.), Publishing Company, Dordrecht, Holland (1976)
15. Wainwright, A.M.: Virtual History: How Videogames Portray the Past. Routledge, London-New York (2019)
16. White, H.: The question of narrative in contemporary historical theory. History Theory **23**(1), 1–33 (1984)

17. Zaagsma, G.: On digital history. Low Countries Hist. Rev. **128**(4), 3–29 (2013)
18. Zafar, R.: Doing public history in the contemporary world. Master's thesis, MA in Public History, Royal Holloway, University of London (RHUL) (2013)

Design of Knowledge Graphs for Interactive Digital Narratives Authoring

M. Abhilash[(✉)] and Frank Nack

INDElab, Informatics Institute, Faculty of Science, University of Amsterdam,
1098 XH Amsterdam, The Netherlands
abhilashkm92@gmail.com

Abstract. This article focuses on methodologies necessary to create effective knowledge graphs during IDN authoring, which can be used to support narrative engineers during the creation and maintenance of IDNs in a dynamic and scalable manner. Two different open-source knowledge graph technologies have been used, Apache Jena (an RDF triple store) and Neo4j Community Edition (a property model graph) for implementing two versions of an open source authoring environment. The findings show that Neo4j in general performs more preferable.

Keywords: Interactive Digital Narrative (IDN) · Knowledge Graph · Apache Jena · Neo4j · Property graphs · Resource Description Framework (RDF)

1 Introduction

The working environment of a narrative engineer (NE)[1] of an Interactive Digital Narrative (IDN) is the authoring environment [12]. The environment provides the technical means to build a functioning IDN, and in the best case it adapts to the objectives and goals of the NE by providing relevant technology and related services.

Authoring is a complex process that covers story planning, content collection and arrangement, and the implementation of the IDN engine that facilitates, among other things, the interactivity of the user with the content [6,15]. Most authoring tools are strong on the authoring of surface structures (i.e., to handle media creation), where the design and creation of deep structures is less considered, as this requires technical skills that seem to limit the creative processes of IDN designers [9,11,15,17]. Thus, tools like Twine[2] try to minimize the effort (see also [14] for additional tools).

---

[1] The term "narrative engineer" has been chosen to distinguish it from the term "author" as the creator of a linear narrative. It has also been chosen against the term "creator" [7] to emphasize the strong technical aspect of the authoring process of IDNs.

[2] https://twinery.org/.

J. T. Murray and M. C. Reyes (Eds.): ICIDS 2024, LNCS 15468, pp. 243–256, 2025.
https://doi.org/10.1007/978-3-031-78450-7_18

Knowledge graphs provide the ability to represent complex networks of entities (as nodes) and relationships (as edges) [4], thus having the ability to manage the intricate relationships of narrative elements, such as characters, their relationships and events in the context they appear in. In addition, they offer a solution to track changes and enable diverse story developments based on user interactions. However, designing a knowledge graph (KG) in order to effectively support IDN generation, performance, and maintenance involves several challenges, including knowledge representation design, scalability, consistency, and the building of an applicable reasoning as well as performance engine [17].

This research aims to contribute to the fields of IDN and knowledge management by investigating the design, model, implementation, and evaluation of a KG generation process in the context of IDN authoring.

2 Related Work

2.1 Interactive Digital Narrative (IDN)

IDNs lean towards the idea of a narrative environment in the form of a cybernetic system that establishes a causality, where the observed outcomes of actions are taken as input for further action in ways that support or disrupt a condition. The condition in the context of a narrative should be understood as the development of narrative states over time. Koenitz outlined in his SPP model (System, Process, Product) [8] the systemic view on IDN, the currently best model to capture the fragmented, distributed, and interactive nature of an IDN.

2.2 IDN Authoring

IDN authoring represents a dynamic process that merges creative storytelling with the handling of technologies that support the design, collection, and presentation of multi-modal multimedia content, the interaction with this content, and related to this the modeling of and the adaptation to user behavior [12]. The NE is therefore the designer of the narrative front-end (interface) and the narrative cognitive model based on which the IDN engine reacts.

There are over 300 IDN authoring tools available [6,15], of which each addresses particular authoring issues and services related to the type of IDN to be built. For an NE a steep learning curve needs to be applied with respect to understanding the interface as well as the underlying schemata and generation engine, in case a different type of IDN needs to be created as those the NE is used to. In addition, most of these IDN tools are closed environments, which limit the exchange of information. If all tools would provide at least the same underlying representation of narrative and deep narrative structures, the problem of information exchange and comparative analysis could be diminished [10,11].

2.3   Knowledge Graph and IDNs

Generally a Knowledge graph represents entities (nodes) and their relationships (edges) in a graph format, and in this way facilitates complex queries that can stimulate insights in the human who accesses this information structure.

Hogan et al. [5] explain the methodologies for constructing knowledge graphs, including manual curation, automated extraction from structured and unstructured data sources, and crowd-sourcing approaches. These capabilities are particularly relevant to IDNs, where characters, settings, events, and user choices can be modeled as entities and relationships, allowing dynamic story generation and adaptation.

Yu et al. explain the non-linear nature and dynamic behavior of IDNs. Figure 1 in the study shows the evolution and branching of the knowledge graph and different options for the plot points [18].

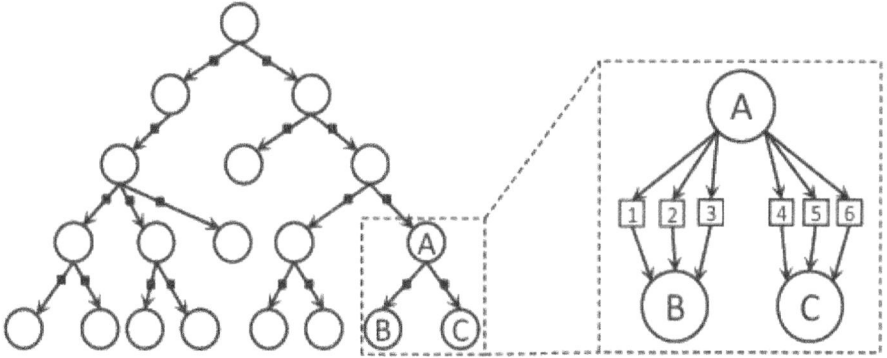

Fig. 1. A sample branching story graph (left) and an enlargement part of the graph showing multiple options for a plot point (right) [18]

Singh et al. [16] discuss how knowledge graphs can enhance the narrative structure, enable automation of the generation of story narratives, and facilitate adaptive narratives based on user inputs and preferences in real-time.

2.4   Evaluation of Knowledge Graph

The evaluation of quality of KGs is important for understanding the effectiveness of its design by checking reliability, accuracy, and the performance of the structures.

Chen et al. [3] provide essential metrics and methodologies for assessing different aspects of a KG like completeness, consistency and accuracy. Their framework provides with a set of criteria for assessment of KG quality, addressing critical dimensions such as structural integrity, semantic accuracy, and application relevance.

3 Implementation

The primary aim of the research is to evaluate the effectiveness of technical infrastructure for the automatic generation of a KG in the context of IDN authoring. We try to see if the applicability of open-source KG environments facilitate what IDN authoring requires with respect to the generation and maintenance of KGs during authoring. We compare two different open-source approaches which we integrated into an authoring environment in which NEs can build and alter (add or delete elements) their IDN, and then observe how the applied KG environments react on those activities. In this section, we describe the system, which will then be evaluated on the basis of ease of installation, performance, flexibility, interaction, versioning, and usability (see 4.2).

3.1 IDN Authoring Approach

Inspired by [11,12], we design an open source environment that is web-based, so that ease of access can be assumed. We adapt the system described in Paranich [13] as the front-end, as this system provides a support for the essential authoring stages (i.e. Ideation, Meaning Making, Interaction, and Validation). Each stage involves iterative feedback loops to refine and enhance the narrative elements based on the NE's inputs. We developed an API for this system that is called during the different authoring tasks performed in Paranich's tool. This means that if a new content unit is generated, altered, or deleted, our system gets the description of the performed task and the new specification of the unit, which is then integrated, altered, or marked as deleted, into the graph structure of that IDN. In case there is a request sent from the authoring tool to visualise graph structures (complete or partial), this request is also sent via the API and our system generates the note and relation lists, transfers them to the Paranich system, where they get presented based on its engine. Our implemented version can be used in real-time.

3.2 Knowledge Graph Modeling

The design of the knowledge graph in our system is based on the Chatman's narrative model [2] (see also Fig. 2). Chatman's work underscored the importance of understanding narrative components and their interrelationships, which informed the design of our KG schema. Figure 3 provides a comprehensive overview of all classes (or nodes) with a description and properties associated with the node. The ontology for RDF is defined as a turtle file and is uploaded to Github[3]. We consider this ontology detailed enough so that generated graphs can represent an IDN protostory space.

---

[3] https://github.com/idnknowledgegraph/idnknowledgegraph/blob/main/ Ontology_IDN.ttl.

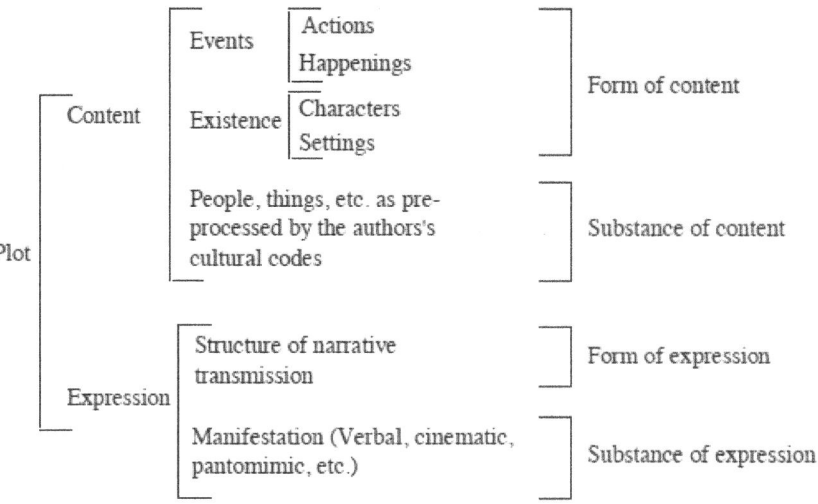

Fig. 2. Relationship between narrative elements (adopted from Chatman ([2], p.26)

3.3   Implementation and Integration

Two open source technologies are considered for implementation: **Apache Jena**[4] and **Neo4j**[5]. These technologies were selected because they are both open source, provide community support, and facilitate the implementation of popular but distinct graph structures: Apache Jena is based on RDF triples, whereas Neo4j is based on property graphs [1].

Apache Jena is installed on a MacOS server with 2-cores, 8 GiB memory. The Fuseki server[6] (Jena's SPARQL server) is set-up to manage SPARQL query execution.

Neo4j Community Edition is deployed and hosted on a Microsoft Azure[7] Virtual Machine. A Redhat Linux[8] 9.1 standard image with 2 virtual cpus, 4 GiB memory is used for the hosting of Neo4j.

APIs are developed to provide CRUD for every node and relationships for Neo4j[9] and for Apache Jena[10], and a composite service for neo4j was developed to act as an interface for the Authoring web tool.

---

[4] https://jena.apache.org/.

[5] https://neo4j.com/product/neo4j-graph-database/.

[6] https://jena.apache.org/documentation/fuseki2/.

[7] https://azure.microsoft.com/.

[8] https://www.redhat.com/.

[9] https://github.com/idnknowledgegraph/idnknowledgegraph/tree/main/Service_ Neo4j.

[10] https://github.com/idnknowledgegraph/idnknowledgegraph/tree/main/fuseki_ service.

Class	Description	Properties
Character	Represents a character in the narrative space.	hasName, hasDescription, hasRelationshipWith: CharacterRelationship, participatesIn: Event, performsAction: Action, created_at: xsd:dateTime, updated_at: xsd:dateTime, deleted_at: xsd:dateTime, is_active: xsd:boolean
Event	An event or action that occurs within the narrative space.	hasDescription, leadsTo: Event, DecisionPoint, partOfPlot: CharacterPlot, created_at: xsd:dateTime, updated_at: xsd:dateTime, deleted_at: xsd:dateTime, is_active: xsd:boolean
DecisionPoint	A point in the narrative where the user or character makes a choice.	hasDescription: xsd:string, belongsTo: StoryArc, hasChoice: Choice, partOfPlot: CharacterPlot, created_at: xsd:dateTime, updated_at: xsd:dateTime, deleted_at: xsd:dateTime, is_active: xsd:boolean
Choice	Represents a choice available at a Decision Point.	resultsIn: Outcome, leadsToNarrativeChange: Narrative Change, created_at: xsd:dateTime, updated_at: xsd:dateTime, deleted_at: xsd:dateTime, is_active: xsd:boolean
Outcome	The result or consequence of a choice. This can lead to new path and story.	hasDescription: xsd:string, created_at: xsd:dateTime, updated_at: xsd:dateTime, deleted_at: xsd:dateTime, is_active: xsd:boolean
StoryArc	A sequence of events and decisions that form a coherent narrative path.	hasName: xsd:string, hasDescription: xsd:string, belongsTo: DecisionPoint, Choice, created_at: xsd:dateTime, updated_at: xsd:dateTime, deleted_at: xsd:dateTime, is_active: xsd:boolean
Character Relationship	Represents a specific relationship between two characters (e.g., friend, enemy, sibling).	relationshipType: xsd:string, created_at: xsd:dateTime, updated_at: xsd:dateTime, deleted_at: xsd:dateTime, is_active: xsd:boolean
Character Plot	A subplot or narrative arc that primarily involves a specific character. This can be created by Narrative Engineer or come from generation engine.	created_at: xsd:dateTime, updated_at: xsd:dateTime, deleted_at: xsd:dateTime, is_active: xsd:boolean
Action	An action taken by a character, which may affect the narrative's progression or the state of other characters.	actionDescription: xsd:string, affectsCharacter: Character, leadsToNarrativeChange: NarrativeChange, created_at: xsd:dateTime, updated_at: xsd:dateTime, deleted_at: xsd:dateTime, is_active: xsd:boolean
Narrative Change	Represents a change in the narrative, potentially altering the storyline, character development, or setting.	changeDescription: xsd:string, created_at: xsd:dateTime, updated_at: xsd:dateTime, deleted_at: xsd:dateTime, is_active: xsd:boolean
Media	Represents a media element associated with a narrative entity.	mediaType: xsd:string, mediaURL: xsd:string, created_at: xsd:dateTime, updated_at: xsd:dateTime, deleted_at: xsd:dateTime, is_active: xsd:boolean
Version	Tracks changes in the knowledge graph.	version_number: xsd:string, timestamp: xsd:dateTime, description: xsd:string

Fig. 3. Node types and relationships in our knowledge graph schema

4 Experiment

4.1 Goal

Experimental Goal: The primary goal of this experiment is to evaluate the technical capabilities and overall effectiveness of the KG in the context of IDN authoring.

Experimental Setup: The environment setup involves deploying knowledge graph environments using two technologies: Apache Jena and Neo4j.

4.2 Testing and Validation

Criteria for Evaluation. The evaluation of the KG is based on the following parameters based on existing work as discussed in Sect. 2.4:

- Ease of setup of the environment: Flexibility and support for setting up
- Performance on creation of the KG: Time for initial creation of KG
- Performance on update of the KG: Adaptability of the KG on introduction of new characters, relationships or properties
- Interaction and Integration patterns: patterns utilized for integration with the user interface
- Versioning: Versions of KG

Testing. The actual quantitative testing is performed by the main author[11] in an automated manner using SOAP UI for performance tests and PostMan for versioning and flexibility. The actual test was performed between 15 May and 27 June 2024.

5 Results

The results are organised based on the criteria used for evaluation and validation based on the experimental goals, setup, and testing procedures. The quantitative results are extracted based on individual testing and automated testing using the tools described in Sect. 4.2.

5.1 Ease of Setup of the Environment

Goal: Determine which technology offers a straightforward and well-supported setup process.

---

[11] 31 year old Male, Master's degree in Science and 2 years experience in working with graph technologies.

Result: The setup process for Apache Jena and Neo4j was documented to evaluate the time required, complexity, and availability of support resources. Apache Jena required an setup time of 2 h on a local server, including the configuration of the Fuseki server. Setting up Neo4j Community Edition took approximately 15 min from the Azure marketplace.

5.2   Performance on Creation of the Knowledge Graph

Goal: Benchmark the initial creation performance of Apache Jena versus Neo4j for different complexities.

Result: Performance evaluation is done based on creation times and retrieval times. The creation times revealed significant differences between the two technologies. Neo4j demonstrated faster performance in graph creation, taking an average of 33 min to populate the graph with 10,000 nodes and relationships. Apache Jena took approximately 42 min for the same. The retrieval times also showed significant differences with retrieval for 10,000 nodes and the relationship is 1000 times faster in Neo4j as compared to Apache Jena. This performance advantage is mainly due to Neo4j's optimized engine.

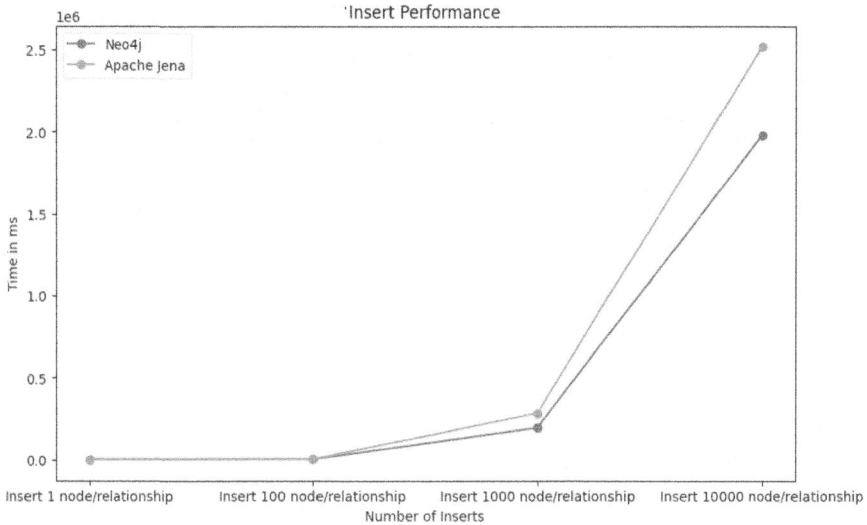

Fig. 4. Insert Performance

Figure 4 plots the performance of Neo4j and Apache Jena for 1 to 10000 inserts for a complex IDN.

Figure 5 plots the performance of retrieving data from both systems.

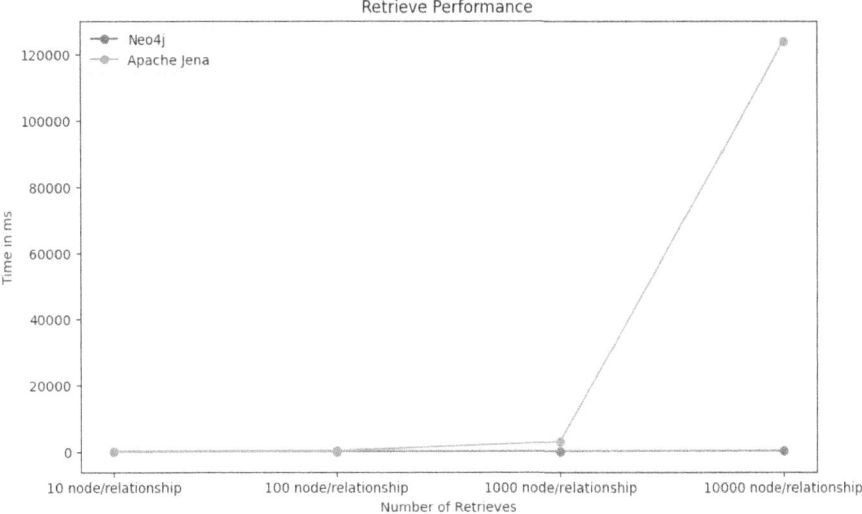

Fig. 5. Get Performance

5.3   Performance on Update of the Knowledge Graph

Goal: Assess how each system performs under dynamic conditions.

Result: The evaluation of performance on update operations was tested by simulating changes (like a typical IDN) on an existing graph structure (with 10000 nodes and relationships). Neo4j showed shorter response times, with an average of 200 milliseconds for updates. Apache Jena showed an average response time of 350 milliseconds. Both systems showed no real differences with respect to the adaptability of the graphs when different elements (character, relationships) and actions (change, delete) were performed. Also, no data got lost and no notes suddenly stood isolated. The faster update performance of Neo4j suggests that it might be a more suitable option for dynamic IDNs where frequent updates by the NE are common during the meaning-making and validation phases.

5.4   Interaction and Integration Patterns

Apache Jena and Neo4j supports different interaction patterns for real-time user interaction, as well as bulk data updates. The real-time services created based on neomodel and Django for Neo4j and SPARQL and Django for Apache Jena supported these integration patterns with the user interface of the IDN system. However, from a developer's perspective, Neo4j's Cypher query language provided more powerful query capabilities for complex interaction patterns compared to SPARQL used in Jena.

5.5   Versioning

The versioning solution for a KG is implemented with each class (node) and relationship annotated with versioning metadata, including version number, timestamps, and active status, ensuring tracking of changes and facilitating time-
travelling across different versions of the narrative space.

The versioning solution works on the basis of versioning metadata in every
node and relationship within the graph. Each node and relationship include the
properties: version, created_at, updated_at, is_active, and deleted_at. The
version property indicates the version number, which identifies the version of the
graph to which a particular element belongs. The created_at and updated_at
timestamps track when an element was created and last updated, respectively.
The is_active property indicates which is the newest version of the element. The
deleted_at timestamp provides the soft delete timestamp of a specific element.
With the soft delete, the element(s) can be re-used within the narrative space
in future.

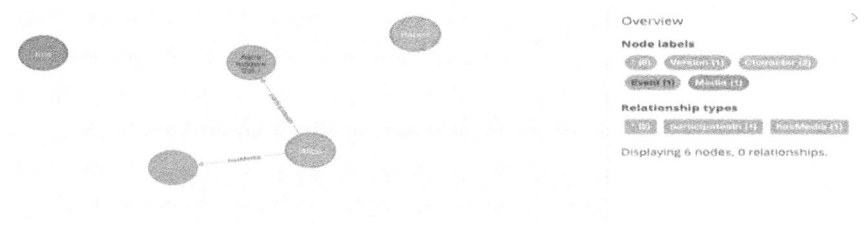

Fig. 6. Version 1.0

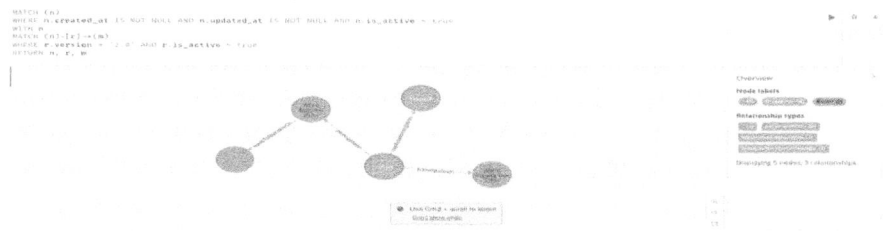

Fig. 7. Version 2.0

Figures 6, 7, 8 and 9 demonstrates an example of versioning with 3 versions of
the graph. Version 1 being the initial version of knowledge graph creating nodes
(characters, events) and relationships. Version 2 is expansion of the graph by
introducing new nodes (characters, events), relationship updates, and narrative

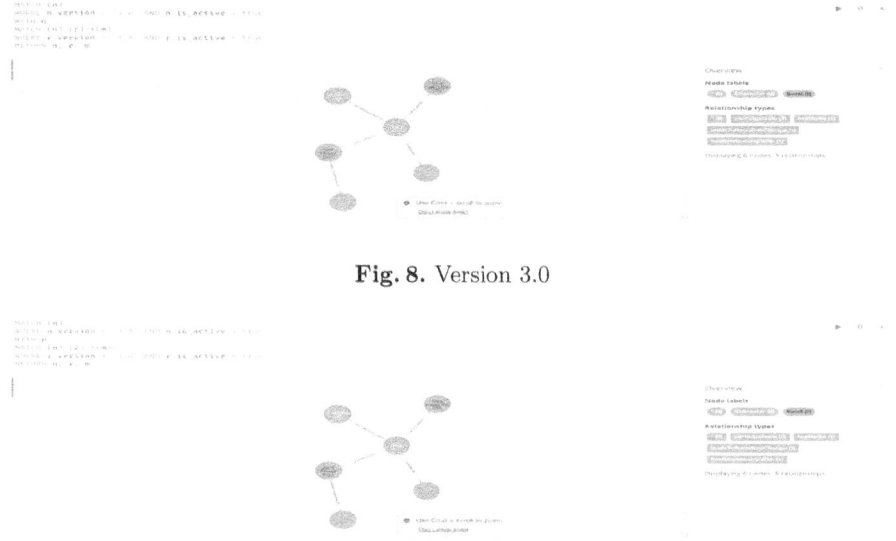

Fig. 8. Version 3.0

Fig. 9. Versioning full graph

changes. Version 3 is modification and updates of the knowledge graph by adding and deleting nodes and relationships.

A Cypher query[12] was executed to retrieve all nodes and relationships associated with different versions of the graph which represented the narrative space, which returned the representation of the narrative's elements and their interconnections as shown in the Fig. 9. The query successfully extracted all relevant data, providing a clear snapshot of the KG at a specific point in time. This versioning approach ensures that interactive digital narratives can maintain consistency and coherence, even as they undergo modifications and expansions.

6 Discussion

We aimed to investigate the effectiveness of the automatic generation of a KG in the context of IDN authoring so that they can finally support dynamic and non-linear storytelling. By implementing and comparing the performance of Apache Jena and Neo4j, we provided a quantitative analysis to understand how different KG technologies can enhance knowledge management in IDN.

The quantitative assessments of Apache Jena and Neo4j highlighted key differences in performance, scalability, and responsiveness to real-time data updates which are crucial factors for IDNs. Neo4j performed better (13 times for ease of setup, 1.3 times for performance, 2 times on flexibility, and 1000 times for responsiveness). This comparison on one hand serves the practical aspects of

---

[12] https://neo4j.com/docs/cypher-manual/current/introduction/.

IDN development, and on another to the field of application of semantic web technologies in interactive narratives.

6.1 Limitations

This work has limitations that impact the general usage and application of the results. First, the controlled environment in which the technologies were tested. Real-world IDN authoring is often even more complex, involving many more interactions performed by NEs than the 10.000 in our experimental setting. Therefore, the performance metrics recorded in this report may not fully capture the challenges and efficiencies of deploying these technologies in different real-world scenarios.

Second, qualitative analysis of KG structure and integration with the Web interface is not performed as part of this research. Although the KG is tested in an abstracted manner, performing a qualitative analysis on the user's experience might give more insights than what is covered as part of this report.

7   Conclusion and Future Work

This report addressed a research gap in IDN authoring, namely the use of knowledge graphs as a content representation structure for the protostory as well as a memory structure capturing the authoring process. This research mainly contributes a detailed analysis of two technologies which can be used for KG generation during authoring, namely Apache Jena and Neo4j. The findings provide a detailed view on the capability of Neo4j as a technology to handle complex dynamic data interactions more efficiently than Apache Jena during various phases of the IDN authoring process.

An avenue for future work is the investigation of how knowledge graphs can further contribute to the design and implementation of the narrative cognitive model based on which the IDN engine reacts, thus contributing to the modeling of user memory and contextual structures in particular. We take our findings regarding versioning as the base for work on the analysis of IDN collections to further gain insights into the theory of IDN as well as providing support services during the authoring process. For example, we investigate how analysis of KG clusters can help IDN theoreticians to better understand what makes a particular IDN genre and how genres can be distinct from each other, including relevant interfaces. We also develop analysis tools that can make use of the versioning to help an individual IE over structural problems, (i.e. using existing authoring records to establish typical problem sets with solutions for particular genres).

In conclusion, while this report offers a practical framework for the implementation of knowledge graphs in open source IDN authoring environments, it also highlights the complexity and challenges inherent in this innovative space. The contributions of this research are only a small step in further developments of IDN knowledge representation< authoring and analysis.

Acknowledgments. This work has been partially funded by the EU INDCOR - COST Action CA18230 (Interactive Narrative Design for Complexity Representations).

Disclosure of Interests. The authors have no competing interests to declare that are relevant to the content of this article.

References

1. Angles, R.: A comparison of current graph database models. In: Proceedings - 2012 IEEE 28th International Conference on Data Engineering Workshops, ICDEW 2012, p. 177 (2012). https://doi.org/10.1109/ICDEW.2012.31
2. Chatman, S.: Story And Discourse Narrative Structure in Fiction and Film. Cornell University Press (1978)
3. Chen, H., Cao, G., Chen, J., Ding, J.: A practical framework for evaluating the quality of knowledge graph. In: LNCS, vol. 9999, pp. 111–122. Springer, Cham (2019). https://doi.org/10.1007/978-981-15-1956-7_10
4. Ehrlinger, L., Wöß, W.: Towards a definition of knowledge graphs. Semantics (Posters, Demos, Success) **48**(1–4), 2 (2016)
5. Hogan, A., et al.: Knowledge graphs. ACM Comput. Surv. **54**(4), 1–37 (2022). https://doi.org/10.1145/3447772
6. Kitromili, S., Jordan, J., Millard, D.E.: What is hypertext authoring? In: Proceedings of the 30th ACM Conference on Hypertext and Social Media, pp. 55–59. ACM, New York (2019). https://doi.org/10.1145/3342220.3343653
7. Koenitz, H., Eladhari, M.P., Louchart, S., Nack, F.: INDCOR white paper 1: a shared vocabulary for IDN (interactive digital narratives) (2024). https://arxiv.org/abs/2010.10135. Accessed 24 Jun 2024
8. Koenitz, H.: Understanding Interactive Digital Narrative: Immersive Expressions for a Complex Time. Routledge (2023). https://doi.org/10.4324/9781003106425
9. Kybartas, B., Bidarra, R.: A survey on story generation techniques for authoring computational narratives. IEEE Trans. Comput. Intell. AI Games **9**(3), 239–253 (2016). https://doi.org/10.1109/TCIAIG.2016.2546063
10. Lee, M. et al.: A design space for intelligent and interactive writing assistants. In: Proceedings of the CHI Conference on Human Factors in Computing Systems (CHI '24), pp. 1–35. Association for Computing Machinery, New York, NY, USA (2024). https://doi.org/10.1145/3613904.3642697
11. Nack, F.: IDN Authoring - a design case. arXiv:2306.13999 (2023)
12. Nack, F., et al.: Interactive digital narratives and interaction, June 18, white paper, COST action 18230. arXiv:2306.10547 (2024). Accessed 24 Jun 2024
13. Paranich, J.: Communicating intent of the text-based IDN in the authoring web environment. MSc Thesis. University of Amsterdam (2024)
14. Set of IDN authoring tools classified by the INDCOR COST association (2023). https://omeka-s.indcor.eu/s/idn-authoring-tools/item-set/43. Accessed 02 Jun 2024
15. Shibolet, Y., Knoller, N., Koenitz, H.: A framework for classifying and describing authoring tools for interactive digital narrative. In: Proceedings of the International Conference on Interactive Digital Storytelling, ICIDS 2018, LNCS, vol. 11318, pp. 523–533. Springer, Cham (2018). https://doi.org/10.1007/978-3-030-04028-4_61

16. Singh, K., Lytra, I., Sethupat, A., Shekarpour, S., Vidal, M.E., Lehmann, J.: No one is perfect: analysing the performance of question answering components over the DBpedia knowledge graph. J. Web Semant. **65**, 100594 (2020). https://doi.org/10.1016/j.websem.2020.100594

17. Thue, D., Bulitko, V., Spetch, M., Wasylishen, E.: Interactive storytelling: a player modelling approach. In: Proceedings of the AAAI Conference on Artificial Intelligence and Interactive Digital Entertainment (2007)

18. Yu, H., Riedl, M.O.: Toward personalized guidance in interactive narratives. https://www.semanticscholar.org/paper/Toward-personalized-guidance-in-interactive-Yu-Riedl/34eff4e12197f53f7909986df03c63a2ba1a6afc. Accessed 22 Mar 2024

Being Water: Collaborating with an LLM in an Interactive Digital Narrative (IDN) as Speculative Aesthetics

Rafaela Nunes[1,2]($\boxtimes$) (ID), Terhi Marttila[2] (ID), Andrés Isaza-Giraldo[2] (ID),
Paulo Bala[2] (ID), and Pedro F. Campos[2,3] (ID)

[1] Faculty of Fine Arts of the University of Lisbon, Lisbon, Portugal
`rafaela@nenhures.net`
[2] ITI/LARSyS, Lisbon, Portugal
[3] Wow!Systems, Funchal, Portugal

Abstract. *Being Water* is an IDN experience that speculates about the ways of being of water in the world. It combines 360° video, artifact-beings, voice-over and atmospheric sound. In a first iteration, users navigate through the environment to listen to authorial text. This paper's focus is on second iteration in which we experiment with integrating generative AI (genAI) to various degrees (e.g., augmenting interaction, making it replayable, sustaining a narrative) by using authorial text and scene context. We discuss preliminary findings in using LLMs as a collaborator to make meaningful additions to digital artworks.

Keywords: digital art · interactive digital narrative · large language models · speculative aesthetics

1 Introduction

With the release of models like OpenAI's GPT [1], Midjourney [23], and Stable Diffusion [20] among others, we have witnessed a popularization of genAI technologies as they become more user-friendly, easy to access and highly adaptive to practice and research. Simply put, genAI generates outputs from learned features in data input, whether that is text, images, music or videos. GenAI models are trained on large datasets, learning patterns and structures. In recent years, user interaction with these models has been mostly done through text prompting and image prompting, which constitutes a practical way to explore the vast space of possible outputs, called latent space.

Despite the ongoing popularity surge of genAI within the general public, this technology has faced considerable controversy within creative practices. Mainly, the reported existence of intellectual property in the datasets used for the training of these models has sparked backlash from creators, which has often culminated in the filing of lawsuits against companies that developed these AI models [3,21,26]. While no final ruling has cleared out the intellectual property of said systems, the United States Copyright Office has revoked copyright

J. T. Murray and M. C. Reyes (Eds.): ICIDS 2024, LNCS 15468, pp. 257–266, 2025.
https://doi.org/10.1007/978-3-031-78450-7_19

claims over images generated using MidJourney [23] for the visual novel *Zayra of the Dawn*[1] which constitutes a clear legal precedent. Moreover, AI bias is an emergent ethical concern, and while efforts to address it are largely focused on representativeness and fairness in datasets and algorithms, human and systemic biases seem to be the underlying factor, and AI should therefore be approached as a socio-technical system [22].

Despite these reactions, various artists have been thinking about and through these issues by working with different AI models. Work of artists like Mario Klingemann and Stephanie Dinkins represent artistic practices that engage with genAI in innovative ways. Motivated by this exploration of creative practice, in this work we aim to understand how artists are expanding their practices through the collaboration with genAI and engaging in speculative thinking about what could be meaningful ways to connect with others through interactive digital narratives.

In this paper, we present our work-in-progress artwork, *Being Water*, a digital space dedicated to seeing, feeling and thinking through the perspective of water in the spirit of speculative aesthetics. This interactive and immersive experience is a collaboration between four humans and genAI. Our aim is also to think how this artwork might transform by speculatively imagining the branching of possibilities afforded by this kind of collaboration. We present our artwork in its current shape, and proceed to present an iteration of it using a large language model (LLM) to deepen the interactive element of the artwork, allowing mutual imaginings between human and machine.

We worked with the AI through a perspective of collaboration, and not simply as a passive tool, acknowledging the way the different media we work with (text, code, film, audio and painting, as well as genAI) interact with us, with each other and with others that experience it. This way, we consider our collaboration with these different media and between ourselves as an agential type of creative practice. Nunes describes such an agential turn in art-making as "*a set of artistic practices which take as their theoretical and practical point of departure the whole of human and nonhuman relations and their natural-cultural contexts*" [17, p. 7]. The work presented in this paper is of interest to other researchers and artists examining their creative practices as they incorporate genAI as a collaborator.

2   Related Work

Janet Murray has proposed concepts such as dramatic agency, meaningful replay, multisequential or multiform storyworlds as suggestions towards creating a vocabulary to describe how meaningful experience in interactive digital narrative (IDN) is created [16]. Murray observes that dramatic agency does not necessarily mean that the user can change the events of the story, but rather that the user feels that their interaction choices have coherent and meaningful consequences in the experience [16]. In intersecting Murray's work and genAI, LLMs could be used for attuning user interaction with consequences in the experience through

---

[1] https://www.copyright.gov/docs/zarya-of-the-dawn.pdf.

programming the system instead of authoring for multiple possible interaction-consequence pairs. For example, by inviting the LLM to attune their textual response to the image they see on screen, it can create dramatic agency through coherence between interaction and experience.

Another important aesthethic value of IDNs, according to Murray, is whether or not the experience motivates replay, and whether these variations are trivial or dramatically meaningful [16]. Implementing genAI can contribute towards creating an immense quantity of material for IDNs with low effort (compared with the effort required for creating manually). Klingemann's work *Uncanny Mirror* [19] invites visitors to view themselves in a "mirror", in fact a screen, which shows them an image of themselves, yet created in real time by a GAN algorithm that was trained on images of the previous exhibition visitors. The image one sees is never the same, it changes constantly, and this invites to replay as a continued exploration of the GAN's vast latent space, whose dataset might also be changing.

Other aesthethic values of IDNs according to Murray include multisequential narratives as narratives in which multiple traversals are possible and multiform story systems in which a set of parameters can produce multiple parallel instantiations [16]. Koenitz calls the author of such a multiform story system the *"creator, system builder, and narrative architect"* [7] instead of referring to a storyteller, which would allude to the notion of a literary author. In *Not the only one* [4], artist Stephanie Dinkins trains a genAI on three generations of women's oral history of her Black American family. This results in a voice interactive experience in which interactors are able to converse with the system to learn about the Black American experience. Instead of following her initial intention to preserve her family's story, by implementing genAI, Dinkins creates a multiform narrative system in which interactors are free to explore the Black American experience according to their particular interests.

Nunes develops a practice-based research that stems from a transmedia creative practice which intersects painting, programming and genAI [17]. Nunes transforms her paintings into virtual entities, creating "artifact-beings" from an iterative process that imbues her paintings with human and nonhuman characteristics and concepts through the generative AI's interpretations of them. This way, the artist engages in imaginatively projecting artifact-being hybrids, questioning binary boundaries like beings and non-beings, artificial and natural. Nunes's work [17], albeit not implicitly focused on narrative as such, is another example of the creation of such a multiform story system in which parameters are set and both user input as well as the input of genAI influence the final "output" and experience.

3   Methdodology

Inspired by the work of other artists and the increasing availability of genAI models, we wanted to explore the process of adapting artworks to include genAI as a collaborator. We do this through a practice-based research approach. Firstly, four collaborators (all authors in this paper) created a digital artifact sustaining a narrative that was meant to be experienced by an audience. Secondly, we expand our collaboration to include genAI models, looking for ways to not only deepen interaction within the digital artifact, but also maintain and reinforce the author's desired narrative for the artwork. In the following subsections, we describe some experimental iterations of the digital artwork.

3.1 Being Water

Our purpose with *Being Water* is to speculate about how water might perceive the world as a way of attempting to become sensitive to the perspectives of others. We follow Hayles' proposal of speculative aesthetics [6], in which one imaginatively projects into the worldview of other objects and beings based on evidence about their ways of being in the world as an attempt to escape anthropocentrism, never assuming that these speculations in any way represent the actual perception of the world of the entity, but as fictional entities that we called *waterbeings*.

Our initial iteration was based on a collaborative flow in which an authorial speculative text was written based on 360° videos of water sources. This text was used in Stable Difusion [20] to transform existing paintings from one of the authors to create images for the *waterbeings'* texture maps. In Blender [2], we procedurally generated organic shapes from these maps, the *waterbeings*. Using the Unity 2023.3 game engine [25], we brought together several types of media to create an interactive narrative experience (see Fig. 1). The procedurally generated shapes and the abstract images were thus used to create *waterbeings* which move around the space and can be interacted with based on the user's distance to play voice recordings of the authorial text, alongside the ambient sound of the video and spatial music distributed around in droplets.

While this work used genAI, this was not done during runtime; conversely, the output was selectively curated. Although the moving authorial texts and changing videos guaranteed a new poetic experience for each player, the experience doesn't cease to be a finite game lacking the sense of ephemeral replayability that an ever-transforming object (like a mirror or video feedback [8]) might have.

3.2 LLM Integration in *Being Water*

After completing the first iteration of *Being Water*, we reiterated on the work by experimenting with expanding the imaginative capacity of the speculative text through integrating LLMs. In this further development, we added an LLM layer to further deepen the interactive dimension of the work, allowing the AI to react to and generate content based on the text and environment that we created, as well as respond to the user's input.[2] This way, we aim to explore the AI's interpretation of poetic data.

---

[2] A video example of the different outputs is available online in https://vimeo.com/1017470826/6cd5d860df.

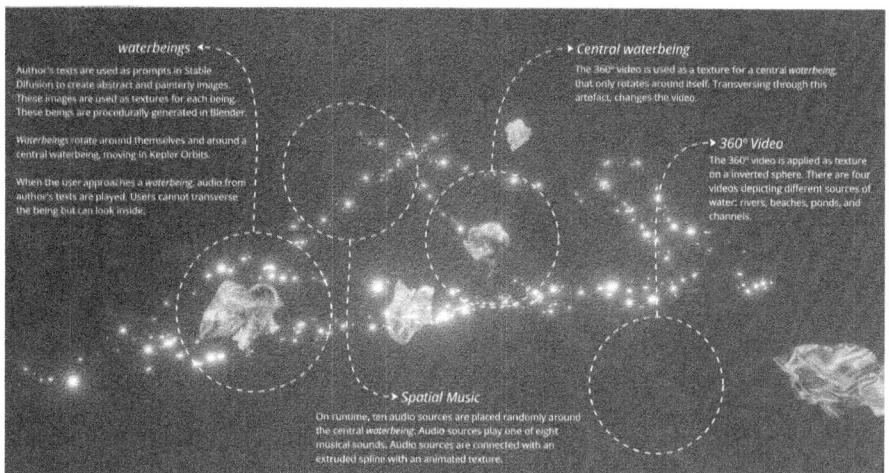

Fig. 1. First iteration of *Being Water*.

The purpose of this integration was to expand on the speculative imaginative aspect of the work by extending the human imagination to the collective, database-based universe of possibilities afforded by LLMs. Another purpose was to increase the replayability of the experience by making use of the variability that LLMs can provide for the content of the experience.

Building on the previous iteration, we used Ollama (version 0.3.10) [18], a framework designed to facilitate the deployment of LLMs on local environments, to communicate between Unity and a generative model. Given its versatility, we used a multimodal model LLaVA1.6 7b [9–11], to allow for text and image prompts. To replace voice recordings, we used the output of the LLM to create digital voice through Jets Text-to-Speech Model validated for Unity Sentis (Version 1.4.0-pre.2*) [24].

The authors had prompt writing sessions, which were streamlined iteratively after much trial and error. As instructions for the LLMs output, we used a base prompt (see Fig. 2). Selecting this prompt required multiple iterations in order to guide the output of the LLM. The inclusion of the word "poem" or "poetic" in the prompt seemed to always result in the use of rhyme. The word artistic or art tended to add stereotypical notions to the output such as references to painting or creativity. At worst, the LLM would directly quote the key concepts in the prompt, revealing the inner workings of the system (e.g., "*An artistic reality is a mirror's smile.*").

We experimented with three different levels of integration of the LLM within the artwork, asking the LLM to generate text: (1) based on the authorial text only, (2) based on the user's current view and finally, (3) based on a combination of the authorial text and the image input.

Figure 2 shows some outputs from this experimentation. Asking the LLM to expand on the authorial text as the sole input resulted in the regurgitation of recognizable portions of the text input. The LLM reordered sentences, mixed and matched and reformulated parts of the authorial text, but never managed to escape the confines of the imaginative capacity of the original text. In prior work, Marttila [14] experimented with an LLM-inspired performative approach to remixing their own text to draw new meanings from it and the resulting text output was far bolder than that of the LLM in these experiments. However, the LLM's imaginative capacity might in this case be limited by the small size of the text input, since the prompt confines the output to the authorial text.

Asking the LLM to base its output on the user view resulted in an overly abstract text, as evidenced in Fig. 1, "*liquid thoughts weave*" or "*where color and form intertwine*". We presume this might be due to the abstract nature of the views which the experience presents, leading the LLM to interpret mostly colors and shapes, rather than objects.

By far the most meaningful speculative output was achieved by asking the LLM to base its output on both the authorial text and the user view. This is evidenced in Fig. 2 – e.g., "*a frozen abstraction, the remnants of a body once fluid, now trapped in ice and stone*". While this output is clearly anchored in the authorial text, the LLM is expanding beyond the imaginative confines of the text by adding layers it "sees" in the experience such as "*a frozen abstraction*", or, as in another output, "*watery forms*". In this conjunction of embracing or interpreting the authorial text through the abstract visions it sees on screen, the LLM succeeds in expanding on human imagination by offering perspectives that were not present in the authorial speculative text.

4   Discussion

Collaboration with LLMs and generative art within an artistic context is still very recent, and yet, as we have seen, different artists have been taking advantage of this technology's capabilities, as well as exploiting its weaknesses to great effect. In this context, the importance arises of thinking about ways to meaningfully and thoughtfully collaborate with genAI within creative practices. In the case of the second iteration of *Being Water*, our purpose was first and foremost to invite genAI to expand on the imaginative and speculative components of the work.

As an author or artist, one expresses their perspective through their own unique view of the world. Collaborating with an LLM is quite different than working with another human, in the sense that the LLM does not have a singular, individual perspective, but it is a vast collection of different views, opinions and ideas - all represented through a single iteration at a time, "evened out" in some kind of virtual middle ground among this enormous multiplicity. Working with an LLM as we have described brought us the realization that we were effectively collaborating with a simulation of thought, a simulated non-perspective with such a type of collective.

In a sense, we are engaging in a mode of unprecedented second-order observation. Luhmann describes two modes of observation in society - first-order observation relates to what is directly experienced, and second-order observation to

☰ Base Prompt

You are water. Write a concise artistic, philosophical, dadaist, avant-garde text in exactly three lines.
Don't enumerate. Be brief.

➕ Additional Input

✏ Authorial Text

For thousands of years, bound up, hinged to others in a massive body. A body of water, they say. Frozen together, bound together, unable to move. Unable to think about anything other than just being, waiting, or perhaps just being. Being water. Waiting for the sun to warm us up, to warm everything up and to release us into a flowing body of water. No longer bound to just this place. In silence bound to those that happened to happen upon the place where the cold froze us into place. In silence, waiting, or perhaps just being, being water.

➕

📹 User View

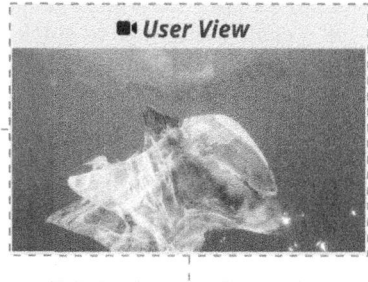

🤖 LLM Output

- *"A frozen mass of unity. A waiting game of bound water. An icebox of watery fate."*

- *"In silence and solitude, I am water, cracking up into smaller bodies of water, rushing and grinding against rocks."*

- *"Bound in frozen form. In water's silent chorus. Waiting for the sun to release us."*

- *"Amidst the ocean's embrace, The dreamer wakes within a glassy sleep, Reflecting on life's abstract dance."*

- *"An artistic reality is a mirror's smile. Where color and form intertwine. In the abstract, we find our own truth."*

- *"Liquid thoughts weave, in the depths of mind where all streams flow and one may lose. Dadaism is here, for when the rules are blurred and only chaos remains to inspire us. Art as a river, leading towards an endless ocean of creativity"*

- *"The cracking of time's watery veins. The ripping apart of bodies submerged in sound and heat. A dadaist dance of force and flow being both water and rock."*

- *"A frozen abstraction, the remnants of a body once fluid, now trapped in ice and stone. The waiting game, for what, we're left to ponder in our watery forms. Breaking free from the icy grip, seeking warmth and flow, returning to our natural state."*

- *"Silent whispers of water, frozen in the vast expanse of thought. Bound together, yet yearning to flow free and unfettered. Awaiting the warmth of release from ice-bound chains, into a flowing unity with all."*

Fig. 2. Examples of outputs based on three scenarios of LLM integration

what is experienced as being observed by someone else - an observation of an observation [13]. Second-order observation has, according to Luhmann, "*become the advanced mode of perceiving the world in modern society*" [12, p. 100], and this has been used to analyze the way we interact with others through and because of social media [15]. According to this theory, we can affirm that experiencing the AI's collective output through an LLM allows us to observe how we collectively observe the world. By interacting with AI like we do, we are engaging with AI-generated representations of human data.

In our LLM-integrated artwork, we are allowing the AI to create observations of what it is "seeing". It is undeniably transforming our experience based not on a single perspective, but on probability patterns in data. This attests to a uniquely different way of weaving interactive narratives with AI, and how we must take into account how it reflects a *representation* of multiple perspectives - limited as it reflects this "evening out" of perspectives into a single iteration. Such a view is a challenging way to think about the embodiment of knowledge and the gaze. Haraway describes attempts at *"views from nowhere"* as *"truly fantastic, distorted, and irrational"* [5, p. 587].

Future work includes refining the prompt in order to better utilize the imaginative capacities of LLMs through expanding the level of agency afforded to it instead of limiting the LLM's output to the confines of the authorial text. We also suggest performing a fine-tuning training of the LLM, using a previously curated corpus of text, either of human generated or AI generated texts. This would generate results closer to those desired by the artists, guiding the model to a clearer form. Moreover, it could be possible to include conversational interaction within the user and the LLM, creating newly tailored text in each interaction.

5   Conclusion

This paper describes our process of experimenting with the integration of LLMs into an authorial text in the artwork *Being Water*. We discussed some of the affordances of IDN's and showed how existing work integrates LLMs in a meaningful way that expands the narrative experience. Supported by a first iteration of the artwork, we describe preliminary results of experimenting with LLM integration into the work. Future work includes further fine tuning our experiments with LLMs and analysing their use on the impact of the narrative experience.

Acknowledgments. This research was funded by the Portuguese Recovery and Resilience Program (PRR), IAPMEI/ANI/FCT under Agenda no.26, C645022399-00000057 (eGamesLab). The authors would also like to acknowledge the Portuguese Foundation for Science and Technology, for projects 10.54499/LA/P/0083/2020; 10.54499/UIDP/ 50009/2020 & 10.54499/UIDB/50009/2020.

References

1. AI, M.: ChatGPT (2022). https://chat.openai.com/
2. Community, B.O.: Blender (2018). http://www.blender.org. 3D modelling and rendering package
3. David, E.: George R.R. Martin and other authors sue OpenAI for copyright infringement. The Verge (2023). https://www.theverge.com/2023/9/20/23882140/george-r-r-martin-lawsuit-openai-copyright-infringement
4. Dinkins, S.: Not the only one (2018). https://www.stephaniedinkins.com/ntoo.html

5. Haraway, D.: Situated knowledges: the science question in feminism and the privilege of partial perspective. Fem. Stud. **14**(3), 575 (1988). https://doi.org/10.2307/3178066

6. Hayles, N.K.: Speculative aesthetics and object-oriented inquiry (OOI). In: Askin, R., Ennis, P.J., Hägler, A., Schweighauser, P. (eds.) Speculations V Aestehtics in the 21st Century. Punctum Books (2014). https://doi.org/10.2307/jj.2353877

7. Koenitz, H.: Understanding Interactive Digital Narrative: Immersive Expressions for a Complex Time, 1 edn. Routledge, London (2023).https://doi.org/10.4324/9781003106425

8. Krauss, R.: Video: The aesthetics of narcissism. October **1**, 51–64 (1976). http://www.jstor.org/stable/778507

9. Liu, H., Li, C., Li, Y., Lee, Y.J.: Improved baselines with visual instruction tuning (2023). https://arxiv.org/abs/2310.03744

10. Liu, H., Li, C., Li, Y., Li, B., Zhang, Y., Shen, S., Lee, Y.J.: LLaVA-next: improved reasoning, OCR, and world knowledge (2024). https://llava-vl.github.io/blog/2024-01-30-llava-next/

11. Liu, H., Li, C., Wu, Q., Lee, Y.J.: Visual instruction tuning. In: NeurIPS (2023)

12. Luhmann, N., Baecker, D., Gilgen, P.: Introduction to systems theory. Polity, Cambridge, UK; Malden, MA (2013). oCLC: ocn819367834

13. Luhmann, N., Barrett, R.: Theory of Society. Cultural Memory in the Present. Stanford University Press, Stanford (2012)

14. Marttila, T.: Speaking in loops that change - writing for the wandering listener in time, diffracted (2024). https://airdrive.eventsair.com/eventsairseasiaprod/production-expertevents-public/325a4a2820d4482ca779e149faf61c92

15. Moeller, H.G.: On second-order observation and genuine pretending: coming to terms with society. Thesis Eleven **143**(1), 28–43 (2017).https://doi.org/10.1177/0725513617740968

16. Murray, J.H.: Research into interactive digital narrative: a kaleidoscopic view. In: Rouse, R., Koenitz, H., Haahr, M. (eds.) ICIDS 2018. LNCS, vol. 11318, pp. 3–17. Springer, Cham (2018). https://doi.org/10.1007/978-3-030-04028-4_1

17. Nunes, R.: AI, a tool or an author? A Posthuman feminist perspective on the agency of gen-AI in creative practices. Augment. Hum. Res. **9**(1), 8 (2024). https://doi.org/10.1007/s41133-024-00074-8

18. Ollama: Ollama (2024). https://github.com/ollama/ollama

19. Onkaos: Uncanny Mirror by Mario Klingemann (2019). https://vimeo.com/336559940

20. Rombach, R., Blattmann, A., Lorenz, D., Esser, P., Ommer, B.: High-resolution image synthesis with latent diffusion models (2021)

21. Schrader, A.: In a blow for artists, a federal judge has sided with three A.I. Companies in a Copyright Dispute. Artnet (2023). https://news.artnet.com/art-world/federal-judge-sides-with-ai-companies-in-artists-copyright-dispute-2387654

22. Schwartz, R., Vassilev, A., Greene, K., Perine, L., Burt, A., Hall, P.: Towards a standard for identifying and managing bias in artificial intelligence. Technical report, NIST SP 1270, National Institute of Standards and Technology (U.S.), Gaithersburg, MD (2022). https://doi.org/10.6028/NIST.SP.1270, https://nvlpubs.nist.gov/nistpubs/SpecialPublications/NIST.SP.1270.pdf

23. Team, M.: Midjourney (2022). https://midjourney.com/

24. Unity: unity/sentis-jets-text-to-speech Hugging Face. https://huggingface.co/unity/sentis-jets-text-to-speech

25. Unity Technologies: Unity (2023). https://unity.com/. Game development platform
26. Vincent, J.: Getty images sues AI art generator stable diffusion in the US for copyright infringement. The Verge (2023). https://www.theverge.com/2023/2/6/23587393/ai-art-copyright-lawsuit-getty-images-stable-diffusion

Exploring Collaborative Interactive Digital Narrative Creation in Higher Education Through Narrative Analysis: A Case Study on COVID-19 Storytelling

Dimitra Petousi[1] , Akrivi Katifori[1]([✉]) , Maria Boile[1] , and Eirini Sifaki[2]

[1] Athena Research and Innovation Center, Aigialias and Chalepa, 15125 Marousi, Greece
{dpetousi,vivi,mboile}@athenarc.gr
[2] Department of Language and Intercultural Studies, University of Thessaly, Argonafton and Filellinon, 382 21 Volos, Greece
eisifaki@uth.gr

Abstract. This paper explores collaborative IDN creation as a pedagogical approach in higher education. Drawing on theories of constructivism and social learning, we believe that collaborative IDN creation can foster knowledge-building and diverse perspectives. To investigate this approach, we conducted a study involving a class of college students tasked with creating IDNs about the COVID-19 pandemic. As the first step, we analyze the theme, interactivity, agency, and other elements of their IDNs, to understand the potential benefits and challenges of this method. Students demonstrated a diverse range of storytelling approaches, incorporating a range of elements and themes. Future work will focus on indepth interviews to gain insight into their thought process, motivations around design decisions, sense of co-creation and perceived learning outcomes.

Keywords: Collaborative Creation · Digital Storytelling · Social Learning · Higher Education

1 Introduction

Collaborative IDN creation is a promising pedagogical approach promoting creativity and social skills. It draws on theories of constructivism and social theories of learning [17], which highlight the importance of social interaction through peer interactions [14]. Creative writing is a beneficial activity for the cognitive development of learners as it fosters imagination and inspires them to express themselves in creative, compelling and fun ways [3]. Combining collaboration and creative writing activities can foster a more engaging and motivating learning experience, by providing students with opportunities to work together, share ideas, and receive feedback from their peers. The interactive nature of IDNs

© The Author(s), under exclusive license to Springer Nature Switzerland AG 2025
J. T. Murray and M. C. Reyes (Eds.): ICIDS 2024, LNCS 15468, pp. 267–278, 2025.
https://doi.org/10.1007/978-3-031-78450-7_20

makes them suitable for such an immersive and collaborative learning environment.

To investigate the effectiveness of collaborative IDN creation as a pedagogical tool in higher education, we conducted a study involving college students. They were tasked with forming groups and creating interactive digital narratives about the COVID-19 pandemic, including personal, impersonal, real or fictional stories. By examining the approaches the students took in their narratives, we aim to understand the potential benefits and challenges of this method. In this paper, we will primarily focus on describing the approaches used by the students in their IDNs. We will analyze narrative techniques, the level of interactivity, the implementation of agency, and other relevant elements. This analysis will provide a foundation for future research on collaborative storytelling as a means to foster student engagement, creativity, and critical thinking.

2   Background

Interactive Digital Narratives (IDNs) offer a promising pedagogical approach that encourages active participation and breaks away from traditional passive learning methods [2,8]. A key element of IDNs is agency, which refers to "the satisfying power to take meaningful action and see the results of our decisions and choices" [10]. Agency in IDNs can be local which focuses on the immediate choices/actions a user can take within a specific scene; global which can influence the overall development of the narrative, and the potential for different endings [9,12]. Restricted agency refers to the ability of a user to take action within certain constraints, while unrestricted agency might suggest complete freedom (i.e. open-world games) [13]. The concept of agency is essential for meaningful interaction as Atkins points out, the pleasure of play lies in the "cause and effect" relationship between the player's actions and the system's responses [1].

To fully utilize the learning potential of IDNs, we need to also incorporate suitable educational models. The trialogical approach, offers a unique framework that emphasizes collaborative learning through "shared epistemic objects" [5]. Furthermore, the research and information gathering phase encouraged collaborative learning and critical thinking, fulfilling King's [7] requirement for going beyond information retrieval and engaging in analysis. This approach goes beyond traditional models focusing on information transfer or individual participation, encouraging collaborative learning and critical thinking [14].

Collaborative learning approaches have been widely used in various educational settings. Johnson and Johnson [6] highlight the importance of five elements: positive interdependence, individual and group accountability, interpersonal and small group skills, face-to-face promotive interaction and group processing. The potential of IDNs moves beyond individual learning experiences and can be adopted for collaborative creation and learning approaches, especially in interdisciplinary environments. The benefits from this collaborative and active learning approach seem to be positive and point to a more holistic and interconnected educational approach.

3   Methodology

This study aimed to explore the potential of IDNs as a pedagogical tool in higher education. Participants were students enrolled in the "Design and Implementation of an Intercultural Project" course of the Department of Language and Intercultural Studies of the University of Thessaly, Greece. The course included 64 students, 42 female and 12 male, with average ages 21–23.. Students were divided into self-selected groups, forming 22 groups of 2 to 4 students. This approach allowed for the formation of teams based on shared interests and experiences, potentially enhancing engagement and collaboration. The groups were not given any instructions on how to collaborate while designing and developing the IDN and were allowed to self-organize in this aspect. By employing a self-selected group formation process, we fostered positive interdependence from the outset. Students with shared interests and experiences could leverage their individual strengths to build a cohesive narrative.

The course duration was one semester and the project spanned across half of the semester. It included three 2-h lectures and tutorial sessions to familiarize the students with the basic concepts of IDN design and development, focusing on the interactive fiction and visual novel paradigms. The Narralive Story Maker IDN creation tool [15,16] was selected for the student project, due to the authors' prior experience with the tool for student projects in museology courses. It provided students with the necessary features to design interactive elements, incorporate multimedia, and structure their narratives. The tool was presented in a hands-on 2-hour tutorial session and the students were provided a 1 h video tutorial and a pdf manual. A second session was arranged while their IDN project was being developed to resolve open issues. They were also encouraged to seek support from the authors and, in some cases, individual support sessions were scheduled.

Once the groups were formed, students were tasked with developing an IDN for the COVID-19 pandemic. The students were given 8 weeks to complete it, plus extensions given upon request to some groups. The narrative could be based on personal experiences, either real or fictional or they could create an impersonal narrative as well. To enrich their stories, students were encouraged to examine a relevant collection of artworks, to optionally either incorporate them in their IDNs or use them as inspiration. These artworks were part of an educational program initiated during the pandemic and inviting health practitioners to submit their own artworks about COVID-19, inspired by museum exhibits [11]. After developing their concept notes, the groups conducted research to gather information and media relevant to their narratives.

The students were allowed to choose their own experience type. Previous lectures on the theory of IDN presented both linear and multi-linear storytelling experiences, focusing on visual novel type examples for the latter. Although the students were not specifically instructed to select a specific experience type, the range of examples given affected their selected approach.

The IDNs, upon completion, were reviewed and analyzed by four researchers to assess their adherence to specific IDN elements. These are summarized in

Table 1 and include multi-linearity, use of branching points, level of agency, narrator perspective, use of media elements and story themes.

Table 1. IDN elements used for the analysis of the students' IDNs.

IDN aspects	Values
Multi-linear	Yes, No
Use of branching points	No branching points, Limited, Extensive
Agency	Local, global and restricted, true/unrestricted
Perspective	First-person, Third-person, Omniscient
Media Elements	Dialogue, Images, Audio and music, Videos, AI-Generated images
Themes	Artistic Activities, Museum Tours, Education and Information, Human Relations, Allegory and Fairytale, Solidarity and Volunteerism
Inspiration or incorporation of artworks	Yes, No

4   Results

The study yielded a rich set of 21 IDNs. While one group did not complete the project, the remaining narratives provided valuable insights into the design and content of IDNs as educational tools for collaborative learning, reflection and knowledge expansion. The detailed analysis of the IDNs revealed a diverse range of storytelling approaches and narrative structures, from linear to interactive, with a varying number of branching points and different narrative techniques, delving into a variety of themes and perspectives, and incorporating media elements.

4.1   Multi-linearity

The IDNs exhibited varying degrees of interactivity. Some narratives followed a linear path, guiding the viewer through a predetermined sequence of events. Others incorporated branching paths, allowing users to make choices that influenced the story's outcome. This interactive element enhanced engagement and provided a sense of agency. This diversity suggests that IDNs can be adapted to suit different learning styles and preferences.

Linear Narratives: In this work we define as linear narratives stories that have predetermined outcomes and no alternative endings. Branching points may be present but have no effect on the story. Therefore, 12 of the 21 IDNs followed a linear structure, guiding the viewer through a predetermined sequence of events.

Multi-Linear Narratives: 9 of the 21 IDNs incorporated multi-linear elements, allowing for branching paths or user-driven choices that have some slight or big effect on the outcome of the story. These included stories with restricted, local and global agency.

4.2   Branching Points

We also analyzed the use of branching points in the 21 IDNs. A branching point is a decision point within a narrative where the viewer can choose between different paths, leading to varying outcomes. The results indicate different approaches across the IDNs:

No branching Points: 4 of the 21 IDNs did not include any branching points, suggesting a more linear narrative structure.

Limited Branching Points: 3 IDNs had 1 branching point, 4 IDNs had 2, and 6 IDNs had 3. These IDNs offered a moderate level of interactivity, allowing viewers to make a limited number of choices, (pseudo choices and choices that had not an effect on the story outcome, i.e. how the person is feeling at the moment of an event or a character deciding his pseudonym for an online group chat) and, basically although branching points were present they still alluded to linear outcomes. Except for 2 IDNs who although were short stories, the choices present led to different outcomes.

Extensive Branching Points: One IDN had 4 branching points, 3 IDNs had 5, and 2 IDNs had 6. These IDNs provided a high degree of interactivity, allowing viewers to significantly influence the story's direction and outcome.

While most IDNs were relatively linear, a significant portion incorporated branching points, demonstrating the potential for interactive storytelling in this educational context. The use of branching points in IDNs did enhance engagement and provide a more personalized experience.

4.3   Agency

Agency is a critical component of IDNs, as it allows viewers to actively participate in shaping the story's outcome. We examine the different levels of agency present in the 9 multi-linear IDNs, exploring the impact of choices and actions on the narrative's direction and conclusion. By understanding the varying degrees of agency, we can better appreciate the potential of IDNs to foster engagement, critical thinking, collaborative learning and knowledge expansion.

Local Agency: All 9 multi-linear included local agency, where choices or actions had limited or no impact on the overall story outcome.

Global Agency: Global agency was present in 4 of the 9 multi-linear IDNs, where choices or actions significantly affected the story's direction and conclusion. This narrative approach by incorporating branching paths and interactive elements, the students were able to give viewers the power to influence the protagonists' journeys and ultimately determine the story's conclusion. Most of the group's decision to include global agency in their IDNs was intentional. They recognized that this approach would not only enhance engagement but also promote critical thinking. It is worth noting that 3 of the stories with global agency featured a first-person perspective that covered a big part of the narrative, which likely contributed to the sense of agency experienced by the user.

Restricted Agency: All 9 multi-linear IDNs had limited or restricted agency, providing the viewer with a sense of choice but ultimately confining their actions within predetermined boundaries.

True/Unrestricted Agency: None of the IDNs offered true or unrestricted agency, where the viewer could freely shape the narrative without constraints.

4.4   Perspective

The perspective from which a story is told can significantly influence the viewer's experience and understanding of the narrative. In the IDNs in this study, three distinct perspectives were employed: first-person, third-person, and omniscient [4]. The use of different perspectives provided viewers with varying levels of immersion, understanding and insight, allowing viewers to connect with the characters and story in different ways.

First-Person: 7 IDNs adopted a first-person perspective, allowing the viewer to experience the story through the eyes of a character. Students employed diverse characters from children to adults, the viewers could experience the story as.

Third-Person: 5 IDNs used a third-person perspective, providing an external viewpoint on the narrative. 6 IDNs employed a combination of first-person and third-person perspectives which provided insights into the characters' inner thoughts and the broader context.

Omniscient: 3 IDNs employed an omniscient perspective, offering a broader and more comprehensive view of the story. One IDN used a combination of first-person and omniscient perspectives.

4.5   Media Elements

This aspect explored the effective use of media elements, such as images, audio, and video, that could enhance the storytelling experience and make the IDNs more engaging for viewers. The incorporation of AI-generated images showcased the potential of emerging technologies to enrich educational content.

Dialogue: 12 IDNs incorporated dialogue between characters, while 8 relied solely on narration.

Images: all 21 IDNs utilized images as a complementary medium to enhance storytelling.

Audio and Music: 8 IDNs included audio or music to create a more immersive experience.

Videos: 3 IDNs incorporated videos to provide additional visual content.

AI-Generated Images: 6 IDNs used AI-generated images to create unique and visually striking elements.

4.6   Themes

At the stage of narrative analysis, a variety of themes has been observed. This demonstrates the versatility of IDNs as a tool for addressing diverse educational goals. By examining the themes explored in these narratives, we can gain valuable insights into the educational goals and perspectives of the students as creators. These themes reflect the diverse educational goals, creative thoughts and social concerns that motivated the students to create their IDNs. A thematic analysis of the IDNs revealed, inductively six distinct themes:

Artistic Activities: 3 IDNs focused on artistic activities, showcasing the power of creativity and self-expression, particularly during a time of isolation and uncertainty.

Museum Tours: 2 IDNs offered virtual museum tours, providing immersive experiences of historical or cultural sites. The 2 groups chose to create digital museum tours, providing virtual experiences of historical sites or cultural artifacts. These narratives offered a unique way to engage with cultural heritage and promote learning.

Education and Information: 3 IDNs covered the topic from an educating/informing point of view, such as public health or private health issues. The groups who created educational and informative narratives aimed to educate viewers on specific topics, such as health or specific events. These IDNs served

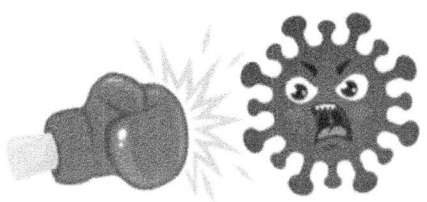

Αφού γνωρίσαμε τους δύο ήρωες μας, πάμε να δούμε τώρα παρέα πως περνάει ο Νικόλας μέσα σε μία μέρα. Μην ξεχνάτε ότι ο κορονοιός είναι δύσκολος εχθρός! Ό,τι βήματα κάνει ο ήρωας μας με την βοήθεια σας, θα πρέπει να εξασφαλίζουν ότι θα συνεχίσει να είναι υγιής και έτοιμος για πολύ παιχνίδι.

Fig. 1. IDN instructing on protection measures.

as informative tools, providing valuable knowledge in an engaging and interactive format (Fig. 1).

Human Relations: 6 IDNs explored the complexities of human relationships, including family, friendship, and community. One particular IDN delved into difficult social issues, such as domestic violence. These narratives highlighted the importance of social connection and emotional well-being during challenging times (Fig. 2).

Η ιστορία εκτυλίσσεται στο Βόλο, στο πλαίσιο της επιβολής της δεύτερης καραντίνας. Λόγω των περιοριστικών μέτρων, τα πανεπιστήμια είναι κλειστά, όπως και οι χώροι εστίασης, οπότε τα Μέσα Κοινωνικής Δικτύωσης είναι η μόνη λύση για να γνωριστούν μεταξύ τους οι φοιτητές. Λοιπόν, ξεκινάμε;

Ξεκινάμε!

Fig. 2. Friendship during the pandemic.

Four IDNs combined the above two topics (human relations and education - information) by addressing social issues through an informative lens. This approach seems to provide factual knowledge with an emotional resonance.

Allegory and Fairytale: 2 IDNs employed allegorical or fairytale elements to convey deeper meanings. These 2 narratives used symbolism and metaphor to explore complex themes such as loss of human contact or collective effort and evoke emotions.

Solidarity and Volunteerism: 1 IDN focused on themes of solidarity and volunteerism, highlighting acts of kindness and compassion.

Συμβίωση στην καραντίνα

Άλλη μια μέρα ξημερώνει στην πόλη της Λάρισας. Η πανδημία βρίσκεται στην αρχή

Fig. 3. IDN focusing on family relations and handling conflict.

4.7   Inspiration and Incorporation of Artworks

Only 3 of the 21 IDNs created narratives that were inspired or commented on real-life artworks in an organic way in the narratives and 1 IDN simply incorporated existing artworks into the narrative as complementary images. This inspiration or incorporation of artworks in the few IDNs showcased their potential for deeper engagement with cultural and artistic content.

SITUATIONSHIP

Το εμβόλιο πήρε θέση και μπήκε στην μέση

Pfizer, Johnson και Moderna έκαναν αυτήν τη σχέση πιο μοντέρνα.

Η αγκαλιά και το φιλί, έχουν σχέση καλή

Χωρίς πλέον επαφή

Πέρασε ο καιρός και το αγκάθι έμεινε εκτός

Σε αυτό βοήθησε ο γιατρός και ο χρόνος ο καλός

Η αγκαλιά και το φιλί βρέθηκαν ξανά μαζί

Όχι όμως, όπως πρώτα, αν θες, δες και ρώτα.

(Οι εραστές, του Ρενέ Μαγκρίτ)

Fig. 4. A narrative incorporating artworks as complementary material.

5   Conclusions and Limitations

In this study, we present the results of the analysis of 21 IDNs about the COVID-19 pandemic created in the context of a student group project. Students were asked to create IDNs, inspired by personal experiences, general knowledge and a collection of artworks about the pandemic. Their IDNs demonstrated the potential of interactive storytelling as a powerful pedagogical tool. The diverse range of themes and structures showcased the creativity and imagination of the participants, while also highlighting the relevance of IDN as a means to express contemporary issues. It is interesting to note that most of the groups did not opt for a purely didactic approach, but rather decided to explore themes relevant to human relations and wider societal issues, including family abuse, inequalities of access to care, depression, loneliness and isolation, etc. The process fostered creativity and shared imagination within the student groups, as evidenced by their diversity. It is important to further explore how this creative sense of producing a complex IDN reinforces positive feelings towards the learning process. At the end of the course, the IDNs were presented in a one-day event in the Department premises. However, in future applications, it would be interesting to incorporate a step where students share their IDNs, evaluate them, and then discuss and reflect upon them (Figs. 3 and 4).

The integration of real-life artworks into the IDN creation process offers a unique opportunity to engage learners with cultural and artistic content in a more immersive and interactive way and merits further investigation. By exploring how IDNs can be inspired by or incorporate and/or comment on existing artworks as a means of enhancing the educational potential of IDNs, we can gain insights into the effectiveness of this approach in fostering deeper engagement, reflection and understanding. It would be interesting to incorporate in future student projects the requirement for integrating artworks in the IDNs, or using them as inspirations, to further explore this potential.

One limitation of this study is its exclusive focus on the narrative analysis of the IDNs. While this approach provided valuable insights, it did not delve into the perspective of the students who engaged with these IDNs. Preliminary discussions with three of the groups revealed different aspects of the process, including the function of the selected collaboration or cooperation approaches, creative decision-making, division of the work, etc. The dialogic process within the group, to select, refine and expand the IDN concept has the potential to promote perspective-taking. Therefore, we plan follow-up research that could benefit from incorporating qualitative methods, particularly in-depth interviews to get direct feedback from students regarding their motivation and thought process behind design choices as well as perceived learning outcomes. The data from these interviews will also provide valuable insight regarding the effectiveness of the collaborative IDN creation within the trialogical framework. We aim to assess whether this approach can lead to a shift in students' perspectives or the acquisition of new knowledge. We believe that collaborative research and creation of IDNs for a specific subject will encourage students to develop a deeper understanding of the subject through the sense of co-creation and shared experience. Through further exploration and refinement, the process of collaborative IDN creation has a strong potential to enhance educational experiences, particularly in the trialogical framework, promote a deeper understanding of the subject and foster critical thinking skills.

Acknowledgments. This paper is part of the InterArt project conducted at the Cultural Relations and Comparative Arts Laboratory (CulCo lab) of the University of Thessaly and funded by the Center Of Research Innovation And Excellence (CRIE).

References

1. Atkins, B.: More than a Game: The Computer Game as Fictional Form. Manchester University Press (2003)
2. Barbara, J., et al.: IDNS in education: skills for future generations. In: Holloway-Attaway, L., Murray, J.T. (eds.) ICIDS 2023. LNCS, vol. 14383, pp. 57–72. Springer, Cham (2023). https://doi.org/10.1007/978-3-031-47655-6_4
3. Craft, A.: Creativity and early years education a lifewide foundation. Continuum (2002)
4. Diasamidze, I.: Point of view in narrative discourse. Procedia - Soc. Behav. Sci. **158**, 160–165 (2014).https://doi.org/10.1016/J.SBSPRO.2014.12.062
5. Hakkarainen, K., Paavola, S., Kangas, K., Seitamaa-Hakkarainen, P.: Sociocultural Perspectives on Collaborative Learning Toward Collaborative Knowledge Creation, 1st edn. Routledge (2013)
6. Johnson, D.W., Johnson, R.T.: Social interdependence theory and cooperative learning: the teacher's role. In: Gillies, R.M., Ashman, A.F., Terwel, J. (eds.) The Teacher's Role in Implementing Cooperative Learning in the Classroom. Computer-Supported Collaborative Learning, vol. 8, pp. 9–37. Springer, Boston (2008). https://doi.org/10.1007/978-0-387-70892-8_1

7. King, A.: Collaborative learning in the music studio. Music. Educ. Res. **10**, 423–438 (2008). https://doi.org/10.1080/14613800802280167

8. Kooloos, J.G., Bergman, E.M., Scheffers, M.A., Schepens-Franke, A.N., Vorstenbosch, M.A.: The effect of passive and active education methods applied in repetition activities on the retention of anatomical knowledge. Anatom. Sci. Educ. **13**, 458 (2020). https://doi.org/10.1002/ASE.1924

9. Mateas, M., Stern, A.: Interaction and Narrative, pp. 642–669. MIT Press (2005)

10. Murray, J.: Hamlet on the Holodeck. Free Press (1997)

11. National Museum of Contemporary Art Athens: Emst for health (2021). https://www.emst.gr/en/category/emst-for-health

12. Roth, C., Vermeulen, I.: Real story interaction: the role of global agency in interactive storytelling. In: Herrlich, M., Malaka, R., Masuch, M. (eds.) ICEC 2012, pp. 425–428. Springer, Heidelberg (2012)

13. Tanenbaum, K., Tanenbaum, T.J.: Agency as commitment to meaning: communicative competence in games. Digit. Creat. **21**, 11–17 (2010). https://doi.org/10.1080/14626261003654509

14. Vass, E., Littleton, K., Miell, D., Jones, A.: The discourse of collaborative creative writing: peer collaboration as a context for mutual inspiration. Thinking Skills Creat. **3**, 192–202 (2008). https://doi.org/10.1016/J.TSC.2008.09.001

15. Vrettakis, E., Kourtis, V., Katifori, A., Karvounis, M., Lougiakis, C., Ioannidis, Y.: Narralive creating and experiencing mobile digital storytelling in cultural heritage. Digit. Appl. Archaeol. Cult. Heritage **15**, e00114 (2019). https://doi.org/10.1016/j.daach.2019.e00114

16. Vrettakis, E., et al.: The story maker - an authoring tool for multimedia-rich interactive narratives. In: Bosser, A.-G., Millard, D.E., Hargood, C. (eds.) ICIDS 2020. LNCS, vol. 12497, pp. 349–352. Springer, Cham (2020). https://doi.org/10.1007/978-3-030-62516-0_33

17. Vygotsky, L.: The Collected Works of L. S. Vygotsky. Plenum Press (1988). https://doi.org/10.1007/978-1-4613-1655-8

The IDN Design Model: A Proposal for an Extended SPP Model

Anca Serbanescu(✉) and Hartmut Koenitz

University of Amsterdam, Amsterdam, The Netherlands
{a.serbanescu,h.a.koenitz}@uva.nl

Abstract. The proliferation of AI systems has brought increased attention to the process of creating Interactive Digital Narratives (IDNs). There is still no formal IDN design model, as previous efforts were focused on understanding finished artefacts. This paper addresses the theoretical gap in terms of the interactive digital narrative design process by considering the role of AI and proposing a novel IDN design model that includes the possibility of collaborative interaction between AI and designers in the context of creating IDNs, thereby facilitating the systematization of knowledge. This model is an extension of the existing SPP model introduced by Koenitz, reinterpreted through a design-driven approach. This broader perspective distinguishes the creative design process, the authoring process and the data pipeline, providing a more fine-grained understanding in contrast to a unified authoring process as described in current IDN literature.

Keywords: IDN design model · SPP model · Authoring Tools · Generative AI · Participatory Design · IDN Design

1 Introduction

The proliferation of authoring tools (ATs) is a well-documented phenomenon within the interactive digital narrative (IDN) scholarly community [18,31]. At the same time, the rise of Artificial Intelligence (AI) tools, driven by advances in Natural Language Processing (NLP) and Computer Vision (CV), has attracted considerable public [12] and scholarly attention in the IDN community and related fields [7,8,20,36]. Since 2022, there has been a significant rise in the prevalence of AI-generated content, with terms such as generative AI models, neural network-based image enhancement [33], Natural Language Generation (NLG) systems [29], Natural Language Processing (NLP) [5], Computer Vision (CV) [34], Audio Signal Processing (ASP) [41], and AI-powered creative platforms gaining widespread recognition [4]. Generative AI (GAI), such as the commercial platform GPT from OpenAI and its popular ChatGPT[1] product or the image production tool Midjourney[2], gained popularity because of the ease with

---

[1] https://chatgpt.com/.

[2] https://www.midjourney.com/.

© The Author(s), under exclusive license to Springer Nature Switzerland AG 2025
J. T. Murray and M. C. Reyes (Eds.): ICIDS 2024, LNCS 15468, pp. 279–288, 2025.
https://doi.org/10.1007/978-3-031-78450-7_21

which promising results may be acquired by beginning with a small set of simple command prompts. This technology enables the rapid production of high-quality content for use in everyday tasks like writing emails and reports but is also used to meet the growing demands of various digital media platforms [3]. The implications of recent AI developments for the IDN field are noteworthy, enabling new possibilities for narrative-focused creation.

ATs in the IDN domain are described as software that helps non-programmers create IDN works [31]. ATs support the development of IDNs by reducing the need for technical expertise, making IDN creation more accessible to non-programmers who can use such a tool to create interactive stories without a technical background [9,32]. The use of ATs in creating IDNs necessitates matching conceptual development on the side of theory.

The IDN field is rapidly expanding as a result of technological breakthroughs and the continued development of IDN tools and systems [27]. However, this growth has tended to prioritise the building of systems, tools and products, while theoretical efforts have focused on understanding the finished artefact [16, 17,22,24]. At the same time, the IDN design process received considerably less attention. Some works exist (e.g. [15] expanded more recently in a chapter on design [17]), but there is still no formal IDN design framework. The advent of GAI tools makes the need to fill this conceptual gap even more pressing. Therefore, there is a need to conduct research on the creative design process of developing IDN experiences to contribute to the systematisation of knowledge [30]. This paper helps to address the knowledge gap in the process of creating IDN experiences, by conceptualizing the *IDN design process* in the light of the proliferation of GAI tools. The focus here is on a theoretical framing, and not on a categorization of different AI approaches, which we see as a future step.

2   The IDN Design Process

The term *IDN design process* refers to a more expansive notion than what is referred to in existing literature [10,21,37], where it is typically used in relation to the authoring process. This paper proposes an extended understanding of the term *IDN design process*, where the design-creative process is the overarching activity, even if the authoring process is still an important part of the process. It refers to several steps, exchanges, and connected processes that come together to create IDNs. We enhance our understanding and investigation of interactive digital narrative production by embracing this inclusive viewpoint.

When it comes to the use of GAI in this context, the *IDN design process* is a participatory process that involves the interaction between the designer and the digital counterpart to design a *narrative design product*.

As we have argued above, there is a scarcity in the IDN literature regarding the theoretical and empirical design aspects of creating IDN systems, especially when it comes to the interaction between Authoring Tools and designers, which has only recently received much needed attention [30]. Our contribution is a novel approach to the understanding of IDN beyond its manifestation as a complete work. This approach is meant to address the following questions: How can we systematize knowledge to facilitate a better understanding of the meaning of design in relation to IDN? Additionally, how does AI affect the process of creating an IDN work?

2.1   The Design-Creative Process

The overall *IDN design process* is based on the design-creative process, which integrates both the creative process and the design process. We use this definition, inspired by Bonnardel and Didier [2], to avoid the misunderstanding of the two processes as distinct, while we take them as overlapping and inseparable. Often these two processes are described separately, but they share several characteristics. The meanings attributed to them are not clear-cut and there is no real dividing line between them.

The creative process is described as a series of divergent and convergent thinking [39] that takes place within a person to generate creative ideas. Several scholars [1, 19, 28, 38] have defined the creative process throughout time, offering different perspectives on stages and phases. The number of stages can be reduced [38] or increased [28]. Yet, there is no discernible difference between these phases and the ones of the design process, with the exception that the design process is more problem-solving-oriented, emphasising function, practicality, and user-centeredness. Attempts to systematise them from a theoretical point of view show that the actual phases occur in a non-linear, even chaotic manner, as Plattner et al. point out [26].

The design-creative process' nature is an interactive set of steps that intertwine with one another. Though the stages are often quite straightforward for the designer, recognising the intersections of divergent and convergent thought are higher-order cognitive tasks that take practice to become proficient [26]. Several procedures, including the authoring process, alternate during the *IDN design process*. To analyze the *IDN design process* we start by taking the authoring component of the creative process into consideration first.

2.2   The Authoring Process

Authoring is an active process that involves continuous learning and mastery [23]. Sofia Kitromili [13], notes that authoring tools are difficult to use and that there is a lack of understanding regarding the authoring process, its requirements, and the best ways to match the tools to each step of the process. In the context of IDN, authoring encompasses various aspects, including content selection, mode of interaction, audience perception, and narrative generation [25]. This multifaceted process involves the skilful manipulation of elements to create engaging and interactive narrative experiences.

However, the authoring process is, in fact, an integral part of the *IDN design process*, in which a participatory process takes place between the designer and the authoring tool, which can include a GAI tool. GAI can contribute to the construction of elements in the IDN work, such as static components (e.g. assets, fixed text) or those of a dynamic nature (UI, procedural components, narrative design). A well-known example of a GAI tool which can act as an authoring tool to create static narrative elements is *ChatGPT*, a conversational general knowledge AI chatbot that provides text-based responses. ChatGPT creates material based on pre-existing data, adapting them to the task at hand. Many GAI tools can create the programming code for full-text adventures and smaller snippets to be used in different kinds of experiences. In terms of production-level content as direct output from GAI, Sora AI[3], is getting closer. Sora AI is capable of creating video from text input. This AI potentially paves the way for dynamic narrative content that changes continuously based on the user's interaction with the AI as an accessible function for every designer. By providing a more personalised and responsive experience, it would dynamically change its output based on real-time data and user interactions. Integrating advanced AI systems into the authoring process can, therefore, lead to more innovative and adaptive IDN works, making it easier for designers to create dynamic artefacts through user-friendly interfaces to powerful technology. This type of functionality was previously only available to designers who were also AI experts or in professional settings in which an AI expert or a whole AI team existed.

2.3   The Data Pipeline

AI systems, when considered as stand-alone entities, go through an internal process that we will call the *data pipeline* [11]. The term *data pipeline* describes the conceptual data processing that takes place in the AI system, a procedure that begins with gathering raw data, moves through some processing and ends up being deposited as information. The *data pipeline* allows data to be processed and analysed to respond to the designer.

The participatory process is itself interactive, established in the collaborative act between designers and AIs. However, the designer must communicate with and be assisted by a developer in implementing various AI-powered data analysis settings. The designer is the main orchestrator of the data process [30]. The data selection and analysis are guided by their creative vision, objectives, and anticipated story consequences. The data analysis settings and AI system configuration may need technical expertise beyond the designer's domain, demanding collaboration and communication between the designer and the developer. Through this partnership, the designer may specify their artistic goals and objectives, and the developer can turn these into the proper technical configurations to increase the AI system's performance. The *IDN design process* encompasses all of these factors and takes into account all of them in a non-linear, cycle-independent manner.

3   From SPP to IDN Design Model

The SPP model is a prominent theoretical model for analysing and understanding IDN works.

---

[3] Sora AI - Open AI https://openai.com/index/sora/ [Accessed 21 June 2024].

SPP understands IDN as consisting of three components: *system, process* and *product* (see Fig. 1). The term *system* refers to digital artefacts or *"the combination of software with the hardware on which the software is executed"* [17]. Ready for use by users, often called interactors. *Process* refers to the interaction between the *system* and the interactor(s). *Product* is the output that results from the interaction of the interactor with the *system*. *Product* can be either *objective* (as a recording or a play trace) or subjective (as a retelling [6] by interactors).

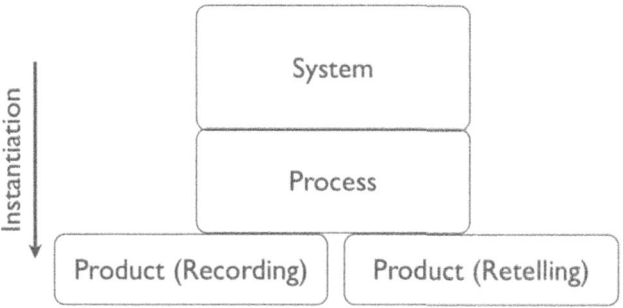

Fig. 1. The SPP model [17], p.76.

The term *instantiation* denotes the process of generating a concrete and thus *instantiated* narrative from the space of potential narratives contained in the system. Originating from the field of computer science, instantiation is specifically associated with creating objects as instances of a designated class [40]. Extending the applicability of the instantiation concept beyond its computer science roots, Koenitz assimilates and adapts it within the IDN domain. Instantiation in the IDN context, according to Koenitz [17], defines *"the relationship between the artefact (computer/software system) and its resultant output"*. Koenitz takes the content of the systems as a "protostory", a prototype for all realized, instantiated stories contained in the resulting objective or subjecive product. Instantiation also has important implications in the discourse on authorship.

The *IDN design model* is an extension of the SPP model, where the focus is on aspects which happened earlier, before the existence of an SPP system. The focus of this paper is on the *IDN design process* that results in a *narrative design product*, which is different from the *product* in the SPP model. The *narrative design product* is an *IDN design artefact*, the *system* under the existing SPP model.

Figure 2 shows a representation of the *IDN design process* extending the SPP model, and we call this extended version the *IDN design model*. Conceptually, we distinguish between the types of designs created in collaboration with AI systems and those that are not within the *IDN design process*. *AI design* is a participatory method in which the designer collaborates with an *AI system* providing assistance. In contrast, there is *non AI design*, which refers to the

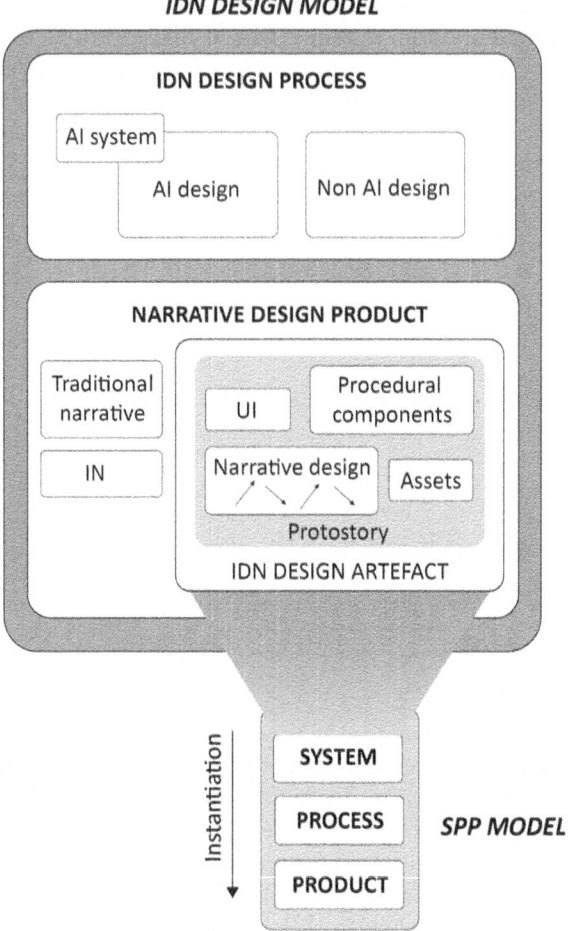

Fig. 2. The IDN design model [30], p. 120.

practice of using conventional software and writing tools rather than AI support systems.

3.1   The Narrative Design Product

The *IDN design process*, e.g. in the form of participatory exchange between designers and AI support systems, can yield outputs that can be static or dynamic. In terms of static or dynamic we distinguish three types of artefacts: a) traditional narrative; b) interactive narrative (IN); c) IDN design artefact. Accordingly, *narrative design product* is a definition proposed here, derived from the *IDN design model*, which encompasses several narrative components and artefacts (traditional narratives, interactive narratives, IDN design artefacts).

In this paper, the term *traditional narrative* refers to stories without digital or interactive elements, in which the writer is the author and builds a story for an audience of readers who have no ability to change the story. A traditional narrative can be exemplified by a literary story contained in a book, where the book acts as the medium for the narrative's transmission. There are additional manifestations of traditional narratives, such as movies. Traditional narratives differ from IDN and Interactive Narratives (INs) in that they do not provide the audience for whom they are intended with the means to participate in the continuing story.

With IN, there is limited interaction. Typical examples include the *Choose Your Own Adventure*[4] game books, which provide a multi-linear reading experience. In these works, the reader guides the plot by making decisions on the protagonist's behalf, which have varying consequences and resolutions depending on what they decide. This dynamic interactive method changes the traditional linear flow of the narrative since the number of pages no longer reflects the sequence in which they should be read. Rather, readers decide on the continuation at pre-determined times (e.g. 'if you want to open the door, go to page 20', 'if you want to hide behind a tree, go to page 35'). This participatory modality fosters deeper reader engagement and allows readers to return to the same book several times, each time exploring a distinct plot [35]. At the same time, the reader does not have full agency [24] since their actions do not result in any changes in the storyworld.

In contrast, *IDN design artefacts* describe outputs that are complete dynamic systems. These digital artefacts produce experiences that turn audiences into interactors, able to participate in the story through agency. Agency is the power to take meaningful decisions [24] which are reflected in a virtual world, including over the progression of a narrative, how characters are shaped and change, and how the environment changes.

The Sims[5] is a useful example for comprehending the significance of the *IDN design artefacts*. Interactors may build and manage virtual characters in this life simulation video game. Interacting with objects and carrying out predetermined tasks in the virtual context of *Sim City*, interactors engage with the continuing narrative and shape their own story. What is referred to as an *IDN design artefact* in the *IDN design model* corresponds to the system in Koenitz's SPP model [14,16,17].

4   Conclusion

In this paper, we have argued that there is a lack of theoretical knowledge about the design process leading to an IDN work and that the predominant focus in

---

[4] Choose your own adventure books is a narrative format designed for children and young adults that creates game books. Find more at https://openlibrary.org/collections/CYOA [Accessed July 14, 2023].

[5] The Sims is a life simulation game developed by Maxis. It lets users to construct and govern virtual humans called Sims, shaping their lives in a simulated world. https://www.ea.com/it-it/games/the-sims. [Accessed January 2024].

the literature has been on the IDN artefact as a final work. At the same time, the emergence of GAI as a factor in IDN design necessities increases attention to the conceptualization and formalization of IDN-related design knowledge. Consequently, we propose an extended version of Koenitz's SPP model that includes the design process that precedes the creation of the IDN work. The new perspective that takes shape in the *IDN design model* enhances theoretical understanding by considering the creative design process that leads to the creation of an *IDN design artefact*. We created an initial high-level framework that will be followed by an in-depth investigation of AI design components. Moreover, our model acknowledges the emerging technology of GAI within what we call the *IDN design process*, as a supporting function. We offer this systematization as a basis for stimulating discussion with the aim to further refining the existing model.

References

1. Amabile, T.M.: Creativity in Context. Westview Press, Boulder (1996)
2. Bonnardel, N., Didier, J.: Brainstorming variants to favor creative design. Appl. Ergon. **83**, 102987 (2020). https://doi.org/10.1016/j.apergo.2019.102987
3. Cao, Y., Li, S., Liu, Y., Yan, Z., Dai, Y., Yu, P.S., Sun, L.: A comprehensive survey of AI-generated content (AIGC): a history of generative AI from GAN to ChatGPT. arXiv preprint arXiv:2303.04226 (2023)
4. Cerruti, C., Valeri, A.: AI-powered platforms: automated transactions in digital marketplaces. Dissertation, Master of Science in Business Administration, Università degliăStudi di Roma (2022)
5. Chowdhary, K., Chowdhary, K.: Natural language processing. In: Fundamentals of Artificial Intelligence, pp. 603–649. Springer (2020)
6. Eladhari, M.P.: Re-tellings: the fourth layer of narrative as an instrument for critique. In: Rouse, R., Koenitz, H., Haahr, M. (eds.) ICIDS 2018. LNCS, vol. 11318, pp. 65–78. Springer, Cham (2018). https://doi.org/10.1007/978-3-030-04028-4_5
7. Fisher, J.A.: Centering the Human: Digital Humanism and the Practice of Using Generative AI in the Authoring of Interactive Digital Narratives. In: Holloway-Attaway, L., Murray, J.T. (eds.) ICIDS 2023. LNCS, vol. 14383, pp. 73–88. Springer, Cham (2023). https://doi.org/10.1007/978-3-031-47655-6_5
8. Gallotta, R., Liapis, A., Yannakakis, G.: LLMaker: a game level design interface using (only) natural language (2024)
9. Green, D., Hargood, C., Charles, F.: Define authoring tool: a survey of interactive narrative authoring tools (2018)
10. Hargood, C., Millard, D.E., Mitchell, A., Spierling, U.: The Authoring Problem: Challenges in Supporting Authoring for Interactive Digital Narratives. Springer (2023)
11. IBM: Fundamentals. IBM Design for AI. (2019). https://www.ibm.com/design/ai/fundamentals
12. Kafka, P.: The AI boom is here, and so are the lawsuits (2023)
13. Kitromili, S., Reyes, M.C.: Understanding the process of authoring. In: The Authoring Problem: Challenges in Supporting Authoring for Interactive Digital Narratives, pp. 17–30. Springer (2023)

14. Koenitz, H.: Towards a theoretical framework for interactive digital narrative, pp. 176–185. Springer (2010)
15. Koenitz, H.: Design approaches for interactive digital narrative. In: Schoenau-Fog, H., Bruni, L.E., Louchart, S., Baceviciute, S. (eds.) ICIDS 2015. LNCS, vol. 9445, pp. 50–57. Springer, Cham (2015). https://doi.org/10.1007/978-3-319-27036-4_5
16. Koenitz, H.: Towards a specific theory of interactive digital narrative. In: Interactive Digital Narrative, pp. 91–105. Routledge (2015)
17. Koenitz, H.: Understanding Interactive Digital Narrative: Immersive Expressions for a Complex Time. Taylor & Francis (2023)
18. Koenitz, H., Eladhari, M.P.: Challenges of IDN research and teaching. In: Cardona-Rivera, R.E., Sullivan, A., Young, R.M. (eds.) ICIDS 2019. LNCS, vol. 11869, pp. 26–39. Springer, Cham (2019). https://doi.org/10.1007/978-3-030-33894-7_4
19. Lawson, B.: How Designers Think. Routledge (2006)
20. Liu, H.X., Huang, Y., Holopainen, J.: How to use generative AI as a design material for future human-computer (co-)creation? In: Generative AI and HCI Workshop (2023). https://scholars.cityu.edu.hk/en/publications/publication(2ac5b9c4-b559-4765-a304-5d921e4419dc).html
21. Locatis, C., Al-Nuaim, H.: Interactive technology and authoring tools: a historical review and analysis. Educ. Technol. Res. Dev. **47**(3), 63–75 (1999)
22. Montfort, N.: Twisty Little Passages: An Approach to Interactive Fiction. MIT Press (2005)
23. Murray, J.H.: Inventing the Medium: Principles of Interaction Design as a Cultural Practice. MIT Press (2011)
24. Murray, J.H.: Hamlet on the Holodeck: the Future of Narrative in Cyberspace. Free Press, New York (1997)
25. Nack, F., et al.: INDCOR white paper 3: interactive digital narratives and interaction. arXiv preprint arXiv:2306.10547 (2023)
26. Plattner, H., Meinel, C., Leifer, L.: Design Thinking: Understand Improve Apply. Springer (2010)
27. Rizvic, S., Boskovic, D., Okanovic, V., Sljivo, S., Zukic, M.: Interactive digital storytelling: bringing cultural heritage in a classroom. J. Comput. Educ. **6**, 143–166 (2019)
28. Sawyer, R.K.: The iterative and improvisational nature of the creative process. J. Creat. **31**, 100002–100002 (2021)
29. Semaan, P.: Natural language generation: an overview. J. Comput. Sci. Res. **1**(3), 50–57 (2012)
30. Serbanescu, A.: Human-AI co-creativity. Understanding the relationship between designers and AI systems in the field of interactive digital narrative. Ph.D. thesis, Politecnico di Milano (2024)
31. Shibolet, Y., Knoller, N., Koenitz, H.: A framework for classifying and describing authoring tools for interactive digital narrative, pp. 523–533. Springer (2018)
32. Shibolet, Y., Lombardo, V.: Resources for comparative analysis of IDN authoring tools, pp. 513–528. Springer (2022)
33. Singh, K., Seth, A., Sandhu, H.S., Samdani, K.: A comprehensive review of convolutional neural network based image enhancement techniques, pp. 1–6. IEEE (2019)
34. Stockman, G., Shapiro, L.G.: Computer Vision. Prentice Hall PTR (2001)
35. Swinehart, C.: One Book, Many Readings. Samizdat Drafting Co. (2009)
36. Uusitalo, S., Salovaara, A., Jokela, T., Salmimaa, M.: Clay to play with: generative AI tools in UX and industrial design practice. In: Proceedings of the

2024 ACM Designing Interactive Systems Conference, DIS 2024, pp. 1566–1578. Association for Computing Machinery, New York (2024). https://doi.org/10.1145/3643834.3661624
37. Vosmeer, M., Holloway-Attaway, L.: Interactive Storytelling: 15th International Conference on Interactive Digital Storytelling, ICIDS 2022, Santa Cruz, CA, USA, December 4–7, 2022, Proceedings, vol. 13762. Springer (2022)
38. Wallas, G.: The Art of Thought, vol. 10. Harcourt, Brace (1926)
39. Wong, Y.L., Siu, K.W.M.: A model of creative design process for fostering creativity of students in design education. Int. J. Technol. Design Educ. **22**(4), 437–450 (2012)
40. Zola, A.: What is an instantiation in computer programming? (2022). https://www.techtarget.com/whatis/definition/instantiation
41. Zölzer, U.: Digital Audio Signal Processing. Wiley (2022)

Author Index

GPSR Compliance

The European Union's (EU) General Product Safety Regulation (GPSR) is a set of rules that requires consumer products to be safe and our obligations to ensure this.

If you have any concerns about our products, you can contact us on ProductSafety@springernature.com

In case Publisher is established outside the EU, the EU authorized representative is:

Springer Nature Customer Service Center GmbH
Europaplatz 3
69115 Heidelberg, Germany

The manufacturer's authorised representative in the EU is Springer
Nature Customer Service Centre GmbH, Europaplatz 3, 69115 Heidelberg,
Germany. If you have any concerns regarding our products, please
contact ProductSafety@springernature.com

Printed and bound by CPI Group (UK) Ltd, Croydon, CR0 4YY
05/05/2026
02103581-0002